SuSE Linux
ADMINISTRATION GUIDE

Third edition 2002

Copyright ©

This publication is intellectual property of SuSE Linux AG.

Its contents can be duplicated, either in part or in whole, provided that a copyright label is visibly located on each copy.

All information found in this book has been compiled with utmost attention to detail. However, this does not guarantee complete accuracy. Neither SuSE Linux AG, the authors, nor the translators shall be held liable for possible errors or the consequences thereof.

Many of the software and hardware descriptions cited in this book are registered trademarks. All trade names are subject to copyright restrictions and may be registered trade marks. SuSE Linux AG essentially adheres to the manufacturer's spelling. Names of products and trademarks appearing in this book (with or without specific notation) are likewise subject to trademark and trade protection laws and may thus fall under copyright restrictions.

Please direct suggestions and comments to documentation@suse.de

Authors:	Frank Bodammer, Stefan Dirsch, Olaf Donjak, Torsten Duwe, Roman Drahtmüller, Thorsten Dubiel, Karl Eichwalder, Thomas Fehr, Stefan Fent, Werner Fink, Carsten Groß, Franz Hassel, Hendrik Vogelsang, Klaus Kämpf, Hubert Mantel, Anas Nashif, Johannes Meixner, Lars Müller, Matthias Nagorni, Peter Pöml, Siegfried Olschner, Marcus Schaefer, Klaus Singvogel, Klaus G. Wagner, Christian Zoz
Translators:	Daniel Pisano, Olaf Niepolt
Editors:	Antje Faber, Dennis Geider, Roland Haidl, Jana Jaeger, Edith Parzefall, Peter Reinhart, Marc Rührschneck, Thomas Schraitle, Martin Sommer, Rebecca Walter
Layout:	Manuela Piotrowski, Thomas Schraitle
Setting:	LaTeX

This book has been printed on 100 % chlorine-free bleached paper.

Contents

Preface	1
Changes to the Administration Manual	2
Typographical conventions	3
A Word of Thanks	4

I Installation   5

1 The Installation   7

Text-Based Installation with YaST2	8
The Start Screen	8
linuxrc: The Basics	9
Starting SuSE Linux	13
Special Installations	16
Installation Without a Supported CD-ROM Drive	16
Tips and Tricks	18
Booting from Disk (SYSLINUX)	18
Booting with CD 2	18
Creating a Boot Disk in DOS	19
Creating a Boot Disk in a UNIX-Related System	20
Supported CD-ROM Drives	21
ATAPI CD-ROM Hangs While Reading	21
Problems with CD-ROM Drives on Parallel Port	23

		Loadlin Does Not Have Enough Memory to Load the Kernel	. . .	23
		Loadlin Does Not Start		23
	Partitioning for Experts			24
		Size of Swap Partition		24
		Implementation of the Computer		25
		Optimizations		26

2 Updating the System and Package Management 29

	Updating SuSE Linux	30
		Preparations	30
		Updating with YaST2	32
		Manual Update	32
		Updating Individual Packages	33
	Software Changes From Version to Version	34
		From 6.x to 7.0	34
		From 7.0 to 7.1	38
		From 7.1 to 7.2	39
		From 7.2 to 7.3	40
		From 7.3 to 8.0	40
		From 8.0 to 8.1	42
	RPM — the Distribution Package Manager	43
		Verifying Package Authenticity	44
		Managing Packages: Install, Update, and Uninstall	44
		RPM Queries	46
		Installing and Compiling Source Packages	49
		Other Tools for Working with RPM Archives	50

II Configuration 53

3 YaST2 in Text Mode (ncurses) 55

	Explanation of ncurses	56
	Invocation and Usage	56
	Module Operation	57
	Invoking the Various Modules	59
	YaST Online Update	59

4 YaST2 in Graphics Mode   61

Starting YaST2 62
Software 62
    Change Installation Source 63
    YaST Online Update (YOU) 63
    Patch CD Update 64
Install and Remove Software 64
System Update 64
Hardware 65
    Graphics Card and Screen 66
    Partitioning 66
    Expert Partitioning 66
    Logical Volume Manager (LVM) 67
    Soft RAID 72
Network/Basic 76
    E-Mail 76
Network/Advanced 77
    Configuring an NFS Server 77
    Configuring NIS 77
    Host Name and DNS Configuration 78
    Configuring Routing 78
Security and Users 78
    Firewall 78
System 78
    Runlevel Editor 79
    Sysonfig Editor 79
Miscellaneous 80

SuSE Linux – Administration Guide   v

5 Booting and Boot Managers 81

Booting a PC 82
Boot Concepts 83
Map Files, LILO, and GRUB 84
An Overview of LILO 85
Configuring LILO 87
    Structure of lilo.conf 88
    Other LILO Configuration Options 91
Installing and Uninstalling LILO 94
Sample Configurations 97
    DOS/Windows 95/98 and Linux 97
    Windows NT or Windows 2000 and Linux 98
LILO Problems 99
Booting with GRUB 100
    The Menu 100
    Names for BIOS devices 101
    Installation Using the GRUB Shell 102
Creating Boot CDs 102
    Procedure 103
    Boot CD with ISOLINUX 103
Configuring the Boot Mechanism with loadlin 104

6 The X Window System 113

Historical Background 113
Version 4.x of XFree86 114
Configuration of the X Window System with SaX2 116
    Differences Between the X Server and the Window Manager 116
    About SaX2 116
    Start-Up and Hardware Recognition 117
    Configuration 117
    Controlling the Mouse with the Keyboard 118
    Adjusting the Image Geometry 125

	Starting the Graphical Interface	126
	Further Configurations	126
	The X Server Log File	130
	Starting the X Window System	132
	FAQ and Troubleshooting	133
	Optimizing the Installation of the X Window System	138
	Integrating Additional (True Type) Fonts	143
	OpenGL — 3D Configuration	146
7	**Sound with ALSA**	**151**
	Basic PCM Types	152
	Compressing Audio Data	152
	Buffering and Latencies	153
	ALSA and MIDI	154
	Loading Sound Fonts (SB Live! and AWE)	155
8	**Printer Operation**	**157**
	Printing Basics	158
	Making the Printer Work	161
	Configuring a Printer with YaST2	165
	Print Queues and Configurations	165
	Printer Configuration with YaST2: The Basics	166
	Automatic Configuration	168
	Manual Configuration	168
	Printer Configuration in Application Programs	172
	Printing from the Command Line	172
	Using the LPRng and lpdfilter System	172
	Using the CUPS System	172
	Manual Configuration of Local Printer Ports	173
	Parallel Ports	173
	USB Ports	176
	The IrDA Printer Interface	178
	Serial Ports	179

Manual Configuration of the LPRng and lpdfilter Printing System . . . 179
The LPRng and lpdfilter Print Spooler 179
Command-Line Tools for LPRng 180
    Managing Local Queues 181
    Managing Remote Queues 183
The Print Filter of the LPRng and lpdfilter Printing System 184
Custom Print Filters for the LPRng Spooler 194
The CUPS Printing System 198
    Naming Conventions 198
    IPP and Server 198
    Configuration of a CUPS Server 199
    Network Printers 201
    Internal CUPS Print Job Processing 202
    Tips & Tricks 203
Command-Line Tools for the CUPS Printing System 205
    Managing Local Queues 205
    Managing Remote Queues 208
Working with Ghostscript 210
Working with a2ps 213
Reformatting PostScript with psutils 215
    psnup 216
    pstops 216
    psselect 220
    Using Ghostscript to View the Output 221
ASCII Text Encoding 221
Printing in a TCP/IP Network 224
    Terminology 224
    Remote Printer Troubleshooting 232
    Print Servers Supporting Both LPD and IPP 235

9 Hotplugging Services — 237
- Hotplugging in Linux 238
- Hotplugging and Coldplugging 238
- USB 239
- PCI and PCMCIA 240
- Network 241
- Firewire (IEEE1394) 242
- Other Devices and Further Development 242

10 Configuring and Using Laptop Computers — 243
- PCMCIA 244
  - The Hardware 244
  - The Software 244
  - Configuration 246
  - Switching Configurations — SCPM 248
  - Troubleshooting 248
  - Installation via PCMCIA 252
  - Other Utilities 253
  - Updating the Kernel or PCMCIA Package 254
  - For More Information 254
- IrDA — Infrared Data Association 254
  - Software 255
  - Configuration 255
  - Usage 255
  - Troubleshooting 256

III System — 259

11 The Linux Kernel — 261
- Kernel Update 262
- Kernel Sources 262
- Kernel Configuration 263

Kernel Modules	264
Settings in the Kernel Configuration	266
Compiling the Kernel	267
Installing the Kernel	267
Cleaning Your Hard Disk After Compilation	268

12 Special Features of SuSE Linux — 269

Linux Standards	270
File System Hierarchy Standard (FHS)	270
Linux Standard Base (LSB)	270
teTeX — TeX in SuSE Linux	270
Example Environments for FTP and HTTP	270
Hints on Special Software Packages	271
Package bash and /etc/profile	271
cron Package	271
Log Files — the Package logrotate	272
Man Pages	274
The Command ulimit	274
The free Command	275
The File /etc/resolv.conf	275
Booting with the Initial Ramdisk	276
Concept of the Initial Ramdisk	276
The Order of the Booting Process with initrd	276
Boot Loaders	277
Using initrd in SuSE	278
Possible Difficulties — Self-Compiled Kernels	279
Prospects	280
linuxrc	280
The SuSE Rescue System	285
Preparations	286
Starting the Rescue System	287
Working with the Rescue System	288
Virtual Consoles	291
Keyboard Mapping	291
Local Adjustments — I18N/L10N	292

13 The SuSE Linux Boot Concept — 295
The init Program 296
Runlevels 296
Changing Runlevels 298
Init Scripts 298
The YaST2 Runlevel Editor 301
SuSEconfig, /etc/sysconfig, and /etc/rc.config 301
Using the YaST2 sysconfig Editor 303
System Configuration: Scripts and Variables 303

IV Network — 333

14 Linux in the Network — 335
TCP/IP — The Protocol Used by Linux 336
    Layer Model 337
    IP Addresses and Routing 339
    Domain Name System 342
IPv6 — The Next Generation's Internet 344
    A New Internet Protocol 344
    Structure of an IPv6 Address 345
    IPv6 Netmasks 348
    For More Information About IPv6 348
Network Integration 349
    Preparing 349
    Configuration Assisted by YaST2 349
    Hotplug and PCMCIA 351
    Configuring IPv6 351
Manual Network Configuration 352
    Configuration Files 353
    Start-Up Scripts 359
Routing in SuSE Linux 359
DNS — Domain Name Service 361

        Starting the Name Server BIND 361
        The Configuration File /etc/named.conf 362
        For More Information 369
    NIS — Network Information Service 371
        NIS Master and Slave Server 371
        Manual Installation of an NIS Client 373
    NFS — Shared File Systems 375
        Importing File Systems with YaST2 375
        Importing File Systems Manually 375
        Exporting File Systems with YaST2 375
        Exporting File Systems Manually 376
    DHCP 379
        The DHCP Protocol 379
        DHCP Software Packages 379
        The DHCP Server dhcpd 380
        Assigning Fixed IP Addresses to Hosts 382
        The Finer Points 383

15 Heterogenous Networks   385
    Samba 386
        Installing and Configuring the Server 387
        Samba as Login Server 391
        Installing Clients 392
        Optimization 393
    Netatalk 394
        Configuring the File Server 395
        Configuring the Print Server 398
        Starting the Server 399
    Netware Emulation with MARSNWE 401
        Starting the Netware Emulator MARSNWE 401
        The Configuration File /etc/nwserv.conf 401
        Access to Netware Servers and Their Administration 404
        IPX Router with ipxrip 405

16 Internet — 407

- Configuring an ADSL or T-DSL Connection 408
  - Default Configuration 408
  - DSL Connection by Dial-on-Demand 408
- Proxy Server: Squid 409
  - About Proxy Caches 409
  - Some Facts About Cache Proxying 410
  - System Requirements 412
  - Starting Squid 413
  - The Configuration File /etc/squid.conf 414
  - Transparent Proxy Configuration 419
  - Squid and Other Programs 422
  - More Information on Squid 426

17 Network Security — 427

- Masquerading and Firewalls 428
  - Masquerading Basics 428
  - Firewalling Basics 430
  - SuSEfirewall2 431
- SSH — Secure Shell, the Safe Alternative 433
  - The OpenSSH Package 434
  - The ssh Program 434
  - scp — Secure Copy 435
  - sftp — Secure File Transfer 435
  - The SSH Daemon (sshd) — Server-Side 435
  - SSH Authentication Mechanisms 436
  - X, Authentication, and Other Forwarding Mechanisms 438
- Network Authentication — Kerberos 438
  - Kerberos Terminology 439
  - How Kerberos Works 440
  - Users' View of Kerberos 443
  - For More Information 444
- Security and Confidentiality 445
  - Basic Considerations 445
  - Local Security and Network Security 446
  - Some General Security Tips and Tricks 454
  - Using the Central Security Reporting Address 456

SuSE Linux – Administration Guide _____ xiii

V Appendixes   457

A File Systems in Linux   459

    Glossary 460

    Major File Systems in Linux 460

        Ext2 461

        Ext3 461

        ReiserFS 462

        JFS 463

        XFS 464

    Some Other Supported File Systems 465

    Large File Support in Linux 466

    For More Information 467

B Manual Page of e2fsck   469

C The GNU General Public License   473

Bibliography   481

Preface

[SuS02b] showed how easy it is to install and operate your new SuSE Linux, how to install your hardware and software, how various applications are operated, and where you can find quick help. You are now holding the new *Administration Manual* in your hands. Experienced SuSE Linux users probably know the predecessor to this book, titled *The Reference*.

This book offers an introduction to the technology of SuSE Linux, including details of system administration and the configuration of special system components. It also describes the theoretical foundation of certain properties of Linux and especially of SuSE Linux. This includes background information about the X Window System, the boot concept, printing with Linux, and the kernel.

The operation with and in networks has always been one of the strengths of Linux. This is why great part of the book has been dedicated to the theory, configuration, and administration of networks with their various protocols and services, to routing, NFS and NIS, to heterogenous networks with Samba and Netatalk as well as to proxies and the Apache web server. A comprehensive chapter on the delicate topic of security and its enforcement in networks concludes the book.

Changes to the Administration Manual

This section lists the changes to the documentation from the last version to the current:

- The following chapters have been greatly modified due to many innovations:
  - ▷ Adjustment of *The SuSE Linux Boot Concept* on page 295 to the current version (variables, /etc/sysconfig, etc.)
  - ▷ YaST2: Complex aspects were moved from the user manual to the administration maual.
  - ▷ Printing with CUPS and in a TCP/IP network
- The following chapters were added:
  - ▷ GRUB, an alternative boot manager.
  - ▷ Hotplug. How to connect or remove computer hardware during the runtime of the system. (ref. page 237).
  - ▷ Kerberos, an authentication mechanism (siehe Seite 438).
  - ▷ Comparison of Linux file systems (siehe Seite 459).

Typographical conventions

The following typographical conventions are used in this book:

Text layout	Meaning
YaST	programs
`/etc/passwd`	file or directory names
⟨*parameter*⟩	when entering a command, `parameter` should be replaced by the actual value, excluding the angle brackets.
`PATH`	the environment variable `PATH`
`192.168.1.2`	the value of a variable. In this case, 192.168.1.2
`ls`	the command `ls`
`news`	the user `news`
`earth:~ #` **`ls`**	Input of `ls` in the command shell of the user `root` in his home directory of the host "Earth"
`newbie@earth:~ >` **`ls`**	Input of `ls` in the command shell of user `newbie` in his home directory on the host "Earth"
`C:\>` **`fdisk`**	DOS prompt with the command input `fdisk`
Alt	A key to press. Keys to press sequentially are separated by spaces.
Ctrl + Alt + Del	Keys to press simultaneously are grouped with the '+' sign.
"Permission denied"	System messages
'System Update'	Menu items, buttons, labels

A Word of Thanks

The list of all people who contributed to the success of this distribution would fill a book alone. We would therefore like to generally thank here all people who have contributed with their relentless efforts to presenting you an excellent and better than ever SuSE Linux.

The developers of Linux promote the becoming of Linux with their immense voluntary effort in world-wide cooperation. We thank them for their commitment for this distribution would not exist without them.

And last but not least, our special thanks goes naturally out to Linus Torvalds!

Have a lot of fun!

Your SuSE team

Part I

Installation

The Installation

SuSE Linux can be installed according to a number of local requirements. The various methods span from manual installation to fully automated installation.

The following sections cover the various installation methods, like for instance the text-based installation with YaST2, inform about various installation sources (CD-ROM, FTP, NFS) as well as about automated installation sources. A comprehensive description of the standard graphical installation can be found at the beginning of the user manual. This chapter concludes with installation troubleshooting and a tutorial on resolving problems should they arise.

Text-Based Installation with YaST2	8
Starting SuSE Linux	13
Special Installations	16
Tips and Tricks	18
Partitioning for Experts	24

/WichtigThis administration guide only describes special installation methods. A comprehensive description of the standard graphical installation routine can be found at the beginning of the user manual.

Text-Based Installation with YaST2

Background Information

In addition to installation with the assistance of a graphical interface, SuSE Linux can also be installed with the help of the YaST2 text menus (console mode). All modules are available in this text mode. The text mode is especially useful if you do not need a graphical interface (e.g., for server systems) or if the graphics card is not supported by the X Window System.

The Start Screen

Insert CD 1 into the drive and restart the computer. If the computer does not boot the CD, reset the boot sequence in the BIOS to CDROM, C, A.

The start screen appears. Select 'Manual Installation' within ten seconds so YaST2 does *not* automatically start. Enter boot parameters in the boot options after manual, if your hardware requires such parameters. However, such parameters are usually not needed. To switch to text mode, select (F2=Text) then press (↵).

Now, a box appears with the progress display "Loading Linux kernel". The kernel boots and linuxrc is started.

The menu-driven linuxrc application waits for user entries.

Possible Problems

- If your CD-ROM drive (ATAPI) crashes when booting the system, refer to Section *ATAPI CD-ROM Hangs While Reading* on page 21.

- CD 1, which features an optimized kernel for Pentium processors, is not recognized as a boot medium. Try the "boot floppy" or CD 2. Refer to Sections *Booting from Disk (SYSLINUX)* on page 18 and *Booting with CD 2* on page 18.

- For graphics cards, including FireGL 1, 2, and 3, the graphical mode does not boot (framebuffer). In this case, text-based installation is required.

- The start option 'Installation – Safe Settings' is provided whenever DMA leads to difficulties.

linuxrc: The Basics

Make installation settings using linuxrc. If necessary, load drivers as kernel modules. Finally, linuxrc launches the YaST installation tool, starting the actual installation of the system software and other applications.

Use ⟨↑⟩ or ⟨↓⟩ to choose menu items and ⟨←⟩ or ⟨→⟩ to select a command, such as 'Ok' or 'Cancel'. Run the command by pressing ⟨↵⟩.

Thorough documentation of linuxrc can be found in *linuxrc* on page 280.

Settings

The linuxrc application opens with language and keyboard selection options.

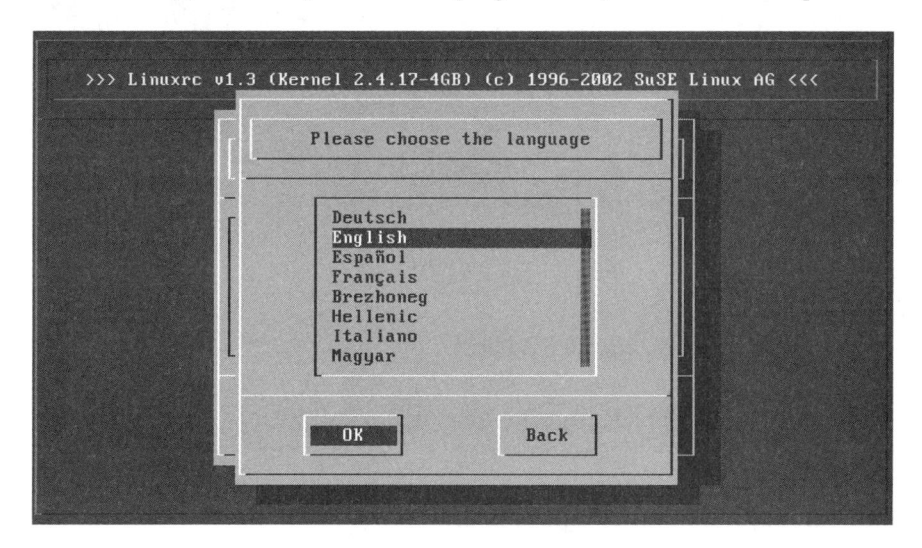

Figure 1.1: Language Selection

- Select the installation language (e. g., 'English') and confirm with ⟨↵⟩.
- Next, select the keyboard layout (e. g., 'English').

Possible Problems

- linuxrc does not provide a selection for your preferred keyboard layout. If this is the case, select an alternative layout. Following the installation, use YaST later to switch to the exact layout.

Main Menu in linuxrc

Now, you find yourself in the main menu in linuxrc (Figure 1.2).

```
>>> Linuxrc v1.3 (Kernel 2.4.17-4GB) (c) 1996-2002 SuSE Linux AG <<<

                        ┌─────────────────────────┐
                        │       Main menu         │
                        └─────────────────────────┘
                   ┌──────────────────────────────────┐
                   │            Settings              │
                   │        System information        │
                   │   Kernel modules (hardware drivers) │
                   │     Start installation / system  │
                   │          Exit / Reboot           │
                   │           Power off              │
                   │                                  │
                   │      ┌──────┐      ┌──────┐     │
                   │      │  OK  │      │ Back │     │
                   │      └──────┘      └──────┘     │
                   └──────────────────────────────────┘
```

Figure 1.2: Main Menu in linuxrc

The following options are offered here:

'Settings' Adjust the language, monitor, or keyboard here. This was configured in the previous sections.

'System Information' Find information about the hardware here, if recognized by the kernel and activated by the loaded modules.

'Kernel Modules (Hardware Drivers)' You may need to launch hardware-compatible modules here. These also include additional file systems to load (ReiserFS).

As a rule, you do *not* need to use this menu item if your hard disks and CD-ROM drive (ATAPI) are connected to an (E)IDE controller, as the (E)IDE support is already built into the kernel.

'Installation/System boot' Continues installation

'Cancel/Reboot' Cancel the installation.

'Power off' Shuts down the system and cuts off the power.

Integrating the Hardware Using Modules

Select loading of kernel modules with 'Kernel module' only if you need support for SCSI or for PCMCIA or if you do *not* have an ATAPI drive. At present, other components are also be swapped out as modules (e.g., IDE) or added (e.g., USB, FireWire, or file systems). Read about how modules are loaded in Section *linuxrc* on page 280. In the following submenu, choose which modules to load. Possible choices are:

A SCSI module if you have a SCSI hard disk or SCSI CD-ROM drive.

A CD-ROM module if your CD-ROM drive is *not* connected to the (E)IDE controller or the SCSI controller.

A network module if you want to install via NFS or FTP, but this is not discussed here.

One or more file systems such as ReiserFS or ext3.

--- Tip ---

If you cannot find any support for your installation medium (proprietary CD-ROM drive, parallel port CD-ROM drive, network cards, PCMCIA) among the standard modules, you may find what you need on the `modules` floppy disk, which contains additional drivers. To do this, go to the end of the list and select the item '-- More modules --'. You are then asked to insert the `modules`.

--- Tip ---

Starting Installation

Since you have already selected 'Installation/System boot', press ⏎ to begin the installation.

The following items are available:

'Start Installation/Update' Prepare for an installation or an update of the existing system.

'Boot Installed System' You will probably need this item later if you encounter problems when booting your system.

'Boot Rescue System' This option is currently only offered for X86-compatible systems.

SuSE Linux – Administration Guide   11

Figure 1.3: linuxrc *Installation Menu*

'Eject CD'   Eject CD electronically.

To begin the installation, press ⏎ to access the menu item 'Start Installation/Update'. Then, choose the source medium. Usually, the cursor can be left at the default selection: 'CD-ROM'.

Now press ⏎. The installation environment will be loaded directly from the CD 1.

As soon as this procedure is completed, YaST2 starts in the text-based version (ncurses). The installation thens continue as described in [SuS02a], Chapter *Installation*.

Possible Problems

- The SCSI adapter is not detected:
    - ▷ Try loading a module for a compatible driver.
    - ▷ Use a kernel with the appropriate integrated SCSI driver. Create a boot floppy as described in Section *Creating a Boot Disk in DOS* on page 19.

- The ATAPI CD-ROM drive hangs when reading the data. See *ATAPI CD-ROM Hangs While Reading* on page 21.

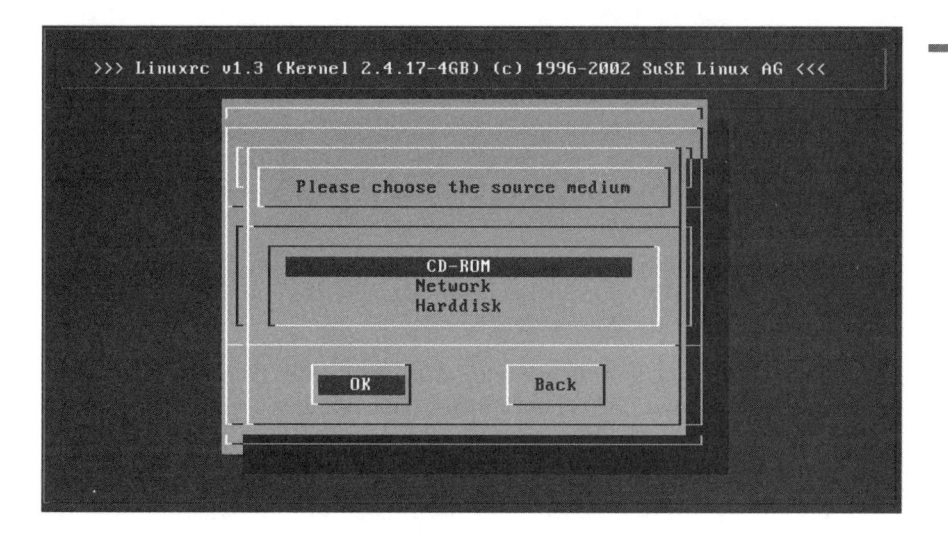

Figure 1.4: Selecting the Source Medium in linuxrc

- For reasons still unknown, sometimes problems occur when loading data to the RAM disk, so YaST2 cannot be started. If this situation arises, the following procedure can often lead to efficient results:

  Select 'Settings' → 'Debug (Experts)' in the linuxrc main menu. There, select no in 'Force root image'. Then go back to the main menu and restart installation.

Starting SuSE Linux

After installation, the question remains as to how you want to boot your system normally.

The following section describes the options you have for booting your SuSE Linux system. The best boot method for you depends on the intended use of your Linux system.

Boot disk You can boot Linux from a *boot disk* ("boot floppy"). This choice will always work (as long as the boot disk does not get corrupted) and it is easy. The boot disk may have been created during the installation.

loadlin The loadlin boot option can be configured as follows:

- The computer must be running either in DOS Real mode or have a VCPI server in virtual 8086 mode [1] In other words, this method will *not* function in Unix, OS/2, Windows NT, or in a DOS window on a Windows 95/98 machine. It does, however, function well from MS-DOS or from Windows 95/98 in DOS mode.
- Your computer must have enough DOS memory available: there must be 128 KB available below the 640 KB limit, the rest can be on extended/EMS/XMS memory.

loadlin is fairly labor intensive to set up, but it can be easily integrated into the Windows 95/98 boot menus. This requires a manual editing of configuration files. One of the biggest advantages of loadlin is that nothing is installed into the MBR (*Master Boot Record*) of the hard disk. To other operating systems, Linux partitions appear as an unknown type.

To install loadlin, you need to know a little about Linux and DOS. You should also be able to create configuration files with an editor. Find details in Section *Configuring the Boot Mechanism with loadlin* on page 104. If you make a mistake in the Windows 95/98 boot menus, this could cause problems. In the event of an extreme error, you may loose access to your Windows hard drive. *Before* you start modifying your Windows boot menu, make sure you can boot your Windows operating system with a boot floppy.

Linux bootloader The universal and technically elegant solution for booting your system is the employment of a Linux bootmanager like LILO (LInux LOader) or GRUB, which both allow to choose among different operating systems prior to booting. The boot loader can either be configured during installation later with the help of YaST.

⌐ **Caution** ───

There are BIOS variants that check the structure of the boot sector (MBR) and, after a LILO installation, erroneously display a virus warning. This problem can be easily removed by entering the BIOS and looking for corresponding adjustable settings. For example, you should switch off 'virus protection'. You can switch this option back on again later. It is unnecessary, however, if Linux is the only operating system you are using.

─── **Caution** ⌋

---
[1] A VCPI server is accessed by the program emm386.exe.

A detailed discussion of various boot methods, especially of LILO, GRUB and loadlin, can be found in Chapter *Booting and Boot Managers* on page 81.

The Graphical SuSE Screen

Starting with SuSE Linux 7.2, the graphical SuSE screen is displayed on the first console, as long as the option "vga=771" has been provided as a kernel parameter. If you install using YaST2, this option is automatically activated.

Disabling the SuSE Screen

Basically there are three ways to achieve this:

- Disabling SuSE screen on an as-needed basis:

    Enter the command

    `earth:~ #` **`echo 0 >/proc/splash`**

    to disable the graphical screen. The following command activates the screen again.

    `earth:~ #` **`echo 0x0f01 >/proc/splash`**

- Disabling the SuSE screen by default:

    Add the kernel parameter `splash=0` to your boot loader configuration. Chapter *Booting and Boot Managers* on page 81 offers more information on this. However, if you prefer the old text mode anyway (which was the default with previous versions), you should set this to `"vga=normal"`.

- Completely disabling the SuSE screen:

    Compile a new kernel after disabling the option `Use splash screen instead of boot logo` in the menu 'framebuffer support'.

    ⌐ **Tip** ─────────────────────────────────

    Removing the framebuffer support from the kernel will automatically disable the splash screen as well. SuSE cannot not provide any support for your system if you run it with a custom kernel.

    ─────────────────────────────── **Tip** ⌡

Special Installations

Installation Without a Supported CD-ROM Drive

What do you do if a standard installation via the CD-ROM drive is not possible? Your CD-ROM drive might not be supported if it is an older, "proprietary" model. It might be your second computer, a notebook, for example, which might not even have a CD-ROM drive, but instead has an Ethernet adapter or a PLIP cable. SuSE Linux provides ways of installing over a network connection to such a machine without using a supported CD-ROM drive. NFS or FTP via Ethernet or via PLIP (Section *Installation from a Network Source* on this page) is available.

Installation from a Network Source

We do not offer support for this method of installation. It is only recommended for experienced computer users.

There is *no* CD-ROM installed on the machine on which you want to install Linux. You are able to connect to a remote machine over the network that has an installed CD-ROM drive (and CD) or that has a copy of the CD on its hard disk. In addition, it is necessary to copy the files .S.u.S.E-disk* from the CD-ROM to the hard disk. This can be abbreviated in the following way:

```
earth:~ # cp /media/cdrom/.S* /emil
earth:~ # cp -a /media/cdrom/suse /emil
```

This "other" computer must "export" the directory in a suitable manner.

> **Tip**
> Alternatively, it is sufficient to start the rescue system on the remote machine and directly export the CD 1.
> **Tip**

Installation Steps

1. Start the installation of the client as specified in Section *Text-Based Installation with YaST2* on page 8.

2. Continue with the installation as described in Section *linuxrc: The Basics* on page 9, but:

- when you come to 'Kernel modules', select 'Networking cards' and load the necessary driver. This is not necessary if you are installing via PLIP.

- when prompted by linuxrc to specify the 'Source medium', select 'Network (NFS)' then configure the network using the available menus. As an alternative, install via FTP or SMB.

3. Finish up the installation as described in [SuS02a], Chapter *Installation*.

Possible Problems

- The installation aborts before it has actually started, because the installation directory of the "other" machine was not exported with `exec` permissions. Correct this and start again.

- The server does not know the computer on which SuSE Linux should be installed. Enter the name and IP address of the computer to install into the file `/etc/hosts` of the server.

Tips and Tricks

Booting from Disk (SYSLINUX)

The "boot disk" method can be used as a fallback solution if you have to deal with special installation requirements (e. g., the CD-ROM drive is not available). For more information on creating the boot disk, read *Creating a Boot Disk in DOS* on the next page and *Creating a Boot Disk in a UNIX-Related System* on page 20.

The bootstrapping process is initiated by the boot loader SYSLINUX (package `syslinux`). SYSLINUX is configured so that some minimal hardware detection is performed at start-up. Basically this includes the following steps:

- Checking whether the BIOS provides VESA 2.0 compliant framebuffer support and making sure the kernel is booted accordingly.

- Reading out any available monitor information (DDC info).

- Reading the first sector of the first hard disk (the "MBR") to arrange for the LILO configuration later, where BIOS IDs will be assigned to Linux device names. This involves a test to read out the sector using the BIOS's lba32 function to find out whether the BIOS supports the corresponding features.

> **Tip**
>
> If you keep (⇧ Shift) pressed when SYSLINUX is started, all of the above steps will be skipped. To ease troubleshooting, add the line `verbose 1` to your `syslinux.cfg`, in which case the boot loader will tell you which action is being performed.
>
> **Tip**

Possible Problems

If the machine does not want to boot from a floppy, change the boot sequence in the BIOS to `A, C`.

Booting with CD 2

As well as CD 1, the second CD is also bootable. On CD 1, a 2.88 MB boot image is used. The second CD contains a traditional image of 1.44 MB in size.

Use CD 2 when you know for certain that you can boot from CD, but when things do not work with CD 1 (the "fallback" solution). Unfortunately, not every BIOS correctly recognizes the large images.

Creating a Boot Disk in DOS

Requirements

You need a formatted 3.5" floppy disk and a bootable 3.5" floppy drive.

Additional Information

CD 1, in the directory /disks, contains a number of disk images. Such an image can be copied to a disk with help from suitable auxiliary programs. This disk is then called a boot disk. These disk images also include the "loader", SYSLINUX, and the program linuxrc. SYSLINUX allows selection of a specific kernel for the booting process and to add parameters for your hardware, if necessary. The program linuxrc supports the loading of kernel modules for your hardware then starts the installation.

Procedure

The DOS application rawrite.exe (CD 1, directory \dosutils\rawrite) is useful for generating the SuSE boot and module disks. Requirements for this are a machine with a DOS (e.g., FreeDOS) or Windows.

The procedure described in the following is for working with Windows:

1. Insert the SuSE Linux CD 1.

2. Open a DOS window (in the start menu under 'Applications' → 'MS-DOS Prompt').

3. Start the rawrite.exe application by giving the correct path name for the CD drive. The following example takes place on the C: drive in the Windows directory and your CD drive is D:

   C:\Windows> **d:\dosutils\rawrite\rawrite**

4. After starting the application, it will prompt you for the source and destination of the file to copy. The image of the bootdisk is stored on CD 1 under \disks. The file is simply named bootdisk. Do not forget to specify the path for your CD drive here either.

   C:\Windows> **d:\dosutils\rawrite\rawrite** RaWrite 1.2 -- Write disk file to raw floppy diskette

SuSE Linux – Administration Guide   19

```
Enter source file name:  d:\disks\bootdisk Enter destination
drive:  a:
```

As soon as you have specified the destination drive `a:`, rawrite will prompt you to insert a formatted disk then press (Enter). You will subsequently be shown the copy progress. This process can be terminated with (Ctrl) + (C).

In this manner, you can also create the other floppy images, `modules1` and `modules2`. These are required if you have SCSI devices or a network card and want to access them during installation. If you have trouble with this, you can use the image `i386` instead as fallback.

Creating a Boot Disk in a UNIX-Related System

Requirements

You need access to a Unix or Linux system with a CD-ROM drive and a formatted disk.

To create a boot disk:

1. If you need to format the disks first:

   ```
   earth:~ # fdformat /dev/fd0u1440
   ```

2. Mount the first CD 1 to `/cdrom`, for example:

   ```
   earth:~ # mount -tiso9660 /dev/cdrom /cdrom
   ```

3. Change to the `disks` directory on CD:

   ```
   earth:~ # cd /cdrom/disks
   ```

4. Create the boot disk with

   ```
   earth:~ # dd if=/cdrom/disks/bootdisk of=/dev/fd0 bs=8k
   ```

   In the `README` file in the directory `disks`, read about what features specific kernels have. These files can be read with `more` or `less`.

In this manner, you can also create the other floppy images, `modules1` and `modules2`. These are required if you have SCSI devices or a network card and want to access them during installation. If you have trouble with this, you can use the image `i386` instead.

Somewhat more complex is using a self-compiled kernel during installation. In this case, write the default image (`bootdisk`) to the disk then overwrite the actual kernel (`linux`) with your own kernel (refer to Section *Compiling the Kernel* on page 267):

```
earth:~ #  dd if=/cdrom/disks/scsi01 of=/dev/fd0 bs=8k
earth:~ #  mount -t msdos /dev/fd0 /mnt
earth:~ #  cp /cdrom/suse/images/eide.ikr /mnt/linux
earth:~ #  umount /mnt
```

Supported CD-ROM Drives

Almost every CD-ROM drive is now supported by Linux.

- Using ATAPI drives (those drives connected to an EIDE controller), there should be no problems at all.

- A key issue for SCSI CD-ROM drives is whether the SCSI controller connected to the CD-ROM drive is supported. The supported SCSI controllers are listed in the `http://cdb.suse.de/`. However, if your SCSI controller is not supported and your hard drive is connected to it, you will have a problem anyway.

- Many proprietary CD-ROM drives are supported under Linux. Here is the most likely place for problems to occur. If your drive is not mentioned, try choosing a similar type.

- Parallel port CD-ROM drives have become very popular. Unfortunately, there is no standard, leading to unexpected trouble. SuSE Linux contains a number of alpha drivers for some devices. If none of them works, install via DOS. Keep in mind that you may access some of these devices only after they have been set up under DOS. You might need a warm reboot.

ATAPI CD-ROM Hangs While Reading

If your ATAPI CD-ROM is not recognized or it hangs while reading, this is most frequently due to incorrectly installed hardware. All devices must be connected to the EIDE controller in the correct order. The first device is master on the first controller. The second device is slave on the first controller. The third device should be master on the second controller, and so forth.

It often occurs that there is only a CD-ROM besides the first device. The CD-ROM drive is sometimes connected as master to the second controller (secondary IDE controller). This is wrong and can cause Linux not to know what to do with this "gap". Try to fix this by passing the appropriate parameter to the kernel (`hdc=cdrom`).

Sometimes one of the devices is just "misjumpered". This means it is jumpered as slave, but is connected as master, or vice versa. When in doubt, check your hardware settings and correct them where necessary.

In addition, there is a series of faulty EIDE chipsets, most of which have now been identified. There is a special kernel to handle such cases. See the `README` in `/disks` of the installation CD-ROM.

If booting does not work immediately, try using the following kernel parameters:

hd⟨x⟩=cdrom   ⟨x⟩ stands for a, b, c, d, etc., and is interpreted as follows:

- a — Master on the first IDE controller
- b — Slave on the first IDE controller
- c — Master on the second IDE controller
- ...

An example of ⟨*parameter to enter*⟩: `hdb=cdrom`

With this parameter, specify the CD-ROM drive to the kernel, if it cannot find it itself and if you have an ATAPI CD-ROM drive.

ide⟨x⟩=noautotune   ⟨x⟩ stands for 0, 1, 2, 3, etc., and is interpreted as follows:

- 0 — First IDE controller
- 1 — Second IDE controller
- ...

An example of ⟨*parameter to enter*⟩: `ide0=noautotune`

This parameter is often useful for (E)IDE hard disks.

Problems with CD-ROM Drives on Parallel Port

All available drivers are listed by linuxrc at the installation. Normally there are no peculiarities.

Unfortunately, lots of drives (e. g., Freecom) are not supported yet. It may be that you cannot use them although the manual claims that the type is identical to a supported one. The manufacturer apparently has changed the internals without making these changes public.

Some devices need to be initialized by the DOS driver before making them available under Linux:

1. Boot DOS and load the CD-ROM driver.
2. Insert a Linux boot disk.
3. Warm reboot the machine.

If your drive is not supported, install from a DOS partition (see Section *Special Installations* on page 16).

For current information on parallel port programming, have a look at http://www.torque.net/linux-pp.html.

Loadlin Does Not Have Enough Memory to Load the Kernel

You do not have enough free memory within the first 640 KB. Try to remove drivers from your start-up files (`config.sys`, `autoexec.bat`) or shift them to memory after the first 640 KB. If you use compressed drives under Windows 95/98 and shifting the driver to high memory does not work, decompress those drives.

Loadlin Does Not Start

If you encounter any problems using loadlin, start `loadlin` using the following options: `-v`, `-t`, or `-d`. It is best to write the debug information into a file, `debug.out`.

`C:\> `**`loadlin -d debug.out`** ⟨*other parameters*⟩

You could send this file to the SuSE support. For ⟨*other parameters*⟩, enter your system-specific values (see Section *Required Files for loadlin* on page 105).

Partitioning for Experts

This section provides detailed information for tailoring a system that best suits your needs. This section is mainly of interest for those who want an optimized system as far as security and performance are concerned and who are prepared to reinstall the complete system where necessary.

It is absolutely essential that you have extensive knowledge of the functions of a UNIX file system. You should be familiar with the topics mount point and physical, extended, and logical partitions.

It should be mentioned here that there is *no* golden rule for all, but many rules for each situation. However, you will find concrete figures in this section to help you.

First, you need to gather the following information:

- What is the purpose of the machine (file server, compute server, stand-alone machine)?

- How many people are going to work with this machine (simultaneous logins)?

- How many hard disks are installed? How big are they and what kind (EIDE, SCSI, or even RAID controllers)?

Size of Swap Partition

Quite often you will read: "Swap should be at least as large as physical RAM". This is a relic of times when 8 MB was regarded as a lot of RAM memory.

Applications that need considerable memory have shifted these values up. Generally, 64 MB of virtual swap should be sufficient. Do not be stingy. If you compile a kernel in X and want to have a look at the manual pages using Netscape and have an emacs running, you will already take up all 64 MB.

To be safe, opt for at least 128 MB of virtual memory. One thing you should never do is not assign swap space at all. Even on a machine with 256 MB RAM, there should be a swap partition. The reasons for this are outlined in Section *Processing Speed and Size of Main Memory* on page 28.

If you want to run extensive simulations with a memory requirement of several gigabytes, read Section *Using as a Compute Server* on page 26 (Example: compute server).

installation	required disk space
minimum	180 MB to 400 MB
small	400 MB to 800 MB
medium	800 MB to 4 GB
large	4 GB to 8 GB

Table 1.1: Examples of Disk Space Requirements for Different Installations

Implementation of the Computer

Computer Used as Stand-Alone Machine

The most common use for a Linux machine is as a stand-alone computer. To make decisions as easy as possible for you, we provide you with some concrete figures you can use at home or at your company. Table 1.1 is an overview of size requirements for different Linux systems.

Example: stand-alone machine (small)

You have a 500 MB spare hard disk to hold Linux: use a 64 MB swap partition and the rest for / (root partition).

Example: stand-alone machine (average)

You have 1,2 GB available for Linux. A small boot partition `/boot` (5–10 MB or 1 cylinder), 128 MB for Swap, 800 MB for /, and the rest for a separate `/home` partition.

Example: stand-alone machine (deluxe)

If you have more than 1.2 GB available, there is no standard way to partition. Read Section *Optimizations* on the next page.

Using as a File Server

Here, hard disk performance is *really* crucial. You should use SCSI devices if possible. Keep in mind the performance of the disk and the controller. A file server is used to save data centrally. This data might be home directories, a database, or other archives. The advantage of this is that administration of the data is simple.

If the file server will serve a huge net (20 users and more), optimizing hard disk access is essential. Suppose you want to provide a file server for 25 users (their home directories). If the average user requires 100–150 MB for personal space, a 4 GB disk mounted under `home` will probably do.

If there are fifty such users, you will need an 8 GB disk. In this case, it would be better to split `home` into two 4-GB disks, as now they would then share the load (and access time).

> **Tip**
>
> The web browser cache should absolutely be stored locally on the user's hard disk.

Using as a Compute Server

A compute server is generally a powerful machine that carries out extensive calculations over the net. Normally, such a machine is equipped with extensive main memory (512 RAM or greater). The only point where fast disks are needed is for the swap space. If you have a number of hard disks, you can spread swap partitions across them.

Optimizations

The disks are normally the limiting factor. To avoid this bottleneck, there are two possibilities that should be used together:

- separate the load onto multiple disks
- use an optimized file system (e.g., `reiserfs`).
- equip your file server with enough memory (at least 256 MB)

Using Multiple Disks in Parallel

This needs some further discussion. The total amount of time needed for transferring data can be separated into five factors:

- time elapsed until the request reaches the controller
- time elapsed until this request is send to the disk
- time elapsed until the hard disk manages to set its head
- time elapsed until the media has turned to the right sector

- time elapsed for transferring data

The first factor depends on the network connection and has to be regulated elsewhere. We do not cover this here. The second factor can be ignored, because it depends on the controller. The third factor is the vital part. The time is counted in milliseconds. Relative to the access time of main memory (measured in nanoseconds), this is a factor of one million. The fourth factor depends on the disk rotation speed. The fifth factor depends on the rotation speed, the number of heads, and the actual position of the data (inside or outside).

For optimized performance, consider factor three. Here, the SCSI feature "disconnect" comes into play. Look at what happens:

The controller sends the command (in this case to the hard disk) "Go to track x, sector y" to the device. Now the disk motor has to start. If this is an intelligent disk (if it supports disconnect) and the driver itself is also able to do disconnect, the controller sends a disconnect and the disk separates itself from the SCSI bus. Now other SCSI devices can do work. After a time (depending on the strategy or load on the SCSI bus), a connection to the disk is reestablished. Normally, the device has now reached the requested track.

On a multitasking, multiuser system like Linux, there are lots of optimizations that can be done here. Look at an output of the command df (see Output 1).

```
Filesystem         Size  Used Avail Use% Mounted on
/dev/sda5          1.8G  1.6G  201M  89% /
/dev/sda1           23M  3.9M   17M  18% /boot
/dev/sdb1          2.9G  2.1G  677M  76% /usr
/dev/sdc1          1.9G  958M  941M  51% /usr/lib
shmfs              185M     0  184M   0% /dev/shm
```

Output 1: Example of df Command Output

How does this parallelizing benefit us? Suppose we enter in /usr/src:

root@earth:/usr/src/ > **tar xzf package.tgz -C /usr/lib**

Here, package.tgz will be untarred into /usr/lib/package. To do so, the shell launches tar and gzip (located in /bin, so on /dev/sda) then package.tgz in /usr/src is read (on /dev/sdb). Last, the extracted data is written to /usr/lib (on /dev/sdc). Using parallelizing, positioning as well as read and write of the disks' internal buffers can be activated at the same time.

This is only one example. There are many more. If this example were a frequent processing requirement and if there are many disks (with the same speed), as a rule of thumb, /usr and /usr/lib should physically be placed on different disks. Here /usr/lib should have approximately seventy percent of the capacity of /usr. /, due to its access, should be placed on the disk containing /usr/lib.

>From a certain number of SCSI disks onwards (4–5), consider buying a RAID controller. Thus, operations on the disks are not merely semiparallel but parallel. Fault tolerance is one of its famous by-products.

Processing Speed and Size of Main Memory

The size of main memory is more important in Linux than the processor itself. One reason, if not the main reason, is Linux's ability to dynamically create buffers of hard disk data. Here, Linux uses lots of tricks, such as "read ahead" (getting sectors in advance) and "delayed write" (saving writes until there is a bundle to write). The latter is the reason why you should not switch off your Linux machine. Both factors contribute to the fact that the main memory seems to fill up over time as well as to Linux's high speed. See also Section *The free Command* on page 275.

2 Updating the System and Package Management

SuSE Linux provides the option of updating an existing system without completely reinstalling it. There are two types of updates: *updating individual software packages* and *updating the entire system*. Packages can also be installed by hand using the package manager RPM.

Updating SuSE Linux 30
Software Changes From Version to Version 34
RPM — the Distribution Package Manager 43

Updating SuSE Linux

Software tends to "grow" from version to version. Therefore, we recommend first taking a look at the available partition space with df *before* updating. If you suspect you are running short of disk space, secure your data before updating and repartition your system. There is no general rule of thumb regarding how much space each partition should have. Space requirements depend on your particular partitioning profile, the software selected, and the version numbers of SuSE Linux 8.1.

> **Note**
>
> It is recommended to read the README and, in DOS/Windows, README.DOS file on your CD. You will find notes there regarding any additional changes made *after* this manual went to print.
>
> **Note**

Preparations

Before you begin your update, copy the old configuration files to a separate medium just to be on the safe side. Such media can include streamers, removable disks, floppy drives, ZIP drives. This primarily applies to files stored in /etc. Also, review the configuration files in /var/lib. Furthermore, it cannot hurt to write the current user data in /home (the HOME directories) to a backup medium. Back up this data as root. Only root has read permission for all local files.

Before starting your update, make note of the root partition. The command df / lists the device name of the root partition. According to the Output 2, the root partition to write down is /dev/hda7.

```
Filesystem        Size  Used Avail Use% Mounted on
/dev/hda1         1.9G  189M  1.7G  10% /dos
/dev/hda7         3.0G  1.1G  1.7G  38% /
/dev/hda5          15M  2.4M   12M  17% /boot
shmfs             141M     0  141M   0% /dev/shm
```

Output 2: List with df -h

The root partition can be recognized as the one mounted as /.

Possible Problems

PostgreSQL
>   Before updating PostgreSQL (package `postgres`), it is usually best to "dump" the databases. See the man page for `pg_dump` (`man pg_dump`). This is, of course, only necessary if you actually *used* PostgreSQL prior to your update.

Promise Controller   The hard disk controller manufactured by Promise is currently found on high-end motherboards in numerous computer models, either as a pure IDE controller (for UDMA 100) or as an IDE-RAID controller. As of SuSE Linux 8.0, these controllers are directly supported by the kernel and treated as a standard controller for IDE hard disks. The additional kernel module `pdcraid` is required before you can aquire RAID functionality.

>   For some updates, hard disks on the Promise Controller may be detected before disks on the standard IDE controller. If so, the system will no longer boot following a kernel update and usually exit with "Kernel panic: VFS: unable to mount root fs". In this case, the kernel parameter ide=reverse must be passed when booting to reverse this disk detection process.Ssee Section *The Start Screen* on page 8. To apply this parameter universally when using YaST2, enter it in the boot configuration. See the information about YaST2 in the [SuS02a] manual.

> ⌐ **Caution** ─────────────────────────────────────
>
>   Only the controllers activated in the BIOS are detectable. In particular, subsequently activating or deactivating the controllers in the BIOS has a direct effect on the device names. Use caution or risk being unable to boot the system.
>
> ───────────────────────────────────── **Caution** ⌐

>   *Technical Explanation*
>   The controller sequence depends on the motherboard. Each manufacturer wires its supplementary controllers differently. The `lspci` shows this sequence. If the Promise Controller is listed before the standard IDE controller, the kernel parameter ide=reverse is required after updating. With the previous kernel (without direct Promise support), the controller was ignored so the standard IDE controller was detected first. The first disk was then `/dev/hda`. With the new kernel, the Promise Controller is detected immediately and its (up to four) disks are registered as `/dev/hda`, `/dev/hdb`, `/dev/hdc`, and `/dev/hdd`. The previous `/dev/hda` disk becomes `/dev/hde` so is no longer detectable in the boot process.

Updating with YaST2

Following the preparation procedure outlined in Section *Preparations* on page 30, you can now boot.

Boot the system as you did to install it originally then select 'Update existing system' in YaST2 after confirming the language. YaST2 then tries to determine the available root partitions and which packages to update. In addition, you have the option of enhancing your system with important new software components.

Manual Update

Updating the Base System

Since basic system components, such as libraries, must be exchanged when updating a base system, an update cannot be run from within a currently running Linux system. First, set up the update environment. This is normally done using the CD or DVD or with a custom boot disk. If you are carrying out manual modifications during the update or prefer to perform the entire update with YaST2 in text mode, follow the steps already described in detail in Section *Text-Based Installation with YaST2* on page 8. Below is a summary of this procedure.

1. Immediately after booting the kernel from the "boot disk" or from the CD or DVD, linuxrc automatically starts.

2. In linuxrc, specify the language and keyboard settings under 'Settings' and click 'Ok' to confirm each setting.

3. You might need to load the required hardware and software drivers via 'Kernel Modules'. See Section *linuxrc: The Basics* on page 9 for more details on how to proceed and *Loading Modules* on page 282 for a description of linuxrc.

4. Go to the menu items 'Start Installation / System' → 'Start Installation/Update' to select the source medium (see on page 284).

5. The installation environment is loaded from linuxrc then YaST2 started.

In the YaST opening screen, select 'Update existing system' after YaST2 has verified the language and hardware. Next, YaST attempts to determine the root partition. Select the root partition from the list (for example, /dev/sda3). YaST2 then reads the "old" `fstab` on this partition. YaST will analyze the file systems specified there then mount them. Then, you can request a backup copy of the system files

In the following dialog, either determine whether only the already-installed software should be updated or whether important new software components should be added to your system ("upgrade mode"). It is recommended to accept one of the default selections (e. g., 'Base System'). In the warning dialog, select 'Yes' to start the software installation.

First, the RPM database is checked, then the main system components are updated. YaST automatically creates backups of files modified in the running system since the last installation. In addition, old configuration files are backed up with the endings .rpmorig and .rpmsave (see Section *Managing Packages: Install, Update, and Uninstall* on page 44). The installation or update procedure is logged in /var/adm/inst-log/installation-* and can be viewed later at any time.

Updating the Rest of the System

After the base system is updated, you will be switched to YaST's update mode. This mode allows you to tailor the rest of the system update to your needs.

Complete the procedure as you would a new installation. Among other things, select a new kernel. The available options are presented by YaST.

Tip

If you boot with loadlin, save the *new* kernel and, possibly, the initrd into the loadlin directory of your DOS partition.

Tip

Possible Problems

- If certain shell environments no longer behave as expected after the update, you should by all means check to see if the current "dot" files in the home directory are still compatible with your system. If not, use the current versions in /etc/skel. For example:

  newbie@earth:~ > **cp /etc/skel/.profile ~/.profile**

Updating Individual Packages

Regardless of your overall updated environment, you can always update individual packages. From this point on, however, it is your responsibility to ensure that your system remains consistent. Update advice can be found at http://www.suse.de/en/support/download/updates/.

You can assemble components of the YaST package selection list as desired. If you select a package essential for the overall operation of the system, YaST issues a warning. Such packages should be updated only in the update mode. For instance, numerous packages contain "shared libraries". If you update these programs and applications in the running system, things might malfunction.

Software Changes From Version to Version

The individual aspects changed from version to version are outlined in the following sections in detail. This summary indicates, for example, whether basic settings have been completely reconfigured, whether configuration files have been moved to other places, or whether common applications have been significantly changed. Only the modifications that would affect the daily use of the system at either the user or the administrator level are mentioned below. The list is by no means exhaustive or complete. The following also makes references to SDB (Support Database) articles. These articles are in the package sdb_en, series doc.

Problems and bugs for each version have been published on the web server as soon as they were recognized. See the links listed below. Important updates of individual packages can be accessed at http://www.suse.de/en/support/download/.

From 6.x to 7.0

Problems and peculiarities:
file:/usr/share/doc/sdb/en/html/bugs61.html
file:/usr/share/doc/sdb/en/html/bugs62.html
file:/usr/share/doc/sdb/en/html/bugs63.html
file:/usr/share/doc/sdb/en/html/bugs64.html
file:/usr/share/doc/sdb/en/html/bugs70.html

- Kernels of varying optimization levels are available for installation. These kernels use an "initrd", or initial ramdisk. This aspect should be kept in mind when generating this type of kernel. See Section *Possible Difficulties — Self-Compiled Kernels* on page 279 and file:/usr/share/doc/sdb/en/html/adrian_6.3_boot.html.

- All kernel modules ("drivers") are components of the kernel you have installed (single, multiprocessor, etc.). This ensures that the properly compiled module are installed. package `kernmod` and package `kernmods` are no longer required. The configuration files of the installed kernel are stored in `/boot` as `vmlinuz.config-pentium`, e.g., `vmlinuz.autoconf.h` and `vmlinuz.version.h`.

- The configuration file for the kernel modules has a similar file name pattern as other configuration files: `/etc/modules.conf` (formerly `/etc/conf.modules`).

- The nscd (name service cache daemon) is also included in the glibc. It is configured in the `/etc/nscd.conf` file. See the man page for `nscd` (`man 8 nscd`) for more information.

- The current glibc has ushered in the final migration to "Unix98 PTY" devices, which requires the mounting of the `devpts` file system. This is defined by the following line in `/etc/fstab`:

```
none        /dev/pts    devpts     gid=5,mode=620      0  0
```

Refer to the documentation in `/usr/src/linux/Documentation/Changes` under the kernel sources (package `kernel-source`, series d).

- PAM (Pluggable Authentication Modules): In addition to `/etc/login.defs`, there are now `/etc/securetty`, `/etc/security/limits.conf`, and `/etc/security/pam_env.conf`. See on page ??.

- Valid *login shells* are specified in `/etc/shells`. See the man page for shells (`man 5 shells`). If a user is designated `/bin/true`, this user can only log in over the X Window System— this user does not have a shell. If `/bin/false` defines the "login shell" for a given user, that user cannot log in at all.

- The X Window System 4.0 no longer supports some older graphics cards. It also does not support some newer cards yet. See Section *Version 4.x of XFree86* on page 114. The setup application will recognize this situation, in which case, it will automatically fall back to the previous package version 3.3.x.

- To heighten security, the XDM is now preconfigured to *not* accept XDMCP or Chooser requests. To access from X terminals, for example, comment out the option line DisplayManager.requestPort in `/etc/X11/xdm/xdm-config` (formerly `/var/X11R6/lib/xdm/`

xdm-config) with an exclamation mark. See the man page for xdm (man xdm).

- RPM (see also Section *RPM — the Distribution Package Manager* on page 43) is available in Version 3.0. The format of the RPM database has changed. The database must be converted as soon as rpm is installed. In the course of a normal update of the (Base) system with YaST, this conversion will take place at the right time in the background.

- According to the FHS (Filesystem Hierarchy Standard), the architecture-independent documentation is now found under /usr/share/doc (formerly /usr/doc).

- The manual pages are stored in /usr/share/man and the info pages in /usr/share/info, according to the FHS.

- makewhatis (package makewhat) now uses the tool manpath to search for *manual pages*. The environment variable MANPATH should no longer be set in rc files.

- A newer version of tar has been included. The overwrite behavior when unpacking existing files has changed. If you rely on the old mode, use the --overwrite option.

- In X, the Compose button ("multikey") can be accessed using the key combination (⇧ Shift) + (Ctrl) (right). See Section *Keyboard Mapping* on page 291

- For reasons of security, *anonymous FTP* is no longer allowed automatically. To allow anonymous FTP with the ftp daemon, in.ftpd the comment sign '#' in /etc/pam.d/ftpd must be removed at the beginning of the line:

```
auth      sufficient      /lib/security/pam_ftp.so
```

- Changing *password* with PAM *Pluggable Authentication Modules*. pam_unix can also change NIS passwords and understands md5 hashes as passwords. Caution!

  There is now a new pam_pwcheck module which takes over the verification of new passwords. The old entry:

```
password required      /lib/security/pam_unix.so      #strict=false
```

must be changed (written in one line, or with \ at the end of the line):

```
password required    /lib/security/pam_pwcheck.so  \
                     nullok #use_cracklib
password required    /lib/security/pam_unix.so     \
                     nullok use_first_pass use_authtok
```

This manual intrusion is only necessary if rpm is not able to change the configuration files itself because the system administrator has made changes. This is the case for all PAM configuration files located in `/etc/pam.d`.

- `ldconfig` is only run if there is a `/lib` directory newer than `/etc/ld.so.cache`. This may be run in the background. Force `ldconfig` to run by setting the environment variable `run_ldconfig` to `true`. You can also set this at the boot prompt with "run_ldconfig=true".

- The package `apache` package has been divided. If you need special enhancements, also install the `mod_*` subpackages. Documentation on PHP can be found in the package `phpdoc`. For a good overview, take a glance at `/var/log/httpd`.

- package `openssh`: For heightened security, "X11 forwarding" is disabled in the default setting. The parameter `-X` allows the activation of this feature. Forwarding can be globally or locally (only for certain machines) activated by entering the line ForwardX11 yes in `/etc/ssh/ssh_config`. Users can also specify this option in `~/.ssh/config`.

- `ypserv` from the package `ypserv` is no longer linked to the "tcp-wrapper" library, but instead uses `/var/yp/securenets`. After an update, the settings from `/etc/hosts.allow` or from `/etc/hosts.deny` should be transferred to `/var/yp/securenets`.

- The portmapper is started via `/etc/init.d/portmap` (since SuSE Linux 7.1) or with the command `rcportmap`. `/sbin/init.d/rpc` is now obsolete.

- On the package `cron`: in accordance with the FHS, the cron tables are located in `/var/spool/cron/tabs`. See Section *cron Package* on page 271.

- On the package `postgres`: PostgreSQL and all of its components have been reorganized on the basis of the original packages. The package `pg_datab` with the initialization database is no longer needed. If needed, initialization is performed by the start-up script.

- Regarding package `mutt`: several details have been changed. The configuration files `/etc/Muttrc` and `/etc/skel/.muttrc` attempt to preserve its familiar behavior as much as possible. The lines:

  ```
  set autoedit=yes
  set edit_headers=yes
  ```

  ensure that the editor is immediately started in `.muttrc` to compose an e-mail. There are also some key aspects that require new system behavior, such as PGP. Read the relevant documentation for more information on this.

From 7.0 to 7.1

Problems and Special Features:
`http://sdb.suse.de/sdb/en/html/bugs71.html`.

- *Kernel:* The "low-level" drivers for special EIDE chip sets are integrated into the standard kernel. `k_eide` or `eide` are no longer necessary as separate images. This means you no longer need to create your own boot disk if you require this driver.

- The runlevels have changed. See Table 13.1 on page 297. The `init` scripts are now located in `/etc/init.d`. If your have already created your own scripts, you should make sure they are backed up before updating.

- DEFAULT_LANGUAGE: New name for the former variable LANGUAGE in `/etc/rc.config` (as of SuSE Linux 8.0 in `/etc/sysconfig/language`). See Section *Local Adjustments — I18N/L10N* on page 292.

- The `/etc/resolv.conf` is now written directly from YaST as well as YaST2, not by SuSEconfig. Since version 7.2, this task is performed by the script `/sbin/modify_resolvconf`, included in package `aaa_base`.

- The limitation of the package names to eight characters has been removed and many packages may now have more descriptive names.

- The functionality of the package `dochost` has been integrated into the package `susehelp`, making `dochost` obsolete.

- Regarding the former package `ypclient`: This package is now divided into ypbind and yp-tools and the init-script is called `ypbind`.

- Regarding package `jade_dsl`: To avoid conflict with package `rzsz`, the command line tool `sx` is now called `s2x` and `sgml2xml`.

From 7.1 to 7.2

Problems and Special Features:
`http://sdb.suse.de/sdb/en/html/bugs72.html`.

- package `nkitb` no longer exists. The different programs were moved into several packages: talk, rsh, finger, rwho, telnet, etc.

  A number of programs are already IPv6-ready. For this reason, ensure that DNS is correctly configured — otherwise you might have to wait for the DNS time out for IPv6 queries. Also, in `/etc/nsswitch.conf`, replace the entry `dns` with `dns6`.

- Renaming of several packages (see on the facing page); e.g.: package `docbook-dsssl-stylesheets`, package `docbook_3` and package `docbook_4`.

- You have to install package `mod_php4` instead of package `mod_php` now.

- Emacs was split into several packages:

  ▷ Base package emacs.

  ▷ In addition, you have to install package `emacs-x11`, which includes the program *with* X11 support.

  ▷ package `emacs-nox` contains the program *without* X11 support.

  ▷ package `emacs-info`: Online documentation in the info format.

  ▷ package `emacs-el` contains uncompiled library files written in Emacs Lisp — not required for a runtime environment.

  ▷ Numerous additional packages which can be installed, if required: package `emacs-auctex` (for LaTeX); package `psgml` (for SGML/XML); package `gnuserv` (for a client-server environment), etc.

- Changes to follow the current FHS (see Section *File System Hierarchy Standard (FHS)* on page 270):

▷ `/media` (was `/cdrom` and `/floppy`)

Compatible links will be available for a transitional period.

From 7.2 to 7.3

Problems and Special Features:
http://sdb.suse.de/sdb/en/html/bugs73.html.

- Kernel 2.4, which is included in SuSE Linux, has IDE-DMA turned on by default. If you have any problems related to DMA, you can always fall back on the 'Installation — Safe Settings' boot option. Also see on page 8.

- Apart from the DISPLAYMANAGER variable as defined in `rc.config` (as of SuSE Linux 8.0 in `/etc/sysconfig/displaymanager`), the correct runlevel needs to be set in `/etc/inittab`. YaST2 is able to take care of this. Also see Section *Runlevel Editor* on page 79.

- Samba: The configuration files have been moved to the `/etc/samba` directory to improve clarity.

- MySQL now uses the TCP wrapper library for extended security.

  The new subpackage `mysql-Max` offers all the new and enhanced features, which are automatically available after installation.

- To save space (more than 30 MB), package `allman` is no longer included. The manual pages are, however, still included in the packages.

- DocBook documents, which use certain "features", are accepted by `db2x.sh` (package `docbktls`). Users who depend on compatible documents should work with the `--strict` option.

From 7.3 to 8.0

Problems and peculiarities:
http://sdb.suse.de/sdb/en/html/bugs80.html.

- Boot disks are shipped only as floppy images (directory `disks`). A boot disk is only required if you cannot boot from CD. Depending on your hardware or installation preferences, you can also create floppies from the images `modules1` (formerly `modules`) and `modules2`. Read

Creating a Boot Disk in DOS on page 19 and *Creating a Boot Disk in a UNIX-Related System* on page 20 for information about creating these disks.

- YaST2 has completely replaced YaST1, even in the text and console mode.

- Some BIOS's require the kernel parameter `realmode-power-off`, which was known as `real-mode-poweroff` up to kernel version 2.4.12.

- The START variables of the `rc.config` for launching services are no longer required. Services are started if the respective links exist in the runlevel directories. These links are created with `insserv`.

- System services are configured by variable lines in the files located under `/etc/sysconfig`. The settings in `/etc/rc.config.d` will be applied to the update.

- `/etc/init.d/boot` is comprised of several scripts and moved to other packages if necessary (see package `kbd`, package `isapnp`, package `lvm`, etc.). See on page 300.

- There have also been some changes made in the network arena. Read Section *Network Integration* on page 349 for more information on this.

- logrotate is used to manage log files. `/etc/logfiles` is no longer necessary. See Section *Log Files — the Package logrotate* on page 272.

- The `root` login over telnet or rlogin can be permitted by entering specifications in the files under `/etc/pam.d`. Due to security risks, ROOT_LOGIN_REMOTE can no longer be set to `yes`.

- PASSWD_USE_CRACKLIB can be activated with YaST2.

- If NIS files for `autofs` will be distributed over NIS, the YaST2 NIS client module should be used for configuration. There, select 'Start Automounter'. This aspect has made the `USE_NIS_FOR_AUTOFS` variable obsolete.

- The locate tool for quickly finding files is no longer included in the standard software installation. If desired, install it later. If installed, the updatedb process — just as it did in previous versions — will be automatically activated about fifteen minutes after starting your computer.

- The mouse support for pine is activated. This means that pine in an xterm can also be operated with a mouse (or a similar input device) by clicking the menu items. This, however, also means that, as usual, cut and paste only works by using ⇧ Shift when the mouse support is activated. This is deactivated with a new installation. It is, however, not excluded that the function is still active following an update (when an older ~/.pinerc is present). The option enable-mouse-in-xterm can be deactivated in the configuration for pine.

From 8.0 to 8.1

Problems and peculiarities:
http://sdb.suse.de/sdb/de/html/bugs81.html.

- Changes in the user and group names: To attain compliance with UnitedLinux, some entries in /etc/passwd and /etc/group have been adjusted accordingly.

    ▷ Changed users: ftp is now in group ftp (and not in daemon any more).

    ▷ Renamed groups: www (was wwwadmin); games (was game).

    ▷ New groups: ftp (with GID 50), floppy (with GID 19), cdrom (with GID 20), console (with GID 21), utmp (with GID 22).

- Changes related to FHS (see *File System Hierarchy Standard (FHS)* on page 270):

    ▷ An environment for HTTPD (Apache) is created at /srv/httpd (was /usr/local/httpd).

    ▷ An environment for FTP is created at /srv/ftp (was /usr/local/ftp).

- To ease access to the desired software, the single packages are not stored in a few bulky series any more, but rather in accessible "RPM groups". This also means the CDs do not contain spurious and cryptic directories under suse any more, but only few directories named after architectures, for example, ppc, i586, or noarch.

- The following programs are now installed or not automatically installed during a new installation:

    ▷ The boot loader GRUB, which offers more possibilities than LILO. LILO is preserved when updating the system.

▷ The mailer postfix instead of sendmail.

▷ The modern mailing list application mailman is installed instead of majordomo.

▷ Select harden_suse manually when needed and read the current documentation for it.

- Split packages: `rpm` to `rpm` and `rpm-devel`; `popt` to `popt` and `popt-devel`; `libz` to `zlib` and `zlib-devel`.

  `yast2-trans-*` is now split by languages: `yast2-trans-cs` (Czech), `yast2-trans-de` (German), `yast2-trans-es` (Spanish), etc. Not all languages are installed to save hard disk space. Install the required packages for the YaST2 language support as needed.

- Renamed packages: `bzip` to `bzip2`.

- Packages no longer: `openldap`. Use `openldap2` now.

RPM — the Distribution Package Manager

In SuSE Linux, RPM (`rpm`), the "Red Hat Package Manager", serves as the package manager. It makes the powerful RPM database available to everyone: users, system administrators, and, of course, package builders. Detailed information about installed software can be queried from the database at any time.

Essentially, `rpm` has three modes. In one mode, it compiles software applications from "pristine" sources and packages them for installation. In the second, it installs, upgrades, and cleanly uninstalls software packaged in the RPM format. Finally, in the third, it supports queries about packages and maintains the RPM database of installed packages.

Installable RPM archives are packed in a special binary format. These archives consist of the program files to install and certain meta information used during the installation by `rpm` to configure the software package or stored in the RPM database for documentation purposes. RPM archives normally have the extension `.rpm`.

`rpm` allows the administration of LSB-compliant packages. Refer to *Linux Standard Base (LSB)* on page 270 for more about LSB.

> **Tip**
>
> For a number of packages, the components needed for software development (libraries, headers, include files, etc.) have been put into separate packages. These development packages are only needed if you want to compile software *yourself*, for example, the most recent GNOME packages. These development packages can be identified by the name extension -devel (previously: dev or d): package alsa-devel, package gimp-devel, package kdelibs-devel.
>
> **Tip**

Verifying Package Authenticity

Since Version 7.1, the SuSE RPM packages have a GnuPG signature:

```
1024D/9C800ACA 2000-10-19 SuSE Package Sign-
ing Key <build@suse.de>
Key fingerprint = 79C1 79B2 E1C8 20C1 890F  9994 A84E DAE8 9C80 0ACA
```

With the command rpm -verbose -checksig apache-1.3.12.rpm, verify the signature of an RPM package to determine whether it really originates from SuSE or from another trustworthy facility. This is especially recommended for update packages downloaded from the Internet. Our public package signature key normally resides in /root/.gnupg/.

Managing Packages: Install, Update, and Uninstall

Normally, RPM installation can be done simply with
rpm -i ⟨package⟩.rpm. With this command, the package will be installed — but only if its dependency requirements are met and if it does not conflict with another package. With an error message, rpm requests those packages that need to be installed to fulfill dependencies. In the background, the RPM database ensures that no conflicts will arise — a specific file can only belong to one package. By choosing different options, you can force rpm to ignore these defaults, but be sure to know what you are doing. Otherwise, risk compromising the integrity of the system and possibly jeopardize the ability to update the system.

Use -U or --upgrade to update a package. This option will remove the files of the old version and immediately install the new files. rpm updates configuration files more cautiously:

- If a configuration file has *not* been changed by the system administrator, `rpm` will install the new version of the appropriate file. No action by the system administrator is required.

- If a configuration file was changed by the system administrator *before* the update, `rpm` will save the changed file with the extension `.rpmorig` or `.rpmsave` (backup file) and install the version from the new package, but only when the originally installed file and the newer version are different. If this is the case, compare the backup file (`.rpmorig` or `.rpmsave`) with the newly installed file and make your changes again in the new file. Afterwards, be sure to delete all `.rpmorig` and `.rpmsave` files to avoid problems with future updates.

- `.rpmnew` files appear if the configuration file already exists *and* if the `noreplace` label was specified in the `.spec` file.

Following an update, `.rpmsave` and `.rpmnew` files should be removed after comparing them, so they do not hinder future updates. The `.rpmorig` extension is assigned if the file has not previously been recognized by the RPM database. Otherwise, `.rpmsave` is used. In other words, `.rpmorig` results from updating from a foreign format to RPM. `.rpmsave` results from updating from an older RPM to a newer RPM. `.rpmnew` does not disclose any information as to whether the system administrator has made any changes to the configuration file. Some configuration files (like `/etc/httpd/httpd.conf`) purposely are not overwritten to enable a seamless takeover of the running operations using the personal settings.

The `-U` switch is *not* just an equivalent to uninstalling with the (`-e`) option and installing with the (`-i`) option. Use `-U` whenever possible.

> **Note**
>
> After every update, check all backup files created by `rpm`. These are your old configuration files. If necessary, incorporate your customizations from the backup files in the new configuration files. After this process, the files with the extensions `.rpmorig` and `.rpmsave` should be deleted.
>
> **Note**

To remove a package, enter the command:

```
earth:~ #  rpm -e ⟨package⟩
```

`rpm` will only delete the package if there are no unresolved dependencies. It is theoretically impossible to delete Tcl/Tk, for example, as long as another application requires it. Even in this case, RPM calls for assistance from the database. If such a deletion is — for whatever reason and under unusual circumstances — impossible, even if *no* additional dependencies exist, it may be helpful to rebuild the RPM database using the option `-rebuilddb`. See the side notes below regarding the RPM database (Section *RPM Queries* on page 48).

RPM Queries

With the `-q` option, `rpm` initiates queries, making it possible to inspect an RPM archive (by adding the option `-p`) and also to query the RPM database of installed packages. Several switches are available to specify the type of information required (see Table 2.1).

`-i`	Package information
`-l`	File list
`-f` ⟨FILE⟩	Query a package owned by ⟨FILE⟩ (the full path must be specified with ⟨FILE⟩)
`-s`	File list with status information (implies `-l`)
`-d`	List only documentation files (implies `-l`)
`-c`	List only configuration files (implies `-l`)
`--dump`	File list with complete details (to be used with `-l`, `-c` or `-d`)
`--provides`	List features of the package that another package can request with `--requires`
`--requires, -R`	Capabilities the package requires
`--scripts`	(Un)installation scripts (preinstall, postinstall, uninstall)

Table 2.1: The Most Important RPM Query Options (`-q` [`-p`] ... ⟨package⟩)

For example, the command

earth:~ # **rpm -q -i wget**

displays the information shown in Output 3.

```
Name        : wget                    elocations: (not relocateable)
Version     : 1.8.1                       Vendor: SuSE AG, Nuern-
berg, Germany
```

```
Release      : 142                    Build Date: Fri Apr  5 16:08:13 2002
Install date: Mon Apr  8 13:54:08 2002 Build Host: knox.suse.de
Group        : Productivity/Networking/Web/Utilities   Source RPM: wget-
1.8.1-142.src.rpm
Size         : 2166418                License: GPL
Packager     : feedback@suse.de
Summary      : A tool for mirroring FTP and HTTP servers
Description :
Wget enables you to retrieve WWW documents or FTP files from a server.
This might be done in script files or via command line.
[...]
```

Output 3: rpm -q -i wget

Option `-f` only works if you specify the complete file name with its full path. You can name as many file names as you want. For example,

```
earth:~ #  rpm -q -f /bin/rpm /usr/bin/wget
```

leads to the following result:

```
rpm-3.0.3-3
wget-1.5.3-55
```

If only part of the file name is known, a shell script must be implemented (see File 1). The file name found is passed as a parameter when running the script.

```
#! /bin/sh
for i in $(rpm -q -a -l | grep  $1); do
    echo "\"$i\" ist in Paket:"
    rpm -q -f $i
    echo ""
done
```

File 1: Script to Search for Packages

With the command `rpm -q --changelog rpm`, display a precise list of information (updates, configuration, modifications, etc.) about a specific package. This example is on the package *rpm*. However, only the last five change entries in the RPM database are listed. All entries (dating back the last two years) are included in the package itself. This query only works if CD 1 is mounted at `/cdrom`:

```
earth:~ #   rpm -qp --changelog /cdrom/suse/a1/rpm.rpm
```

With the help of the installed RPM database, verification checks can be made. These checks are initiated with the option `-V` (or `-y` or `--verify`). With this option, `rpm` will show all files in a package that have been changed since installation. `rpm` uses eight character symbols to give some hints about the following changes:

5	MD5 check sum
S	File size
L	Symbolic link
T	Modification time
D	Major and minor device numbers
U	Owner
G	Group
M	Mode (permissions and file type)

Table 2.2: RPM Verify Options

In the case of configuration files, the letter c will be printed. For example, if you have changed /etc/wgetrc from the package wget, you may see:

```
earth:~ #   rpm -V wget
```

```
S.5....T c /etc/wgetrc
```

The files of the RPM database are placed in /var/lib/rpm. If the partition /usr has a size of 1 GB, this database can occupy nearly 30 MB, especially after a complete update. If the database is much larger than expected, it is useful to rebuild the database with the option `--rebuilddb`. Before doing this, make a backup of the old database. The cron script cron.daily makes daily copies of the database (packed with gzip) and stores them in /var/adm/backup/rpmdb. The number of copies is controlled by the variable ⟨*MAX_RPMDB_BACKUPS*⟩ (default: 5) in /etc/rc.config. The size of a single backup is approximately 3 MB. (This value is valid for a 1 GB /usr partition.) Take this space requirement into account when deciding how large the root partition should be. If /var has its own partition, you do not have to worry about this.

Installing and Compiling Source Packages

All source packages of SuSE Linux carry an `.spm` extension ("Source RPMS").

> **Tip**
>
> These packages can be handled in the same way as all other packages. The packages, however, will not be found in the RPM database (and are not marked with an `[i]` in YaST), as only "installed" software is listed. This is because the source packages are not incorporated in the RPM database. Only *installed* operating system software is listed in the RPM database.
>
> *Tip*

The rpm directories in `/usr/src/packages` must exist (if none of your own settings have been made, for example, in `/etc/rpmrc`).

SOURCES   this is for the original sources (`.tar.gz` files, etc.) and for distribution-specific adjustments (`.dif` files).

SPECS   for the ".spec" files, similar to a meta Makefile, which control the "build" process.

BUILD   All the sources are unpacked, patched, and compiled in this directory.

RPMS   This is where the completed "binary" packages are stored.

SRPMS   here are the "source" RPMs.

> **Note**
>
> Do not experiment with essential system packages, such as package `libc`, package `rpm`, or package `nkit`. This could lead to a malfunctioning system.
>
> *Note*

When you install a source package with YaST, all the necessary components will be installed in `/usr/src/packages`: the sources and the adjustments in SOURCES, the relevant `.spec` file in SPECS. To "create packages" see [Bai97]. More information can be obtained from the man page for `rpm`.

This example uses the `wget.spm` package. After you have installed the package with YaST, you should have the following files:

`/usr/src/packages/SPECS/wget.spec` `/usr/src/packages/SOURCES/wget-1.4.5.dif` `/usr/src/packages/SOURCES/wget-1.4.5.tar.gz`

`rpm -b ⟨X⟩ /usr/src/packages/SPECS/wget.spec` starts the compilation. Here ⟨X⟩ is a wild card for different stages of the build process (see the output of `rpm --help` or the RPM documentation). Here is a short explanation:

-bp Prepare sources in `/usr/src/packages/BUILD`: unpack and patch.

-bc the same as -bp, but with additional compilation.

-bi the same as -bp, but with additional installation of the built software. Caution: if the package does not support the BuildRoot feature, you might overwrite configuration files.

-bb the same as -bi, but with the additional creation of the "binary" package. If the compile was successful, the binary should be in `/usr/src/packages/RPMS`.

-ba the same as -bb, but with the additional creation of the "source RPM". If the compilation was successful, the binary should be in `/usr/src/packages/SRPMS`.

-short-circuit lets you skip specific steps.

This binary RPM may now be installed by invoking `rpm -i` or, even better, with `rpm -U` (to make it appear in the RPM database).

Other Tools for Working with RPM Archives

Midnight Commander (`mc`) is able to "browse" RPM archives and to operate on parts of them. This tool works on an RPM package archive as if the archive were a regular file system. Using mc, view HEADER information with F3 and copy parts of an archive with F5. Incidentally, there is now even an Emacs front-end for rpm.

xrpm is a new graphical RPM manager, written in Python, which supports commands to FTP-accessed archives. KDE can use the tool krpm, a graphical interface in the X Window System, for RPM management. krpm is currently in an early development stage.

Using the Alien (`alien`) Perl script, it is possible to convert or install an "alien" binary package. This tries to convert "old" TGZ archives to RPM before installing. This way, the RPM database can keep track of such a package after it has been installed. Beware: `alien` is still "alpha" software, according to its author — even if it already has a high version number.

YaST2, as described in *Software* on page 62, is also useful.

Part II

Configuration

YaST2 in Text Mode (ncurses)

This chapter addresses system administrators and experts who do not run an X server on their systems and who rely on the text-based installation tool. It provides basic information on starting and operating YaST2 in text mode (ncurses). It furthermore explains to update your system online automatically to keep it as up-to-date as possible.

Explanation of ncurses	56
Invocation and Usage	56
Module Operation	57
Invoking the Various Modules	59
YaST Online Update	59

Explanation of ncurses

The text-based version of YaST2 replaces YaST1 after its development was discontinued. A text-mode YaST2 had already been provided, but was rarely used. YaST2 in text mode is operated with the keyboard just like YaST1. YaST2-ncurses has a different look and feel and YaST1 shortcuts no longer function.

Invocation and Usage

To start YaST2 in text mode, enter `yast` as `root` at the prompt. Usage may be unfamiliar, but is very simple. The whole program can, in principle, be operated with (Tab), (Alt) + (Tab), (Space), Arrow ((↑) and (↓)), and (Enter) as well as with shortcuts. When Yast2 is started in text mode, the main window appears first (see Figure 3.1).

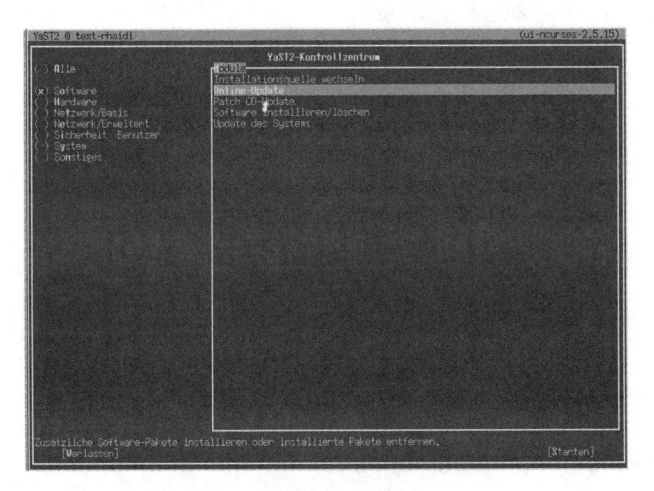

Figure 3.1: The YaST2-ncurses Main Window with Active Module Frame

There are three areas here: The left column features the categories to which the various modules belong. The modules of the category selected with an x are in a white frame to the right. The two buttons for aborting or starting the module marked in the frame are at the bottom.

After starting, the cursor is placed on the topmost field 'All', so the field is color-highlighted (normally green). However, 'Software' is selected, which

can be recognized by the bracketed "x". Pressing (Tab) switches from one item
to the next in the left column. The green-colored category is activated with
(Space). The modules of this category then appear in the right-hand frame.
The coloring of the marked items depends on the current terminal settings.
Press (Tab) repeatedly until the thin white frame to the right becomes
prominent. Normally, it is possible to move backwards (Alt) + (Tab) or with
(⇧ Shift) + (Tab) (see Section *Module Operation* on the current page). Highlighting the white frame switches focus to the right-hand window in which
a module can be selected for starting. The arrow keys move back and forth
among the modules. Start the desired module by pressing (Enter) when it is
marked green. Alternatively, press (Tab) to select 'Start'. Then start the selected module by pressing (Enter).

Different buttons or selection fields also contain a differently-colored letter
(yellow with the standard settings). The combination (Alt) + (letter) selects the
button directly, bypassing the TAB navigation.

Restriction of Key Combinations

It is possible that the (Alt) combinations in YaST do not work if system-wide
(Alt) key combinations are set by a running X server. It is also possible that
keys like (Alt) or (⇧ Shift) are captured for the terminal used.

Replacing (Alt) with (Esc): (Alt) shortcuts can be executed with (Esc) instead of
(Alt). For example, (Esc) + (H) replaces (Alt) + (H).

Replacement of backward and forward navigation by (Ctrl) + (F) and (Ctrl) + (B):
If the (Alt) and (⇧ Shift) combinations are occupied by the window manager or the terminal, the combinations (Ctrl) + (F) (forward) and (Ctrl) +
(B) (backward) can be used instead.

Restriction of function keys: In SuSE Linux 8.1, the function keys are also
shortcuts (see *Module Operation* on the following page). Certain function
keys could equally be occupied by the choice of terminal and are possibly not available for YaST The (Alt) key combinations and function keys
should, however, be fully available on a pure text console.

Module Operation

In the following, it is assumed that the (Alt) key combinations are functional.
Make appropriate substitutions or switch to a pure text console, if needed.

Navigation between buttons and selection lists: (Tab) and (Alt) + (Tab) navigates back and forth between buttons and frames containing selection lists and among the frames.

Navigation in selection lists: (↑) and (↓) always navigate among the single items within an activated frame containing a selection list. These can, for instance, be the single modules of a module group in the control center.

Checking of radio buttons and check boxes The selection of buttons with empty square brackets (check box [ ]) or of the module groups with parentheses (radio buttons ( )) on the left-hand side of the control center is done in the same way as the selection of packages during installation with (Space) or (Enter). The buttons at the bottom of the various modules or of the control center are activated with (Enter) when color-highlighted or with (Alt) + (yellow key).

The function keys: The function keys ((F1) to (F12)) provide quick access to the various available buttons. Which function keys are actually mapped to buttons depends on which YaST module is active, because the different modules offer different buttons. These include details, info, add, and delete. Like in YaST, 'OK', 'Continue', and 'Cancel' have been assigned to (F10). The various functions mapped to the function keys are explained in the help, accessible with (F1).

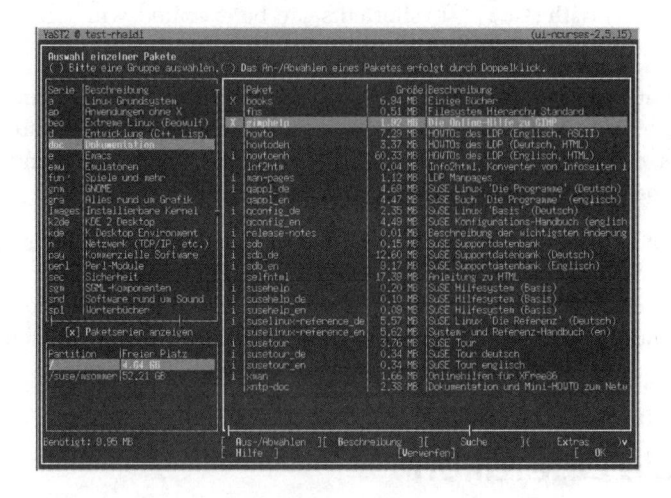

Figure 3.2: The Software Installation Module

Invoking the Various Modules

Each YaST module can also be started directly. The modules can simply be started with `yast` ⟨*module name*⟩. The network module, for instance, is started with the command `yast lan`. Access a list of the names of the modules available on a system by running `yast -l` or `yast --list`. The various module descriptions can be found on page 65.

YaST Online Update

The YaST Online Update YOU can be operated and started from the console. As administrator, it is easy to create a weekly cron job that keeps the system up-to-date with YOU.

The cron Job for YOU

The following are basic instructions for creating the cron job. Basically, there are two different possibilities for setting up a cron job. The simpler method for this is described here. The following steps are necessary:

1. Become `root`.

2. Start the crontab editor with `crontab -e`.

3. Press `i` for the insertion mode of vi.

4. Enter the following lines:

   ```
   MAILTO=" "
   13 3 * * 0 /sbin/yast2 online_update auto.get
   53 3 * * 0 /sbin/yast2 online_update auto.install
   ```

   The first five elements of the last two lines have the following meaning when read from left to right: minutes, hours, day of the month, month of the year, day of the week (0 is Sunday). `*` disregards that value. In this example, the first entry starts the cron job every Sunday at 3:13 a.m. The second job starts forty minutes later at 3:53 a.m. The line `MAILTO" "` prevents root from receiving the output of YaST2-ncurses as an e-mail and can, of course, be omitted.

> **Caution**
>
> Enter arbitrary times of the hour for the cron jobs and preferably not the times from the example above because this would overload the FTP server.
>
> **Caution**

5. Save the cron job by sequentially pressing (Esc) :wq or alternatively (Esc) ZZ.

The cron daemon is automatically restarted and your cron job is added to /var/spool/cron/tabs/root.

YaST2 in Graphics Mode

YaST2 assists in extending your SuSE Linux system with additional hardware components, such as a printer or sound card, configuring and installing system services, Internet access, and software, or deleting undesired packages. The [SuS02a] manual contains a description of various ways of accessing YaST2.

Starting YaST2	62
Software	62
Install and Remove Software	64
System Update	64
Hardware	65
Network/Basic	76
Network/Advanced	77
Security and Users	78
System	78
Miscellaneous	80

Starting YaST2

After starting YaST2, the YaST2 Control Center opens. The left window panel is divided into the categories 'Software', 'Hardware', 'Network/Basic', 'Advanced Network', 'Security & Users', 'System', and 'Miscellaneous'. When an icon is clicked, the corresponding modules are displayed to the right as icons. The configuration of the various modules is usually a multistaged process.

YaST2 guides through all the dialogs with 'Next'. A help text listing all possible inputs to each topic is shown in the left-hand part of the window. Once all the required values have been entered, the process is concluded with 'Finish' in the last configuration dialog. The configuration is then saved.

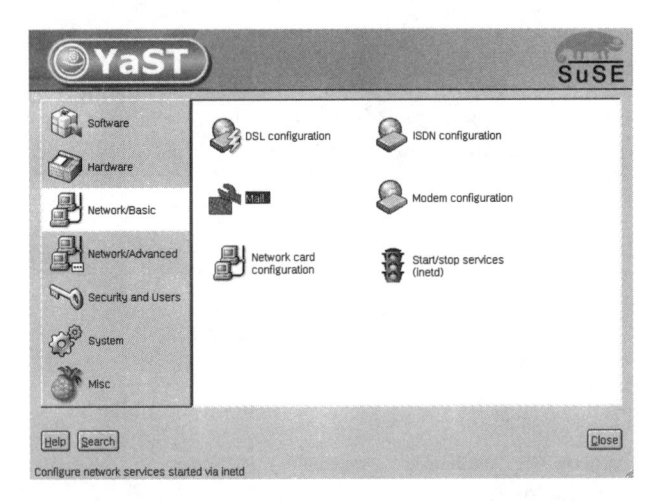

Figure 4.1: YaST2 System Configuration and Administration

Software

Use this module to install or delete software or to change the installation source. There are furthermore two update tools: one for the "normal" system update and one for the online update which is served by our FTP server. The "Configuration" manual provides more information on this.

4

Change Installation Source

The installation source is the medium which provides the software that is to be installed. You can install from CD (the general case), from a network server or from hard disk. (More on this can be read in chapter *YaST2 – Configurations* → *Software* of [SuS02b] and in the comprehensive help text for YaST2).

YaST Online Update (YOU)

YaST Online Update enables the installation of important upgrades or improvements. The corresponding patches are made available for downloading on the SuSE FTP server. The installation of the current packages can proceed completely automatically. 'manual update' allows however also the possibility of personally determining which patches are applied to your SuSE Linux system.

Selecting 'weiter' downloads a list of all available patches (in case that 'manual update' was chosen). Then the software installation module (ref. *Install and Remove Software* on the following page) starts and lists the patches which have been downloaded. It is possible to simply accept the suggested list of packages marked for installation. They are then installed like normal packages.

Online Update from the Console

For the benefit of system administrators, the Online Update can be started in a shell. As `root`, load the current patch list and all related RPMs from the first server in the `/etc/suseservers` list using the command:

earth:/root # **yast2 online_update .auto.get**

To load only certain patches, add options to the command. Among these options are `security`, `recommended`, `document`, `YaST2`, and `optional`. `security` retrieves security-related patches, `recommended` fetches updates recommended by SuSE, `document` provides you with information on the patches or on the FTP server, `YaST2` fetches YaST2 patches, and `optional` gets minor updates. Information on these patches is stored in `/var/lib/YaST/patches/i386/update/X.Y/patches`, where X.Y represents the SuSE Linux version number. This information is only readable for root.

The command for downloading the security patches, for example, is:

```
earth:/root #  yast2 online_update .auto.get security
```

When you enter `.auto.get`, by default the SuSE FTP server list is loaded into `/etc/suseservers`. To disable this, deactivate the function in the `/etc/rc.config`. To do this, set `yes` to `no` in the line `YAST2_LOADFTPSERVER="yes"`.

The patches can now be installed with

```
earth:/root #  yast2 online_update .auto.install
```

This command installs all fetched patches. To just install a group, use the same options as in `.auto.get`.

This method can be fully automated. The system administrator is able to download the packages overnight, for example, then install the ones needed the next morning.

Patch CD Update

As opposed to the online update, the patches are not retrieved from the FTP server, but instead scanned from CD. This CD is available for "SuSE Linux Enterprise Server" customers. The advantage is that it goes a lot quicker with a CD.

After the patch CD is inserted, all the patches stored on the CD will be read into and displayed in this YaST2 module screen. Select which one to install from the patch list. If you forgot to put the CD into the drive, a warning will appear. Then insert the CD and resume updating the patch CD.

Install and Remove Software

This module provides services for installing, updating and removing software from your system. It has been completely revised for SuSE Linux 8.1 and offers more functionality and flexibility than ever before. This module is described in detail in chapter *Yast2 – Configurations* → *Software* of [SuS02b].

System Update

Use this module to keep your system up to date. It can be started at different stages in the process. YaST2 recognizes which packages need to be updated or you can decide on your own which package should be updated.

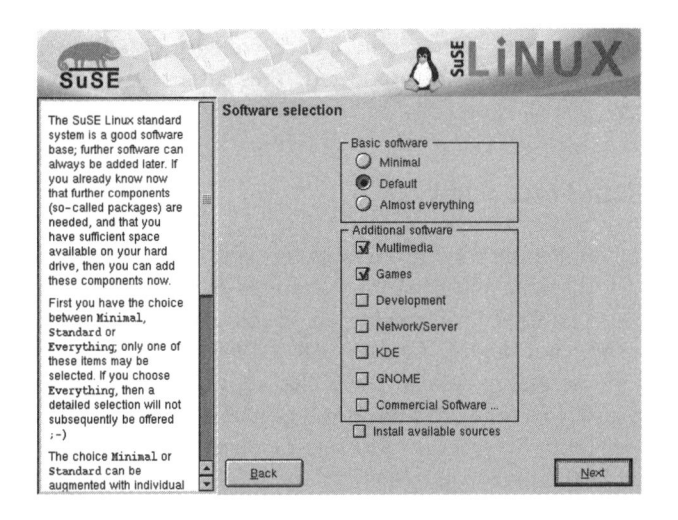

Figure 4.2: YaST2: *Installing and Removing Software*

However, the base system itself cannot be updated using this method. It can only be updated by booting from the installation medium, such as the CD. More information can be found in chapter *Updating the System and Package Management* on page 29.

Hardware

New hardware must first be installed and connected according to the vendor's instructions. Connect the external devices such as printer or modem and start the corresponding YaST2 module. The majority of conventional devices will automatically be recognized by YaST2, at which point, the technical information is displayed. If autodetection fails, YaST2 will present a device list (model, manufacturer, etc.) from which to select the appropriate device.

The configuration tools needed for configuring the various devices can be found under 'Hardware'. Refer to the hardware information for data pertaining to the hardware autodetected by YaST2. This is especially useful for support requests.

This book describes only some of the configuration tools in detail. A description all available hardware configuration modules can be found in the [SuS02b].

All printers connected to your system can be configured with this module. Local and network printers are supported. This discussed in more detail in chapter *Printer Operation* on page 157.

Graphics Card and Screen

This module handles the configuration of the graphical interface X11, that is, the settings for displays and grpaphics adapters including multihead. This module can also be used for changing an already existing X11 configuration (for instance the color depth). Chapter *The X Window System* on page 113 provides all the necessary details. SaX2 also allows the configuration of mouse, keyboard, touchscreens and graphics tablets. The description of the module can be found in section *YAST2 — Configuration → Display and Input devices (SaX2)* of the [SuS02b].

Partitioning

Section *User-defined installation → Partitioning* of the [SuS02b] contains simple instructions for partitioning.

Expert Partitioning

The partitioning module for professionals enables editing and deletion of existing partitions, as well as the creation of new ones. Access Soft RAID and LVM configuration from here.

> **Note**
>
> Lots of background information and partitioning tips can be found in chapter *Partitioning for Experts* on page 24.
>
> **Note**

In normal circumstances, partitions are specified during installation. However, it is possible to integrate a second hard disk in an already existing Linux system. First, the new hard disk must be partitioned. Then it must be mounted and entered into the /etc/fstab file. It may be necessary to copy some of the data to move an /opt partition from the old hard disk to the new one.

Use caution if you want to repartition the hard disk you are working on — this is essentially possible, but you will have to reboot the system right afterwards. It is a bit safer to boot from CD then repartition it.

The 'Experts...' button reveals a pop-up menu containing the following commands:

Reread Partition Table Rereads the partitioning from disk. For example, you will need this for manual partitioning in the text console.

Adopt Mount Points from Existing /etc/fstab This will only be relevant during installation. Reading the old `fstab` is useful for completely reinstalling your system rather than just updating it. In this case, it is not necessary to enter the mount points by hand.

Delete Partition Table and Disk Label This completely overwrites the old partition table. For example, this can be helpful if you have problems with unconventional disk labels. Using this method, all data on the hard disk will be lost.

Logical Volume Manager (LVM)

The Logical Volume Manager (LVM) enables flexible distribution of hard disk space over several file systems. As it is difficult to modify partitions on a running system, LVM was developed: it provides a virtual "pool" (Volume Group — VG for short) of memory space, from which logical volumes (LV) can be generated if needed. The operating system will access these instead of the physical partitions.

Features:

- Several hard disks or partitions can be combined into a large logical partition.

- If a LV (e.g., `/usr`) is full, it can be enlarged with the appropriate configuration.

- With the LVM, even append hard disks or LVs in a running system. However, "hot–swappable" hardware, designed for these types of interventions, is required for this.

Implementing LVM already makes sense for heavily used home PCs or small servers. If you have a growing data stock, as in the case of databases, MP3 archives, or user directories, the Logical Volume Manager is just the right thing for you. This would allow you file systems that are larger than physical hard disk. Another advantage of the LVM is up to 256 LVs can be added.

Keep in mind that working with the LVM is very different than working with conventional partitions.

Instructions and further information on configuring the "Logical Volume Manager" (LVM) can be found in the official LVM HOWTO and the SuSE documentation:

- http://www.sistina.com/lvm/Pages/howto.html
- http://www.suse.com/us/support/oracle/.

LVM Configuration with YaST2

Prepare the LVM configuration in YaST2 by creating an LVM partition when installing. To do this, click 'Partitioning' in the suggestion window then 'Discard' or 'Change' in the screen that follows. Next, create a partition for LVM by first clicking 'Add' → 'Do not format' in the Partitioner then clicking '0x8e Linux LVM'. Continue partitioning with LVM immediately afterwards or wait until after the system is completely installed. To do this, highlight the LVM partition in the Partitioner then click 'LVM...'.

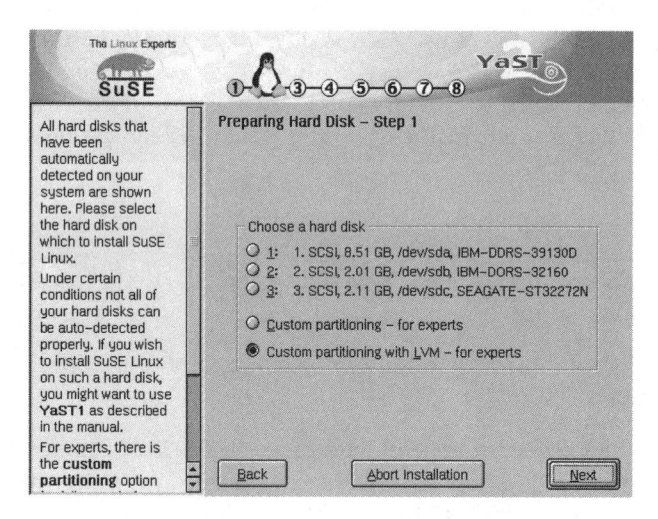

Figure 4.3: YaST2: *Activating LVM During Installation*

LVM — Partitioner

After you select 'LVM...' in the partitioning section, you will then be be presented with a dialog where you can repartition your hard disks. Delete or modify existing partitions here or add new ones. A partition to use for LVM must have the partition label 8E. These partitions are indicated by "Linux LVM" in the partition list (see last Section).

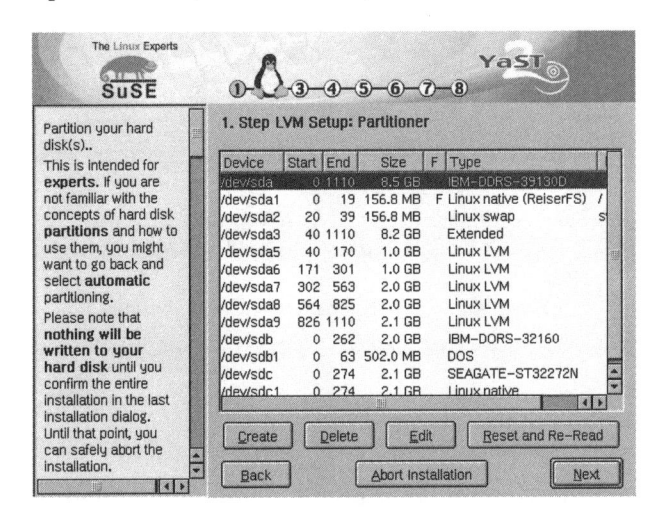

Figure 4.4: *YaST2: LVM Partitioner*

You do not need to individually set the 8E label for all partitions designated for LVM. If need be, YaST2 will automatically set the partition label of a partition assigned to an LVM Volume Group to 8E. For any unpartitioned areas on your disks, create LVM partitions in this dialog. These partitions should then be designated the partition label 8E. They do not have to be formatted and no mount point can be entered in respect to these.

If a working LVM configuration already exists on your system, it will be automatically activated as soon as you begin configuring the LVM. If this is successfully activated, any disks containing a partition belonging to an activated volume group can no longer be repartitioned. The Linux kernel will refuse to read the modified partitioning of a hard disk as long as only one partition on this disk is being used. Of course, repartitioning disks not belonging to an LVM volume group is not a problem at all. If you already have a functioning LVM configuration on your system, repartitioning is usually not necessary. In this screen, configure all mount points not located on LVM Logical Volumes. The root file system in YaST2, at least, must be stored on a normal partition. Select this partition from the list and specify this as root file system using the 'Edit' button. To ensure LVM's optimal flexibility, we recommend that you pool all additional file systems onto LVM logical volumes. After specifying

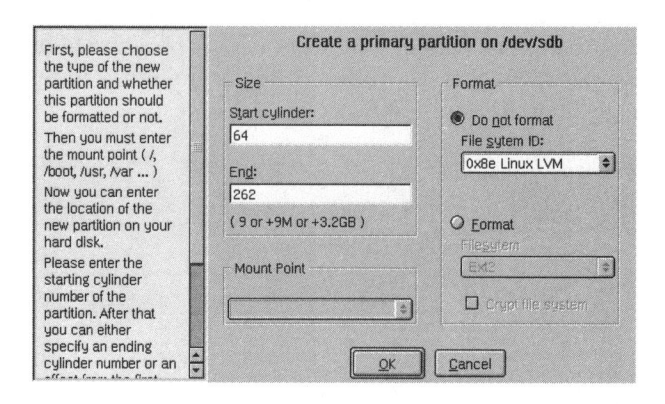

Figure 4.5: YaST2: Creating LVM Partitions

the root partition, exit this dialog.

LVM — Configuring Physical Volumes

This dialog is responsible for managing LVM volume groups (often indicated by "VG"). If no volume group exists on your system yet, you will be prompted in a pop-up window to add one. "System" is suggested as a name for the volume group where the SuSE Linux system files are located. Physical Extent Size (often indicated by PE Size) defines the maximum size of a physical and logical volume in this volume group. This value is normally set to 4 megabytes. This allows for a maximum size of 256 gigabytes for physical and logical volumes. The physical extent size should only be increased if you need larger logical volumes than 256 gigabytes (e.g., to 8, 16, or 32 megabytes).

In the following dialog, all partitions are listed which have either the "Linux LVM" or "Linux native" type. Therefore, all swap and DOS partitions will not be shown. If a partition is already assigned to a volume group, the name of the volume group will be shown in the list. Unassigned partitions are indicated by "—".

The volume group currently being edited can be modified in the selection box above, to the left. The buttons in the upper right enable creation of additional volume groups and deletion of existing volume groups. In any case, only volume groups can be deleted to which no other partitions are assigned. No more than one volume group needs to be created for a normally installed SuSE Linux system. A partition assigned to a volume group is also referred to as a physical volume (often indicated by PV).

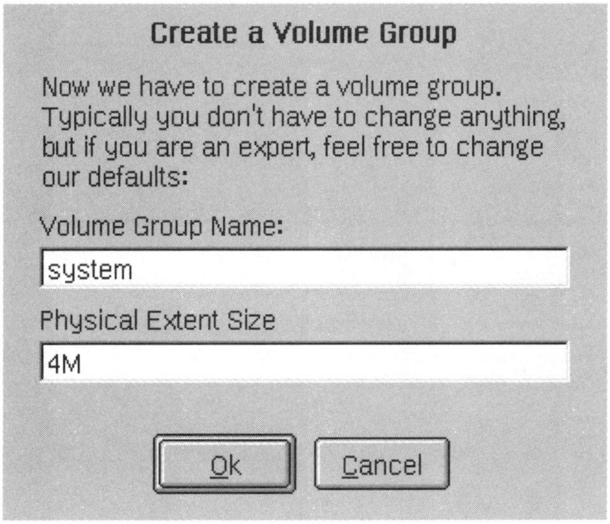

Create a Volume Group

Now we have to create a volume group. Typically you don't have to change anything, but if you are an expert, feel free to change our defaults:

Volume Group Name:

    system

Physical Extent Size

    4M

    [Ok]   [Cancel]

Figure 4.6: YaST2: Adding a Volume Group

To add a previously unassigned partition to the selected volume group, first click on the partition then the 'Add Volume' button below the selection list. At this point, the name of the volume group is entered next to the selected partition. Assign all partitions reserved for LVM to a volume group. Otherwise, the space on the partition will remain unused. Before exiting the dialog, every volume group has to be assigned at least one physical volume.

Logical Volumes

This dialog is responsible for managing logical volumes (often indicated by just "LV").

Logical volumes are assigned, one to each volume group, and have a particular given size. Normally, a file system is created on a logical volume (e. g., reiserfs, ext2) and is then designated a mount point. The files stored on this logical volume can be found at this mount point on the installed system. All normal Linux partitions to which a mount point is assigned, all swap partitions, and all already existing logical volumes are listed here. If you have already configured LVM on your system, the existing logical volumes will have to be entered now.

Before you proceed, assign the appropriate mount point to these logical volumes. If you are configuring LVM on a system for the first time, no logical

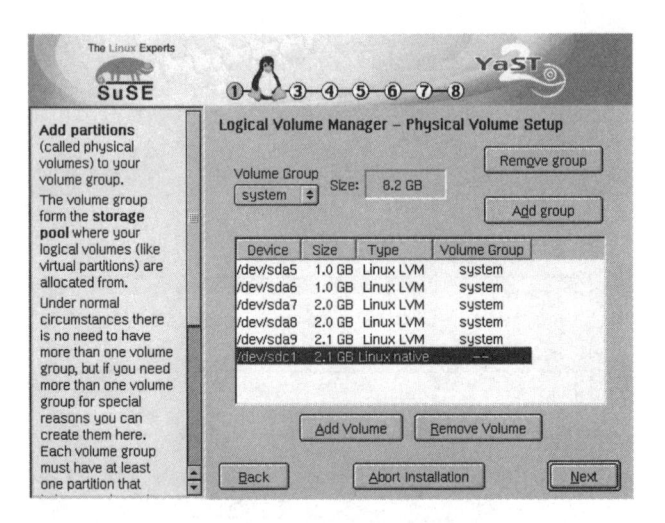

Figure 4.7: YaST2: Partition List

volumes will be displayed in this screen yet. A logical volume must be generated for each mount point (using the 'Add' button). You will also need to specify the size, the file system type (e. g., reiserfs or ext2), and the mount point (e. g., `/var`, `/usr`, `/home`).

If you have created several volume groups, switch between the different volume groups in the selection list above and to the left. The added logical volumes are listed in the volume group displayed there. Once you have created all the logical volumes as required, the LVM configuration will be complete. At this point, exit the dialog and go on to software selection if you are still in the installation process.

┌─ **Caution** ─────────────────────────────────────

Using LVM is associated with increased risk factors such as loss of data. Risks also include application crashes, power outage, and faulty commands. Save your data before implementing LVM or reconfiguring volumes — in other words, never work without a backup.

─────────────────────────────────── **Caution** ─┘

Soft RAID

The purpose of RAID (Redundant Array of Inexpensive Disks) is to combine several hard disk partitions into one large "virtual" hard disk for the opti-

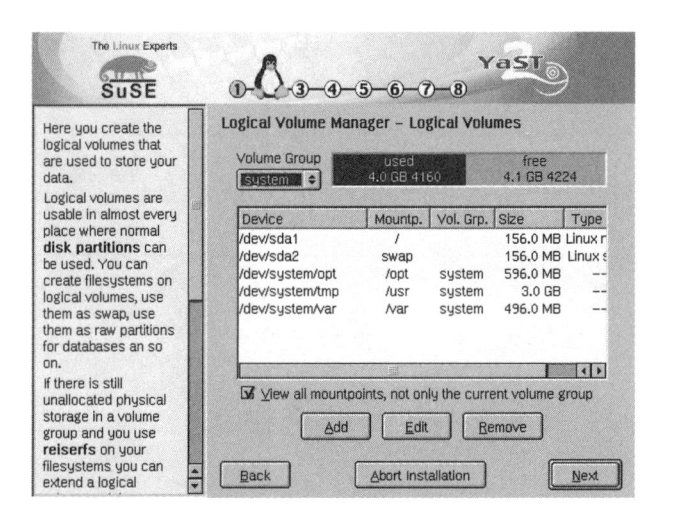

Figure 4.8: YaST2: Logical Volume Management

mization of performance and data security. Using this method, however, one advantage is sacrificed for another. "RAID level" defines the pool and common triggering device of the all hard disks, known as the RAID controller. A RAID controller mostly uses the SCSI protocol, because it can drive more hard disks better than the IDE protocol. It is also better able to process parallel running commands.

Instead of a RAID controller, which can often be quite expensive, the Soft RAID is also able to take on these tasks. SuSE Linux offers the option of combining several hard disks into one Soft RAID system with the help of YaST2 — a very reasonable alternative to Hardware RAID.

Customary RAID Levels

RAID 0 This level improves the performance of your data access. Actually, this is not really a RAID, because it does not provide data backup, but the name "RAID 0" for this type of system has become the norm. With RAID 0, two hard disks are pooled together. The performance is very good — although the RAID system will be destroyed and your data lost, even if just one of the many remaining hard disks fails.

RAID 1 This level provides more than adequate backup for your data, since the data is copied to another hard disk 1:1. This is known as "hard

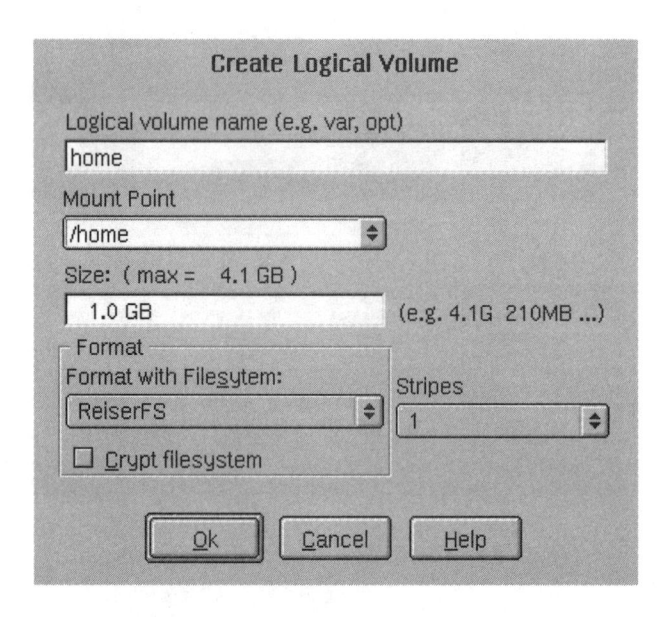

Figure 4.9: YaST2: Creating Logical Volumes

disk mirroring" — if a disk is destroyed, a copy of its contents is located on another one. All of them except one could be damaged without endangering your data. The writing performance suffers a little in the copying process when using RAID 1 (ten to twenty percent slower), but read access is significantly faster in comparison to any one of the normal physical hard disks, because the data is duplicated so can be parallel scanned.

RAID 5 RAID 5 is an optimized compromise between the two other levels in terms of performance and redundancy. The hard disk potential equals the number of disks used minus one. The data is distributed over the hard disks as with RAID 0. "Parity blocks", created on one of the partitions, are there for security reasons. They are linked to each other with XOR — thus enabling the contents, via XDR, to be reconstructed by the corresponding parity block in case of system failure. With RAID 5, no more than one hard disk can fail at the same time. If one is destroyed, it must be replaced as soon as possible to save the data.

Soft RAID Configuration with YaST2

Access Soft RAID configuration by way of the 'RAID' module under 'System' or via the partitioning module under 'Hardware'.

1st Step: Partitioning

First, see a list of your partitions under 'Expert Settings' in the partitioning tool. If the Soft RAID partitions have already been set up, they will appear here. Otherwise, you will have to set them up from scratch. For RAID 0 and RAID 1, at least two partitions are needed — usually for RAID 1, exactly two and no more. If RAID 5 is being used, at least three partitions will be required. It is recommended to only take partitions of the same size. The RAID partitions should be stored on various hard disks to insure against the risk of losing data if one is defective (RAID 1 and 5), as well as to optimize the performance of RAID 0.

2nd Step: Setting Up RAID

Click on 'RAID' and a dialog will appear where you can choose between RAID levels 0, 1 and 5. In the following screen, you will have the option of assigning the partition to the new RAID. The 'Expert options' button opens the settings options for the "chunk size" — fine-tune the performance. Clicking on the check box 'Persistent superblock' ensures that the RAID partitions will be recognized as such when booting.

After completing the configuration, you will then see the `/dev/md0` device and others indicated on the expert page in the partitioning module by "RAID".

Troubleshooting

Find out whether a RAID partition has been destroyed by the file contents `/proc/mdstats`. The basic procedure in case of system failure is to shut down your Linux system and replace the defective hard disk with a new one partitioned the same way. Then restart your system and give the `raidhotadd /dev/mdX /dev/sdX` command. This will enable the hard disk to be integrated automatically into the RAID system and be fully reconstructed.

Configuration instructions and more details for Soft RAID can be found in the HOWTOs at:

- `/usr/share/doc/packages/raidtools/Software-RAID-HOWTO.html`
- `http://www.LinuxDoc.org/HOWTO/Software-RAID-HOWTO.html`

or over a Linux RAID mailing list, such as:

- http://www.mail-archive.com/linux-raid@vger.rutgers.edu.

There you will find help if unexpected complications arise.

Network/Basic

Under 'Network/Basic', YaST2 provides basic configuration tools to pave your way into the Internet: configuration of ADSL, T-DSL (in Germany), network card, ISDN, modem, host name, and DNS. Documentation for this is also located in the [SuS02b].

E-Mail

The e-mail configuration module has been reworked to bring it in line with recent developments. Support for e-mail transfer with postfix has been added and sendmail continues to be supported. Find this configuration module under 'Network/Advanced'. The first dialog lets you select the type of your network connection:

'Host with permanent network connection'
This is normally a "leased line", as is often found at companies or other institutions that work with the Internet. The Internet connection is always running so no dial-up is necessary. This menu item is also meant for members of a local network where no permanent Internet connection exists, but where a central mail server is used for sending e-mail.

'Host with temporary network connection (Modem or ISDN)'
Most home users need this option. It is for computers not on a local network that connect to the Internet via modem, T-DSL, ADSL, or ISDN.

'No network connection'
If you do not have an Internet connection and if the machine does not belong to any other network, sending or receiving e-mails on this machine will (of course) not be possible.

In the following steps, you will be prompted to provide the server name for outgoing messages and to define at least one local user. If you have a dial-up connection, you will have the possibility to set individual POP servers for incoming mail on a per-user basis.

The module also allows you to define aliases and address masks and set up virtual domains. Exit the configuration with 'Finish'.

Network/Advanced

For advanced Internet users and network administrators, there are modules for starting and stopping system services such as inetd, Sendmail (with expert configuration), NFS client and server, routing, expert networking, and NIS client. 'Network for Experts' offers the same functionality as 'Network card configuration' under 'Network/Basic', so you can still configure your modem and ISDN here.

Detailed information about networking and related subjects can be found in the comprehensive chapters on networks in this manual.

Configuring an NFS Server

A system on your network can very quickly be turned into an NFS server with the help of YaST2. This is a server that makes directories and files available to those clients permitted access. Many applications and files can, for example, be made available to multiple users without installing them locally on each system. Details on the configuration of a system as an NFS server can be found in *NFS — Shared File Systems* on page 375.

Configuring NIS

As soon as various Unix systems in a network seek access to common resources, it must be ensured that the user and group IDs are harmonized across all systems. The network becomes transparent and the user always encounters the same environment no matter which system is used.

NIS — Network Information Service on page 371 describes how NIS can be configured as a client and as a server.

Host Name and DNS Configuration

The host name and the DNS data are set here. A later modification of these settings should be avoided as these parameters are necessary for the proper operation of the network. Refer to *Network Integration* on page 349 and *DNS — Domain Name Service* on page 361.

Configuring Routing

Routing equally represents an important parameter for the configuration of a network. *Network Integration* on page 349 contains a complete explanation of routing under Linux.

Security and Users

Here, YaST2 offers tools for simple user and group administration. The configuration module 'System Security' provides various preconfigured levels and expert setting options. Read more about this in *YaST2 — Configuration: Security and Users* in the *User Guide*.

Firewall

The SuSE Firewall 2 can very easily be turned on and configured with this module. Security is essential while connected to the Internet as the possibilities for an attack are enormous. The SuSE firewall offers solid protection. Detailed background information on masquerading, firewalls, and the SuSE firewall can be found in *Masquerading and Firewalls* on page 428. A description of the module can be found in *Yast2 — Configuration: Security and Users* of the [SuS02a].

System

Under 'System', you have the option of reconfiguring the boot mode, creating a boot or module disk, or setting the language and time zone. Modules for backing up and restoring data can also be found here. The profile manager allows the creation of and fast switching between complete sets of individual system configurations. [SuS02b] contains the necessary instructions for the operation of the various modules of this group. The sysconfig and runlevel editors as well as the LVM partitioner are briefly described below. Detailed background information about partitioning and the boot loader can befound in the following sections:

- *Partitioning for Experts* on page 24
- *Booting and Boot Managers* on page 81

Runlevel Editor

The runlevel of the system, its "operation mode", starts after your system boots. In SuSE Linux this is usually runlevel 5 (full multiuser operation with network and KDM, the graphical login). The standard runlevel can be adjusted with this module. Also adjust which services are started in which runlevel. See Table 13.1 on page 297. Runlevels in Linux are described in more detail in *Runlevels* on page 296.

'Edit' continues to an overview of all the services and daemons, supplemented with information as to whether they have been activated on your system and for which runlevels. Highlight a line with the mouse and activate the check boxes for runlevels '0', '1', '2', '3', '5', '6', and 'S' and, with that, state which service or daemon should be activated for which runlevel. Runlevel 4 is undefined — this is always reserved for custom settings.

With 'Start' and 'Stop', decide whether a server should be implemented. The current status is checked via 'Update', if this has not already been done automatically. 'Reset to default value' allows you to restore the default settings to their initial state following installation. 'Activate service' only appears if the service is currently disabled. 'Reset all services to default value' restores all services to their original state following installation. 'Finish' saves the system configuration.

Caution

Do not experiment here. This is an expert tool. If certain service settings are wrong, the system may not be able to restart, possibly requiring a reinstallation from scratch, or security gaps could turn up in your system.

Caution

Sysonfig Editor

The files where the most important SuSE Linux settings are stored are located in the /etc/sysconfig directory. This directory used to be a central file,

/etc/rc.config, where all the configurations were stored. The sysconfig editor presents the settings options in an easy-to-read manner. The values can be modified and subsequently added to the individual configuration files in this directory. Detailed information about the sysconfig editor and the sysconfig variables can be found in *SuSEconfig, /etc/sysconfig, and /etc/rc.config* on page 301.

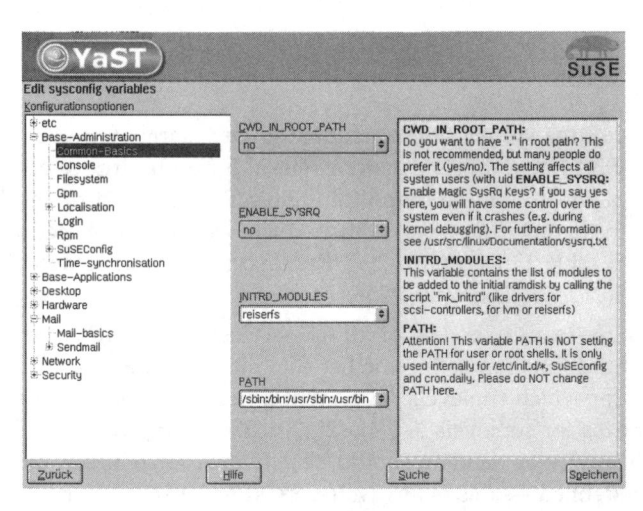

Figure 4.10: YaST2: Configuring the sysconfig Editor

Miscellaneous

'Miscellaneous' offers the option of loading vendor-supplied driver CDs. The start-up protocol (/var/log/boot.msg) and the system protocol (/var/log/messages can be be viewed respectively with this module. Another module enables sending a request to installation support. These modules are described in more detail in [SuS02b].

Booting and Boot Managers

This chapter introduces various methods for booting your installed system. The basics of the boot process can be applied to different boot managers. LILO is used as an example. After a detailed description of LILO, GRUB is explained with comparisons to LILO. A brief introduction to loadlin is also included.

LILO is the boot loader normally used with previous SuSE Linux releases. If you update to this release, LILO will continue to be used. If you have a new installation, GRUB will be used as default.

Booting a PC	82
Boot Concepts	83
Map Files, LILO, and GRUB	84
An Overview of LILO	85
Configuring LILO	87
Installing and Uninstalling LILO	94
Sample Configurations	97
LILO Problems	99
Booting with GRUB	100
Creating Boot CDs	102
Configuring the Boot Mechanism with loadlin	104

Booting a PC

After turning on your computer, the first thing that happens is that the BIOS (Basic Input Output System) takes control, initializes the screen and keyboard, and tests the main memory. Until this task is completed, no external devices or external storage media are known to the system.

Once the basic system has finished its internal setup, it starts to verify the hardware around it. Date, time, and information about some of the most important external devices are read from the CMOS settings (usually referred to as the CMOS setup). After reading the CMOS, the BIOS should recognize the first hard disk, including details such as its geometry. It can then start to load the operating system (OS) from there.

To load the OS, the system loads a 512-byte data segment from the first hard disk into main memory and executes the code stored at the beginning of this segment. The instructions contained there determine the rest of the boot process. This is the reason why the first 512 bytes of the hard disk are often called the *Master Boot Record* (MBR).

Up to this point (loading the MBR), the boot sequence is independent of the installed operating system and is identical on all PCs. Also, all the PC has to access peripheral hardware are those routines (drivers) stored in the BIOS.

Master Boot Record

The layout of the MBR always follows a standard independent of the operating system. The first 446 bytes are reserved for program code. The next 64 bytes offer space for a partition table for up to four partitions. See Section *Partitioning for Experts* on page 24. Without the partition table, no file systems exist on the hard disk — the disk would be virtually useless without it. The last two bytes must contain a special "magic number" (AA55). Any MBR containing a different number is rejected.

Boot Sectors

Boot sectors are the first sectors on a hard disk partition, except the extended partition that serves as a "container" for other partitions. They offer 512 bytes of space and are designed to contain code able to launch an operating system on this partition. Boot sectors of formatted DOS, Windows, and OS/2 partitions do exactly that. In contrast, Linux boot partitions are empty at the very start. A Linux partition cannot be started directly, although it may contain a kernel and a valid root file system. A boot sector with a valid start code contains the same "magic number" as the MBR in its last two bytes.

Booting DOS or Windows 95/98

The DOS MBR of the first hard disk contains information that determines which partition of a hard disk is "active" — which partition should be searched for the operating system to boot. Therefore, DOS has to be installed on the first hard disk. The executable code in the MBR ("first stage boot loader") tests whether the marked partition contains a valid boot sector.

If this is the case, the "second stage boot loader" can be started from there. DOS system programs can now be loaded and you will see the usual DOS prompt. In DOS, only primary partitions can be marked active. Therefore, you cannot use logical partitions inside an extended partition as bootable DOS partitions.

Boot Concepts

The simplest boot concept affects only one machine with one operating system installed. The boot process for this case has already been outlined. The same concept can be used for a Linux-only machine. In this case, you could theoretically skip the installation of LILO. The big disadvantage of doing this is that you cannot pass additional parameters to the system kernel at boot time. As soon as there is more than one operating system installed, there are a number of new boot possibilities.

Booting another OS from a floppy disk: One OS can be booted from the hard disk. Other operating systems can be booted using boot disks.

- *Requirements:* the floppy drive must be bootable
- *Example:* install Linux in addition to Windows, but boot Linux from a floppy disk
- *Advantage:* no boot loader needs to be installed
- *Disadvantage:* requires working boot disks and the boot process takes longer
- Depending on the purpose of the computer, it is an advantage or disadvantage that Linux cannot be booted without a disk.

Boot chaining of additional systems: The same OS is always booted. Others can be optionally started from within the first OS.

- *Requirements:* adequate programs for chain booting of operating systems must be available
- *Example:* loading Linux from DOS or Windows using loadlin.exe or starting a NetWare server from DOS with server.exe (see Section *Configuring the Boot Mechanism with loadlin* on page 104).

Installing a boot manager: Theoretically, this allows you to use an arbitrary number of operating systems on a single machine. The choice of systems is done at boot time. Changing operating systems requires a reboot. Of course, the boot manager must work smoothly with all installed operating systems.

Map Files, LILO, and GRUB

The main obstacle for booting an operating system is the fact the kernel usually is a file within a file system on a partition on a disk. These concepts are unknown to the BIOS.

To circumvent this, "maps" and "map files" were introduced. These maps simply note the physical block numbers on the disk that comprise the logical files. When such a map is processed, the BIOS loads all the physical blocks in sequence as noted in the map, building the logical file in memory.

The main difference between LILO and GRUB is that LILO relies almost entirely on maps, whereas GRUB tries to get rid of fixed maps during boot as early as possible. This is accomplished by introducing *File System Code* to the boot loader, so files can be found by their path names rather than block numbers. This difference has historical reasons: in the early days of Linux, many file systems were competing for dominance. Werner Almesberger wrote a boot loader that did not need to know what kind of file system the kernel to boot actually resided in. The idea behind the GRUB approach, however, is even older, from the ages of traditional Unix and BSD. These usually had a single file system of choice and often had a reserved space at its beginning in which to embed a boot loader. This boot loader knew the data structures of the file system in which it was embedded and kernels could be found by name in the root directory of that file system.

Another fundamental difference is that the LILO boot code is written in 16-bit assembler while as much of GRUB as possible is written in 32-bit portable C. The impact of this, however, is mostly beyond the scope of this book.

The following section describes the installation and configuration of a boot manager, using the Linux boot manager LILO. A complete description of LILO's features can be found in [Alm94]. This reference can be located in `/usr/share/doc/packages/lilo/user.dvi`, viewed on screen with applications like `xdvi`, or printed with: `lpr /usr/share/doc/packages/lilo/user.dvi`

GRUB is compared to LILO in Section *Booting with GRUB* on page 100. This is followed by a description of loadlin.

An Overview of LILO

The Linux boot loader LILO is usually installed in the MBR (details in Sections *LILO Locations* on the next page and *Installing and Uninstalling LILO* on page 94). LILO has access to two real mode hard disks and is able to find all the data it needs from the *raw* hard drives without requiring any partitioning data. Because of this, operating systems can also be booted from the second hard disk. The entries in the partition table are ignored when using LILO.

> **Tip**
>
> A raw device is a block device (such as a hard disk, partition, or floppy disk) accessed directly via a device file and not a file system.
>
> **Tip**

An important difference from the standard DOS boot sequence is that you can select any of the installed systems at boot when using LILO. After loading the MBR into memory, LILO is started and displays the boot menu with all the installed operating systems. The first in the list is booted by default if no selection is made. LILO then loads the boot sector of the partition from which to boot the operating system or it loads the Linux kernel and boots Linux. It also provides the important option of passing a command to the kernel. For security reasons, this can be protected totally or partially with a password.

The Components of LILO

The LILO boot mechanism consists of the following components:

- the beginning, or *first stage*, of the LILO code in a boot sector that activates the system boot

> **Tip**
>
> The boot sectors installed by LILO contain a byte sequence similar to that characteristic for boot sector viruses. Therefore, it is not unusual for DOS virus scanners to claim to have detected the AIRCOP boot sector virus in files such as `/boot/chain.b` or `/boot/os2_d.b`.
>
> **Tip**

- the *heart* of the LILO code, located in `/boot/boot-menu.b`
- a *map* file, normally `/boot/map`, where LILO enters the location of Linux kernels and other data during its installation
- optional: the *message file* `/boot/message`, which displays the graphical boot menu from which the operating system can be selected
- the different Linux kernels and boot sectors LILO should offer

> **Caution**
>
> Any write access (even through file movements) to any of these files corrupts the map file, requiring you to *update* LILO (see *Updating After Changing the Configuration* on page 95). This is especially important when changing kernels.
>
> **Caution**

LILO Locations

This section refers to the *first stage* of LILO mentioned above. Consider this general restriction: depending on the BIOS version on your computer, it may be required that the kernel image `/boot/vmlinuz` be located on the *first 1024 cylinders* of the hard disk. This can be achieved with a small extra partition that can be "mounted" in the directory `/boot`, all of which is located within the first 1024 cylinders. Further information is provided in the SuSE support database:

`http://sdb.suse.de/en/sdb/html/1024_Zylinder.html`

The following locations are suitable for storing the LILO *boot sector*.

- **on a *floppy disk*.**
  This is the simplest, but also the slowest method for booting with LILO. Choose this alternative if you do not want to change the existing boot sector.

- **in the boot sector of a primary Linux partition on the first hard disk.**
  This leaves the MBR untouched. Before it can be booted, the partition must be marked active. Start fdisk as `root` with the command `fdisk -s <partition>`. The program will ask for a command. 'm' gives you a list of possible entries and 'a' marks the selected partition as active. If Linux is completely installed on logical drives or partitions on the second hard disk, LILO can only be installed in the boot sector of the extended drive of the first hard disk, if there is one. Linux fdisk can also activate such a partition.

  For booting multiple systems from the hard disk, this is extremely awkward. Every time you want to boot, you have to activate the corresponding boot sector *beforehand*. The next two variants are much less cumbersome.

- **in the *Master Boot Record*.**
  This variation offers the highest flexibility. It is the only alternative possible if all of the Linux partitions reside on the second hard disk and there is no extended partition on the first drive. Every setting of the MBR must be edited with extreme care since errors may have severe consequences. The safety aspects are described in Section *Installing and Uninstalling LILO* on page 94.

- **in a boot sector booted by *another boot manager*.**
  Try this if you have used another boot manager and want to continue using it. Depending on its flexibility and power, there are several variations. A common case: you have a primary Linux partition on the second hard disk from which you boot Linux. Your boot manager is able to boot this partition via a boot sector. Then you can activate your Linux partition by installing LILO into this boot sector and telling your boot manager that it is active.

> **Caution**
>
> Be careful if you try to make a *logical* Linux partition bootable by installing LILO onto it. Success *is not guaranteed*, even if your other boot manager is able to launch logical partitions.
>
> **Caution**

Configuring LILO

LILO is a flexible boot manager that offers many ways of adapting a configuration to your needs. The most important options and meanings are described below. For more detail, look at [Alm94].

LILO is configured in /etc/lilo.conf. If you are installing LILO for the first time, use YaST to configure LILO. Fine-tune by editing /etc/lilo.conf later.

> **Note**
>
> /etc/lilo.conf should only be readable for root, as it could contain passwords (see Section *Other LILO Configuration Options* on page 91). This is the default setting with SuSE Linux.
>
> **Note**

It is recommended to keep a backup of the previous lilo.conf file. Your settings only take effect when you update LILO after changing /etc/lilo.conf (see Section *Installing and Uninstalling LILO* on page 94).

Structure of lilo.conf

/etc/lilo.conf starts with a global section followed by one or more system sections for each operating system LILO should start. A new section is started by a line beginning with either image or other.

The order of entries in /etc/lilo.conf only matters because the first one in the list is booted by default unless the default option is used or the user selects another entry. This can be set to delay and timeout.

A sample configuration for a computer with both Windows and Linux is shown in File 2. There is a new Linux kernel (/boot/vmlinuz and a fallback kernel /boot/vmlinuz.shipped) and Windows on /dev/hda1. The program MemTest86 is also available.

```
### LILO global section
boot    = /dev/hda             # LILO installation target: MBR
backup  = /boot/MBR.hda.990428 # backup file for the old MBR
                               # 1999-04-28
vga     = normal               # normal text mode (80x25 chars)
read-only
menu-scheme = Wg:kw:Wg:Wg
lba32                          # Use BIOS to ignore
                               # 1024 cylinder limit
prompt
password = q99iwr4             # LILO password (example)
timeout = 80                   # Wait at prompt for 8 s before
                               # default is booted
```

```
message = /boot/message      # LILO's greeting

### LILO Linux section (default)
  image  = /boot/vmlinuz     # Default
  label  = linux
  root   = /dev/hda7         # Root partition for the kernel
  initrd = /boot/initrd

### LILO Linux section (fallback)
  image  = /boot/vmlinuz.shipped
  label  = Failsafe
  root   = /dev/hda7
  initrd = /boot/initrd.suse
  optional

### LILO other system section (Windows)
  other  = /dev/hda1         # Windows partition
  label  = windows

### LILO memory test section (memtest)
  image  = /boot/memtest.bin
  label  = memtest86
```

File 2: Sample Configuration of /etc/lilo.conf

Anything between a '#' and the end of a line is regarded as a comment. Spaces and comments are ignored by LILO and can be used to improve readability.

The mandatory entries are explained here. The additional options are described in Section *Other LILO Configuration Options* on page 91.

- **Global section** (Parameter part)

    ▷ boot=⟨*bootdevice*⟩

    The device on whose first sector LILO should be installed. ⟨*bootdevice*⟩ may be a floppy disk drive (/dev/fd0), a partition (e. g., /dev/hdb3), or an entire disk (e. g., /dev/hda). The last means installing LILO in the MBR. Default: if this option is missing, LILO is installed on the current root partition.

    ▷ lba32

    With this option, ignore the 1024-cylinder limit of LILO if your BIOS supports this.

▷ prompt

Forces the LILO prompt to be displayed. The default is no prompt (refer to Section *Other LILO Configuration Options* on the next page, option delay). This is recommended if LILO needs to manage more than one system. timeout should be set to guarantee an automatic reboot if nothing is entered at the prompt.

▷ timeout=⟨*tenth-seconds*⟩ Sets a time-out for selecting an operating system to boot. Afterwards, the default system is booted. Specify the time-out in ⟨*tenth-seconds*⟩ (0.1 second increments). Pressing ⇧ Shift or the arrow keys disables the timeout option and LILO waits for orders. Default is set to 80.

- **Linux section**

    ▷ image=⟨*kernelimage*⟩

    Enter the name of the kernel image to boot, including its directory location. With a new system, this is most likely `/boot/vmlinuz`.

    ▷ label=⟨*name*⟩

    This name must be unique in `/etc/lilo.conf`. Otherwise, freely choose a name for the system (e. g., Linux). Maximum length is 15 characters. Use only letters, numbers, and underscore in names — no blanks or special characters. For more on the specific rules for which characters to use, see [Alm94], as described in Section *Boot Concepts* on page 84. The default is the file name of the kernel image (e. g., `/boot/vmlinuz`).

    By this name, select which system to boot from the menu. It is recommended, if there are several systems installed, to use a message file displaying the possible selections (see Section *Other LILO Configuration Options* on the next page, option message).

    ▷ root=⟨*rootdevice*⟩

    This gives the kernel the name of the root partition (e. g., `/dev/hda2`) of your Linux system. This is recommended for security reasons. If this option is omitted, the kernel takes its own root partition ⟨*kernelimage*⟩.

- **Linux part** (Linux — Safe Settings)

    Even if you installed a customized kernel, you are still able to boot the SuSE standard kernel.

▷ optional

If you decide to delete /boot/vmlinuz.shipped (*not recommended*), this section will be skipped without an error message during LILO installation.

- **Other systems**

    ▷ other=⟨*partition*⟩

    other tells LILO to start the partitions of other systems (e. g., /dev/hda1).

    ▷ label=⟨*name*⟩

    Select a name for the system. This is recommended, because the default — the raw device name — is not very informative.

- **Memory Test**

    Entry for the memory test program memtest86.

Other LILO Configuration Options

The previous section covered the entries required in /etc/lilo.conf. Other useful options are discussed below. They are either marked as global or image options of /etc/lilo.conf.

- backup=⟨*backup*⟩ (global)

    The file where LILO backs up the boot sector. The default is /boot/boot.xxxx, where xxxx is the internal device number of the installation partition.

    We do not recommend use of a cryptic name. You will not be able to use the implemented uninstall feature of LILO, but we think it is better to do this carefully by hand, anyway. (see Section *Uninstalling LILO* on page 96)

    ┌─ **Caution** ─────────────────────────────

    If the backup file exists, LILO does *not* create a new one. Make sure you use a name not already in use.

    ─────────────────────────── **Caution** ─┘

- compact (image)

    This option is recommended if you want to install LILO on a floppy disk. If enabled, LILO tries to read more sectors at a time, resulting in a faster boot process. This does not work on every machine. We do not recommend setting this as the normal way is safer and it only provides a difference of one or two seconds.

- loader=⟨*boot loader*⟩ (image)
  To load a boot sector belonging to another operating system, LILO constructs a *pseudo MBR* in its map file. At boot time, LILO first starts this pseudo MBR, which, in turn, starts the other boot sector. This option specifies the file where the code for the pseudo MBR is found.
  Default: /boot/chain.b (usually, this is correct).

When booting another operating system in this way, it is possible to swap hard disks according to their device numbers. This allows an OS, such as DOS, that must be installed on the first hard disk to actually be installed on a later hard disk. For this, the options map-drive=⟨*number*⟩ and to=⟨*number*⟩ are used. See File 3.

```
# Booting DOS from the second hard disk
# DOS bootable partition config begins
other = /dev/hdb1
  label = DOS
  loader = /boot/chain.b
    map-drive = 0x80    #  first hd: BIOS number 0x80
    to        = 0x81    #  second hd: BIOS number 0x81
    map-drive = 0x81
    to        = 0x80
  table = /dev/hdb
# DOS bootable partition config ends
```

File 3: Extract from /etc/lilo.conf: Booting DOS from a Second Hard Disk

- table=⟨*ptable*⟩ (image)
  ⟨*ptable*⟩ sets the source device for the partition table written into the pseudo MBR (normally /dev/hda or /dev/sda).

- disk=⟨*device file*⟩ (global)
  bios=⟨*BIOS device number*⟩
  cylinders=⟨*amount*⟩
  heads=⟨*amount*⟩
  sectors=⟨*amount*⟩
  LILO can be told precisely which BIOS device number and geometry to use. This is rarely needed. There is one major exception: *IDE-SCSI* system. If you own a BIOS that is capable of switching the boot devices

SCSI prior to IDE and want to use this feature, tell LILO the switched order from the perspective of the BIOS. This is achieved by an extra entry in the global section of `lilo.conf`. An example for a system with one SCSI and one IDE disk can be seen in File 4.

```
# Enable LILO to correctly access /dev/sda and /dev/hda
# at boot time if their boot order is interchanged in
# the BIOS:
disk = /dev/sda    #    The SCSI disk is regarded as ...
    bios = 0x80    #    ... first BIOS disk;
disk = /dev/hda    #    the IDE disk is regarded as ...
    bios = 0x81    #    ... second BIOS disk.
```

File 4: Extract from lilo.conf: Boot Sequence — SCSI Before IDE

- linear (global)
  Giving this option when installing LILO causes all references to hard disk sectors to be stored as logical addresses instead of physical addresses, so they are independent of any hard disk geometry. This option is intended for cases where, when booting, the BIOS detects a different geometry than that of the Linux system running. Only needed in rare cases.

  The linear option does *not* release you from the constraints of the 1024--cylinder limit, which is determined by the BIOS geometry of the boot hard disk. Refer also to `/usr/share/doc/sdb/en/html/kgw_lilo_linear.html`.

- message=⟨*message-file*⟩ (global)
  Points to a file creating the boot screen and displaying the selection of operation systems. SuSE Linux normally uses a PCX image instead of the classical start-up message. To learn more about this, read `file: /usr/share/doc/sdb/de/html/jkoeke_bootgrafik_72.html`.

  Note
  If this option is set, the message file becomes part of the LILO boot machinery and, after every change to this file, LILO must be updated (Section *Installing and Uninstalling LILO* on the next page).

- password=⟨*password*⟩ (global or image)
  May be located either in the global or one of the system-specific image sections. Provides secure access to LILO services or booting the corresponding system by means of a password. If you take this seriously, remove the password from `lilo.conf` after using it. As `root`, you can set a new password for LILO any time you like (you just need to update LILO afterwards). It is recommended also to set the option restricted, otherwise it could be possible to launch a shell. See the man page about lilo.conf (`man lilo.conf`).

- read-only (global)
  LILO uses this image option to instruct the kernel initially to mount the root partition read-only, as is usually customary for booting Linux systems. If this option is omitted, the kernel will use its own default setting, which is shown by the `rdev -R` ⟨*kernelimage*⟩ command.

- delay=⟨*tenth-seconds*⟩ (global)
  If the prompt is *not* explicitly set, access a prompt by pressing ⇧ Shift, Ctrl, or Alt. The delay= option sets the time to elapse before LILO boots the first system in its list. The default is 0 — no waiting. The delay option has no effect if a prompt is specifically requested by prompt.

- vga=⟨*mode*⟩ (global)
  Selects VGA mode at start-up. Valid modes are `normal` (80x25), `ext` (80x50), or `ask` (asks when booting). For a framebuffer-enabled kernel, possible values are listed and described in `/usr/src/linux/Documentation/fb/vesafb.txt`.

- append="⟨*parameter*⟩" (image)
  Image option for Linux kernel. Enables kernel parameters to be specified, for example, for hardware components, in the same way as at the LILO prompt. The kernel first reads the append line then the prompt. Therefore, if the parameters given at the append line are different from those specified at the prompt, the latter ones will be used.

  For example: append="mcd=0x300,10"

Installing and Uninstalling LILO

During a new Linux installation or at a later time, YaST leads you through the steps of installing LILO interactively. In this section, we assume that some action is required that goes beyond what YaST2 can accomplish and we take a closer look at how LILO works during the installation and uninstallation process.

> **Caution**
>
> The installation of a boot manager is tricky. Ensure *in advance* that you are completely able to boot Linux and other mounted systems. You must have fdisk installed on a crash recovery disk. Otherwise, you might find yourself unable to access your hard disk at all.
>
> **Caution**

Updating After Changing the Configuration

If any of the LILO components have changed or you have modified your configuration in `/etc/lilo.conf`, update LILO. This is easily done by launching the *Map Installer* as root with `/sbin/lilo`.

LILO creates a backup of the target boot sector, writes its *first stage* into it, then generates a new map file (see also Section *The Components of LILO* on page 85). LILO issues a report on each installed system as shown in Output 4.

```
Added linux *
Added suse
Added windows
Added memtest86
```

Output 4: *Output After Launching LILO*

When the installation is completed, the machine can be rebooted with `shutdown -r now`. While rebooting, the BIOS first performs its system test. Immediately afterwards, see LILO and its command prompt, where you can enter parameters and select a boot image from the recently installed configurations. (Tab) shows a list of all systems installed.

Installation After Recompiling a Kernel

For including a freshly-compiled kernel in your LILO boot setup, the Linux kernel Makefile offers an all-in-one solution. All the commands to configure and create the kernel are put together in the file `/usr/src/linux/Makefile`. Here, `INSTALL_PATH=/boot` is specified. This `Makefile` has a target called bzlilo that, after a kernel compilation, automatically copies the currently installed kernel `/boot/vmlinuz` (this used to be `/vmlinuz`) to

SuSE Linux – Administration Guide   95

/boot/vmlinuz.old, the new kernel to /boot/vmlinuz, then reinstalls LILO. This can be done by entering the command make bzlilo instead of make zImage. This is only useful if you have edited /etc/lilo.conf *in advance* and if your current kernel really is located in /boot/vmlinuz. The new and the old kernels should now be listed. See File 2 on page 88 for an example of the resulting /etc/lilo.conf.

At the LILO prompt, launch either of the two kernels. This makes your boot more secure, because you can still boot your old kernel if the new one fails. For more on creating a new kernel, see Chapter *The Linux Kernel* on page 261.

Uninstalling LILO

Caution

Uninstalling a boot manager is tricky. Ensure *in advance* that you are able to boot Linux and other systems with their respective boot disks.

To uninstall LILO, copy the former content of the boot sector over LILO. This requires a valid backup of that former content. See Section *Other LILO Configuration Options* on page 91, option backup.

Caution

A boot sector backup is no longer valid if the partition in question has a new file system. The partition table of an MBR backup becomes invalid if the hard disk in question has been repartitioned since the backup was created. Obsolete "backups" are time bombs. It is best to delete them as soon as possible.

It is very simple to regain a DOS or Windows MBR. Just enter the MS-DOS command (available since 5.0)

C:\> **FDISK /MBR**

or, on OS/2,

C:\> **FDISK /NEWMBR**

These commands only write the first 446 bytes (the boot code) into the MBR and leave partitions untouched.

For other restorations, first make a backup of the LILO sector in question — just to be on the safe side. Now check carefully whether your old backup file is the correct one and if it is exactly 512 bytes in size. Finally, write it back with the following commands:

- If LILO resides in partition yyyy (e. g., hda1, hda2):

  ```
  earth:~ # dd if=/dev/yyyy of=New-File bs=512 count=1
  earth:~ # dd if=Backup-Date of=/dev/yyyy
  ```

- If LILO resides in the MBR of zzz (e. g., hda, sda):

  ```
  earth:~ # dd if=/dev/zzz of=New-File bs=512 count=1
  earth:~ # dd if=Backup-Date of=/dev/zzz bs=446 count=1
  ```

The last command is "cautious" and does not overwrite the partition table. Again, *do not forget:* with `fdisk`, mark the desired starting partition as *bootable*.

Sample Configurations

If Linux is the only operating system on your machine, there is nothing left to do. All the required steps have already been taken by YaST2. More information for multisystem computers can be found under `/usr/share/doc/howto/en/html/mini/Linux+*`.

DOS/Windows 95/98 and Linux

Requirements: There must be at least a primary partition each for DOS/Windows 95/98 and Linux below the 1024-cylinder limit (Section *LILO Locations* on page 86).

For this case, we have already discussed a configuration (File 2 on page 88) — only the settings for root, image, and other need adaptation. LILO is installed in the MBR.

Save your `/etc/lilo.conf` and be sure you have a Linux boot disk. Windows 95/98 is especially inclined to eliminate "foreign" MBRs. If you can still boot Linux using your boot disk, this problem is quickly solved with the command

```
earth:~ # /sbin/lilo
```

This completes your LILO installation.

Windows NT or Windows 2000 and Linux

In general, the boot concepts of Windows 2000 and Windows NT are identical. Therefore the following explanations only refer to Windows NT, but are valid for Windows 2000 as well.

1. If Windows NT and Linux need to coexist on the same hard disk, use the NT boot manager for booting. This can either start the kernel images or the boot sectors themselves. Execution of the following steps prepares everything for a peaceful coexistence of Linux and Windows NT:

   - Install NT.
   - Partition the NT disks (using FAT so Linux can write to them).
   - Install Linux as usual (in our example, the root partition is on /dev/sda3). Mount either the DOS partition or an error-free DOS floppy disk (for example, on /dos).
   - Install LILO, but install it in Linux's root partition (/dev/sda3), **not** in the MBR (/dev/sda). You may still configure a selection of Linux kernels for LILO. See File 5.

   ```
   # LILO Configuration file
   # Start LILO global Section
   boot=/dev/sda3                   # Target of installation
   backup=/boot/boot.sda3.020428    # Backup previous
                                    # boot sec-
   tor; 28. Apr 2002
   prompt
   timeout=100      # Wait at prompt: 10 s
   vga = normal     # force sane video state
   # End LILO global section
   # Linux bootable partition config begins
   image = /vmlinuz              #   default image to boot
       root = /dev/sda3          # Here the root partition!
       label = Linux
   # Linux bootable partition config ends
   ```
   File 5: lilo.conf for a Boot Disk

   After editing lilo.conf, install LILO as usual with /sbin/lilo.
   - Copy the LILO boot sector to a location where NT can find it. For example,
     ```
     earth:~ #  /bin/dd if=/dev/sda3 bs=512 count=1 \
     
                    of=/dos/liloboot.lin
     ```

This step, as well as the following, must be performed after every kernel update.

- Boot NT. Copy `liloboot.lin` from the data disk to the main directory of NT's system drive, if it is not already there.
- In `boot.ini` (first setting attributes), supplement, at the end, `c:\liloboot.lin="Linux"`.
- After the next boot (if everything went smoothly), there should be an entry in NT's boot manager.

2. *Another possibility, but not always feasible: Install LILO to the MBR* and pretend that it is DOS (as described in the above example). This method apparently no longer works for newer NT versions, as it only seems to start if it detects special (undocumented) sequences in the MBR, which are, unfortunately, not recognized by LILO.

⎡ **Caution** ─────────────────────────────────

NT 3.5x and 4.0 do not recognize Linux partition types 82 and 83. Make sure that no NT program tries to "repair" your partition table. This would result in loss of data. Always have valid backups of the LILO boot sector available.

────────────────────────────────── **Caution** ⎦

LILO Problems

Some Guidelines

Some simple initial guidelines will prevent most LILO problems (this is taken from the LILO documentation [Alm94]):

- Always have an up-to-date and tested *boot disk* at hand.
- SuSE Linux contains a rescue system on its boot disk and installation CD (see Section *The SuSE Rescue System* on page 285) to give you access to all your Linux partitions. Tools are included for fixing almost any problems that can occur.
- Check `/etc/lilo.conf` *before* using the map installer (`/sbin/lilo`).

Booting with GRUB

Except the points mentioned earlier, most of the LILO features also apply to GRUB. Some differences will be apparent to the user, however.

Like LILO, GRUB also consists of two stages — a 512-byte first stage to be put into an MBR or a partition boot block and a larger "stage2" found using a map file. From here on, however, things work differently with GRUB. stage2 contains code to read file systems. Currently supported are ext2 (and thus ext3, for GRUB's read-only purposes), reiser FS, jfs, xfs, minix, and the DOS FAT FS as used by Windows. Any file contained in such a file system on a supported BIOS disk device can be displayed, used as a command or menu file, or loaded into memory as a kernel or initrd, just by issuing the appropriate command followed by the BIOS device and a path.

The big difference to LILO is that once GRUB is installed, kernels and menu entries can be added or changed without any further action required. At boot time, GRUB will dynamically locate and reread the files' contents.

The Menu

For the computer user, the most important GRUB file, once GRUB is installed, is the menu file, by default /boot/grub/menu.1st. This file contains all information about other partitions or operating systems that may be booted using the menu.

Because of its own code to read file systems, GRUB does a fresh read of the menu file on each boot, so there is absolutely no need to update GRUB each time you make changes to the file — just use YaST2 or your favorite editor.

The menu file contains commands. The syntax is quite simple. Each line consists of a command followed by optional parameters separated spaces, as in the shell. Some commands allow an equal sign before their first parameter for historical reasons. Comments introduced by the hash sign ('#').

To identify the menu entries in the menu summary presentation, give each entry a name or title. After the keyword title, spaces are skipped and the rest of the line appears as a selectable item when the menu is shown. All commands up to the next title will be executed when this menu entry is chosen.

The simplest case is the chain loading of another operating system's boot loader. The command is called chainloader and the argument is usually another partition's boot block in GRUB's *block notation*, for example:

```
chainloader (hd0,3)+1
```

GRUB's device naming is explained in Section *Names for BIOS devices* on the current page. This example means one block from the beginning of a partition.

The command to specify a kernel image is just `kernel`. The first argument is taken as a path to a kernel file on a partition. The remainder is passed to that kernel when it is started.

If the kernel does not have the necessary built-in file system or disk drivers to access the root partition, an `initrd` must be specified. This is a separate GRUB command and takes the path to the initrd file as its only argument. This command must follow the `kernel` command, as the loading address of the initrd will be written into the already-loaded kernel image.

The `root` command simplifies the specification of kernels and initrds. In a strict sense, this command really does not do anything, but is just a shorthand. `root` takes a GRUB device or partition as its only argument and all kernel, initrd, or other file paths that do not explicitly specify a device will have this device prepended, up to the next `root` command.

Implicitly at the end of each menu entry there is a `boot` command, so there is no need to write it into the menu file. Should you, however, come into a situation to interactively type GRUB commands by hand during the boot process, you will have to finally issue the `boot` command. `boot` takes no arguments. It just executes the loaded kernel image or chain loader.

Once you have written all your menu entries, specify which entry number to use as `default`. Otherwise, the first one (number 0) will be used. You can also specify a time-out in seconds after which this should occur. `timeout` and `default` are usually written before the menu entries.

Names for BIOS devices

The origin of GRUB is revealed by the way it gives names to BIOS devices. A BSD-like scheme is used: the floppy disk devices `0x00`, `0x01` are called fd0 and fd1, respectively, and all hard disks recognized by the host BIOS or added by add-on controllers `0x80`, `0x81`, `0x82` are simply called hd0, hd1, and so on, regardless of their specific type. The problem of linux device name correspondence to BIOS devices is common to both LILO and GRUB. Both use similar heuristics to establish a mapping, but GRUB stores the result in a file that can be corrected.

Partitions on hard disks are expressed by appending their number with a separating comma. A complete GRUB path consists of a device name, which is always written in parenthesis, and a file path on that device or partition, always with a leading slash. So, for example, on a system with only a single IDE disk and Linux on its first partition, a bootable kernel might be

(hd0,0)/boot/vmlinuz

> **Note**
>
> Partition numbers in GRUB are zero-based. (hd0,0) corresponds to /dev/hda1.

Installation Using the GRUB Shell

Because GRUB is 32-bit C code, it is quite easy to replace the BIOS calls with Linux system calls to get an identical GRUB program that is able to function within a Linux environment. This program is called the *GRUB shell*. The functionality to install a GRUB onto a disk is present within GRUB itself as the install or setup command and is thus available via the GRUB shell when Linux is running and when GRUB has just been loaded during the boot process. This greatly eases the rapair of a damaged system.

The Linux environment is where the BIOS mapping heuristics come into play: the GRUB shell reads a file device.map, which consists of one line specifying the GRUB device and the path name to a Linux device node separated by spaces. Some SCSI adaptor BIOSes allow their disks to be inserted *before* the IDE disks instead of appended after them, some BIOSes are capable of switching first and second hard disk, and others give you full control over the sequence of disks attached to on-board interfaces and all add-on cards. On current PCs, there is no reliable way to detect this. So, in case of trouble, first make sure device.map reflects the actual BIOS numbering of your disks. device.map is found in the default GRUB directory, /boot/grub/.

Creating Boot CDs

This concerns problems arising when attempting to boot a system with the LILO boot manager configured with YaST2. The creation of a system boot disk fails with more recent SuSE Linux versions because the space available on a floppy disk is no longer sufficient for the start-up files.

Procedure

It is possible to create a bootable CD-ROM containing the Linux start-up files if your system has an installed CD writer. This solution is only a workaround. It should normally be possible to configure LILO properly. Refer to the documentation about this subject in `/usr/share/doc/packages/lilo/README`, the man page for `lilo.conf` (`man lilo.conf`), and the man page for `lilo` (`man lilo`).

Boot CD with ISOLINUX

It is easiest to create a bootable CD with the ISOLINUX boot manager. The SuSE installation CDs are also made bootable with isolinux.

- Boot the installed system first using the following alternate procedure:
  - ▷ Boot from the installation CD or DVD as for installation.
  - ▷ Choose the preselected option 'Installation' during the boot sequence.
  - ▷ Choose the language and keyboard map next.
  - ▷ In the following menu, choose 'Boot installed system'.
  - ▷ The root partition is automatically detected and the system is booted from it.

- Install package `syslinux` with YaST2.

- Open a root shell. The following commands create a temporary directory and copy the files required for the booting of the Linux system (the isolinux boot loader as well as the kernel and the initrd) into it:

  ```
  earth:~ # mkdir /tmp/CDroot
  earth:~ # cp /usr/share/syslinux/isolinux.bin /tmp/CDroot/
  earth:~ # cp /boot/vmlinuz /tmp/CDroot/linux
  earth:~ # cp /boot/initrd /tmp/CDroot
  ```

- Create the boot loader configuration file `/tmp/CDroot/isolinux.cfg` with your preferred editor. Enter the following content:

  ```
  DEFAULT linux
  LABEL linux
    KERNEL linux
    APPEND initrd=initrd root=/dev/hdXY [boot parameter]
  ```

Enter your root partition for the parameter `root=/dev/hdXY`. It is listed in the file `/etc/fstab`. Enter additional options for the setting `[boot parameter]`, which should be used during booting. The configuration files could, for example, look like this:

```
DEFAULT linux LABEL linux KERNEL linux APPEND initrd=initrd
root=/dev/hda7 hdd=ide-scsi
```

- The following command (entered at a command prompt) then creates an ISO-9660 file system for the CD.

  ```
  mkisofs -o /tmp/bootcd.iso -b isolinux.bin -c boot.cat
    -no-emul-boot -boot-load-size 4
    -boot-info-table /tmp/CDroot
  ```

  The complete command must be entered as one line.

- The file `/tmp/bootcd.iso` can be written to CD after that with either graphical CD writing applications, like KonCD or XCDroast, or simply at a command prompt:

  ```
  cdrecord -v speed=2 dev=0,0,0 /tmp/bootcd.iso -eject
  ```

  The parameter `dev=0,0,0` must be changed according to the SCSI ID of the writer. This can be determined with the command `cdrecord -scanbus`. Also, refer to the man page for `cdrecord` (`man cdrecord`).

- Test the boot CD. Reboot the computer to verify whether the Linux system is started correctly from the CD.

Configuring the Boot Mechanism with loadlin

loadlin will be introduced in the following sections as another method of booting SuSE Linux. loadlin is a DOS application capable of booting a Linux kernel stored in a DOS directory. loadlin can be seamlessly integrated into an already existing DOS/Windows 9x environment and easily started with the help of the Windows boot manager. As there is no entry in the MBR, Windows will not know that Linux is installed, but only "see" one or more partitions possessing IDs Window does not recognize. Undesired side effects that could result from Linux coexisting on your Windows system are minimized that way.

The procedure described here works for Windows 95 and Windows 98. The configuration files shown below were developed for Windows 95. Therefore, the following only directly refers to Windows 95.

You will have to make some preparations before using loadlin to boot Linux. Depending on your system environment, you will also have to modify certain boot files.

loadlin can be activated in two ways: by selecting from several configurations in the boot menu or by starting loadlin from a running system then switching to Linux. Both methods have their advantages and disadvantages:

- Using the boot menu, avoid starting Linux from within another operating system.

- You can integrate other configurations into a boot menu.

- However, you must modify the boot files to set up a boot menu. You might have to try out different options. Some helpful tips can be obtained in the DOS help files after typing `help menu`.

- Switching to Linux at the DOS prompt is quite simple.

- The Linux boot can be nicely built into the graphical interface of Windows 95. Switch to Linux by double-clicking an icon. You can also set up a boot menu in Windows 95 (Windows 95 runs on DOS 7.0).

─ Tip ─────────────────────────────────
If possible, use a boot menu if you want to boot Linux as soon as you switch on the computer. The DOS prompt or the double-click method can additionally be used to switch to Linux from DOS/Windows 95. Only a summary of using Windows boot menus is included here.
──────────────────────────────── Tip ─┘

Required Files for loadlin

The following is needed (in DOS, Windows 3.x, and Windows 95):

1. If loadlin is not already installed, install it from CD 1 by entering the command `setup`.

2. Switch to the `c:\loadlin` directory (in MS-DOS). You will find a file `linux.par` there. In this directory, create a file with the name `startlin.bat` in an editor (use another name if desired) as in the file 6.

```
c:\loadlin\loadlin c:\loadlin\linux.par
```

File 6: Sample batch file for booting Linux

Now edit the following lines in the `linux.par` file:

```
c:\loadlin\zimage    # first value must be
                     # the file name of the Linux kernel
initrd=c:\loadlin\initrd
root=/dev/xxx        # the device mounted as root FS
ro                   # mount root read-only
```

File 7: Sample parameter file for booting Linux

Replace xxx with the device name of your root partition. The `initrd` entry is only required if, for example, you need to boot SCSI support as well (for more on the "initial ramdisk" concept, see Section *Booting with the Initial Ramdisk* on page 276). Start Linux at the DOS prompt at any time using the `startlin.bat` file. The file `linux.par`, used by `startlin.bat` and by `config.sys`, contains all the parameters necessary for booting Linux. When you are more familiar with Linux, you can add or substitute other boot parameters in `linux.par`. If you compile your own kernel later, copy it from the Linux file system to the `c:\loadlin\zimage` file and, from that point on, your new kernel will boot. If necessary, also store a newly-generated `initrd` in that file.

Setting Up Boot Menus

Configure a boot menu in DOS or Windows 3.x as follows:

1. First, set up a boot menu in the `c:\config.sys` file. Edit it according to the sample file in File 8.

   ```
   [Menu]
   menuitem=Win, Boot Windows...
   menuitem=DOS, Boot MS-DOS...
   menuitem=Linux, Boot Linux...
   menucolor=15,1
   menudefault=Win,5
   ```

File 8: Sample config.sys for Booting Linux (Part 1)

Set up the boot menu items under the [Menu] label. Also set the menu's color, the time after which the default system should boot, and which one is the default.

2. Enter the labels [Common], [Win], [DOS], and [Linux] further below. Write the global entries under Common. Under the other labels, enter the specifications that should only apply to certain entries. Use the lines as in File 9.

```
[Common]
device=c:\dos\himem.sys /testmem:off
device=c:\dos\emm386.exe noems
dos=high,umb
files=30
buffers=10
shell=c:\dos\command.com

[Win]
devicehigh=c:\dos\dblspace.sys /move
devicehigh=c:\cd\slcd.sys /D:SONY_000 /B:340 /M:P /V /C

[DOS]
devicehigh=c:\dos\dblspace.sys /move
devicehigh=c:\cd\slcd.sys /D:SONY_000 /B:340 /M:P /V /C

[Linux]
shell=c:\loadlin\loadlin.exe @c:\loadlin\linux.par

[Common]
rem Remains empty
```

File 9: Sample config.sys for Booting Linux (Part 2)

Finally, save the file.

3. Now open the c:\autoexec.bat file. Enter the same labels in the file, along with their corresponding entries. The notation will, however, be somewhat different. The label selected in the boot menu is stored in the variable %config%. File 10 is an example.

```
@echo off

rem Entries for all configurations
```

```
switches= /f
set comspec=c:\dos\command.com
prompt $p$g
loadhigh c:\dos\keyb gr,,c:\dos\keyboard.sys
loadhigh c:\dos\doskey
set temp=c:\temp
loadhigh c:\dos\mscdex.exe /D:SONY_000 /E /V /L:H
c:\logimaus\mouse.exe

goto

:Win
c:\dos\smartdrv.exe a- b- c+ 2048 1024
path c:\windows;c:\dos;c:\util;
win
c:\dos\smartdrv /C
goto end

:DOS
path c:\dos;c:\util;
goto end

:end
echo * Goodbye *
```

File 10: Sample autoexec.bat for Booting Linux

4. Now, when you boot your computer, the boot menu will appear and you will have five seconds to select the system to boot. Otherwise, after five seconds, Windows will automatically boot. If you select 'Linux', Linux will start and prompt you for your login.

Booting from Windows

Go through the following steps to configure a start icon for Linux, which you can use to boot Linux from a running Windows 95 system.

1. Click into the c:\loadlin folder, select the file startlin.bat, and select 'Edit' → 'Copy'.

2. Go to the folder or position on your desktop to which to save your Linux icon. Press the right mouse button and click 'Add Link'.

3. Highlight the link you just made, press the right mouse button and click 'Properties'. Go to the 'Application' tab and click the button 'Advanced' below. Check the box 'MS-DOS Mode' in the dialog. Confirm with 'OK'.

4. You can use the 'Other Icon' browse button to search for a nice icon then give the link a suitable name. Done!

5. Double-clicking the new icon takes you to a dialog confirming that Windows 95 is now entering MS-DOS mode. If this dialog bothers you, disable it in the link properties.

The Windows Boot Menu

Configure a boot menu for Windows 95:

1. First, edit the file `c:\msdos.sys`. To do so, make the file visible by entering

   `C:>` **`attrib -R -S -H c:\msdos.sys`**

   This is a text file in which you need to enter some lines to activate the special Windows 95 boot menu. The lines below the `[Options]` label should look similar to those shown in File 11.

```
[Options]
BootGUI=0
BootDelay=0
BootMenu=0
Logo=0
```

File 11: msdos.sys *for Booting Linux*

The `Logo=0` parameter is optional and prevents Windows 95 from switching to graphical mode before booting. This will speed up the booting process and make things easier later, in case at some point you want to use the DOS emulator in Linux.

The `BootGUI=0` parameter causes Windows 95 to boot directly to DOS mode. After editing the file, reset the attributes. Then enter

`C:>` **`win`**

at the DOS prompt to start Windows, although our sample file `c:\autoexec.bat` will already do this, if you have chosen Win95 in the menu.

2. Next, you must set up your own boot menu in the file `c:\config.sys` by entering similar information as shown at the beginning of File 12.

```
[Menu]
menuitem=Win95, Booting Windows 95...
menuitem=DOS, Booting MS-DOS...
menuitem=Linux, Booting Linux...
menudefault=Win95,5
```

File 12: Sample config.sys (Part 1) for Booting Linux in Windows 95

Set up the boot menu items under the `[Menu]` label. Select the default system and the amount of time until it is automatically booted if no other choice is made by the user.

3. Further below, you will see the `[Win95]`, `[DOS]`, `[Linux]`, and `[Common]` labels. Enter global settings under `[Common]` (there will only be a few in Windows 95). Enter other boot menu–related settings under the remaining labels. Use the lines from your present `config.sys` for this. The example in File 13 gives a general idea.

```
[Win95]
dos=high,umb
device=c:\windows\himem.sys /testmem:off

[DOS]
device=c:\plugplay\drivers\dos\dwcfgmg.sys
dos=high,umb
device=c:\windows\himem.sys /testmem:off
device=c:\windows\emm386.exe noems I=B000-B7FF
devicehigh=c:\cdrom\torisan.sys /D:TSYCD3 /P:SM

[Linux]
shell=c:\loadlin\loadlin.exe @c:\loadlin\linux.par

[Common]
accdate=C+ D+ H+
switches= /F buffers=20
```

File 13: Sample `config.sys` (Part 2) for Booting Linux in Windows 95

Finally, save the file.

4. Now open the `c:\autoexec.bat` file. Enter the same labels in this file, along with their corresponding entries. However, the notation will be somewhat different. The label selected in the boot menu is stored in the variable %config%. You may want to enter something like in File 14.

```
@echo off
loadhigh keyb gr,,c:\windows\command\keyboard.sys
goto %config%

:Win95
win
goto end

:DOS
path c:.;d:.;c:\windows\command;c:\util;
loadhigh c:\windows\command\mscdex.exe /D:TSYCD3 /L:x
loadhigh c:\windows\command\doskey
c:\windows\command\mouse.exe
goto end

:end
echo * And now? *
```

File 14: Sample `autoexec.bat`This macro is not allowd. Please consult the documentation. for Booting Linux in Windows 95

5. Now, when you boot your machine, your self-designed boot menu will appear. You will have five seconds to select the system to boot. Otherwise, Windows 95 will boot automatically. If you select 'Linux', Linux will boot and prompt for a login.

The X Window System

Historical Background

The X Window System is the de facto standard GUI for UNIX. Yet the X Window System is far more than this — X11 is a network-based system. Applications running on the machine `earth` can display their results on the machine `sun`, provided the two machines are connected via a network. The network could be a local one (LAN) or a connection between computers thousands of miles away via the Internet.

X11 was first developed as an enterprise of DEC (Digital Equipment Corporation) and the project Athena at MIT (Massachusetts Institute of Technology). The first release of X11R1 was in September 1987. Since release 6, the X Consortium, Inc. has been responsible for the development of the X Window System.

XFree86 ™ is a freely available implementation of X servers for PC systems. It was developed by a handful of ambitious programmers who founded the XFree86 team in 1992. In 1994, this team went on to found The XFree86 Project, whose aim is to continue research and development on X11 and to provide it to the public. Since March 2000, the completely revised major release XFree86-4.0 has been available for download from `http://www.XFree86.org`. By default, SuSE Linux installs XFree86-4.0. Below, take a closer look at the features of this version.

SuSE would like to thank the XFree86 team for their help and for their permission to include beta servers on our CD's[1], without which their production would have been much more difficult, if at all possible.

---

[1] Parts of this documentation are taken from chapter *XFree86 Konfigurieren* from [HHMK96] which was kindly given to us by Dirk Hohndel

The next sections are about configuring the X server. For this purpose SaX2 [2] and xf86config will be discussed, simple tools for configuring the X Window System.

In contrast to the text-based xf86config, SaX2 works directly with the X server and can be operated with the mouse.

To make optimal use of the hardware available (graphics card, monitor, keyboard), optimize the configuration manually. Certain aspects of this optimization will be explained. Even more detailed information on configuring the X Window System can be found in the directory `/usr/share/doc/packages/xf86` as well as in the the man page for `XF86Config` (`man XF86Config`).

Caution

Be very careful when configuring your X Window System. Never start the X Window System until the configuration is finished. A wrongly configured system can cause irreparable damage to your hardware (this applies especially to fixed-frequency monitors). The authors of this book and SuSE cannot be held responsible for damage. This information has been carefully researched, but this does not guarantee that all methods presented here are correct and will not damage your hardware.

Caution

Version 4.x of XFree86

This version of SuSE Linux comes with version 4.x of XFree86 which differs from the previously used version 3.3 in a number of ways. Overall there are hardly any differences for the user when operating the graphical desktop. Applications, such as the graphical desktops KDE or GNOME, behave with the new version in the same way as version 3.3.6 included in earlier distributions.

Advantages

The new X server is no longer a monolithic program, but just a relatively small basic scaffolding to which the necessary program modules can be later

---

[2]SaX: *SuSE Advanced X Configuration Tool* The configuration program SaX2 (sax2) to configure XFree86-4.0 makes XF86Setup (package `xfsetup`) obsolete.

added, if and when required. For example, there are no longer many different X servers for different graphics cards as in the previous version, but just one executable program called XFree86, which can be found in the directory `/usr/X11R6/bin`. This is also the actual X server. The graphics driver, which then takes on the task of controlling the graphics card, is a loadable module.

A similar method is used to support the various input devices, fonts, or X protocols. This again consists of individual modules that can be later loaded by the X server. As a rule, you do not need to worry about these modules. The configuration of the modules to operate the graphical desktop on your computer is managed as far as possible by SaX2.

Through this module concept, it is easy for a vendor to implement a driver for exotic hardware, such as touch screens or new graphics cards. The developers have even ensured that the necessary modules for various operating systems only need to be made available once, which means that a graphics driver module compiled in FreeBSD, for example, can also be used in Linux and vice versa. This portability, however, is limited to the same hardware platform: a module compiled for Linux on PowerPCs cannot be used on an Intel PC.

Support for the mouse has also been significantly improved. Especially under heavy loads, the reaction of the mouse to mouse movements is considerably faster and more direct than with the previous XFree86 X server. Overall, the output speed has also been improved, so graphics operations are generally performed more quickly than on the old X server due to the completely revised XAA (*XFree86 Acceleration Architecture*).

Compared to XFree86 3.3.x, the configuration file has a slightly different format and is now located in `/etc/X11/XF86Config`. For fine-tuning your X configuration, details on the structure of the configuration file and how it functions can be found in Section *Optimizing the Installation of the X Window System* on page 138.

Error logging has also been improved. The X server creates a very detailed log file, which you can always find after the X server has started in the file `/var/log/XFree86.0.log`. One of the further features of this version is the support of special options, such as True Type fonts. Other features also include the provision of the 3D protocol extension, glx, gamma correction of the screen, and the support of multiple graphics cards for Multihead configurations. More information on this can be found in Section *Optimizing the Installation of the X Window System* on page 138.

SuSE Linux – Administration Guide 115

Configuration of the X Window System with SaX2

Differences Between the X Server and the Window Manager

In Linux, a graphical interface is any component that ensures all necessary hardware components are supported. This service is referred to simply as the *X server*.

The graphical interface, the X server, allows your hardware to communicate with your software. This is how desktops like KDE and GNOME can display information on screen with which the user can interact. These desktops and similar applications are often called *window managers*. In Linux, there are several window managers, which can differ greatly in appearance and performance.

Without a functioning graphical interface — without an activated X server — there would be no graphical user environment. SuSE offers the application SaX2 to ease the configuration of your graphical interface as much as possible.

About SaX2

The application SaX2 (**SuSE Advanced X11 Configuration**) is responsible for the setup of X Window System, the graphical interface. SuSE Linux finds itself in one of these states following a standard installation:

The system is already in graphical mode — In this case, the graphical user interface has already been set up during installation by YaST2. This is possible since SaX2 is a modular system so some parts of the application can be used in other applications. YaST2 uses a module called ISax in the installation for this setup. In this case, SaX2 can be used to adjust the already existing configuration. Before starting SaX2, switch to text mode to avoid any potential conflicts with the already activated X server.

You will have the following options:

1. Switch to a text console using (Ctrl) + (Alt) + (F1)
2. Log in to the system as user `root`
3. Enter the command `init` 3. After this command has run, the system will be in text mode.

The system is already text mode — There are a number of reasons why a graphical interface cannot be started following installation. Perhaps you did not configure a graphical interface during the installation. In this case, the graphical interface can be set up rather quickly with SaX2.

> **Note**
>
> In the following sections, we assume your system is in text mode and that you have logged in as user `root`.
>
> **Note**

Start-Up and Hardware Recognition

To start SaX2, enter the command `sax2`. The application will now start detecting the hardware for the mouse, keyboard, graphics card, monitor, and 3D capabilities. These first four are the basic components. If these are not set up, the X server cannot be started. 3D capabilities in Linux are still in their developmental phase. If SaX2 detects a card with 3D capabilities supported by Linux, you will be asked if you want to use these features. More on this topic can be found in Chapter 3.

Configuration

After SaX2 has finished detecting the hardware, a temporary configuration will be generated that SaX2 uses to run the configuration interface. In many cases, the default settings are sufficient. You will have the following selection options in this first dialog:

- 'Save' — You are satisfied with the default configuration and want to save it.

- 'Adjust' — You are satisfied with the configuration, but want to change the position of the screen because it is not exactly in the middle or is too big or too small. More information on adjusting the screen geometry can be found in Section *Adjusting the Image Geometry* on page 125.

- 'Change configuration' — You are not satisfied and want to change the configuration.

- 'Cancel' — Exits SaX2 and returns you to the text console.

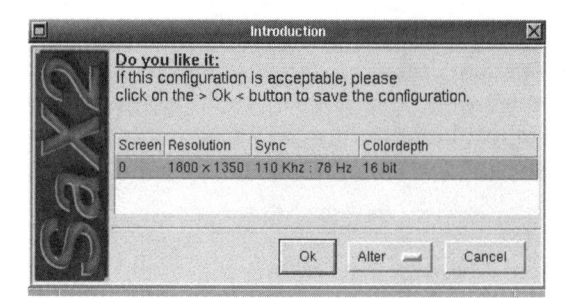

Figure 6.1: Initial Introduction

Controlling the Mouse with the Keyboard

After SaX2 starts, you will see a field highlighted in white in the lower right sector of the screen bearing the label: *Is your mouse not working ? -> Press 5 in the number pad....* If you follow these instructions and press ⑤, a window will appear as such:

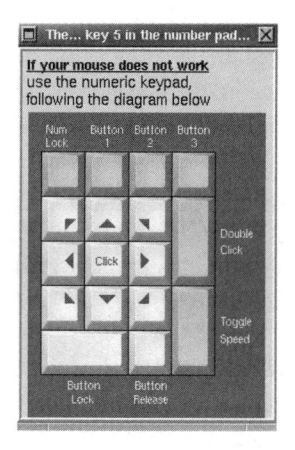

Figure 6.2: Using the Virtual Mouse

You cannot carry out any actions in this window. This image is only there for informational purposes. It represents the number pad on the keyboard and describes which mouse functions correspond to which keys.

- In the image: **Button 1** corresponds to the (%) key. This key activates the left mouse button.

- In the image: **Button 2** corresponds to the (X) key. This key activates the middle mouse button.

- In the image: **Button 3** corresponds to the (-) key. This key activates the right mouse button.

- In the image: **Click** corresponds to the (5) key. This key triggers a click with the previously activated mouse button. If no mouse button is activated, the left mouse button will be used. After the click, button activation is reset to default.

- In the image: **Double-Click** corresponds to the (+) key. This key acts like the (5) key, except it triggers a double-click.

- In the image: **Button Lock** corresponds to the (0) key. This key acts like the (5) key, except it triggers a single-click then locks it.

- In the image: **Button Release** corresponds to the (Del) key. This key releases a mouse button locked by the (0) key.

- In the image: **Upper left arrow** corresponds to the (7) key. This key moves the mouse to the upper left.

- In the image: **Up arrow** corresponds to the (8) key. This key moves the mouse straight up.

- In the image: **Upper right arrow** corresponds to the (9) key. This key moves the mouse to the upper right.

- In the image: **Left arrow** corresponds to the (4) key. This key moves the mouse to the left.

- In the image: **Right arrow** corresponds to the (6) key. This key moves the mouse to the right.

- In the image: **Lower left arrow** corresponds to the (1) key. This key moves the mouse to the lower left.

- In the image: **Down arrow** corresponds to the (2) key. This key moves the mouse straight down.

- In the image: **Lower right arrow** corresponds to the (3) key. This key moves the mouse to the lower right.

Changing the Configuration

If you have selected the item 'Change Configuration', SaX2's main screen loads. If a configuration is already available, SaX2 gives the option in the first dialog of loading this data. All the necessary information can be found in the /etc/X11 directory in the XF86Config file.

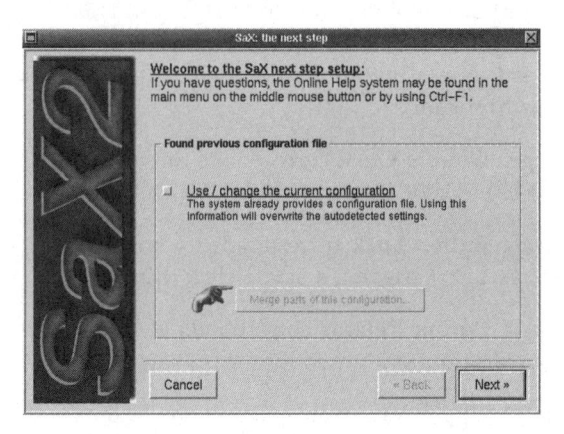

Figure 6.3: Loading the Configuration

> **Note**
>
> If you are uncertain as to whether you should have the existing configuration loaded, continue to the next page without loading it.
>
> **Note**

Configuring the Mouse

If no configuration exists, SaX2 starts with this dialog page. Otherwise, it proceeds to the mouse configuration right after the dialog page about loading an existing configuration.

If your mouse is working, you will not have to do anything else here. The configuration of special input devices, such as setting up graphics tablets or touch screens, also takes place in this screen, but is addressed in Section *Further Configurations* on page 126. If the mouse does not function, however, control the cursor using the number pad on the keyboard as described in Section *Controlling the Mouse with the Keyboard* on page 118. If you are familiar with the protocol and mouse connection, the procedure as described in Chapter *FAQ and Troubleshooting* on page 136 should be applied.

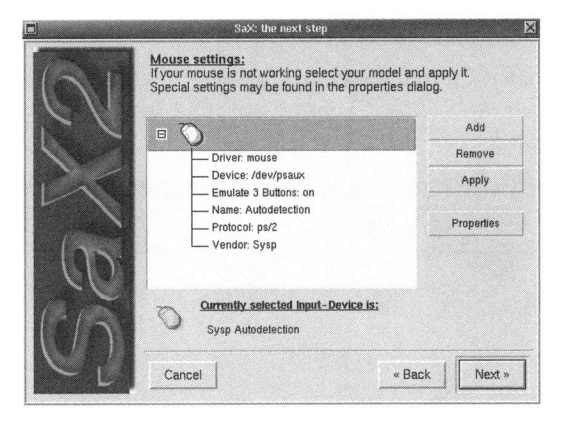

Figure 6.4: Mouse Configuration

Keyboard Configuration

First, check the language settings. If the language is not set correctly, modify the item accordingly then click 'Apply'. Now, switch to the 'Velocity' tab and enter some characters in the test field located there. If not all the characters are displayed correctly, go to the 'General' tab and change the keyboard type. Then, click 'Apply' again so the changes take effect.

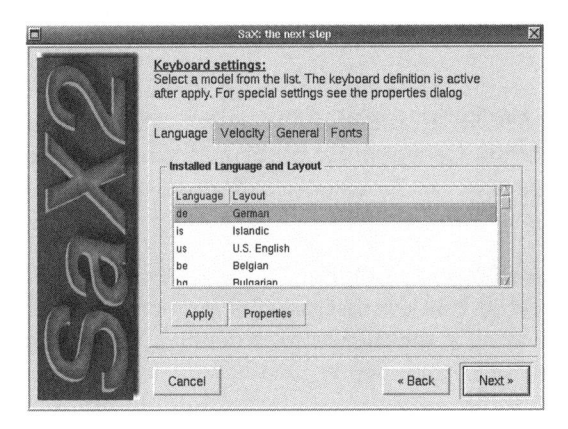

Figure 6.5: Keyboard Configuration

Configuring the Graphics Card

In this dialog, make settings for your graphics card. In this context, it is important that your graphics card is listed and that the right driver has been defined for the card.

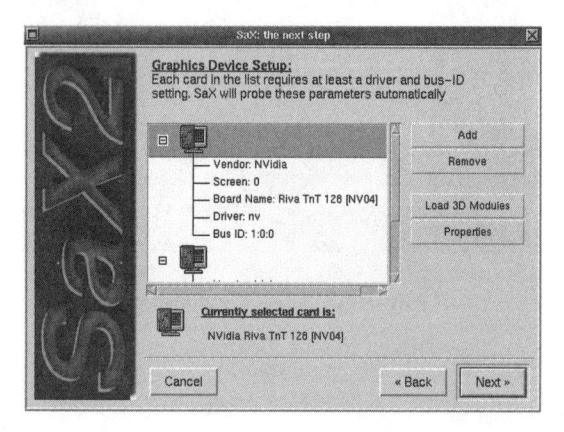

Figure 6.6: Configuration of the Graphics Card

Typically, you do not need to make any changes in this dialog. If you have installed more than one graphics card on your system but only want to use one particular card, individually select the cards you do not want to use and click 'Remove'.

Configuring the Monitor and Resolution

Essentially, colors and resolution are configured here. Under certain circumstances, it may be necessary to enter specifications pertaining to your monitor, because it is not always detected automatically.

- **Changing colors and resolution**
  Click 'Properties'. In the first tab, find both relevant fields. The uppermost field contains the current color depth. Click the right arrow and select the desired color depth. Do the same in the resolution field.

  ┌─ Note ───

  Select or deselect several resolutions. The resolutions will be used in the order selected. If you do not want to use a resolution, deselect it.

  ─── Note ─┘

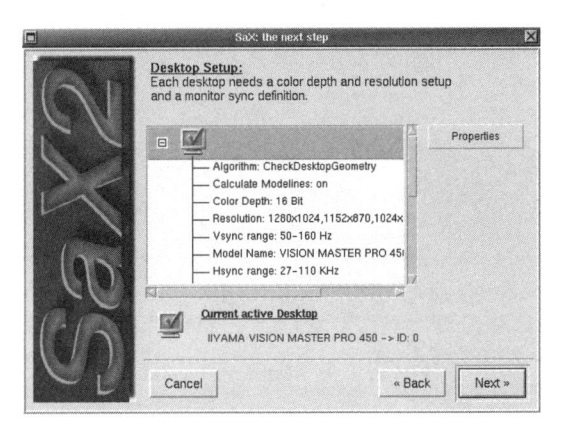

Figure 6.7: Resolution, Color Depth, and Monitor Properties

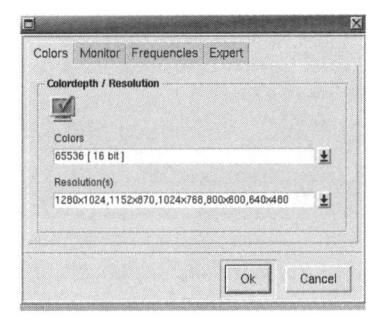

Figure 6.8: Color Depth Selection

- **Changing the Monitor Properties**

  After you have selected the colors and the resolution, change to the monitor tab.

  If the monitor has been detected, it is preselected. If this is the selection you want, you do not need to do anything else. If no monitor or just a "VESA-compatible monitor" has been selected, select the proper monitor model from the list provided. If the monitor is not included in the list, switch tabs to 'Frequency' and enter the appropriate frequency ranges for your monitor for the *horizontal* and the *vertical* deflection frequency in the corresponding fields.

  The corresponding frequency values can be found in the manual sup-

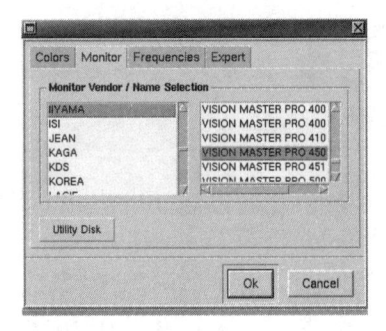

Figure 6.9: Monitor Selection

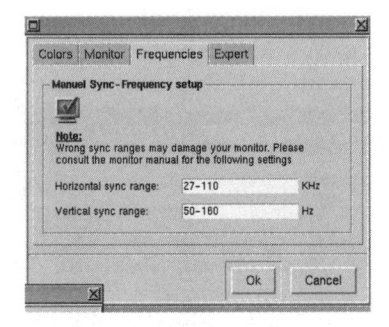

Figure 6.10: Manual Frequency Selection

plied by the monitor's manufacturer. Close the properties window and proceed to the next item.

Testing and Saving the Configuration

After clicking 'Done' in the last dialog, a reference display window appears where you can make the following selections.

- 'Cancel' — Aborts the changes just made. Returns to the previous screen.

- 'Save' — Saves the configuration. Afterwards, you will be asked if you want to exit SaX2.

- 'Start' — Starts another X server applying the new settings and provides the opportunity to adjust the position and size of the image to

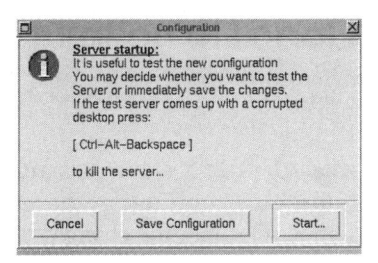

Figure 6.11: Completing the Configuration

the new environment. Refer to Section *Adjusting the Image Geometry* on the current page

If you have modified monitor or resolution settings during the course of configuration, it is recommended to start the test X server to adjust the image if needed. All other settings can be applied without restarting the test X server if no new hardware components were added.

Adjusting the Image Geometry

SaX2 provides an independent application called XFine2. This application starts whenever the image is modified in terms of position or size.

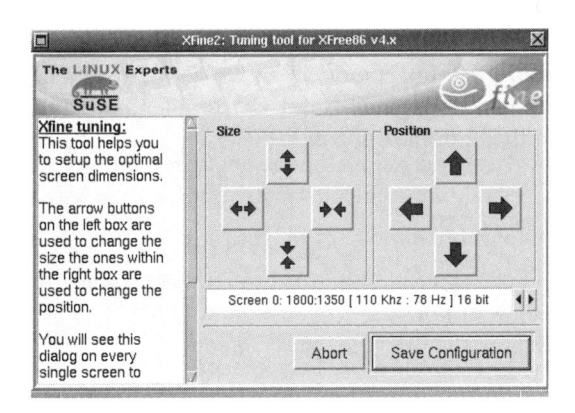

Figure 6.12: Adjusting the Image Geometry

SuSE Linux – Administration Guide   125

Changes to the image geometry are incorporated into the current configuration when you click 'Save'. There are usually two ways to start XFine2 in SaX2:

- **XFine2 is loaded when the test X server is started**
  In this case, if you click 'Save' or 'Cancel', the test X server will quit and, depending on your selection, the changes will either be saved to your image geometry or discarded. After exiting the test X server, you will be returned to SaX2. The test X server works *completely independently* of the X server used by SaX2 itself. The properties shown by the test X server will be saved if you have clicked 'Save', but they will not be transferred to the X server on which SaX2 itself is running.

- **XFine2 is started via the menu item 'Adjust'**
  In this case, if you click 'Save' or 'Cancel', SaX2 will quit and you will be returned to text mode. The changes made to the image geometry will only be saved if you first click 'Save'.

To make changes inside the graphical user environment at a later point in its operation, *XFine2* can be invoked manually at any time. To do this, simply enter the command `xfine2`.

Starting the Graphical Interface

Once you have saved your configuration and exited SaX2, you will find yourself once again in text mode and, from there, can switch to the graphical login level. To do this, use the command `init 5`. Now you can graphically log in to the system. The graphical user environment will automatically be started following this graphical login.

Further Configurations

The following chapter serves as stimulation and as brief instructions to enhanced configuration in terms of X11. We cannot offer any assistance in the form of free installation support for these configurations.

Side Note Regarding Keyboards

The topic of keyboards does not lend itself to quite the same in-depth discussion as other input devices, as you do not normally need to make any specific configurations for your keyboard.

The following applications and files can be of use in certain circumstances. xkeycaps, package `xkeycaps`, lets you see your current changes to the keyboard layout in action or test different settings. Make changes to the individual characters and symbols permanent in the `~/.Xmodmap` file. Refer to the the man page for `xmodmap` (`man xmodmap`) regarding the structure of this file.

KDE offers the kikbd tool ("international keyboard layout"). It enables you to easily switch back and forth between various keyboard layouts. This is useful, for example, if you need the special characters in Spanish or German.

When using the "international keyboard layout" for writing in foreign languages with special characters, note that many X applications only recognize the characters belonging to your locally configured, country-specific character settings. If this is the case, other characters will be ignored. So it is also necessary to correctly configure the "locale". This is done by resetting the environment variable LANG to the desired country setting *before starting the application*. Refer to the man page for `locale` (`man locale`) for all the possible options.

Automatic Configuration (Laptops)

If you have a notebook, configuring it is even easier in many cases due to the special hardware properties for notebooks. In the typical scenario, the notebook is operated with its own predesignated internal display — with an LCD/DSTN or TFT matrix display.

SaX2 recognizes the size of the display. Simply enter the command

```
sax2 -a
```

SaX2 will begin hardware detection and automatically create the configuration without requiring any additional entries on your part. Start the graphical environment after this command has run as described in Section *Starting the Graphical Interface* on the facing page.

Reconfiguration (Fastpath)

The current version of SaX2 allows you to adjust certain aspects of the current configuration from a running graphical user environment. "FastPaths" are made available for this purpose. SaX2 currently implements the following fastpaths:

1. **mouse** Configuration of input devices, in particular, the mouse

2. **keyboard** Keyboard and font configuration

3. **desktop** Color and resolution configuration

4. **layout** Configuration of the arrangement of the various screens (only available for multihead configurations)

To change the mouse configuration from a running session, for example, enter:

```
sax2 -F mouse
```

This will cause SaX2 *not* to start hardware recognition, but, instead, load the existing configuration and display the corresponding dialog. The X server has to be restarted following any changes for these to take effect.

Multihead

The XFree86 Version 4 addresses more than one graphics card. This is referred to as a "multihead environment". SaX2 automatically recognizes when multiple graphics cards are located on your system and will prepare the configuration accordingly. Configuration is limited to two aspects:

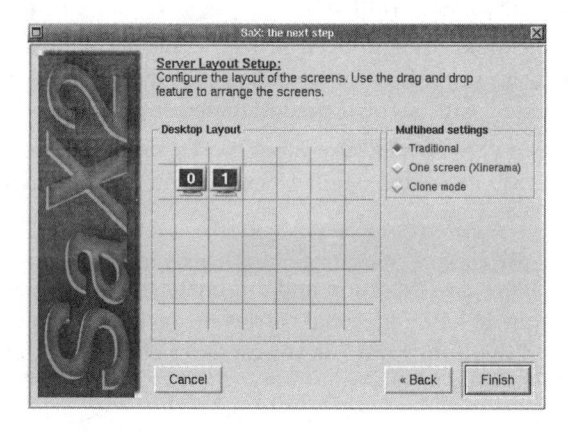

Figure 6.13: Adjusting the Monitor Arrangement

- **Selecting the multihead type**
  SaX2 differentiates between three types of multihead environments

    1. 'Traditional multihead' — Every monitor is treated as an independent display

2. 'Xineramafied multihead' — All monitors are consolidated into one large display

3. 'Cloned multihead' — There is one display for which all other displays are identical copies

- **Defining the multihead layout**
  The layout of a multihead environment is the arrangement and partnerships between the monitors. SaX2 normally creates a default layout following the order in which the graphics cards are detected, which arranges all the monitors in a line, from left to right. Modify this layout by moving the respective screen (depicted as an icon in the layout dialog) to a new position using the left mouse button.

Test your new configuration by clicking 'Start' after completing the layout dialog — you should be aware that the image geometry can only be modified in the *traditional multihead*, since this is the only option where each monitor is independent of one another. The following procedure is advisable:

1. Define the new layout as already described.

2. Set the multihead type to 'Traditional'.

3. Click 'Done' then 'Start'.

4. Adjust the image geometry to fit all the monitors and save this status.

5. Answer the prompt asking whether SaX2 should be ended with 'No'.

6. Set your preferred multihead type.

7. Click 'Done' then 'Save'.

8. Confirm the question as to whether SaX2 should be ended with 'Yes'.

Linux does not currently feature 3D support in a multihead environment. SaX2 will, in this case, deactivate 3D support.

Graphics Tablets

Currently, only Wacom graphics tablets are supported by XFree86. SaX2 provides USB and serial configuration. Unfortunately, at the moment, automatic detection and setup of a tablet connected to the system is not available. From a configuration perspective, a graphics tablet is viewed as an input device — like a mouse. The following procedure is recommended:

1. Start SaX2 and switch to the mouse configuration dialog.

2. Click 'Add' and add a graphics tablet.

3. In the same manner, add the pens to the tablet. Note that the pen and the eraser are considered separate.

4. Test the connection of all the devices added to the serial tablet: `/dev/ttyS0` represents the first serial port, `/dev/ttyS1` the second, and so forth.

5. Save the configuration. Testing the configuration is optional.

Touch Screens

Currently, Microtouch and Elographics touch screens are supported by XFree86. However, SaX2 can only automatically detect the monitor, not the toucher. The toucher is, again, viewed in the same way as a mouse and is therefore configured in the SaX2 mouse dialog. The following procedure is recommended:

1. Start SaX2 and switch to the mouse configuration dialog.

2. Click on the 'Add' button and add a touch screen.

3. Save the configuration. Testing the configuration is optional.

Touch screens feature a multitude of options and usually have to be calibrated first. There is, unfortunately, no tool available for this in Linux. However, you can define the size proportions in SaX2 under the 'Advanced' tab when adding the touch screen. These dimensions depend heavily on the hardware used.

The X Server Log File

For analyzing problems with the X server, there is a very detailed log file that the X server creates when it starts. This file is created by the XFree86-4.0 X server according to the following pattern `/var/log/XFree86.Display.Screennumber.log`. If you start just one X server (the normal case) and this display is assigned the number "0", the file name of this log file is usually `/var/log/XFree86.0.log`. Note that SaX2 here is an exception to this rule: here, at least temporarily, *two* X servers are running (Display :0) for the configuration dialogs and, later, a second one (Display :1) to test settings.

The format of this file has changed drastically compared to XFree86-3.3.x. Now a much clearer distinction is made between information messages, values taken from the configuration file, data originating from the computer hardware, and warnings and errors.

SaX2 allows you to view the X server log file with the middle mouse button. Here, the various types of messages (error, informal, warning, etc.) are shown in different colors. This helps you to find the problem quickly if the X server does not start.

In general the beginning of such a log file appears as shown in 15.

```
%
%
XFree86 Version 4.0 / X Window System
(protocol Version 11, revision 0, vendor release 6400)
Release Date: 8 March 2000
        If the server is older than 6--12 months, or if your card is
        newer than the above date, look for a newer version before
        reporting problems.   (see http://www.XFree86.Org/FAQ)
Operating System: Linux 2.2.13 i686 [ELF] SuSE
Module Loader present
(==) Log file: "/var/log/XFree86.0.log", Time: Sat May 20 13:42:15 2000
(==) Using config file: "/etc/X11/XF86Config"
Markers: (--) probed, (**) from config file, (==) default setting,
         (++) from command line, (!!) notice, (II) informational,
         (WW) warning, (EE) error, (??) unknown.
(==) ServerLayout "Layout[all]"
(**) |-->Screen "Screen[0]" (0)
(**) |    |-->Monitor "Monitor[0]"
%
```

File 15: Taken from the X Server Log File

This provides the following information:

This is an XFree86 X server in version 4.0 compatible with X11R6.4 "vendor release 6400". The release date is 8th March, 2000. The line Operating System: Linux 2.2.13 i686 [ELF] SuSE refers to the system on which the X server was compiled. The kernel version and CPU definition can thus be different from your own system.

After these version messages, the first login entries appear that the X server creates when it starts. First of all, is this the correct log file? Next to Time:,

Symbol	Meaning
(==)	Defaults of the X server
(--)	Values taken from the system by automatic hardware detection.
(**)	Settings fixed in the configuration file.
(++)	Parameters entered at the command line.
(!!)	Here, the X server tells you in detail what it "is doing".
(II)	Version numbers of X server modules, etc., are usually recorded as "informational messages".
(WW)	Warnings: here the X server tells you why it is not carrying out certain actions specified in the configuration file or that should be activated by default.
(EE)	Error! These messages cancel the start procedure or crash the X server. Look out for lines in the log file starting with (EE) if the X server does not start. You can remedy most errors yourself by evaluating these messages.

Table 6.1: Message Types in the X Server Log File

the time when the log file was created is specified. Sometimes you might be searching in the wrong log file.

The same thing is valid for the configuration file. If you did not specify a different file at the command line, this will always be /etc/X11/XF86Config on a normal SuSE Linux system.

The following table 6.1 explains the meaning of the two bracket characters at the beginning of other lines:

If something unexpected happens when starting SaX2 or during the configuration steps, all errors and steps concerning SaX2 are logged in the file /var/log/SaX.log. X server errors are logged, as described above, in the file /var/log/XFree86.0.log. By means of these files, find clues on how to proceed.

Starting the X Window System

The X Window System is started with the command startx. A preconfigured GUI for the KDE window manager is provided for all users. We recommend starting the X Window System from a regular user account, *not* as root. X11 server error messages are saved in the ~/.X.err file. and

`/var/log/XFree86.0.log`. The `startx` command has a few options. For instance, you can select 16-bit color depth by typing `startx -- -bpp 16`.

FAQ and Troubleshooting

1. **How can the installed graphics card be detected?**
   If you do not know what graphics card is on your system, query a list of all the cards installed and supported on your system with `sax2 -p`.

2. **How can I accelerate the start-up of SaX2?**
   Provided that the hardware has **not** been modified since SaX2 was last started, significantly accelerate start-up using the `sax2 -q` command. In this case, no hardware recognition takes place. This option is quite useful, especially when reconfiguring. If you have started SaX2 via a fastpath, do not give the `-q` option, because the fastpath automatically sets this.

3. **What if the graphics card is not supported?**
   If no driver exists for the card's graphics chipset, you still have the option of using the graphics card's framebuffer. This has the advantage that it functions with almost any modern graphics card and practically any laptop. Since the card's graphics controller has to be circumvented in the absence of a driver, the display is accelerated. The X server simply accesses the framebuffer directly after having already been switched to graphics mode when the kernel starts.

   This works as follows: The Linux kernel loads the card's VGA BIOS at start-up and instructs it to switch to a given VESA graphics mode. The text console will be displayed in this configured graphics mode. Unfortunately, the VGA BIOS is written in 16-bit code so cannot be loaded in a running Linux system. As a consequence, the video mode determined when booting is retained until shutdown.

   To use this VESA framebuffer, support must be provided by the kernel and the graphics mode selected when booting. The SuSE Linux kernel, of course, includes VESA framebuffer support. Select your desired graphics mode when booting the system. Pass the parameter vga=x to the LILO boot prompt, where x stands for a value obtained from Table 6.2 on the next page.

   Alternatively, specifically state this as a vga parameter in the file `/etc/lilo.conf`. This value is not incorporated into the append line, but, instead, written directly to the configuration file as vga=x.

Preferred Color Depth	Resolution in Pixels			
	640×480	800×600	1024×768	1280×1024
256 (8 Bit)	769	771	773	775
32 768 (15 Bit)	784	787	790	793
65 536 (16 Bit)	785	788	791	794
16,7 Mill. (24 Bit)	786	789	792	795

Table 6.2: Available VESA Modes

After starting the Linux system, log in again as user root and start SaX2 as follows:

earth:/root # **sax2 -m 0=fbdev**

Note that 0 is a zero and not an uppercase o. This instructs the X server to utilize the driver as framebuffer. Since the resolution, color depth, and image repetition rate are strictly defined, you can — if you are satisfied with your mouse and keyboard settings — have SaX2 instantly save the automatically detected data then exit SaX2 again.

4. **Which file contains the results of the configuration?**
   The entire X11 configuration is stored in a file called XF86Config. Find this file under /etc/X11/XF86Config

5. **What if the graphics card is supported but not recognized by SaX2?**
   In very rare instances, you may have a graphics card that is supported by XFree86, but not recognized by SaX2. In this case, it will be necessary to specify the name of the driver module the card supports using the command sax2 -m 0=<driver>. The option -m assigns a number to a driver name. For example, if you want to assign the module nvidia to the primary card that always bears the number 0, the command would read sax2 -m 0=nvidia. A complete list of all the driver modules can be found at http://www.xfree86.org/4.1.0/Status.html

6. **What if SaX2 crashes when testing the X server?**
   In rare cases, SaX2 or even the system can crash when a completed configuration is followed by an X server test. This usually means that the driver is faulty, which is only significant if more than one X server is started at a time. To prevent this, proceed as follows:

   - Save the configuration *without* testing the X server

- Start the X11 System via `startx` or by logging in graphically
- If the image geometry is incorrect, start the `xfine2` program as user `root` and adjust the image.

7. **SaX2 starts YaST2. Why?**
   There are cases when SaX2 recognizes that the configuration requested cannot be performed without updating or installing software. If so, SaX2 will start YaST2 to update already installed software or to install missing software.

8. **Anti-aliasing does not work in multihead environments**
   Anti-aliasing support, which mainly affects applications linked to QT libraries, can only function in a multihead environment if all the drivers support the RENDER extension. Use the program `xdpyinfo` to find out whether the RENDER extension is activated on all displays.

9. **What should be included in support requests?**
   If you wish to consult support regarding a problem with SaX2, it is of utmost importance that you attach a current log file to the request. This file is generated in the following manner:

   (a) Run SaX2 without parameters. If SaX2 starts, exit the application using (Ctrl) + (Alt) + (←).

   (b) The current log file will then be located in `/var/log/SaX.log`.

10. **No mouse cursor, just a bar code or a colorful square.**
    It can happen that the mouse pointer is not visible or only displayed as a square, although the mouse is activated. This error can be fixed by entering the following line in the **Device** section in the file `/etc/X11/XF86Config`:

    `Option "sw_cursor"`

11. **Image is too small or compressed. The available monitor settings have already reached their limit.**

    (a) The image repetition rate and the `hsync` frequency are set too high, to the monitor's limit. To resolve this, reduce the `vsync` or `hsync` frequencies.

    (b) Move the image using the program xfine2. One of the modes may not be quite right here.

    (c) Append the parameter `+hsync +vsync` to the mode line and try replacing + with –.

Protocol	Mouse Type
PS/2	2 or 3 button mouse with PS/2 connection.
IMPS/2	ADB mouse, USB mouse, or wheel mouse with 3 or more buttons and one or more scroll wheels connected to the USB port.
Microsoft	2 and sometimes 3 button mice, connected to the serial port.
MouseSystems	3 button mice on the serial port.
Intellimouse	Wheel mouse with 3 or more buttons and with one or more scroll wheels, connected to the serial port.
Auto	Automatic detection of the serial mouse.

Table 6.3: Mice and Their Protocols

12. **What if the mouse is not working?**
    The mouse is identified by the port to which it is connected and by the protocol that defines the data format. If SaX2 is not able to recognize the mouse, the mouse can be navigated using the emulation on the key pad. Otherwise, run SaX2 and specify the correct data as to the mouse's connection and its protocol. The command for forwarding this data to SaX2 while launching it is `sax2 -t <protocol> -n <connection>`. Table 6.3 shows the various mouse protocols:

    A more exact description of supported mice can be found in the file `/usr/X11R6/lib/X11/doc/README.mouse`.

13. **Using the mouse in X with the GPM**
    The GPM has the capability of functioning as a "repeater". In this case, GPM makes the mouse's data available over the `/dev/gpmdata` device. Enable the repeater option by adding the option **-R** following the GPM parameters in the **GPM_PARAM** variable in the `/etc/sysconfig/mouse` file. By way of the command `rcgpm restart`, the GPM now only runs as a repeater. To also use the mouse in X over the GPM, start SaX2 using the following command:

    ```
    sax2 -g
    ```

14. **Moving the windows leaves behind hash marks, parts of windows, or other fragments. They do not disappear after I have stopped moving them. I can only get rid of them by refreshing the desktop. What do I do?**

(a) Reduce the image repetition rate or resolution.

(b) Depending on your chipset, apply the relevant options from the README files in /usr/X11R6/lib/X11/doc/, such as the options `fifo_conservative` or `slow_dram`. This depends on the graphics chipset.

(c) Options `noaccel`, `no_imageblt`, or `no_bitblt` may be sufficient.

15. **"Noise"** — image distortions when moving windows or viewing videos — that disappears when the contents of the image are static.

    (a) Reduce image repetition rate, color depth, or resolution.

    (b) Lower the card's clock speed or remove or add a wait state. Sometimes this works with `set_mclk` (but not for all chipsets). Find out more in the README directory. *Caution:* this option is risky (the card can be put into overdrive).

    (c) The bus may also be in overdrive. Check the bus speed of the PCI/VLB or ISA bus.

16. **The screen goes blank when XFree86 is started.**

    (a) Reduce the repetition rate.

    (b) Check the BIOS settings of the computer. Deactivate any "optimization settings" of the BIOS. You may need to consult the manual for your motherboard. Common problem factors are the Video memory cache mode options, AGP Aperture size, and any options that control PCI bus access, such as PCI Peer concurrency. You will almost always find these settings in a menu labeled Advanced Chipset Features.

    (c) Consider other possible causes: Check system for IRQ conflicts (such as a PS/2 mouse requires IRQ 12).

17. **Configuration with xf86config**
    If your X11 system can not be configured with SaX2, a very simple text-based t tool called xf86config4 can be used for this purpose. It is started as user **root** by giving the command `xf86config4`

Optimizing the Installation of the X Window System

This section describes the configuration file, /etc/X11/XF86Config. Each *section* starts with the keyword Section <name of section> and ends with EndSection. Below is a rough outline of the most important sections.

Afterwards, learn how to integrate additional fonts, how to configure input devices, and how 3D acceleration is implemented. This is also managed in certain sections of the XF86Config file, of course, although integrating an additional font requires the help of external programs, which are included with SuSE Linux or are part of the default installation. The methods discussed here aim to illustrate the possibilities available and serve as an incentive, but they do not claim to cover all eventualities.

The programs SaX2 and xf86config (for XFree86-4.0) create the file XF86Config, by default in /etc/X11. This is the primary configuration file for the X Window System. Find all the settings here concerning your graphics card, mouse, and monitor.

XF86Config is divided into several sections, each one dealing with a certain aspect of the configuration. A section always has the same form:

```
Section ⟨name of section⟩
   entry 1
   entry 2
   entry n
EndSection
```

The following types of sections exist:

Files	This section describes the paths used for fonts and the RGB color table.
ServerFlags	General switches are set here.
InputDevice	Input devices are configured in this section. In contrast to XFree86-3.3, keyboards, mice, and special input devices (touch pad, joysticks, etc.) are configured via this section. Important terms here are Driver and the options defined by Protocol and Device.

Table 6.4: continued overleaf...

Monitor	Describes the monitor used. The individual elements of this are the name, which is referred to later in the Screen definition, the bandwidth, and the allowed sync frequencies (HorizSync and VertRefresh). Settings are given in MHz, kHz, and Hz. Normally, the server refuses any mode line that does not correspond with the specification of the monitor. This is to prevent too high frequencies from being sent to the monitor by accident.
Modes	The mode line parameters are stored here for the specific screen resolutions. These parameters can be calculated by SaX2 on the basis of the values given by the user and normally do not need to be changed. You can intervene manually at this point, however, if, for example, you want to connect a fixed frequency monitor. An exact explanation of the individual parameters would be too much for this book. Find details on the meaning of individual number values in the HOWTO file `/usr/share/doc/howto/en/XFree86-Video-Timings-HOWTO.gz`.
Device	This section defines a specific graphics card. It is referenced by its descriptive name.
Screen	This section puts together a Driver (e.g., vga2), a monitor, and a Device to form all the necessary settings for XFree86. In the Display subsection, specify the size of the virtual screen (Virtual, the ViewPort, and the Modes) used with this virtual screen.
ServerLayout	This section defines the layout of a single or multihead configuration. The input devices InputDevice and the display devices Screen are combined into one section.

Table 6.4: Sections in `/etc/X11/XF86Config`

We will now take a closer look at Monitor, Device, and Screen. Further information on the other sections can be found in the man page for `XFree86` (`man XFree86`) and the man page for `XF86Config` (`man XF86Config`).

There can be several different Monitor sections in `XF86Config`. Even multiple Screen sections are possible. Which one is started depends on the server started.

Screen Section

First, we will take a closer look at the screen section. As mentioned above, this combines a monitor with a device section and determines which resolution using which color depth should be used.

A screen section might look like the example in File 16.

```
Section "Screen"
  DefaultDepth  16
  SubSection "Display"
    Depth       16
    Modes       "1152x864" "1024x768" "800x600"
    Virtual     1152x864
  EndSubSection
  SubSection "Display"
    Depth       24
    Modes       "1280x1024"
  EndSubSection
  SubSection "Display"
    Depth       32
    Modes       "640x480"
  EndSubSection
  SubSection "Display"
    Depth       8
    Modes       "1280x1024"
  EndSubSection
  Device        "Device[0]"
  Identifier    "Screen[0]"
  Monitor       "Monitor[0]"
EndSection
```

File 16: The Screen Section of the File /etc/X11/XF86Config

The line Identifier (here Screen[0]) gives this section a defined name with which it can be uniquely referenced in the following ServerLayout section.

The lines Device and Monitor specify the graphics card and the monitor that belong to this definition. These are just links to the Device and Monitor sections with their corresponding names or "identifiers". These sections are discussed later in more detail.

Using DefaultColorDepth, select which color depth mode the server will use if this is not explicitly stated. There is a Display subsection for each color depth. Depth assigns the color depth valid for this subsection. Possible values for Depth are 8, 16, 24, and 32. Not every X server supports all these modes. For most cards, 24 and 32 are basically the same. Some take 24 for packed pixel 24bpp mode, whereas others choose 32 for padded pixel mode.

After the color depth, a list of resolutions is set (Modes). This list is checked by the server from left to right. For each resolution, a suitable Modeline is searched, which has to correspond to one of the given clock rates or a clock rate to program the card.

The first resolution found is the Default mode. With Ctrl + Alt + + (on the number pad), switch to the next resolution in the list to the right. With Ctrl + Alt + − (on the number pad), switch to the left. This enables you to vary the resolution while X is running.

The last line of the Display subsection with Depth 16 refers to the size of the virtual screen. The maximum possible size of a virtual screen depends on the amount of memory installed on the graphics card and the desired color depth, not on the maximum resolution of the monitor. Since modern graphics cards have a large amount of video memory, you can create very large virtual desktops. You should note, however, that you may no longer be able to use 3D functionality if you fill most of the video memory with a virtual desktop. If the card has 16 MB video RAM, for example, the virtual screen can be up to 4096x4096 pixels in size at 8-bit color depth. Especially for accelerated cards, however, it is not recommended to use up all your memory for the virtual screen, since this memory on the card is also used for several font and graphics caches.

Device Section

A device section describes a specific graphics card. You can have as many device entries in `XF86Config` as you like, as long as their names are differentiated, using the keyword Identifier. As a rule — if you have more than one graphics card installed — the sections are simply numbered in order the first one is called Device[0], the second one Device[1], and so on. In the following file, you can see the section from the Device section of a computer in which a Matrox Millenium PCI graphics card is installed.

```
Section "Device"
  BoardName     "MGA2064W"
  BusID         "0:19:0"
  Driver        "mga"
  Identifier    "Device[0]"
  VendorName    "Matrox"
  Option        "sw_cursor"
EndSection
```

If you use SaX2 for configuring, the device section should look something like the above diagram. Both the Driver and BusID are dependent on the hardware installed in your computer and are detected by SaX2 automatically. The BusID defines the PCI or AGP slot in which the graphics card is installed. This matches the ID displayed by the command lspci. Note here that the X server wants details in decimal form, but lspci displays these in hexadecimal form.

Via the Driver parameter, specify the driver to use for this graphics card. If the card is a Matrox Millenium, the driver module is called mga. The X server then searches through the ModulePath defined in the Files section in the `drivers` subdirectory. In a standard installation, this is the directory `/usr/X11R6/lib/modules/drivers`. For this purpose, simply `_drv.o` is added to the name, so, in the case of the mga driver, the driver file mga_drv.o is loaded.

The behavior of the X server or of the driver can also be influenced through additional options. An example of this is the option sw_cursor, which is set in the device section. This deactivates the hardware mouse cursor and depicts the mouse cursor using software. Depending on the driver module, there are various options available, which can be found in the description files of the driver modules in the directory `/usr/X11R6/lib/X11/doc`. Generally valid options can also be found in the man page for `XF86Config` (`man XF86Config`) and the man page for `XFree86` (`man XFree86`).

Monitor Section

Monitor sections each describe, in the same way as the device sections, one monitor. The configuration file `/etc/X11/XF86Config` can again contain as many Monitor sections as you want. The server layout section specifies which monitor section is relevant.

Monitor definitions should only be set by experienced users. A critical part of the monitor section is the mode lines, which set horizontal and vertical timings for the appropriate resolution. The monitor properties, especially the allowed frequencies, are stored in the monitor section.

┌─ **Caution** ───

Unless you have an in-depth knowledge of monitor and graphics card functions, nothing should be changed in the mode lines, since this could cause severe damage to your monitor.

── **Caution** ─┘

For those who want to develop their own monitor descriptions, the documentation in `/usr/X11/lib/X11/doc` might come in handy. The section

[FCR93] deserves a special mention. It describes, in detail, how the hardware functions and how mode lines are created.

Luckily a "manual" setting of the mode lines is hardly ever needed nowadays. If you are using a modern multisync monitor, the allowed frequencies and optimal resolutions can, as a rule, be read directly from the monitor by the X server via DDC, as described in the SaX2 configuration section. If this is not possible for some reason, you can also use one of the VESA modes included in the X server. This will function with practically all graphics card and monitor combinations.

Integrating Additional (True Type) Fonts

A standard X11R6 X server installation also includes a large number of fonts. These can be found in the directory `/usr/X11R6/lib/X11/fonts`, each divided into logically connected groups in subdirectories. Make sure that only subdirectories of the X server are used that:

- are entered in the files section, Files of the file `/etc/X11/XF86Config` as FontPath.

- contain a valid `fonts.dir` file.

- were not closed while the X server was running using the command xset −fp or were started while the X server was running using the command xset +fp.

Since version 4.0, XFree86 can use not only its own format Type1 (a Postscript format) for scalable fonts and pcf for bitmap ones, but also the ttf (True Type font) fonts. As described in Section *Version 4.x of XFree86* on page 114, this support is provided via loadable modules of the X server. Thus, you can also use directories containing True Type fonts together with the X server. To do this, hardly any preparation is needed.

A big advantage of most True Type fonts, apart from their very good scalability, is that these fonts almost always contain more than the normal 255 characters of the font for western Europe coded in "iso-8859-1". With these fonts, you can display Cyrillic, Greek, or eastern European languages without any problem and, with special software, even Asian languages.

This description is essentially about the use of fonts as 8-bit character sets. If you want to use characters of Asian languages (Japanese, Chinese, etc.), use special editors, which are also available in SuSE Linux.

An 8-bit character set contains 255 characters and basically consists of the US-ASCII character set, which defines only the first 128 of 255 possible characters, and expands it with further characters. One text character occupies 8-bits in the computer memory. As 127 characters are certainly not enough to record the special characters, for example, of all European languages, the various languages are combined into groups and this group is then given a short name. The relevant character set is named according to the appropriate norm as the "iso-8859-x" character set, where the x stands for a number from 1 to 15. The exact order of characters in the iso-8859-1 character set can be found in the man page for `iso-8859-1` (`man iso-8859-1`).

The more well-known codings are listed in Table 6.5 : further ones can be taken from the above-mentioned manual page.

Font	Supported regions, contains special characters
iso-8859-1	West European languages: Spanish, German, French, Swedish, Finnish, Danish, and others
iso-8859-2	Central and Eastern Europe: Czech, Rumanian, Polish, German, and others
iso-8859-5	Cyrillic characters for Russian
iso-8859-7	Greek characters for Greek
iso-8859-9	Turkish characters
iso-8859-15	As `iso-8859-1`, but with characters for Turkish and the Euro sign.

Table 6.5: Important Font Codings

The user must then — depending on the language used — select the matching encoding. Especially when transferring texts between different computers, the encoding used must also be transferred. The advantage of this procedure is obvious: To receive support for regional special characters, you only need to select the correct encoding and immediately most programs will be able to portray these special characters, since almost all programs use an 8-bit value (one byte) to represent a text character. If the wrong encoding is chosen, the special characters will be wrongly depicted. With most X applications, as well as with the KDE desktop, you can usually select the coding of the character set when you are configuring the font to use. In X applications, the encoding is usually referred to as Encoding.

The disadvantage of this method is that some language combinations are impossible: You cannot, for example, easily write a German text with umlauts in which you mention Russian place names in Cyrillic.

This dilemma can only be solved using a different approach — with the use of Unicode. Unicode codes characters, unlike ASCII, with two or even more bytes, allowing considerably more characters to be represented. Only if you use Unicode can you depict Asian languages with more than 127 characters, such as Chinese, Japanese, or Korean, on the computer. The disadvantage of this method is that most existing software cannot handle these characters and that you can only read or write texts yourself with Unicode characters using special software. For more information on using Unicode fonts in Linux, see http://www.unicode.org. It is expected that, in the future, more and more programs will support Unicode characters. SuSE Linux offers the program yudit to enter texts in Unicode. The program yudit can be found in the package yudit and, after installation, via the SuSE menu, under Office →Editors.

After these observations, we now have a step-by-step description of the installation of additional fonts, using the example here of True Type fonts.

Locate the fonts to install in your X Window System. If you have licensed True Type fonts, you can simply use these on your system. Mount the partition containing these fonts.

You should create a font directory — if this does not yet exist — and change to it. SuSE Linux already has a directory called `/usr/X11R6/lib/X11/fonts/truetype`. You can copy the relevant fonts to this directory.

earth:/root # **cd /usr/X11R6/lib/X11/fonts/truetype**

Create links to the ttf files and create the font directory. For True Type fonts, you will additionally need a special program called ttmkfdir, package ttmkfdir, to create the file `fonts.dir`. Traditional X fonts are only included using the command mkfontdir. Instead of the path ⟨`/path/to/the/fonts`⟩, set the corresponding path in which these fonts are located.

earth:/usr/X11R6/lib/X11/fonts/truetype #
    ln -s ⟨**/pfad/zu/den/fonts**⟩**/*.ttf .**

earth:/usr/X11R6/lib/X11/fonts/truetype #
    ttmkfdir | sed s/^[0-9]*// >fonts.scale.myfonts

earth:/usr/X11R6/lib/X11/fonts/truetype #
    /sbin/conf.d/SuSEconfig.fonts

If the X server is already running, you can now make the fonts dynamically available. To do this enter:

earth:~ # **xset +fp /usr/X11R6/lib/X11/fonts/truetype**

> **Tip**
>
> The `xset` command accesses the X server via the X protocol. It must therefore have access permissions for the X server currently running. You can find more on this in the man page for `xauth` (`man xauth`)
>
> **Tip**

To set up the fonts permanently, add this search path to the file `XF86Config`. You can use SaX2 to do this. To change the fonts path, you must select the 'Custom' configuration mode of SaX2. In 'Path dialog', add the directory, with 'Add', to the directories already listed.

Test if the fonts were set up correctly. To do this, use the command xlsfonts. If the fonts are correctly installed, the list of all installed fonts, including the newly installed True Type Fonts, is displayed. You can also use the KDE font manager, which displays the installed fonts with an sample text. This can be started in the KDE Control Center.

earth:~ # **xlsfonts**

These newly installed fonts can then be used in all X applications.

OpenGL — 3D Configuration

OpenGL and GLIDE are 3D interfaces for 3Dfx Voodoo cards in Linux. Almost all modern 3D applications use the OpenGL interface, so 3D hardware acceleration can only be implemented over the OpenGL interface, even in the case of 3Dfx Voodoo cards. Only older applications still use the GLIDE interface directly. The OpenGL driver for 3DfxVoodoo cards also uses the GLIDE interface. Direct3D from Microsoft is not available in Linux.

Hardware Support

SuSE Linux includes several OpenGL drivers for 3D hardware support. Table 6.6 on the facing page provides an overview.

If you are installing with YaST2 for the first time, activate 3D support during installation, if the related YaST2 support is recognized. nVidia graphics chips are the only exception. For these, the "dummy" driver included must be replaced by the official nVidia driver. Use YaST Online Update (YOU) to update the `NVIDIA_GLX` and `NVIDIA_kernel` packages. If updating with YOU

OpenGL driver	Supported hardware
Mesa software rendering (very slow)	for all cards supported by XFree86
nVidia GLX / XFree86 4.x	nVidia Chips: all except for Riva 128(ZX)
DRI / XFree86 4.x	3Dfx Voodoo Banshee 3Dfx Voodoo 3/4/5 Intel i810/i815 Matrox G200/G400/G450 FireGL 1/2/3/4 ATI Rage 128(Pro)/Radeon 3Dlabs Glint MX/Gamma
Utah GLX / XFree86 3.3	ATI Rage Pro nVidia Riva 128
Mesa/Glide	3Dfx Voodoo Graphics 3Dfx Voodoo II

Table 6.6: Supported 3D Hardware

is not an option, download the appropriate RPM packages NVIDIA_GLX and NVIDIA_kernel from the nVidia web server (http://www.nvidia.com), install them with YaST2, and run the script switch2nvidia_glx. Because of licensing stipulations, we can only offer the "dummy" nVidia driver packages.

If an update is needed made or a new graphics card installed later, 3D hardware support will have to be configured differently. The approach to doing this depends on the OpenGL driver used and is described in further detail in the section below.

OpenGL Driver

Mesa Software Rendering

This OpenGL driver will always be implemented if no 3D support was configured during installation or if no 3D support is available for the particular card in Linux.

Mesa software rendering should only be implemented if the 3D driver causes any problems (representation errors or system instability). Make sure the package mesasoft is installed then run the script switch2mesasoft. If you have an nVidia card, also run the switch2nv script so the nv driver will be used for XFree86 instead of the nvidia driver. With the command 3Ddiag --mesasoft, check to see if the Mesa software rendering has been properly configured.

nVidia-GLX and DRI

This OpenGL driver can be quite easily configured using SaX2. After starting SaX2, answer "yes" to configuring 3D. If you have an nVidia card and did not update, SaX2 will need to replace the SuSE dummy driver packages with the official nVidia drivers via the Online Update. With the command 3Ddiag, test if nVidia-GLX and DRI are configured properly.

For security reasons, only users belonging to the group video may access the 3D hardware. Verify that all users working locally on the machine are members of this group. Otherwise memory access errors will occur when attempting to start OpenGL applications (nVidia-GLX) and the very laborious *Software Rendering Fallback* of the OpenGL driver will be used (DRI). Use the command id to check whether the active user belongs to the group video. If this is not the case, use YaST2 to add the user to the group.

Mesa/Glide

This OpenGL driver needs to be manually configured with the help of the information provided by `3Ddiag`. Details can be found in Section *Diagnosis Tool 3Ddiag* on the current page.

If you have a Mesa/Glide driver, start OpenGL applications as `root`, because only `root` can access the hardware. To allow this, the user currently logged in will have to enable ⟨*DISPLAY*⟩ for `root`. This can be done with the command `xhost localhost`. The resolution used by the OpenGL application requires GLIDE support (resolutions supported are 640×480 and 800×600). Otherwise the very slow "Software rendering fallback" of the OpenGL driver will be used.

Diagnosis Tool 3Ddiag

The diagnosis tool 3Ddiag is available for the purpose of verifying the 3D configuration in SuSE Linux. This is a command line tool that must be invoked inside a terminal.

The application reviews, for example, the XFree86 configuration to verify that 3D support packages are installed and the proper OpenGL library is used with the GLX extension. Follow the directions in 3Ddiag if "failed" messages appear. Ideally, you will only see "done" messages on the screen.

Unless 3D support was already activated during installation, the 3D configuration of the Mesa/Glide OpenGL driver using this diagnosis can be relatively intensive.

`3Ddiag -h` provides information about options for 3Ddiag.

OpenGL Test Applications

Games, such as `bzflag`, `tuxracer`, and `tuxkart` (from the packages with the same name) and `gears` and `glinfo` from the package `mesa`, are suitable as OpenGL test applications. If 3D support has been activated, they can be played well on a somewhat up-to-date computer. These games, however, are not recommended in conjunction with Mesa software rendering because of the resulting slide show effect.

Troubleshooting

If the OpenGL 3D test results are negative (the games cannot be effectively played), use 3Ddiag to make sure no errors exist in the configuration ("failed" messages). If correcting these does not help or if failed messages have not appeared, take a look at the XFree86 log files. Often, you will find the line "DRI is disabled" in the XFree86 4.x file `/var/log/XFree86.0.log`. The exact cause can only be discovered by closely examining the log file — a task requiring some experience.

In such cases, it is common that no configuration error exists, as this would have already been detected by 3Ddiag. Consequently, at this point, your best bet is the Mesa software rendering OpenGL driver, which does not feature 3D hardware support. Take advantage of Mesa software rendering and forego 3D hardware acceleration to avoid OpenGL representation errors or instability. A familiar example for the latter is the use of DRI and bttv (Watching TV in Linux) with ATI Rage 128 cards.

Installation Support

Apart from Mesa software rendering, all OpenGL drivers in Linux are in developmental phases and are therefore considered experimental. The drivers are included in the distribution because of the high demand for 3D hardware acceleration in Linux. Considering the experimental status of OpenGL drivers, we cannot offer any installation support for configuring 3D hardware acceleration or provide any further assistance with related problems. The basic configuration of the graphical user interface X11 does not include 3D hardware acceleration configuration. This chapter answers many questions regarding this topic. If you have problems with 3D hardware support, use Mesa software rendering as already outlined in Section *Mesa Software Rendering* on page 148.

Additional Online Documentation

- nVidia GLX: `/usr/share/doc/packages/nv_glx/`, `/usr/src/kernel-modules/nv_glx/README NVIDIA_GLX` and `NVIDIA_kernel` from the nVidia server)

- DRI: `/usr/X11R6/lib/X11/doc/README.DRI` (package `xf86`)

- Utah GLX: `/usr/share/doc/packages/glx/` (package `glx`)

- Mesa/Glide: `/usr/share/doc/packages/mesa3dfx/` (package `mesa3dfx`)

- Mesa general: `/usr/share/doc/packages/mesa/` (package `mesa`)

Sound with ALSA

ALSA is the Advanced Linux Sound Architecture. This chapter provides technical information to accompany the sound information in the *Users' Guide*. It offers details for configuration and solutions for clicking playback. Also find information about compression formats and advantages.

Basic PCM Types	152
Compressing Audio Data	152
Buffering and Latencies	153
ALSA and MIDI	154

Main PCM Types: hw and plughw

By selecting a given PCM type, the user can influence how ALSA accesses the sound card. The most important PCM types are `hw` and `plughw`. To understand the difference between the two types, it is necessary to know how a PCM device is opened. Setting (at least) the following parameters is required: sample format, sample frequency, number of channels, number of periods (previously referred to as "fragments"), and size of a period. For example, an application may want to play back a WAV file with a sample frequency of 44.1 kHz, but the sound card does not support this frequency. In this case, ALSA automatically converts the data in the plug-in layer to a format the sound card supports. The conversion affects the parameters sample format, sample frequency, and number of channels.

Selecting the PCM type `plughw` activates the plug-in layer. Selecting the PCM type `hw` causes ALSA to attempt to open the PCM devices directly with the parameters required by the application.

The complete designator for a PCM device consists of the PCM type followed by a colon, the card number, and the device number, as in `plughw:0,0`.

Compressing Audio Data

package `cdparanoia`
package `vorbis-tools`

The conversion of audio CDs to WAV files is described in detail in the "Professional Tools for Burning CDs" chapter. Use the command `cdparanoia -B -z "1-3"` to save tracks 1 to 3 as WAV files, where cdparanoia independently searches for a drive with an inserted audio CD.

In KDE, audio CDs can even be ripped by dragging and dropping them. After starting Konqueror and entering `audiocd:/` as the 'URL', the tracks of an inserted audio CD will be listed, along with several virtual directories. Read more about this in the Section "Ripping Audio CDs with Konqueror", in the "Burning CDs with KOnCD" chapter located in the *Applications Manual*.

Uncompressed audio data of CD quality takes up almost 10 MB per minute. For this reason, the MP3 encoding procedure was developed at the Fraunhofer Institute. Unfortunately, this procedure is patented. Companies that sell MP3 encoders must pay licensing fees. Because of this, the high-performance MP3 encoder developed for Linux, Lame, is not included in our distribution, although its source code falls under the GPL. Obtain more information about the legal status at the project's web site, http://lame.sourceforge.net. Using Lame is only permitted for research purposes in some countries, including Germany and the USA.

Ogg Vorbis is a free compressed audio format. The Ogg format is already supported by KOnCD, xmms, terminatorX, and many other players. This project's web site can be found at http://www.xiph.org/ogg/vorbis. The vorbis-tools package includes an encoder and a simple player. The encoder is started at the command line with `oggenc`. The WAV file to compress is the only required parameter. The option `-h` presents a summary of additional parameters. In the latest version, the Ogg encoder even supports coding with variable bit rate. This way, an even higher compression rate can be obtained with the same quality. Parameters can also be specified for the bit rate itself. The parameter `-b` defines the average bit rate. `-m` and `-M` specifies the minimum and maximum bit rate. Instead of the bit rate, the parameter `-q` for the desired quality can be given.

ogg123 is an Ogg player for the command line. As a parameter, specify the device to use for playback. Start the application with a command like `ogg123 -d alsa09 mysong.ogg`.

Buffering and Latencies

This section explains how to guarantee interruption-free audio playback. This is not solely a Linux problem, but a problem that exists for all multitasking operating systems. Normally in a multitasking operating system, several processes are running simultaneously. Since the processor can only only execute one process at a time, each process is given a certain amount of processor time by the operating system's scheduler. The switching action between processes normally happens so quickly that the user does not notice anything at all.

For audio output, however, this phenomenon is noticeable in the form of short interruptions or clicks. Audio programs therefore use a cache (buffering) for output. The audio data stored in the cache will continue to be relayed to the output of the sound card, even when the audio application is interrupted by the scheduler. A cache large enough to bridge the longest interruptions guarantees click-free output.

There are conflicting interests in this. The cache size defines the reaction time, or latency, of the application. Especially given interactive applications, such as real-time synthesizers and DJ mixer consoles, it is important to keep the cache size as small as possible. Basically, the length of interruptions is dependent on system load and process priority. As a consequence, the cache size required for click-free output is lessened by increasing the audio application's priority. Therefore, many audio applications attempt to switch their process to real-time priority. However, this is only possible when these applications are running with `root` privileges.

It is always risky to run an application in `root` mode, because the application is allowed to perform any action. A security risk presents itself if the computer is connected to the Internet. If this is case, unauthorized users could take advantage of security holes in the application to gain access to your system.

> **Caution**
>
> The commands described in the following should *never* be executed on machines accessible from the Internet or on machines that would suffer serious consequences from a system crash or data loss.
>
> **Caution**

You should use the `sudo` mechanism to run an application as `root`. Our example uses the timidity++ application. To enable all users to run timidity++ on their system with `root` privileges, modify the `/etc/sudoers` file. See the man page for `sudo` (`man sudo`) and the man page for `sudoers` (`man sudoers`) for information. Start `visudo` as root and add the following line to the end of the `/etc/sudoers` file:

```
ALL     ALL=(ALL)  /usr/bin/timidity
```

Now all users on the system will be able to start timidity in `root` mode with `sudo timidity`. A request for the user's individual password follows if more than five minutes have passed since the last `sudo` command.

ALSA and MIDI

package `alsa, pmidi, aseqview, vkeybd`
package `awesfx, snd_sf2, kalsatools`

As well as playing PCM data, many sound cards also feature MIDI functionality. The ALSA MIDI sequencer implements a powerful architecture for routing MIDI data.

Many sound cards possess an external MIDI port for connecting MIDI devices, such as synthesizers, keyboards, and sound modules. If the card's

MIDI port is supported by ALSA, you can record MIDI files over this port using a sequencer application (e.g., jazz). Find a list of the MIDI devices provided by your card in the KDE Control Center under 'Sound' → 'Midi'. Also specify which of these devices should be used to play MIDI files. Use the command `pmidi -l` to list all available MIDI devices and their internal ALSA port numbers. For a "Soundblaster Live!" card, for example, this list would appear as follows:

```
Port      Client name                          Port name
72:0      External MIDI 0                      MIDI 0-0
73:0      Emu10k1 WaveTable                    Emu10k1 Port 0
73:1      Emu10k1 WaveTable                    Emu10k1 Port 1
73:2      Emu10k1 WaveTable                    Emu10k1 Port 2
73:3      Emu10k1 WaveTable                    Emu10k1 Port 3
```

File 17: Soundblaster Live! MIDI Devices

The first column contains the internal port numbers by which the device responds to the ALSA driver. Under the remaining columns, find the client and port names of each device. Along with the external MIDI port already mentioned, find several WaveTable ports. Use a command like `pmidi -p 73:0 mysong.mid` to play a MIDI file over one of the ports listed above.

―― **Note** ――――――――――――――――――――――――――――――

Interrupting a MIDI player during playback can leave a continuous sound playing. If this happens, run the `all_notes_off` script or restart ALSA with `rcalsasound restart` as root.

―――――――――――――――――――――――――――――― **Note** ―

Many sound cards, such as Soundblaster AWE and Live!, have an internal WaveTable synthesizer. This converts MIDI events into audible sounds.

These MIDI events can either be relayed to the WaveTable synthesizer by an external MIDI keyboard or by an application (e.g., MIDI player or sequencer). If you have a Soundblaster AWE or a Soundblaster Live! card, initialize the WaveTable synthesizer with sound fonts to make sounds audible. If you do not have such a card, skip the next section.

Loading Sound Fonts (SB Live! and AWE)

The package `awesfx` contains the `sfxload` command for loading sound fonts in Soundblaster AWE and Live! cards. The relevant sound font files can be found on your sound card's driver CD. The ALSA start-up script can automatically load the required sound fonts for the WaveTable synthesis, if the appropriate files pertaining to the Creative Driver CD have been installed with YaST2. Currently, the script only works for one sound card. However, ALSA can easily manage up to eight sound cards. Then load the sound fonts with the command `sfxload -D ⟨n⟩ /usr/share/sfbank/creative/8MBGMSFX.SF2`. ⟨n⟩ stands for the number of the sound card. This number does not necessarily correspond to the order in which the cards were configured. Find the number in YaST2 under 'Hardware'.

If your driver CD is not available, you can also load already installed sound fonts in `/usr/share/sounds/sf2`. The sound font `Vintage_Dreams_Waves_v2.sf2` by Ian Wilson contains 128 analog synthesizer sounds and 8 drum sets. It is compatible with both SB AWE and SB Live! cards. The ROM sound font `gu11-rom.sf2` by Samuel Collins is *only* compatible with SB AWE cards. It provides an extended general MIDI bank for these cards. Review the copyright files and the documentation in `/usr/share/doc/packages/snd_sf2`. More sound fonts can be found on the Internet. See `http://www.hammersound.net`.

Printer Operation

This chapter provides some background about the inner workings of the printing system. The numerous examples show how the different parts of the printing system are related to each other. The chapter should help you find solutions for possible problems and point you in the right direction whenever your printer does not work as expected. Both the LPRng and lpdfilter print system and the CUPS print system are discussed in detail.

Printing Basics	158
Making the Printer Work	161
Configuring a Printer with YaST2	165
Printer Configuration in Application Programs	172
Manual Configuration of Local Printer Ports	173
Manual Configuration of the LPRng and lpdfilter Printing System	179
The LPRng and lpdfilter Print Spooler	179
Command-Line Tools for LPRng	180
The Print Filter of the LPRng and lpdfilter Printing System	184
Custom Print Filters for the LPRng Spooler	194
The CUPS Printing System	198
Command-Line Tools for the CUPS Printing System . . .	205
Working with Ghostscript	210
Working with a2ps	213
Reformatting PostScript with psutils	215
ASCII Text Encoding	221
Printing in a TCP/IP Network	224

Printing Basics

On a Linux system, printers are managed via *print queues*. Before any data is printed, it is sent to the print queue for temporary storage. From there, it is retrieved by a *print spooler*, which sends it to the printing device in the required order.

However, this data is predominantly not available in a form that can be processed by the printer. A graphical image, for example, first needs to be converted into a format which the printer is able to understand. This conversion into a *printer language* is achieved with a *print filter*, a program which is called by the print spooler to translate data as needed, such that the printer can handle them.

Important Standard Printer Languages

ASCII text Most printers are at least able to print ASCII text. The few devices that cannot print ASCII text directly should be able to understand one of the other standard printer languages mentioned below.

PostScript PostScript is the established printer language under Unix and Linux. PostScript output can be printed directly by PostScript-capable printers, but these are relatively expensive. PostScript is a powerful yet complex language that requires the printer itself to perform very CPU-intensive operations before actually putting something on paper. Adding to the price of PostScript printers are licensing costs.

PCL3, PCL4, PCL5e, PCL6, ESC/P, ESC/P2, and ESC/P raster If a PostScript printer is not available, the print filter uses the program Ghostscript to convert PostScript data into one of these other standard languages. Ghostscript uses different drivers for different printers to make use of specific features offered by the various models, such as color settings, as much as possible.

Processing Print Jobs

1. A print job is started by the user either from the command line or from within an application.

2. The corresponding print data is temporarily stored in the print queue, from which it is retrieved by the print spooler, which in turn sends it to the print filter.

3. The print filter will perform the following steps:

   (a) The filter determines the format of print data.

   (b) Print data is converted into PostScript (if not in PostScript format already). ASCII text, for instance, is converted into PostScript using the filter program `a2ps`.

   (c) The PostScript data is converted into another printer language, if necessary.

   - If the printer is a PostScript model, the data is sent to it with no further processing.
   - If the printer is not a PostScript printer, the program Ghostscript is run and uses one of its drivers to convert data into the language of the printer model. This generates the data that is finally sent to the printer.

4. As soon as all the data of the print job has been sent to the printer, the print spooler deletes it from the print queue.

Available Printing Systems

SuSE Linux supports two different printing systems:

LPRng and lpdfilter — This is a traditional printing system consisting of the print spooler LPRng and the print filter lpdfilter. The configuration of this system must be entirely defined by the system administrator. Normal users can only choose between different print queues that have already been set up. To allow users to choose between different options for a given printer, a number of print queues need to be defined beforehand — each for a different printer configuration. For plain black-and-white printers, such as most laser printers, it is sufficient to define just one configuration (the standard queue). For modern color inkjet printers, define several configurations, for example, one for black-and-white printing, one for color printing, and maybe another one for high-resolution photograph printing. Setting up the printer with predefined configurations has the advantage that the system administrator has a lot of control over the way in which the device is used. On the other hand, there is the disadvantage that users cannot set up the printer according to the job at hand, so maybe they will not be able to make use of the many options offered by modern printers unless the administrator has defined the corresponding print queues beforehand.

CUPS — CUPS allows users to set different options for each print job and does not require that the entire configuration of the print queue is predefined by the system administrator. With CUPS, printer options are stored in a PPD (PostScript printer description) file for each queue and can be made available to users in printer configuration dialogs. By default, the PPD file gives users control over all printer options, but the system administrator may also limit printer functionality by editing the file.

Both printing systems cannot be installed at the same time, because there are conflicts between them. However, YaST2 allows you to choose either and to switch between them. See *Configuring a Printer with YaST2* on page 165.

General Troubleshooting Hints

The documentation included with SuSE Linux mostly describes general printing problems and ways to solve them. Many of the more specific issues are covered by articles in the support database. The support database be accessed as part of the SuSE help system, but the most up-to-date version of this database is available online at `http://sdb.suse.de/en/sdb/html/`.

A good starting point to deal with printer problems are the support database articles *Installing a Printer* and *Printer Configuration with SuSE Linux 8.0*, which you can find by searching for the keyword "printer", or online at `http://sdb.suse.de/en/sdb/html/jsmeix_print-einrichten.html` and `http://sdb.suse.de/en/sdb/html/jsmeix_print-einrichten-80.html`. You may also want to read the general support database articles that describe the most important known problems and issues of each SuSE Linux version in one central place: *Known Problems and Special Features in SuSE Linux 8.1* at
`http://sdb.suse.de/en/sdb/html/bugs81.html`
Known Problems and Special Features in SuSE Linux 8.0 at
`http://sdb.suse.de/en/sdb/html/bugs80.html`

If you do not find your problem described in the documentation or in the support database, we are glad to provide help through our support services. Information about these can be found at `http://www.suse.de/en/services/support/index.html`.

8 Making the Printer Work

General Requirements

- Your printer must be supported by SuSE Linux. To see whether this is the case, consult the following sources:

    SuSE printer database — `http://cdb.suse.de` or `http://hardwaredb.suse.de/` (click 'Englisch' to get the English version.) The Ghostscript drivers listed on these pages correspond to the ones that can be selected for the corresponding printer model in the printer configuration dialog of YaST2.

    The linuxprinting.org printer database — `http://www.linuxprinting.org/` → 'The Database' (`http://www.linuxprinting.org/database.html`) or `http://www.linuxprinting.org/printer_list.cgi`

    Ghostscript — `http://www.cs.wisc.edu/~ghost/`

    The SuSE Linux Ghostscript driver list — `/usr/share/doc/packages/ghostscript/catalog.devices` This file lists the Ghostscript drivers included with the current version of SuSE Linux. This is an important detail because sometimes you find Ghostscript drivers mentioned on the Internet that require Aladdin Ghostscript, while SuSE Linux comes with GNU Ghostscript (due to licensing reasons). In most cases, GNU Ghostscript already includes a driver suitable for your printer.

- The printer has been properly connected to the interface over which it will communicate. For details, read *Manual Configuration of Local Printer Ports* on page 173 and *Manual Configuration* on page 168.

- You should be using one of the standard kernels included on CD, *not* a custom kernel built yourself. If you have problems with your printer, install one of the SuSE standard kernels first and reboot before looking further into the problem.

- You should have installed the 'Default System' to make sure that all required packages are there. As long as you have not deselected (uninstalled) any of the packages of the standard system after installation, you are set to continue. Otherwise, install the 'Default System' with YaST2. None of the 'Minimum System' installs fulfill all the requirements to make the printing system work.

Finding the Right Printer Driver

You do not need any particular driver if your printer is a PostScript model. If that is not the case, you need a Ghostscript driver to produce the data for your specific printer. For non-PostScript devices, the Ghostscript driver is the determining factor as far as printer output is concerned. Choosing the right driver and the right options for it has a big influence on its quality. The Ghostscript drivers available for specific models are listed in the sources mentioned in *General Requirements* on the preceding page.

If you cannot find a specific Ghostscript driver for your printer, it may be possible to use another driver already available. Also, some manufacturers support Linux, so your manufacturer might be able to provide specific Ghostscript driver information. If not, they may be able to provide other information to assist in selection:

- Find out whether your printer is compatible with a model supported by Linux. You may then be able to use the driver for the compatible model.

  For printers to be *compatible*, they should be able to work correctly using the same binary control sequences. Both printers must understand the same language on the hardware level without relying on additional driver software to emulate it.

  A similar model name does not always mean the hardware is really compatible. Printers that appear very similar on the outside sometimes do not use the same printer language at all.

- Check if your printer supports a standard printing language by asking the manufacturer or checking the technical specifications in the printer manual.

  PCL5e or PCL6 Printers that understand the PCL5e or PCL6 language natively should work with the ljet4 Ghostscript driver and produce output at a resolution of 600x600 dpi. Often, PCL5e is mistaken for PCL5.

  PCL4 or PCL5 Printers that understand the PCL4 or PCL5 language natively should work with one of the following Ghostscript drivers: laserjet, ljetplus, ljet2p, or ljet3. Output resolution is limited to 300x300 dpi, however.

  PCL3 Printers that understand the PCL3 language natively should work with one of these Ghostscript drivers: deskjet, hpdj, pcl3, cdjmono, cdj500, or cdj550.

ESC/P2, ESC/P or ESC/P raster Printers that understand ESC/P2, ESC/P, or ESC/P raster natively should work with the stcolor Ghostscript driver or with the uniprint driver in combination with a suitable *.upp parameter file (e.g., `stcany.upp`).

The Issue with GDI Printers

Given that most Linux printer drivers are not written by the maker of the hardware, it is crucial that the printer can be driven through one of the generally known languages, such as PostScript, PCL, or ESC/P. Normal printers understand at least one of the common languages. In the case of a GDI printer, the manufacturer has decided to build a device that relies on its own special control sequences. Such a printer only runs under the operating system versions for which the manufacturer has included a driver. Because it cannot be operated through one of the known languages, it must be considered nonstandard and cannot be used with Linux or can only be used with difficulty.

GDI is a programming interface developed by Microsoft for graphical devices. There is not much of a problem with the interface itself, but the fact that GDI printers can *only* be controlled through the proprietary language they use *is* an issue. A better name for them would be "proprietary-language-only printers."

On the other hand, there are printers that can be operated both in GDI mode and in a standard language mode, but they need to be switched accordingly. If you use Linux together with another operating system, it may be possible that the driver set the printer to GDI mode when you last used it. As a result, the printer will not work under Linux. There are two solutions for this: switch the printer back to standard mode under the other operating system before using it under Linux or use only the standard mode, even under the other operating system. In the latter case, it may turn out that printing functionality is limited, such as to a lower resolution.

There are also some very special printers that implement a rudimentary set of a standard printer language, for example, only the operations necessary for the printing of raster images. Sometimes these printers can be used in a normal way, as many Ghostscript drivers only use the printer as a raster image device anyway. On the negative side, you may be unable to print ASCII text directly. This should not be too much of a problem, however, as ASCII text is mostly printed through Ghostscript and not directly. The only problem occurs when some of these printers need to be explicitly switched before they can print raster images. This requires sending a special control sequence to them — something that can only be achieved with a special driver, but not through Ghostscript.

For some GDI printers, you may be able to obtain Linux drivers directly from the manufacturer. There is no guarantee that such vendor-made drivers will work with other or future Linux versions.

In any case, the above is only true for GDI models. By contrast, printers that understand one of the standard languages do not depend on a particular operating system nor do they require a particular Linux version. However, they often produce the highest quality of output when used with a vendor-made driver.

To sum all this up, SuSE Linux does support the GDI printers listed below. They can be configured using the printer configuration module of YaST2. Be aware that their use will always be rather problematic. Some models might refuse to work at all or their functionality might be limited, for example, to low-resolution black-and-white printing. SuSE does not test GDI printers, so cannot guarantee that this list is correct:

- Brother HL 720/730/820/1020/1040, MFC 4650/6550MC/9050, and compatible models.

- HP DeskJet 710/712/720/722/820/1000, and compatible models.

- Lexmark 1000/1020/1100/2030/2050/2070/3200/5000/5700/7000/7200, Z11/42/43/51/52, and compatible models. Lexmark makes its own Linux drivers available at:
  http://www.lexmark.com/printers/linuxprinters.html

- Oki Okipage 4w/4w+/6w/8w/8wLite/8z/400w and compatible models.

- Samsung ML-200/210/1000/1010/1020/1200/1210/1220/4500/5080/6040 and compatible models.

To our knowledge, the following GDI printers are *not supported* by SuSE Linux (this list is not complete by any means):

- Brother DCP-1000, MP-21C, WL-660

- Canon BJC 5000/5100/8000/8500, LBP 460/600/660/800, MultiPASS L6000

- Epson AcuLaser C1000, EPL 5500W/5700L/5800L

- HP LaserJet 1000/3100/3150

- Lexmark Z12/22/23/31/32/33/82, Winwriter 100/150c/200

- Minolta PagePro 6L/1100L/18L, Color PagePro L, Magicolor 6100DeskLaser, Magicolor 2 DeskLaser Plus/Duplex

- Nec SuperScript 610plus/660/660plus

- Oki Okijet 2010

- Samsung ML 85G/5050G, QL 85G

- Sharp AJ 2100, AL 1000/800/840/F880/121

Configuring a Printer with YaST2

Print Queues and Configurations

In most cases, you will want to set up more than one print queue for the following reasons:

- If you have more than one printer, you need at least one queue for each of them.

- The print filter can be configured differently for each print queue. By having different queues for one printer, operate it with different configurations.

If your model is a plain black-and-white printer, such as most laser printers, it will be sufficient to configure just one standard queue. Color inkjets, on the other hand, require at least two different queues (configurations):

- A standard `lp` configuration for quick black-and-white printouts at low cost. An `lp` queue should always be defined, because this is also the traditional name of the default queue under Linux.

- A `color` configuration or queue used for color printing.

Printer Configuration with YaST2: The Basics

Start the YaST2 printer configuration by selecting it from the YaST2 Control Center or by entering `yast2 printer` in a command line as `root`. Enter `yast2 printer .nodetection` to suppress printer autodetection. For more details about autodetection, see *Parallel Ports* on page 173.

The YaST2 printer configuration always defines settings for *both* printing systems *at the same time*. With each change, a configuration is written for both CUPS and LPRng and lpdfilter. This configuration data is stored in the YaST2 printer database `/usr/lib/YaST2/data/printerdb/suse.prdb`. However, not every option is available for both printing systems. Certain options are only supported by either CUPS or LPRng and lpdfilter. YaST2 provides information about this whenever necessary.

Easily switch back and forth between CUPS and LPRng using the YaST2 printer configuration dialog. Configurations that are supported by both printing systems are available for use immediately after switching from one system to another. However, not every configuration is completely identical under both systems even if it valid for both systems, because of their different capabilities.

The YaST2 printer configuration module allows you to select from and to switch between printing systems as described below.

CUPS as a server If you have a printer connected locally to the computer, CUPS needs to run as a server. This requires a number of packages be installed:

- package `cups-libs`
- package `cups-client`
- package `cups`
- package `cups-drivers`
- package `cups-drivers-stp`

CUPS in client-only mode CUPS may be installed as a client only, provided that there is a CUPS network server running within your local network and you want to use its queues for printing. With this setup, only specify the CUPS network server. Only the following packages are needed:

- package `cups-libs`
- package `cups-client`

LPRng The LPRng and lpdfilter printing system should be installed if the local network only offers an lpd network server, not a CUPS one, (see *The LPRng and lpdfilter Print Spooler* on page 179) and if you want to use the queues for printing. The following packages are required for this setup:

- package `lprng`
- package `lpdfilter`

The package `cups-client` and the package `lprng` are mutually exclusive — they must not be installed at the same time. The package `cups-libs` must always be installed because certain programs, such as Samba, are linked against these libraries.

The printing system as a whole requires a number of additional packages, although the 'Default system' should have installed them for you already. The most important ones are:

- package `ghostscript-library`
- package `ghostscript-fonts-std`
- package `ghostscript-x11`
- package `a2ps`
- package `file`

You can run the YaST2 printer configuration even without any of the printing systems installed. YaST2 saves all configuration data to `/var/lib/YaST2/printers`. When you install a printing system later, or when changing from one system to another one, YaST2 relies on this data to create the actual printer configuration.

The YaST2 printer configuration modules display all configurations that could be created without errors. However, as the actual configurations are only written upon finishing the YaST2 printer configuration module, it is a good idea to restart the module afterwards to check for any errors.

The YaST2 printer configuration also strictly distinguishes between queues created through YaST2 itself (YaST2 queues) and queues created through other means (non-YaST2 queues). Non-YaST2 will never be touched by YaST2. Conflicts may arise if queues have identical names. For instance, you may first create a YaST2 queue named `color` for one of the printing systems then change to another printing system manually (not using YaST2). If you created

SuSE Linux – Administration Guide   167

another `color` queue manually at this point and started the YaST2 printer configuration after that, the manually-created queue would be overwritten by the YaST2 queue of the same name.

When editing a queue, you can tell YaST2 whether it shall be in charge of it. For instance, you could turn a YaST2 queue into a non-YaST2 queue to prevent it from being overwritten in the way assumed above. Conversely, you could also use this to turn a non-YaST2 queue into a YaST2 queue to deliberately overwrite an existing configuration with YaST2.

Automatic Configuration

Depending on how much of your hardware can be autodetected and on whether your printer model is included in the printer database, YaST2 will either autoconfigure your printer or offer a reasonable selection of settings that then need to be adjusted manually.

YaST2 can configure your printer automatically if these conditions are fulfilled:

- The parallel port or USB interface was set up automatically in the correct way and the printer model connected to it was autodetected.

- Your printer's ID, as supplied to YaST2 during hardware autodetection, is included in the printer database. Given that this ID may be different from the actual name of the model, you may need to select the model manually.

- The printer database includes at least one configuration for your model, which is assumed to be fully working and valid for both CUPS and LPRng.

Each configuration should be tested with the print test function of YaST2 to see whether it works as expected. For many configurations included in the printer database, there is no absolute guarantee that they will work as they had to be written without any direct help from printer makers. The YaST2 test page also provides important information about the printer configuration selected.

Manual Configuration

If one of the conditions for automatic configuration is not fulfilled or if you want your own customized setup, configure the printer manually, at least to some extent. The following is an overview of the options to set during manual configuration:

Hardware port (interface)

- If YaST2 was able to autodetect the printer model, you may safely assume that the printer connection works as far as the hardware is concerned. You may then leave this part untouched.

- If YaST2 has not autodetected the printer model, there may have been some problem on the hardware level. Some manual intervention is needed to configure the physical connection. Manual configuration requires specification of the port to which the printer is connected. /dev/lp0 is the first parallel port. /dev/usb/lp0 is the port for a USB printer. Always test this setting from within YaST2 to see whether the printer is actually responding at the selected interface.

    A printer connected to the first parallel port is a fairly safe bet. In this case, the BIOS settings for this port should look like this:

    ▷ IO address: 378 (hexadecimal)

    ▷ Interrupt: (not relevant)

    ▷ Mode: Normal, SPP, or Output-Only.

    ▷ DMA: Disabled

    If the printer does not respond at the first parallel port with these settings, you may need to change the IO address to have the explicit form of 0x378 under the BIOS menu item that lets you configure the advanced settings for parallel ports. If your machine has two parallel ports with IO addresses 378 and 278 (hexadecimal), change them to read 0x378 and 0x278, respectively. For further details on the topic, see *Parallel Ports* on page 173.

Queue name The name of the queue is used frequently when issuing print commands. The name should be rather short and consist of lowercase letters (and maybe numbers) only. The following additional options may be defined for the LPRng and lpdfilter printing system:

- Define a queue named raw to use for special cases where print data shall not be converted by a print filter, but sent to the printer in raw form. Accordingly, when printing through the raw queue, print data must already be available in a format (language) your printer model can understand.

- For each queue, define whether an explicit form feed is needed. If enabled, the spooler sends a form feed command at the end of each print job to eject the last page. Normally, the Ghostscript driver takes care of this and you can leave this disabled.

Ghostscript driver and printer language The Ghostscript driver and the printer language depend on your printer model. Select a default configuration suitable for your model then change it in an additional dialog as needed.

For non-PostScript models, all printer-specific data is produced by the Ghostscript driver. Therefore, the driver configuration (both choosing the right driver and the correct options for it) is the single most important factor determining the output quality. Your settings affect the printer output on a queue-by-queue basis.

If your printer was autodetected, which means the model is included in the printer database, you will be presented with a choice of possible Ghostscript drivers and with several output options, for example:

- black-and-white at 300 dpi
- LPRng only: grayscale at 300 dpi
- color at 300 dpi
- CUPS only: color at 600 dpi
- photo at 600 dpi

YaST2 indicates whether these options are supported by each printing system. Each default configuration includes a suitable Ghostscript driver and, if available, a number of options for the driver related to output quality. If there are specific options for the driver, use the extra dialog to change these as needed. Click the respective value. If there are further configuration options, the subitems are indented in the list. Not all combinations of driver options work with every printer model. This is especially true for higher resolutions.

Always check whether your settings work as expected by printing the YaST2 test page. If the output is garbled (for example, with several pages almost empty), you should be able to stop the printer by first removing all sheets then stopping the test print from within YaST2. However, in some cases the printer will refuse to resume work if you do so. It may be better to stop the test print first and wait for the printer to eject all pages by itself.

If your model was not found in the printer database, YaST2 allows you to choose from a number of generic Ghostscript drivers for the standard printing languages. To use a Ghostscript driver not included in the default configuration offered by YaST2, try to find it under the manufacturer name. For the CUPS printing system, the following special configuration options are available:

- With the CUPS system, normally PPD files are stored in `/usr/lib/YaST2/data/printerdb`. These must exactly match the entries in the YaST2 printer database. The YaST2 PPD files are based on the PPD files that come with package `cups-drivers` and package `cups-drivers-stp`. Selecting a printer manually means selecting any other PPD file (instead of a YaST2 PPD file), such as one of the files included with package `cups-drivers` and package `cups-drivers-stp`, which are stored in `/usr/share/cups/model/`. However, as there is no entry for such a PPD file in the YaST2 database, the default configuration provided by the file cannot be changed with YaST2. Change the default settings in a different way, as described in *Specifying Options for Queues* on page 207.

Other special settings These special settings can be accessed through an extra submenu. Unless you are sure what these options mean, do not change the defaults.

For the CUPS printing system, the following special settings are available:

- Restricting printer use for certain users.
- Queue status: whether the queue is started or stopped and whether it is ready to accept new print jobs.
- Banner page: whether to print out a banner (cover) page at the beginning of each print job and which one. Similarly, whether to add a banner page at the end of each print job and which one.

For the LPRng and lpdfilter printing system, change the following hardware-independent settings:

- The page layout can be changed for ASCII text printouts (but not for graphics or documents created with special application programs).
- You can define an `ascii` print queue for special cases. The `ascii` queue forces the print filter to produce ASCII text output, which may be necessary for some text files that the print filter

does not automatically recognize as such, for example, PostScript source code.
- Country-specific settings can be changed to ensure the correct character encoding when sending ASCII text to the printer and when printing plain text in HTML pages from Netscape.

Printer Configuration in Application Programs

Application programs rely on the existing print queues in a way that is very similar to how they are used on the command line. In an application, printer options are not configured directly, but rather through the existing queues of the system.

Printing from the Command Line

Print from the command line using the command `lpr -Plp filename`, where `filename` is the name of the file to send to the printer. In this example, the default print queue used is `lp`, but the `-P` option allows specification another queue. For instance, the command `lpr -Pcolor filename` tells the printing system to use the `color` queue.

Using the LPRng and lpdfilter System

With this printing system, applications can use the `lpr` command for printing. To make this work, use the application's printer configuration to select one of the existing queues (e.g., `lp` or `color`) or use the application's print dialog to directly enter the corresponding command (e.g., `lpr -Plp` or `lpr -Pcolor`).

Using the CUPS System

The package `cups-client` includes some command-line tools to print with CUPS. One of them is the `lpr` command, which enables use of the commands described above under CUPS, too.

In addition, there are several graphical tools for CUPS, such as `xpp` or the KDE program `kprinter`, which allow you to choose among queues and to change both CUPS standard options and printer-specific options as made available through the PPD file.

Manual Configuration of Local Printer Ports

Parallel Ports

For the most part, printers are connected to a Linux system through a parallel port. Printers on parallel ports are handled by the `parport` subsystem of the Linux kernel. The basics of parallel port configuration with YaST2 are described in *Manual Configuration* on page 169. The paragraphs below provide more in-depth information on the topic.

The `parport` subsystem manages parallel ports only through the corresponding architecture-specific kernel modules after these are loaded. Among other things, this allows for several devices, such as a parallel port ZIP drive and a printer, to be linked to one parallel port at the *same* time. Device files for parallel printers are counted beginning with `/dev/lp0`. With a SuSE Linux standard kernel, printing over the parallel port requires that the modules `parport`, `parport_pc`, and `lp` are loaded. This is achieved by kmod (the kernel module loader). Normally, these modules are loaded automatically as soon as some process requests access to the device file.

If the kernel module `parport_pc` is loaded without any parameters, it tries to autodetect and autoconfigure all available parallel ports. This may not work in some very rare cases and cause a system lock-up. If that should happen, configure it manually by explicitly providing the correct parameters for the `parport_pc` module. This is also the reason why printer autodetection can be disabled for YaST2 as described in *Configuring a Printer with YaST2* on page 165.

Manual Configuration of Parallel Ports

The first parallel port (`/dev/lp0`) is configured with an entry in `/etc/modules.conf`, as shown in File 18.

```
alias parport_lowlevel parport_pc
options parport_pc io=0x378 irq=none
```

File 18: /etc/modules.conf: First Parallel Port

Under `io`, fill in the IO address of the parallel port. Under `irq`, keep the default `none` for polling mode. Otherwise, provide the IRQ number for the parallel port. Polling mode is less problematic than interrupt mode as it helps to avoid interrupt conflicts. However, there are combinations of motherboards and printers that only function well if this is set to interrupt mode. Apart from that, interrupt mode ensures a continuous data flow to the printer even when the system is under very high load.

To make the above configuration work, you may still need to change the parallel port settings made available through the menus of your machine's BIOS or firmware:

- IO address: `378` (hexadecimal)

- Interrupt: `7` (not relevant for polling mode)

- Mode: `Normal`, `SPP`, or `Output-Only` (other modes will not always work)

- DMA: `Disabled` (should be disabled as long as the mode is set to `Normal`)

If interrupt `7` is still free, enable it with:

```
alias parport_lowlevel parport_pc
options parport_pc io=0x378 irq=7
```

File 19: /etc/modules.conf: Interrupt Mode for the First Parallel Port

However, before enabling interrupt mode, enter the command `cat /proc/interrupts` to see which interrupts are already in use on your system. The output of this command will only list interrupts that are being used at the given moment, something which may change according to the hardware components active. In any case, the interrupt used for a parallel port must not be occupied by any other device. You are probably best off using polling mode if you are not sure about this.

Configuring Additional Parallel Ports

Configure a second parallel port (`/dev/lp1`) by adding the corresponding entries to `/etc/modules.conf`, as shown in File 20. In this case, the default IO address should be set to `278` (hexadecimal). This may be changeable on the hardware level, for example, by setting a jumper on an ISA expansion card.

```
alias parport_lowlevel parport_pc
options parport_pc io=0x378,0x278 irq=none,none
```

File 20: /etc/modules.conf: Two Parallel Ports

Special ISA PnP and PCI Expansion Cards

If you do not know the IO address of an additional parallel port, find it first.

ISA PnP Cards If the card has a means to set the IO address and the interrupt to a fixed value (by setting a jumper, for instance), do so before proceeding with the configuration.

If that is not the case, the values for IO address, interrupt, and mode are set for the card by the system on boot. To find out which values have been set for your ISA PnP card, look for them in the boot messages, as stored in `/var/log/boot.msg`, or with `pnpdump` (included in package `isapnp`).

PCI Cards Find possible IO addresses and interrupts for PCI cards by entering the command `/sbin/lspci -v`. The output should be similar to Output 5.

```
00:0a.0 Parallel controller: ...
         ... IRQ 10
         I/O ports at b400
         I/O ports at b000
         I/O ports at a800
         I/O ports at a400
```

Output 5: *Partial Output of* `lspci -v` *for a PCI Interface Card*

Each parallel port is assigned a pair of IO addresses set off by 400 (hexadecimal). In our example, one IO port corresponds to `b000` and `b400`. The other one is at `a400` and `a800`. You may need to experiment a bit to see which of the two IO addresses is the right one. The final configuration entry in `/etc/modules.conf` looks like the one shown in File 21.

```
alias parport_lowlevel parport_pc
options parport_pc io=0x378,0xb400,0xa800 irq=none,none,none
```

File 21: */etc/modules.conf: PCI Card with Two Parallel Ports*

Enabling and Testing a Parallel Port

After configuration, the parallel port is enabled when you reboot the machine.

If you do not want to reboot, run the following commands as `root` to update the module dependency list and to unload all kernel modules related to parallel ports.

```
earth:~ #   depmod -a 2>/dev/null
earth:~ #   rmmod lp
earth:~ #   rmmod parport_pc
earth:~ #   rmmod parport
```

After this, reload the modules with:

```
earth:~ #   modprobe parport
earth:~ #   modprobe parport_pc
earth:~ #   modprobe lp
```

If the printer is capable of direct ASCII text printing, the command

```
earth:~ #   echo -en "\rHello\r\f" >/dev/lp0
```

as `root` should print a single page with the word `Hello` on it.

In the above command, the word `Hello` is enclosed in two `\r` ASCII characters to produce carriage returns. The closing ASCII character `\f` is included to produce a form feed. To test a second or third parallel port in the same way, use `/dev/lp1` or `/dev/lp2`, respectively.

USB Ports

First, make sure interrupt is enabled for USB in your machine's BIOS. In an Award BIOS, for example, go to the menu 'PNP AND PCI SETUP' and set the entry 'USB IRQ' to `Enabled`. The wording of these menus and entries may vary depending on the BIOS type and version.

Test whether the USB printer is responding by entering the command `echo -en "\rHello\r\f" >/dev/usb/lp0` as `root`. If there is only one USB printer connected to the machine and this printer is able to print ASCII text directly, this should print a single page with the word `Hello` on it.

Some USB printers may need a special control sequence before accepting data over a USB line. The following command, entered as one line without spaces or line breaks, sends a control sequence for an Epson Stylus Color USB printer:

```
echo -en "\x0\x0\x0\x1b\x01\x40\x45\x4a\x4c
\x20\x31\x32\x38\x34\x2e\x34\x0a\x40\x45\x4a\x4c\x20
\x20\x20\x20\x20\x0a" >/dev/usb/lp0
```

In most cases, you should be able to get information about the printer manufacturer and the product name by entering `cat /proc/bus/usb/devices`. If this does not display any information, it will usually be for one of these reasons:

- The USB system has not detected the device (yet), maybe even because it is disconnected from power, so there is no communication between the system and the printer.

- The USB system has detected the device, but neither the manufacturer or the product name are known to it. Accordingly, nothing is displayed, but the system can communicate with the printer.

Sometimes it may happen that the USB printer does not respond anymore, for instance, after unplugging it in the middle of a print job. In such a case, the following commands should be sufficient to restart the USB system:

earth:~ # **rchotplug stop**
earth:~ # **rchotplug start**

If you are not successful with these commands, terminate all processes that use `/dev/usb/lp0`, unload all USB printer–related kernel modules, and reload these modules. Before doing so, use `lsmod` to check which USB modules are loaded (`usb-uhci`, `usb-ohci`, or `uhci`) and how they depend on each other. For instance, the entry

```
usbcore    ...    [printer usb-uhci]
```

in the output of `lsmod` shows that the module `usbcore` is being used by modules `printer` and `usb-uhci`. Accordingly, modules `printer` and `usb-uhci` need to be unloaded before unloading `usbcore`.

As `root`, enter the following commands (replace `usb-uhci` with `uhci` or `usb-ohci` depending on your USB system):

earth:~ # **fuser -k /dev/usb/lp0**
earth:~ # **rchotplug stop**
earth:~ # **rmmod printer**

```
earth:~ #   rmmod usb-uhci
earth:~ #   umount usbdevfs
earth:~ #   rmmod usbcore
earth:~ #   modprobe usbcore
earth:~ #   mount usbdevfs
earth:~ #   modprobe usb-uhci
earth:~ #   modprobe printer
earth:~ #   rchotplug start
```

If you have more than one USB printer connected to the system, there is a special issue to consider: All connected devices are autodetected by the USB subsystem with the first USB printer being addressed as device /dev/usb/lp0 and the second one as /dev/usb/lp1. Depending on the model, USB printers can be detected even when they are powerless. Some have the built-in capability to be queried by the system even when powered off. Therefore, to avoid that the system confuses different printers, switch on all printers before booting and try to leave them connected to power all the time.

The IrDA Printer Interface

With IrDA, the system uses an infrared interface to emulate a parallel port. To do so, the Linux drivers provide a simulated parallel port under the device name of /dev/irlpt0. A printer connected through infrared is handled in the same way as any other parallel printer except it is made available to the system under the name of /dev/irlpt0 instead of /dev/lp0.

Test the connection to an IrDA printer by entering the command echo -en "\rHello\r\f" >/dev/irlpt0 as root. If the printer is able to print ASCII text directly, this should print a single page with the word Hello on it.

Regardless of the outcome of the above test, the printer should appear in the output of irdadump. If this does not list your printer, there may be some kind of connection problem or the device is powered off. If the above command does not produce any output at all, you have probably not started the IrDA service yet (it is not started automatically upon booting). The IrDA service can be started and stopped with the commands:

```
earth:~ #   rcirda start
earth:~ #   rcirda stop
```

Serial Ports

To use a printer connected to a serial port in combination with the LPRng printing system, read the document `/usr/share/doc/packages/lprng/LPRng-HOWTO.html`, in particular, the section `file:/usr/share/doc/packages/lprng/LPRng-HOWTO.html#SECSERIAL`. More information can be obtained from the man page for `printcap` (`man printcap`) as well as in the support database by searching for the keyword "serial".

Manual Configuration of the LPRng and lpdfilter Printing System

Normally, the printing system is configured with YaST2 as described in *Configuring a Printer with YaST2* on page 165. SuSE Linux also includes the program lprsetup, which is a bare-bones command-line tool for the configuration of the LPRng and lpdfilter printing system. When setting up a printer with YaST2, it collects all necessary data then runs lprsetup internally with all the necessary options to write the actual LPRng and lpdfilter configuration.

lprsetup is intended as an expert tool. As such, it will not provide any help to find the correct values for printer options. To see a brief list of the available command line options for `lprsetup`, enter `lprsetup -help`, or look up the man page for `lprsetup` (`man lprsetup`) and the man page for `lpdfilter` (`man lpdfilter`) for further details.

For information regarding Ghostscript drivers and driver-specific options, read *Finding the Right Printer Driver* on page 162 and *Working with Ghostscript* on page 210.

The LPRng and lpdfilter Print Spooler

The print spooler used by the LPRng/lpd printing system is LPRng (package `lprng`). The print spooler lpd, or line printer daemon, is usually started automatically on boot. More specifically, the script `/etc/init.d/lpd` is run as part of the boot procedure. After this, the print spooler runs as a daemon in the background. Start and stop it manually with `rclpd start` and `rclpd stop`.

These are the configuration files of LPRng:

/etc/printcap definitions of the system's print queues

/etc/lpd.conf   global print spooler configuration

/etc/lpd.perms   permission settings

According to the script `/etc/init.d/lpd`, the command `rclpd start` also runs the command `checkpc -f` as a subprocess, which in turn creates spool directories with the appropriate permissions in `/var/spool/lpd` according to the queues defined in `/etc/printcap`. When started, the print spooler first reads the entries in `/etc/printcap` to see which print queues have been defined. The spooler's task is then to manage any jobs queued for printing. In particular, the spooler:

- manages local queues by passing the print data of each job to a print filter (if necessary) and sending it to the printer or to another queue afterwards

- handles jobs in the order in which they have been queued

- monitors the status of queues and printers and provides status information when requested

- listens on port 515 to accept or rejects print jobs from remote hosts destined for local queues, depending on the configuration

- forwards print jobs to remote print spoolers (listening on port 515 on other hosts) for printing through remote queues.

To learn more about the details of this mechanism, read the *LPRng Howto* (`file:/usr/share/doc/packages/lprng/LPRng-HOWTO.html`) or consult the man page for `printcap` (`man printcap`) and the man page for `lpd` (`man lpd`).

Command-Line Tools for LPRng

This section only provide a short overview of the available tools. For details, consult the *LPRng Howto*, in particular, section `file:/usr/share/doc/packages/lprng/LPRng-HOWTO.html#LPRNGCLIENTS`.

Managing Local Queues

Printing Files

Details on how to use the `lpr` command can be found in the *LPRng Howto* (`file:/usr/share/doc/packages/lprng/LPRng-HOWTO.html#LPR`). The following only covers some basic operations.

To print a file, you normally must enter `lpr -P⟨queuename⟩ ⟨filename⟩`. If you leave out the `-P⟨queuename⟩` parameter, the printing system defaults to the value of the environment variable `PRINTER`. The same is true for the commands `lpq` and `lprm`. See the man page for `lpr` (man lpr), the man page for `lpq` (man lpq), and the man page for `lprm` (man lprm) for more information. The environment variable `PRINTER` is set automatically on login. Display its current value with `echo $PRINTER`. Change it to expand to another queue by entering:

```
newbie@earth:~ > export PRINTER=⟨queuename⟩
```

Checking the Status

By entering `lpq -P⟨queuename⟩`, check the status of print jobs handled by the specified queue. If you specify `all` as the queue name, `lpq` displays information for all jobs in all queues.

With `lpq -s -P⟨queuename⟩`, tell `lpq` to display only a minimum of information. `lpq -l -P⟨queuename⟩` tells `lpq` to be more verbose. With `lpq -L -P⟨queuename⟩`, `lpq` displays a detailed status report, which will come in handy when trying to track down errors.

For further information, see *Managing Remote Queues* on page 183, the man page for `lpq` (man lpq), and section `file:/usr/share/doc/packages/lprng/LPRng-HOWTO.html#LPQ` of the *LPRng Howto*.

Removing Jobs from the Queue

The command `lprm -P⟨queuename⟩ ⟨jobnumber⟩` removes the print job with the specified number from the specified queue, provided that you own the job. A print job is owned by the user who started it. Display both the ownership and the job number of print jobs with `lpq`.

The command `lprm -Pall all` removes all print jobs from all queues for which you have the required permissions. `root` may remove any jobs in any queues regardless of permissions.

More information can be obtained in the man page for `lprm` (man lprm) and in the *LPRng Howto* (`file:/usr/share/doc/packages/lprng/LPRng-HOWTO.html#LPRM`).

Controlling the Queues

The command `lpc option ⟨queuename⟩` displays the status of the specified queue and allows changing it. The most important options are:

`help` Display a short overview of the available options.

`status ⟨queuename⟩` Display status information.

`disable ⟨queuename⟩` Do not accept new jobs for the specified queue.

`enable ⟨queuename⟩` Accept new jobs for the specified queue.

`stop ⟨queuename⟩` Stop printing from the specified queue. If a job is being printed, it will be completed.

`start ⟨queuename⟩` Enable printing from the specified queue.

`down ⟨queuename⟩` Has the effect of `disable` and `stop` combined.

`up ⟨queuename⟩` Has the effect of `enable` and `start` combined.

`abort ⟨queuename⟩` Has the effect of `down`, but aborts all current print jobs immediately. Aborted jobs are preserved, however, and can be resumed after restarting the queue with `up`.

`root` permissions are required to control printer queues with the above commands. Options can be supplied to `lpc` directly on the command line (as in `lpc status all`). You can also run the program without any options, which starts it in dialog mode — it opens the lpc> command prompt. Then enter the options at the prompt. To leave the program, enter either `quit` or `exit`.

If you were to enter `lpc status all`, the output could look like this:

```
Printer          Printing Spooling Jobs Server Subserver
lp@earth          enabled  enabled    2    123       456
color@earth      disabled disabled    0   none      none
laser@earth      disabled  enabled    8   none      none
```

This gives the following information: Queue `lp` is completely enabled and holds two print jobs, one of which is being printed at the moment. Queue `color`, on the other hand, is completely stopped. Finally, the `laser` queue does not print at the moment, but jobs (there are currently eight of them) are still accepted for the queue and are accumulating in the spooler.

Further information can be obtained from the man page for `lpc` (`man lpc`) and the *LPRng Howto* (`file:/usr/share/doc/packages/lprng/LPRng-HOWTO.html#LPC`).

Managing Remote Queues

For each of the commands explained below, replace the `printserver` parameter with the name or IP address of your print server. For ⟨*queuename*⟩, supply the name of the queue to use on that print server.

Printing Files

With the LPRng printing system installed, the `lpr` command allows you to send files straight to a remote queue. The command syntax is `lpr -P`⟨*queuename*⟩`@printserver` ⟨*file*⟩. As a prerequisite, the print server must be configured to accept remote print jobs on its queues. This is enabled by default with LPRng.

Checking the Status

You can check the status of a queue on a remote host by entering:

```
newbie@earth:~ >   lpq -P⟨queuename⟩@printserver
newbie@earth:~ >   lpq -s -P⟨queuename⟩@printserver
newbie@earth:~ >   lpq -l -P⟨queuename⟩@printserver
newbie@earth:~ >   lpq -L -P⟨queuename⟩@printserver
```

or use

```
newbie@earth:~ >   lpc status ⟨queuename⟩@printserver
newbie@earth:~ >   lpc status all@printserver
```

To list the names of and display status information on all queues of a print server, use either `lpq -s -Pall@printserver` or `lpc status all@printserver`, provided that LPRng is used on the print server, too.

If printing over a remote queue does not work, querying the status of the queues helps determine the cause of the problem. If LPRng is installed on the print server, enter `lpq -L -P`⟨*queuename*⟩`@printserver` to get a detailed status report for troubleshooting.

Removing Jobs from the Queue

The commands

```
newbie@earth:~ >   lprm -P⟨queuename⟩@printserver ⟨jobnumber⟩
newbie@earth:~ >   lprm -P⟨queuename⟩@printserver all
```

```
newbie@earth:~ > lprm -Pall@printserver all
```
delete all print jobs in remote queues that have been issued under your user name. `root` has no special privileges on remote queues. The parameter `all` only works if LPRng is used on the print server host as well.

Using Command-Line Tools for LPRng Troubleshooting

Print jobs are kept in the queue even if you shut down a machine during a printout, and thus they are still there after rebooting. To remove a faulty print job, use the commands described above. Rebooting will not remove them.

For example, it sometimes happens that the host to printer connection suffers some kind of fault, after which the printer is unable to interpret data correctly. This can cause it to spit out large amounts of paper with meaningless babble on it.

1. In the case of an inkjet model, remove all paper from the trays. Open the paper tray if you have a laser model.

2. In most cases, the print job is still in the queue after that. Print jobs are removed from the queue only after all data has been sent to the printer. Check with `lpq` or `lpc status` to see which queue is printing then delete the job in question with `lprm`.

3. The printer may produce some output even after deleting the job from the queue. To stop this, use the commands `fuser -k /dev/lp0` for a printer on the first parallel port or `fuser -k /dev/usb/lp0` for the first USB printer to terminate all processes still using the printer device.

4. Do a complete reset of the printer by switching it off. Wait a few seconds before putting the paper back into the trays and switching the device back on.

The Print Filter of the LPRng and lpdfilter Printing System

The print filter used in conjunction with LPRng is lpdfilter, which is installed as a package with the same name. The following is a detailed description of the steps involved in processing a print job. If you need to know about the inner workings of the print filter, read the scripts powering it (in particular, `/usr/lib/lpdfilter/bin/if`) and probably also follow the steps described in *Troubleshooting Hints for lpdfilter* on page 194.

1. The print filter (`/usr/lib/lpdfilter/bin/if`) determines which options to use as passed to it by the print spooler and specified by the print job's control file. Options for the queue to use are also gathered from `/etc/printcap` and `/etc/lpdfilter/⟨queuename⟩/conf` (where ⟨*queuename*⟩ is the name of the actual queue).

2. The filter determines the file type using the script `/usr/lib/lpdfilter/bin/guess` to run `file` on each file in question. The output of `file` is used to determine the type according to the entries in the file `/etc/lpdfilter/types`.

   - If the `ascii` queue has been specified, the print filter is forced to treat the file as ASCII text.
   - If a queue other than `ascii` has been specified, the printer filter tries to autodetect the file type.

3. The file is converted into a printer-specific data stream according to the file type and the type of queue to use:

   - If the `raw` queue has been specified, print data is usually sent straight to the printer or forwarded to another queue. However, data may also undergo a simple conversion through `recode`, if so specified in `/etc/lpdfilter/⟨queuename⟩/conf`. To have an "absolute" `raw` filter — one that bypasses lpdfilter entirely — remove the line `:if=/usr/lib/lpdfilter/bin/if:\` for the corresponding queue in `/etc/printcap`.
   - If the queue specified is not a `raw` queue:
     (a) If the data is not in PostScript format, it is first converted into PostScript by running `/usr/lib/lpdfilter/filter/type2ps` on it (where `type` is the actual file type determined for the data in question). For example, ASCII text is converted into PostScript with `/usr/lib/lpdfilter/filter/ascii2ps`, which in turn relies on a2ps to obtain the correct character encoding defined for the queue. This ensures that country-specific special characters are printed correctly in plain text files. For details, see the man page for a2ps (`man a2ps`).

(b) If necessary, PostScript data can be converted again if a suitable script is placed in /etc/lpdfilter/⟨*queuename*⟩/pre (where ⟨*queuename*⟩ is the name of the actual queue to use).

(c) PostScript data is converted into another printer language, as needed.

▷ If the printer is PostScript capable, the data is sent directly to the printer (or forwarded to another queue). However, data can be further processed using the Bash functions "duplex" and "tray", which are defined in /usr/lib/lpdfilter/global/functions, to enable duplex printing and paper tray selection through PostScript commands (which requires that the PostScript printer has this functionality).

▷ If the printer is not PostScript capable, Ghostscript uses a driver suitable for the native printer language of the model to produce the printer-specific data that is finally sent to the printer (or forwarded to another queue). Ghostscript-relevant parameters are stored either in the cm line of /etc/printcap or in the file /etc/lpdfilter/⟨*queuename*⟩/upp (where ⟨*queuename*⟩ is the name of the actual queue to use). If so desired, the Ghostscript output can be reformatted again, if a suitable script is placed in /etc/lpdfilter/⟨*queuename*⟩/post (where ⟨*queuename*⟩ is the name of the actual queue to use).

(d) The printer-specific data is transferred to the printer (or to another queue). Control sequences for a specific printer can be sent to the printer both before and after the data stream. These must be specified in /etc/lpdfilter/⟨*queuename*⟩/conf.

Configuration of lpdfilter

Normally, the printing system is configured with YaST2 (as described in *Configuring a Printer with YaST2* on page 165), which includes the setup of lpdfilter. Some of the more special settings, however, can only be changed by editing the configuration files of the print filter by hand. For each queue, a dedicated configuration file is written to /etc/lpdfilter/⟨*queuename*⟩/conf (where ⟨*queuename*⟩ is the name of the actual queue to be used).

Customization of lpdfilter

1. By default, files not in PostScript format are converted into that format with `/usr/lib/lpdfilter/filter/type2ps` (where `type` is the actual type of the file in question). If a suitable script is placed in `/etc/lpdfilter/`⟨*queuename*⟩`/type2ps`, it will be used for the PostScript conversion of the file. The script must be able to accept data on `stdin` and to output data in PostScript format on `stdout`.

2. If so desired, an additional step can be performed to reformat PostScript data, which requires a suitable script be placed in `/etc/lpdfilter/`⟨*queuename*⟩`/pre`. This may be a script to add custom PostScript preloads, for example. The script must be able to accept data on `stdin` and to output data in PostScript format on `stdout`. Some programs to reformat PostScript are included in the package `psutils`. In particular, the program pstops is capable of performing extensive transformations. See the man page for `pstops` (`man pstops`) for details.

3. Special Ghostscript parameters: When writing the configuration with YaST2, Ghostscript parameters are stored in `/etc/lpdfilter/`⟨*queuename*⟩`/upp` (where ⟨*queuename*⟩ is the name of the actual queue to use), but custom Ghostscript parameters can also be added to this file manually. For details on Ghostscript parameters, read *Working with Ghostscript* on page 210.

4. If so desired, data can be reformatted again after conversion by Ghostscript. This requires a suitable script be placed in `/etc/lpdfilter/`⟨*queuename*⟩`/post` (where ⟨*queuename*⟩ is the name of the actual queue to use). This script must be able to accept data on `stdin` and to output a data stream suitable for the specific printer model on `stdout`.

A Hardware-Independent Example

For the purposes of this example, suppose there is a queue called `testqueue`, which we want to configure so ASCII text is printed with line numbers along the left margin. Apart from that, we want to print all files with two pages scaled to fit on one sheet. The scripts `/etc/lpdfilter/testqueue/ascii2ps` and `/etc/lpdfilter/testqueue/pre`, as shown below, would achieve that:

```
#!/bin/bash
cat -n - | a2ps -1 --stdin=' ' -o -
```

File 22: */etc/lpdfilter/testqueue/ascii2ps: ASCII to PostScript Conversion*

```
#!/bin/bash
pstops -q '2:0L@0.6(20cm,2cm)+1L@0.6(20cm,15cm)'
```

File 23: */etc/lpdfilter/test/pre: PostScript Reformatting*

These scripts need to be made executable for all users, which can be achieved with the `chmod` command:

earth:~ # **chmod -v a+rx /etc/lpdfilter/testqueue/ascii2ps**
earth:~ # **chmod -v a+rx /etc/lpdfilter/testqueue/pre**

Reformatting files with `pstops` only works with PostScript files created to allow such transformations, as is usually the case.

Using Custom PostScript Preloads

PostScript preloads are small PostScript files containing commands that are prepended to the print data stream to initialize the printer or the Ghostscript program in the desired way. PostScript preloads are mostly used to enable duplex printing on PostScript printers or to activate a special paper tray. They can also be used for margin and gamma adjustments.

To use preloads, the (PostScript capable) printer or Ghostscript must be able to interpret the special commands. Ghostscript, for instance, does not interpret commands related to duplex printing or paper trays.

For this example, the queue `testqueue` is again used:

Duplex printing To enable or disable duplex printing, create the files `/etc/lpdfilter/testqueue/duplexon.ps` and `/etc/lpdfilter/testqueue/duplexoff.ps` with the following contents:

```
%!PS
statusdict /setduplexmode known
{statusdict begin true setduplexmode end} if {} pop
```

File 24: */etc/lpdfilter/testqueue/duplexon.ps: Enabling Duplex Printing*

```
%!PS
statusdict /setduplexmode known
{statusdict begin false setduplexmode end} if {} pop
```

File 25: */etc/lpdfilter/testqueue/duplexoff.ps: Disabling Duplex Printing*

Paper tray selection To enable the default paper tray 0 or tray number 2, create the files `/etc/lpdfilter/testqueue/tray0.ps` and `/etc/lpdfilter/testqueue/tray2.ps`:

```
%!PS
statusdict /setpapertray known
{statusdict begin 0 setpapertray end} if {} pop
```

File 26: */etc/lpdfilter/testqueue/tray0.ps: Enabling Tray 0*

```
%!PS
statusdict /setpapertray known
{statusdict begin 2 setpapertray end} if {} pop
```

File 27: */etc/lpdfilter/testqueue/tray2.ps: Enabling Tray 2*

Margin settings To adjust margin settings, create a file like `/etc/lpdfilter/testqueue/margin.ps`.

```
%!PS
<<
/.HWMargins [left bottom right top]
/PageSize [width height]
/Margins [left-offset top-offset]
>>
setpagedevice
```

File 28: /etc/lpdfilter/testqueue/margin.ps: Margin Adjustments

The margin settings `left`, `bottom`, `right`, and `top`, as well as the paper size measures `width` and `height`, are specified in points (with one point equaling 1/72 inches or about 0.35 mm). The margin offsets `left-offset` and `top-offset` are specified in pixels, so depend on the resolution of the output device.

If you only want to change the position of the printed area, it is sufficient to create a file like `/etc/lpdfilter/testqueue/offset.ps`.

```
%!PS
<< /Margins [left-offset top-offset] >> setpagedevice
```

*File 29: /etc/lpdfilter/testqueue/offset.ps:
Changing the Position of the Printed Area*

Gamma correction To adjust the gamma distribution between colors, use a file like `/etc/lpdfilter/testqueue/cmyk.ps` or `/etc/lpdfilter/testqueue/rgb.ps`:

```
%!PS
{cyan exp} {magenta exp} {yellow exp} {black exp}
setcolortransfer
```

File 30: /etc/lpdfilter/testqueue/cmyk.ps: CMYK Gamma Correction

```
%!PS
\{red exp\} \{green exp\} \{blue exp\} currenttransfer
setcolortransfer
```

File 31: /etc/lpdfilter/testqueue/rgb.ps: RGB Gamma Correction

You need to know which color model is used by your printer (either CMYK or RGB) to make this work. The values to use for `cyan`, `magenta`, `yellow`, and `black` or for `red`, `green`, and `blue` should be determined through testing. Normally, these should be in the range between 0.001 and 9.999.

To get a rough idea of the effect of the above filtering actions on the output, display them on screen. To see how a sample file looks without gamma correction, enter:

earth:~ # **gs -r60 **
   /usr/share/doc/packages/ghostscript/examples/colorcir.ps

To see how it looks with gamma correction according to the above sample filters:

earth:~ # **gs -r60 /etc/lpdfilter/testqueue/cmyk.ps **
   /usr/share/doc/packages/ghostscript/examples/colorcir.ps

earth:~ # **gs -r60 /etc/lpdfilter/testqueue/rgb.ps **
   /usr/share/doc/packages/ghostscript/examples/colorcir.ps

The above commands must be entered as a single line without the backslash ('\').

End the test by pressing Ctrl + C.

Resetting the Printer To reset the printer to its original state each time, use a file like /etc/lpdfilter/testqueue/reset.ps:

```
%!PS
serverdict begin 0 exitserver
```

File 32: /etc/lpdfilter/testqueue/reset.ps: Printer Reset

To activate one of the above PostScript preloads, create a file similar to /etc/lpdfilter/testqueue/pre:

```
#!/bin/bash
cat /etc/lpdfilter/testqueue/preload.ps -
```

File 33: /etc/lpdfilter/testqueue/pre: Activating a PostScript Preload

In this file, replace preload.ps with the name of your custom preload file. In addition, make this script executable and readable for all users, which can be achieved with chmod in the following way:

```
earth:~ #  chmod -v a+rx /etc/lpdfilter/testqueue/pre
earth:~ #  chmod -v a+r /etc/lpdfilter/testqueue/preload.ps
```

Use the mechanism described above to insert PostScript commands not only before the print data, but also after it. For instance, with a script like /etc/lpdfilter/testqueue/pre, reset the printer to its original state after each print job is finished:

```
%

#!/bin/bash
cat /etc/lpdfilter/testqueue/preload.ps -
/etc/lpdfilter/testqueue/reset.ps
```

File 34: /etc/lpdfilter/testqueue/pre: Inserting a PostScript Preload and a PostScript Reset

A Sample GDI Printer Configuration

This section provides an example for the customized configuration of a gdi print queue. As explained in *The Issue with GDI Printers* on page 163, it is often nearly impossible to make such printers run under Linux. However, special driver programs are available for some GDI models. In most cases, they are designed to run as Ghostscript add-ons with the driver reformatting the Ghostscript output into the printer's own language. Often these drivers make limited use of the printer's functionality, however, allowing only black-and-white printing, for example.

If such a driver is available, Ghostscript can be used with it in the following way (also see *Working with Ghostscript* on page 210):

1. Ghostscript converts the PostScript data into a raster of pixel dots then uses one of its drivers to convert the rasterized image into a format appropriate for the GDI driver at a suitable resolution. Data is then passed to the GDI driver.

2. The rasterized image is converted by the GDI driver into a data format suitable for the printer model.

For the steps described below, it is assumed that a GDI printer driver suitable for SuSE Linux 8.1 is already installed or can be downloaded from the Internet. It is also assumed that the driver works in the way described above.

In some cases, you may need some familiarity with the way source code is handled under Unix or how to unpack such sources (from `.zip` or `.tar.gz` archives or maybe from `.rpm` packages.

After unpacking such an archive, you will often find the latest installation instructions included in some of the files, typically in README or INSTALL, or even in a `doc` subdirectory. If you have downloaded a `.tar.gz` archive, you usually need to compile and install the driver yourself.

For the purposes of the example explained below, the following setup is assumed:

- The driver program has been installed as `/usr/local/bin/printerdriver`.
- The required Ghostscript driver is `pbmraw` with an output resolution of 600 dpi.
- The printer is connected to the first parallel port — `/dev/lp0`.

The Ghostscript driver and the resolution may be different for your printer. Read the documentation included with the driver to find out about these.

First, create the `gdi` queue. To do so, log in as `root` and run lprsetup, as follows:

```
earth:~ # lprsetup -add gdi -lprng -device /dev/lp0 \
    -driver pbmraw -dpi 600 -size a4dj -auto -sf
```

This command must be entered as a single line without the backslash ('\').

Now, create the script `/etc/lpdfilter/gdi/post`:

```
#!/bin/bash
/usr/local/bin/printerdriver ⟨gdi_driver_parameters⟩
```

File 35: /etc/lpdfilter/gdi/post: Running the GDI Printer Driver

Read the documentation of the driver program to find out which options exist for it. Specify them under ⟨*gdi_driver_parameters*⟩ as needed. Make the script executable for all users, and restart the print spooler:

```
earth:~ # chmod -v a+rx /etc/lpdfilter/gdi/post
earth:~ # rclpd stop
earth:~ # rclpd start
```

From now on, users should be able to print with this command:

```
newbie@earth:~ > lpr -Pgdi ⟨filename⟩
```

Troubleshooting Hints for lpdfilter

Enable different debug levels for `lpdfilter` by uncommenting (removing the '#' sign in front of) the corresponding line of the main filter script `/usr/lib/lpdfilter/bin/if`.

```
# DEBUG="off"
# DEBUG="low"
DEBUG="medium"
# DEBUG="high"
```

File 36: /usr/lib/lpdfilter/bin/if: Debug Levels

With `DEBUG="low"` enabled, the program logs its `stderr` output to the file `/tmp/lpdfilter.if-$$.XXXXXX` (where $$ is the process ID and XXXXXX a unique random string).

With `DEBUG="medium"` enabled, the program logs, in addition to its own error output, the `stderr` output of the scripts in `/usr/lib/lpdfilter/filter`, if these scripts are run by `/usr/lib/lpdfilter/bin/if`. The debugging output is written to `/tmp/lpdfilter.name-$$.XXXXXX` (where name is the name of the script that is run and $$.XXXXXX a string composed in the way described above).

With `DEBUG="high"` enabled, all error output is logged as above. Additionally, all output normally destined to the printer is redirected to a log file named `/tmp/lpdfilter.out-$$.XXXXXX` (where $$.XXXXXX is a string composed in the way described above).

To avoid loosing control over the logging activity, you may want to remove the log files with `rm -v /tmp/lpdfilter*` before each new test run.

Custom Print Filters for the LPRng Spooler

The aim of this section is not to show you how to build an alternative to lpdfilter, but rather to lay out the inner workings of the Linux printing engine. We do this by demonstrating how to write a custom printer filter. The example explained below has been kept simple to show just the basic mechanism. This is also the reason why no provisions are made in the filter scripts to do any error checking. The following example is based on the assumption that the printer is connected to the first parallel port (`/dev/lp0`).

Any print filter must accept data from the print spooler on standard input. The filter must then convert the data into the printer-specific format and issue it on standard output. Now the print spooler takes care of the data again and makes sure it is transferred from the filter's standard output to the /dev/lp0 printer device. This is where the Linux kernel comes in: it transfers all data arriving at the printer device to the corresponding IO address (e. g., 0x378). The printer receives this data over the parallel line and interprets it to print accordingly.

On most systems, normal users do not have direct access to the printer device, therefore root permissions are needed for the commands below. Also, in any commands like cat ascii-file >/dev/lp0, replace ascii-file with the name of an existing ASCII file.

Basic Filtering Operations

You can print with the simple command
echo -en "\rHello\r\f" >/dev/lp0. This, however, does not activate the print spooler nor does it use any filter. It writes to the printer device /dev/lp0 directly. The command sends the ASCII signs '\r', 'H', 'e', 'l', 'l', 'o', '\r', and '\f' directly to the printer device. The ASCII character for carriage return, '\r', causes the carriage (printer head) to return to its start position. The ASCII form feed character, '\f', causes the printer to eject the page.

The commands cat ascii-file >/dev/lp0 and
echo -en "\f" >/dev/lp0 still do not activate the spooler or a print filter, but again send characters directly to the printer device /dev/lp0. The first command sends the characters of the ASCII file to the printer. The second one adds a form feed character to eject the page.

Under Linux, ASCII text lines are separated only by a line feed character. By contrast, line breaks under DOS/Windows consist of a line feed ASCII character and a carriage return ASCII character. If you enter the commands

earth:~ # **cat /etc/SuSE-release >/dev/lp0**

earth:~ # **echo -en "\f" >/dev/lp0**

to send an ASCII file directly to the printer, the output will probably look like:

```
SuSE Linux 8.1 (i386)
                VERSION = 8.1
```

The reason is that the printer only performs a line feed but no carriage return (since there is actually no carriage return character between the two lines).

However, it is possible to tell printers to perform both a line feed and a carriage return whenever a line feed character is sent. With the escape sequence `\033&k2G`, all printers that understand the PCL3 language can be reconfigured to perform both a line feed and a carriage return upon receiving an ASCII line feed character. Send the escape sequence to the printer with `echo -en "\033&k2G" >/dev/lp0` after which it should interpret line breaks in the expected way when printing an ASCII file.

Another problem may arise when trying to print country-specific characters, such as umlauts. DOS and Windows use an encoding for these that is different from Linux. Printers are mostly preconfigured for the DOS/Windows environment. As a remedy, enter

```
earth:~ #  cp ascii-file ascii-file.ibmpc
earth:~ #  recode lat1..ibmpc ascii-file.ibmpc
```

to first copy `ascii-file` to `ascii-file.ibmpc` then recode it according to the DOS/Windows standard. After that, the commands

```
earth:~ #  cat ascii-file.ibmpc >/dev/lp0
earth:~ #  echo -en "\f" >/dev/lp0
```

should print both the umlauts and the line breaks in the correct way. Note that the special escape sequence to correct the line break behavior is no longer needed, because the file has been recoded to have DOS/Windows line breaks and umlauts.

To sum this up, the sequence of commands

```
earth:~ #  cp ascii-file ascii-file.ibmpc
earth:~ #  recode lat1..ibmpc ascii-file.ibmpc
earth:~ #  cat ascii-file.ibmpc >/dev/lp0
earth:~ #  echo -en "\f" >/dev/lp0
```

should correctly print an ASCII file on any printer that accepts ASCII directly and is preconfigured for the DOS/Windows character encoding. Having arrived at this point, you may want to automate this by creating a print filter that reformats ASCII text for your printer according to the above steps.

A Sample Custom Print Filter

First, become `root` and create a subdirectory for the custom filter then change into that subdirectory:

```
earth:~ #   mkdir /usr/local/myprinterfilter
earth:~ #   cd /usr/local/myprinterfilter
```

Now, create a Bash script (basically a text file) named `asciifilter` with the contents shown in File 37.

```
#!/bin/bash

# make a temporary file
INPUT="$(mktemp /tmp/asciifilter.$$.XXXXXX)"

# first store everything from stdin in $INPUT
# to have the input as a regular file
cat >$INPUT

# recode the INPUT
recode lat1..ibmpc $INPUT

# add a form feed at the end of $INPUT
# to get the last page out of the printer
echo -en "\f" >>$INPUT

# send $INPUT to stdout
cat $INPUT

# remove the INPUT file
rm $INPUT
```

File 37: /usr/local/myprinterfilter/asciifilter

Make this script executable for all users by entering

```
earth:~ #   chmod -v a+x /usr/local/myprinterfilter/
earth:~ #   chmod -v a+rx /usr/local/myprinterfilter/asciifilter
```

Now use `lprsetup` to create a new print queue (enter `lprsetup --help` to see what the options do). The queue name used in our example is `af`, for "ascii filter."

```
earth:~ #   lprsetup -add af -lprng -device /dev/lp0 -raw -sf
```

In the `af` entry of `/etc/printcap`, look for the `if` line, and replace `/usr/lib/lpdfilter/bin/if` with `/usr/local/myprinterfilter/asciifilter`, such that the complete `af` entry looks similar to File 38.

```
af:\
    :cm=lpdfilter drv= method=raw color=no:\
    :lp=/dev/lp0:\
    :sd=/var/spool/lpd/af:\
    :lf=/var/spool/lpd/af/log:\
    :af=/var/spool/lpd/af/acct:\
    :if=/usr/local/myprinterfilter/asciifilter:\
    :la@:mx#0:\
    :tr=:cl:sh:
```

File 38: /etc/printcap: Custom Filter Entry

Finally, stop then restart the print spooler with

earth:~ # **rclpd stop**

earth:~ # **rclpd start**

From now on, every user should be able to print through the new af queue with the command lpr -Paf ascii-file.

The CUPS Printing System

Naming Conventions

Client or *client program* refers to a program that sends print jobs to a CUPS daemon. A *daemon* is a local service that accepts print jobs either to forward them or to process them locally. *Server* refers to a daemon that is able to deliver print data to one or more printers. Each server functions as a daemon at the same time. In most cases, however, there is no special distinction to make between a server and a daemon, neither from the developer or from the user standpoint.

IPP and Server

Print jobs are sent to servers by CUPS-based programs, such as lpr, kprinter, or xpp, and with the help of the *Internet Printing Protocol*, IPP. IPP is defined in RFC-2910 and RFC-2911 (see http://www.rfc-editor.org/rfc.html). IPP is somewhat similar to HTTP with identical headers but different content data. It also uses its own dedicated communication port 631, which has been registered with IANA (the Internet Authority for Number Allocation).

Print data is transferred to a CUPS daemon, which is also acting as a local server in most cases. Other daemons can be addressed using the environment variable `CUPS_SERVER`.

With the help of the broadcast function of the CUPS daemon, locally managed printers can be made available elsewhere in the network (using UDP port 631). They then appear as print queues on all other daemons configured to accept and use these broadcast packets. This makes it possible to "see" printers on other hosts after booting without configuring them locally, something that may be quite useful in corporate networks. On the other hand, this feature may pose a security risk if the host is connected to the Internet. When enabling printer broadcasting, make sure the daemon broadcasts into the local network only, access is limited to clients on the LAN, and the public IP address (the one used for the Internet connection) is not within the local IP range. Otherwise, remote users relying on the same ISP would be able to "see" and use the broadcast printers as well. In addition to that, such broadcasts mean more network traffic so may increase connection costs. Prevent a local printer from broadcasting IPP packets into the Internet by configuring the SuSEfirewall accordingly. No extra configuration is needed to receive broadcast IPP packets. A broadcast address must only be specified for outgoing print jobs. This may be configured with YaST2, for example.

IPP is used for the communication between a local and a remote CUPS daemon or server. More recent network printers also have built-in support for this protocol (there are a number of models from different makers). Find more information about this on the web pages of manufacturers or in your printer's manual. IPP is also supported by Windows 2000 (and newer Microsoft systems), although originally the implementation was somewhat flawed. These problems may have disappeared or it may be necessary to install a Service Pack to repair them.

Configuration of a CUPS Server

There are many ways to set up a printer with CUPS and to configure the daemon: with command-line tools, with YaST2, with the KDE Control Center, or even through a web browser interface. The following sections are limited to the command-line tools and to YaST2.

> **Caution**
>
> When using the web browser interface for CUPS configuration, be aware that there is a risk of compromising the `root` password. The password will be transmitted as plain text if the URL specified includes the real host name. Therefore, you should always use `http://localhost:631/` as the host address.
>
> **Caution**

For the above reason, the CUPS daemon can only be accessed for administration if addressed as `localhost` (which is identical to the IP address `127.0.0.1`) by default. Entering a different address returns an error message, even if it is valid.

To configure a locally connected printer, first set up a CUPS daemon on the local host. To do so, install package `cups` together with the PPD files provided by SuSE as included in package `cups-drivers` and package `cups-drivers-stp`. After that, start the server (as `root`) with the command `/etc/rc.d/cups restart`. If you do the setup with YaST2, the above steps are already covered by selecting CUPS as the printing system and installing a printer afterwards.

PPD (PostScript Printer Description) files contain options for printer models in the form of a standard set of PostScript commands. They are required for printer installation under CUPS. SuSE Linux comes with precompiled PPD files for many printers from a number of manufacturers. The latter may also offer PPD files for their own PostScript printers on web sites and installation CD's (often in an area called something like "Windows NT Installation").

You may also run a CUPS daemon locally in order to have all printers broadcast by other servers available on the local host (even though no printer is connected locally). You can then use these printers from within KDE applications and OpenOffice, for instance, with very little effort.

Broadcasting can be enabled either with YaST2 or in the file `/etc/cups/cupsd.conf`, by setting the `Browsing` directive to `On` (the default) and the `BrowseAddress` directive to a sensible value, for instance `192.168.255.255`. After that, you still need to tell the CUPS daemon explicitly to grant access to incoming packets, either under `<Location /printers>`, or preferably under `<Location />`, where you would have to include a line like `Allow From some-host.mydomain` (see file: `/usr/share/doc/packages/cups/sam.html`). When you are finished editing the file, you should tell the daemon to re-read its configuration, by entering the command `/etc/rc.d/cups reload` as `root`.

Network Printers

Network printers are either printers which have a built-in print server interface (such as the JetDirect interface in some HP printers), or printers connected to a print server box, or to a router box which is also enabled as a print server. Windows machines offering so-called printer shares are not print servers in the strict sense (though CUPS can handle them easily, and in a way similar to print servers).

In most cases, a network printer supports the LPD protocol which uses port 515 for communications. You can check lpd availability with the command:

`netcat -z hostname.domain 515 && echo ok || echo failed`

If such a server is available, CUPS can be configured to access it under a *device URI*, an address which has the form of: `lpd://server/queue`. You can read about the concept of device URI's in `file:/usr/share/doc/packages/cups/sam.html`.

However, you should probably not use the LPD protocol for a network printer anyway, but rather the printer's built-in port 9100 if available (HP, Kyocera, and many others), or port 35 (QMS). In this case, the device URI must have the form of `socket://server:port/`.

To use printers made available through Windows, you have to install package `samba-client` first and configure this package, i.e. you need to enable the correct "Workgroup", etc. A device URI for Windows printers may be specified in several ways, but the most frequent one has this syntax: `smb://user:password@host/printer`. For other configurations, see `file:/usr/share/doc/packages/cups/sam.html`, as well as the the man page for `smbspool` (`man smbspool`).

If you have a small network consisting of several (Linux) machines, and have set up a print server for it, you will want to avoid configuring the printer for each and every client host. You can achieve this by enabling the broadcast function of the daemon (see above). Thus, when you modify the configuration (for instance in order to use the new standard paper size `Letter`), it will be sufficient to do this once on the server side (also see Section *Specifying Options for Queues* on page 207). Even though the configuration is saved locally on the server side, they are propagated to all clients in the network, with the help of the CUPS tools and the IPP protocol.

Internal CUPS Print Job Processing

Conversion into PostScript

Basically the CUPS daemon should be able to handle any file type, though PostScript is always the safest bet. CUPS processes non-PostScript files by identifying the file type according to `/etc/cups/mime.types` first, and then converting the file into PostScript, by calling the appropriate conversion tool for it, as defined in `/etc/cups/mime.convs`. With CUPS, files are converted into PostScript on the server side rather than on the client side (as is the case with the traditional LPR type spoolers). This feature was introduced to ensure that special conversion operations necessary for a particular printer model are only performed on the corresponding server machine, which has both advantages and disadvantages.

Accounting

After conversion into PostScript, CUPS calculates the number of pages for each print job. This is done with the help of *pstops* (an internal version of the program, with the location `/usr/lib/cups/filter/pstops`). The accounting data for print jobs are written to `/var/log/cups/page_log`.

In the latter file, each line contains the following information:

- printer name (for example `lp`)
- user name (for example `root`)
- job number
- date and time (in square brackets)
- current page number
- number of copies

Other Filtering Programs

CUPS may also use other, special filters, if the corresponding printing options have been enabled. These are the most important ones:

psselect: Allows limiting the printout to certain pages of a document.

ps-n-up: Allows the printing of several pages on one sheet.

Read `file:/usr/share/doc/packages/cups/sum.html` on how to enable the various options.

Conversion into the Printer-Specific Language

The next step in the CUPS printing mechanism is the conversion into the printer-specific data format. To do so, CUPS calls a filter (e.g. `/usr/lib/cups/filter/cupsomatic`) which should be specified in the PPD file installed for the printer model. If this is not the case, the system assumes that the printer is a PostScript capable model. All device-dependent printing options, such as the resolution and paper size, are processed by this script.

Note that writing one's own printer-specific filter script is not a trivial task and therefore best left to a specialist.

Transferring Data to the Printer

As the final step, CUPS calls one of its backends. A backend is a special filter which transfers print data to a device, or to a network printer (see `file:/usr/share/doc/packages/cups/overview.html`). The backend maintains the communication with the device or network printer (as specified through a device URI during configuration). If the backend is `usb`, for instance, CUPS calls the program `/usr/lib/cups/backend/usb`, which in turn opens (and locks) the corresponding USB device file, initializes it, and passes on the data coming from the print filter. When the job is finished, the backend closes the device and unlocks it.

At the time of this writing, there are the following backends: `parallel`, `serial`, `usb`, `ipp`, `lpd`, `http`, `socket` (included in package `cups`). There are also `canon` and `epson` (included in `cups-drivers-stp`), and `smb` (included in `samba-client`).

Filterless Printing

If you want to print files without any filtering, you can use the command `lpr` with its `-l` option, or alternatively use the `lp` command with the `-oraw` option. However, printers will mostly not function when doing so, because the Ghostscript interpreter is not called (by `cupsomatic`, for instance), or due to the lack of some other important filtering action. – Filtering may also be disabled with other CUPS tools, which have similar options to achieve this.

Tips & Tricks

OpenOffice

When printing from OpenOffice applications, CUPS is supported such that a running CUPS daemon is autodetected and queried for available printers and options (this is different from StarOffice 5.2, where it was still necessary to perform a setup for each printer). An extra CUPS setup from within OpenOffice should therefore not be necessary anymore.

On the other hand, if you want to use special CUPS programs for printing from OpenOffice, you should not rely on graphical tools (such as `kprinter` or `xpp`) to trigger the actual print command. Graphical tools may insist on opening their own dialog windows, and thus cause OpenOffice to hang whenever they are activated.

Printing to or from Windows Machines

Printers connected to a Windows machine can be addressed through a device URI such as `smb://server/printer` (see above).

In the opposite case, i.e. if you want to print from a Windows machine to a CUPS server, change the Samba configuration file `/etc/samba/smb.conf` to include the entry `printing = cups` or `printing = CUPS`, and then restart the smb server. See `file:/usr/share/doc/packages/cups/sam.html` for details.

Setting up a Raw Printer

A raw printer can be set up by leaving out the PPD file during configuration, which effectively removes all filtering and accounting features from CUPS. However, this also means that data must already be available in the printer-specific format. Tests at SuSE have shown that this often does not work very well, therefore we currently cannot recommend this setup.

Custom Printer Options

Custom printer options (e.g. a different default resolution) can be stored in the file `~/.lpoptions`. But if the corresponding printer is removed on the server side, several CUPS tools such as `kprinter` and `xpp` will assume that the printer is still there, and thus allow you to select it. This will lead to a number of problems, therefore you should probably open `~/.lpoptions` and remove the "offending" lines from the file, at least if you are experienced enough with the printing system.

Compatibility with LPR Type Printing Systems

CUPS can be configured to accept print jobs from LPR type printing systems. You can either use YaST2 to make the necessary changes to `/etc/inetd`.

conf, or use some other means to remove the comment signs from the beginning of the `printer` line in `/etc/inetd.conf`. The following commands, for instance, would allow you to do that, providing you are logged in as `root`:

```
perl -pi -e 's:^\# (printer):$1:' /etc/inetd.conf
rcinetd reload
```

To switch back to LPRng, you need to re-insert the comment sign, which can be achieved with:

```
perl -pi -e 's:^(printer):# $1:' /etc/inetd.conf
rcinetd reload
```

Command-Line Tools for the CUPS Printing System

The command-line tools of the CUPS printing system, as well as their manual pages, are included in package `cups-client`. Further documentation is provided by the package `cups` package and installed in `/usr/share/doc/packages/cups`, in particular the *CUPS Software Users Manual*, found under `file:/usr/share/doc/packages/cups/sum.html`
and the *CUPS Software Administrators Manual*, under `file:/usr/share/doc/packages/cups/sam.html`.
If a CUPS daemon runs locally on your host, you should also be able to access the documentation under
`http://localhost:631/documentation.html`.

As a general rule, it is useful to remember that CUPS command-line tools sometimes require options to be supplied in a certain order. Consult the corresponding manual pages if you are unsure about specific options.

Managing Local Queues

Printing Files

To print a file, you can enter a "System V style" print command like

```
newbie@earth:~ >  lp -d ⟨queuename⟩ ⟨file⟩
```

or a "Berkeley style" command like

`newbie@earth:~ >` **`lpr -P⟨queuename⟩ ⟨file⟩`**

Additional information can be obtained with the the man page for `lpr` (man `lpr`) and the the man page for `lp` (man `lp`), as well as in the Section "Using the Printing System" of the *CUPS Software Users Manual*, under `file:/usr/share/doc/packages/cups/sum.html#USING_SYSTEM`.

The `-o` parameter allows you to specify a number of important options, some of which will directly influence the type of printout. More information is available with the the man page for `lpr` (man `lpr`) and the the man page for `lp` (man `lp`), as well as in the Section "Standard Printer Options" of the *CUPS Software Users Manual*, under `file:/usr/share/doc/packages/cups/sum.html#STANDARD_OPTIONS`.

Checking the Status

To check the status of a queue, you can enter the "System V style" command

`newbie@earth:~ >` **`lpstat -o ⟨queuename⟩ -p ⟨queuename⟩`**

or the "Berkeley style" command

`newbie@earth:~ >` **`lpq -P⟨queuename⟩`**

If you do not specify a queue name, the commands will display information on all queues. With `lpstat -o`, the output will show all active print jobs in the form of a ⟨queuename⟩-⟨jobnumber⟩ listing.

With `lpstat -l -o ⟨queuename⟩ -p ⟨queuename⟩`, the output will be more verbose, and `lpstat -t` or `lpstat -l -t` display the maximum amount of available information.

For additional information, consult the the man page for `lpq` (man `lpq`) and the the man page for `lpstat` (man `lpstat`), and read the Section "Using the Printing System" of the *CUPS Software Users Manual*, under `file:/usr/share/doc/packages/cups/sum.html#USING_SYSTEM`.

Removing Jobs from the Queue

You can enter the "System V style" command

`newbie@earth:~ >` **`cancel ⟨queuename⟩-⟨jobnumber⟩`**

or the "Berkeley style" command

`newbie@earth:~ >` **`lprm -P⟨queuename⟩ ⟨jobnumber⟩`**

to remove the job with the specified number from the specified queue.

For additional information, consult the the man page for `lprm` (`man lprm`) and the the man page for `cancel` (`man cancel`), and read the Section "Using the Printing System" of the *CUPS Software Users Manual*, under: `file:/usr/share/doc/packages/cups/sum.html#USING_SYSTEM`.

Specifying Options for Queues

To see how to specify hardware-independent options affecting the type of printout, you may want to read the Section "Standard Printer Options" in the *CUPS Software Users Manual*, under
`file:/usr/share/doc/packages/cups/sum.html#STANDARD_OPTIONS`.
The Section "Saving Printer Options and Defaults", which is found under `file:/usr/share/doc/packages/cups/sum.html#SAVING_OPTIONS`, explains how to save option settings.

Printer-specific options affecting the type of printout are stored in the PPD file for the queue in question. They can be read out with the command:

`newbie@earth:~ >` **`lpoptions -p ⟨queuename⟩ -l`**

The output will have the following form:

```
option/text: value value value ...
```

The currently active setting is marked with an asterix (`'*'`) to the left, for example:

```
PageSize/Page Size: A3 *A4 A5 Legal Letter
Resolution/Resolution: 150 *300 600
```

According to the above output, the `PageSize` is set to `A4`, and the `Resolution` to `300` dpi.

The command

`newbie@earth:~ >` **`lpoptions -p ⟨queuename⟩ -o option=value`**

SuSE Linux – Administration Guide   207

would change the value for the given option. With the above sample settings in mind, one could use the command

newbie@earth:~ > **lpoptions -p** *⟨queuename⟩* **-o PageSize=Letter**

to set the paper size for the specified queue to Letter.

If the above lpoptions command is entered by a normal user, the new settings are stored for that user only, in the file ~/.lpoptions.

By contrast, if the lpoptions command is entered by root, the settings specified will be stored in /etc/cups/lpoptions, and thus become the default for all local users of the queue. The PPD file is not touched by this, though.

However, if (and only if) you change the contents of a PPD file for a given queue, the new settings will apply to all users in the local network who print through this queue. The system administrator can change the defaults of a PPD file with a command like:

earth:~ # **lpadmin -p** *⟨queuename⟩* **-o option=value**

Accordingly, to change the default paper size of the sample queue to Letter for all users in the local network, one would enter the command:

earth:~ # **lpadmin -p** *⟨queuename⟩* **-o PageSize=Letter**

Managing Remote Queues

In the examples below, replace printserver with the name or the IP address of your actual print server, and queuename with the name of the remote queue on the print server.

Given that this section only covers the basic commands, you may also want to read Section *Managing Local Queues* on page 205 which explains more options and includes pointers to additional sources of information.

Printing Files

You can print a file either with a "System V style" command like

newbie@earth:~ > **lp -d** *⟨queuename⟩* **-h printserver** *⟨filename⟩*

or with a "Berkeley style" command like

```
newbie@earth:~ > lpr -P⟨queuename⟩@printserver ⟨filename⟩
```

which in both cases starts a print job for the specified queue on the given print server.

Naturally the print server must have been configured to accept jobs on its queues from your host. In its default configuration, the CUPS daemon does not allow this, but you can easily enable the feature with the help of the YaST2 printer configuration module, under the submenu entry which lets you change the CUPS server settings.

Checking the Status

You can check the status of a remote queue on a print server with this "System V style" command:

```
newbie@earth:~ > lpstat -h printserver -o ⟨queuename⟩ -p
    ⟨queuename⟩
```

Removing Jobs from the Queue

With the "System V style" command

```
newbie@earth:~ > cancel -h printserver ⟨queuename⟩-⟨jobnumber⟩
```

you can remove the print job with the specified job number from the specified queue on the given print server.

Using Command-Line Tools for CUPS Troubleshooting

In the case of a broken print job, the troubleshooting procedure is basically the same as the one described in Section *Using Command-Line Tools for LPRng Troubleshooting* on page 184, with the difference that CUPS requires different commands for the second step:

1. Remove all paper from the printer so that the printer stops working.

2. Check which queue is currently printing, by entering `lpstat -o` (or `lpstat -h printserver -o`, respectively), then remove the trouble-making print job with `cancel ⟨queuename⟩-⟨jobnumber⟩` (or with `cancel -h printserver ⟨queuename⟩-⟨jobnumber⟩`, respectively).

3. If necessary, use the `fuser` command to kill leftover programs.

4. Do a complete reset of the printer.

Working with Ghostscript

Ghostscript is a program which accepts PostScript and PDF files as input, and converts them into several other formats. Ghostscript includes a number of drivers to achieve this; these are sometimes also referred to as "devices".

Ghostscript converts files in two steps:

1. PostScript data are rasterized, i.e.the graphical image is broken up into a fine-grained raster of pixel dots. This step is performed independently from the Ghostscript driver used later on. The finer the raster (or in other words: the higher the resolution), the higher the output quality. On the other hand, doubling the resolution both horizontally and vertically (for instance) means that the number of pixels has to quadruple. Accordingly, the computer will need four times the CPU time and amount of memory to double the resolution.
2. The dot matrix which makes up the image is converted into the desired format (a printer language, for instance), with the help of a Ghostscript driver.

Ghostscript is not only used as a printer driver solution; it can also process PostScript files to display them on screen, or convert them into PDF documents.

To display PostScript files on screen, you should probably use the program gv (rather than relying on bare Ghostscript commands), which gives you a more convenient graphical interface to work with Ghostscript.

Ghostscript is a very big program package and has a large number of command-line options. Apart from the information available with the the man page for gs (`man gs`), the most important part of the documentation is the list of Ghostscript drivers, which is found in

`file:/usr/share/doc/packages/ghostscript/catalog.devices`

as well as the following files:

```
file:/usr/share/doc/packages/ghostscript/doc/index.html
file:/usr/share/doc/packages/ghostscript/doc/Use.htm
file:/usr/share/doc/packages/ghostscript/doc/Devices.htm
file:/usr/share/doc/packages/ghostscript/doc/hpdj/gs-hpdj.txt
file:/usr/share/doc/packages/ghostscript/doc/hpijs/hpijs_readme.html
file:/usr/share/doc/packages/ghostscript/doc/stp/README
```

When executed from the command line, Ghostscript processes any options and then presents you with its own GS> prompt. You can exit from this dialog mode by entering `quit`.

If you enter `gs -h`, Ghostscript will display its most important options and list the available drivers, or "devices". This listing, however, only includes generic driver names, even for drivers which support many different models, such as `uniprint` or `stp`. The parameter files for `uniprint` and the models supported by `stp` are explicitly named in `/usr/share/doc/packages/ghostscript/catalog.devices`.

Sample Operations with Ghostscript

You can find a number of PostScript examples in the directory `file:/usr/share/doc/packages/ghostscript/examples`.

The "color circle" in `/usr/share/doc/packages/ghostscript/examples/colorcir.ps`, for instance, is well suited for test printouts.

Displaying PostScript under X

Under X, the graphical environment, you can use `gs` to view a PostScript file on screen. To do so, enter the following command as a single line, omitting the backslash ('\'):

```
newbie@earth:~ > gs -r60 \
    /usr/share/doc/packages/ghostscript/examples/colorcir.ps
```

In the above command, the `-r` options specifies the resolution, which must be appropriate for the output device (printer or screen). You can test the effect of this option by specifying a different value, for instance `-r30`. To close the PostScript window, press Ctrl + C in the terminal window from which `gs` was started.

Conversion into PCL5e

The conversion of a PostScript file into the printer-specific format of a PCL5e or PCL6 printer can be achieved with a command like

```
newbie@earth:~ > gs -q -dNOPAUSE -dSAFER -
    sOutputFile=/tmp/out.prn \
    -sDEVICE=ljet4 -r300x300 \
    /usr/share/doc/packages/ghostscript/examples/colorcir.ps \
    quit.ps
```

Again the command must be entered as a single line and without any backslash (`'\'`). Also, with this command it is assumed that the file `/tmp/out.prn` does not exist yet.

Conversion into PCL3

To convert a PostScript file into the printer-specific format of a PCL3 printer, you can enter one of the following commands, for example:

```
newbie@earth:~ >   gs -q -dNOPAUSE -dSAFER -
     sOutputFile=/tmp/out.prn \
     -sDEVICE=deskjet -r300x300 \
     /usr/share/doc/packages/ghostscript/examples/colorcir.ps \
     quit.ps

newbie@earth:~ >   gs -q -dNOPAUSE -dSAFER -
     sOutputFile=/tmp/out.prn \
     -sDEVICE=hpdj -r300x300 \
     -sModel=500 -sColorMode=mono -dCompressionMethod=0 \
     /usr/share/doc/packages/ghostscript/examples/colorcir.ps \
     quit.ps

newbie@earth:~ >   gs -q -dNOPAUSE -dSAFER -
     sOutputFile=/tmp/out.prn \
     -sDEVICE=cdjmono -r300x300 \
     /usr/share/doc/packages/ghostscript/examples/colorcir.ps \
     quit.ps

newbie@earth:~ >   gs -q -dNOPAUSE -dSAFER -
     sOutputFile=/tmp/out.prn \
     -sDEVICE=cdj500 -r300x300 \
     /usr/share/doc/packages/ghostscript/examples/colorcir.ps \
     quit.ps

newbie@earth:~ >   gs -q -dNOPAUSE -dSAFER -
     sOutputFile=/tmp/out.prn \
     -sDEVICE=cdj550 -r300x300 \
     /usr/share/doc/packages/ghostscript/examples/colorcir.ps \
     quit.ps
```

(Again each of the above commands must be entered as a single line, without the backslashes.)

Conversion into ESC/P, ESC/P2, or ESC/P Raster

These are some sample commands to convert a PostScript file into the printer-specific format of an ESC/P2, ESC/P, or ESC/P raster printer:

```
newbie@earth:~ >  gs -q -dNOPAUSE -dSAFER -
    sOutputFile=/tmp/out.prn \
    @stcany.upp \
    /usr/share/doc/packages/ghostscript/examples/colorcir.ps \
    quit.ps

newbie@earth:~ >  gs -q -dNOPAUSE -dSAFER -
    sOutputFile=/tmp/out.prn \
    -sDEVICE=stcolor -r360x360 \
    -dBitsPerPixel=1 -sDithering=gsmono -dnoWeave \
    -sOutputCode=plain \
    /usr/share/doc/packages/ghostscript/examples/colorcir.ps \
    quit.ps
```

The above commands also show that the `uniprint` Ghostscript driver, which is called through a parameter file (`stcany.upp` in our example), requires a different command syntax, as compared to "regular" Ghostscript drivers. Since all driver options are stored in the `uniprint` parameter file, they do not have to be specified on the Ghostscript command line itself.

Sending the Output Directly to the Printer

With each of the above commands, the output is written in the corresponding printer language, and stored in the file `/temp/out.prn`. This file can be sent directly to the printer by `root` (i.e. without the use of a print spooler or any filtering). For a printer connected to the first parallel port, this can be achieved with the command

```
earth:~ #  cat /tmp/out.prn >/dev/lp0
```

Working with a2ps

Before an ASCII file can be printed through Ghostscript, it needs to be converted into PostScript, since this is the input format that Ghostscript expects. This conversion can be achieved with a2ps.

The a2ps program is a powerful, versatile tool which lets you convert simple text files into high-quality PostScript output, and it comes with a large number of command-line options. You can learn about these with the the man page for a2ps (man a2ps), or read the full documentation of a2ps as an info page.

Sample Operations with a2ps

Using a2ps to Prepare a Text File for Printing

As a first example, a2ps can be used to convert a text file into PostScript, with two pages scaled down so that they fit on one sheet. This can be achieved with the command:

```
newbie@earth:~ >   a2ps -2 --medium=A4dj --output=/tmp/out.ps
        textfile
```

The output of a2ps can then be displayed under X with

```
newbie@earth:~ >   gs -r60 /tmp/out.ps
```

to get a preview of the printout. If the printout comprises more than one sheet, you will need to hit ⏎ in the terminal window from which gs was started, in order to scroll down to the next page. To exit gs, enter Ctrl + C.

You can now take the output of a2ps and convert it into your printer's language, by entering:

```
newbie@earth:~ >   gs -q -dNOPAUSE -dSAFER -
        sOutputFile=/tmp/out.prn \
        ⟨driverparameters⟩ /tmp/out.ps quit.ps
```

In the above command, specify your own driver parameters under ⟨driverparameters⟩, as described in the previous section.

Provided that you are logged in as root, you can send the output of Ghostscript directly to the printer (without relying on a spooler or any further filtering) with the command:

```
earth:~ #   cat /tmp/out.prn >/dev/lp0
```

For the above command it is assumed that the printer is connected to the first parallel port, or /dev/lp0.

Printing Business Cards

To demonstrate the possibilities of a2ps, in this section we show you how to use the program in order to make and print a stack of simple business cards.

First we create a plain text file called card which contains the necessary data:

```
Title FirstName LastName
Street
PostalCode City
E-mail: user@domain
Phone: AreaCode-Number-Extension
```

File 39: card: Business Card Data File

We also need to append a form feed character (\f) to this, to ensure that a2ps treats each card as an individual page.

```
newbie@earth:~ >  echo -en "\f" >>card
```

Now we multiply the contents of the file to have a set of 10 cards in one `cards` file:

```
newbie@earth:~ >  for i in $(seq 1 10) ; do cat card >>cards ;
    done
```

This command allows us to find out how many characters the longest line of `cards` contains:

```
newbie@earth:~ >  cat cards | wc -L
```

Now it is time to do the actual PostScript conversion. We want 10 cards per sheet, printed in two columns with 5 cards each, with a box or frame around them. We also want to use the maximum font size, as allowed by the longest line, and no additional header or footer lines. All this can be done with the command:

```
newbie@earth:~ >  a2ps -i -j --medium=a4dj --columns=2 --rows=5 \
    --no-header --chars-per-line=number --output=cards.ps cards
```

This command must be entered on a single line and without the backslash ('\'). Also, for `number` you need to fill in the number of characters in the longest line, as determined above.

Finally, we are able to preview the printout with `gs -r60 cards.ps` and then send the output to the printer, as described in the previous section. Or we could print the file in the normal way (i.e. relying on the printing system) with `lpr card.ps`.

Reformatting PostScript with psutils

To use one of the reformatting programs described below, you should generate a PostScript input file, by printing to (or saving to) a file such as /tmp/

in.ps from within your application. You can check with file /tmp/in.ps to see whether the generated file is really in PostScript format.

The package psutils includes a number of programs to reformat PostScript documents. The program pstops, in particular, allows you to perform extensive transformations. Details can be obtained with the the man page for pstops (man pstops). Given that the package psutils is not included in the standard setup of SuSE Linux, you may still need to install it.

The following commands will only work if the application program has created a PostScript file which is "good for" such reformatting operations. This should mostly be the case, but there are some applications which cannot generate PostScript files in the required way.

psnup

The command

newbie@earth:~ > **psnup -2 /tmp/in.ps /tmp/out.ps**

takes /tmp/in.ps as its input and transforms it into the output file /tmp/out.ps in such a way that two pages are printed side by side on one sheet. Note however that with the contents of two pages being included on one, the complexity of the resulting document is much higher, and some PostScript printers may fail to print it, especially if they are equipped with only a small amount of standard memory.

pstops

The program pstops allows you to change the size and positioning of PostScript documents. For example, the command

newbie@earth:~ > **pstops '1:0@0.8(2cm,3cm)' /tmp/in.ps /tmp/out.ps**

scales the document by a factor of 0.8, which effectively scales down an A4 page from about 21x30 cm to about 17x24 cm. This in turn leaves an additional margin of about 4 cm on the right and 6 cm on the top. Therefore, the document is also shifted by 2 cm towards the right and 3 cm towards the top, in order to get roughly the same margins everywhere.

This pstops command shrinks the page by quite an amount and also provides for relatively wide margins, so it should generate a page which is almost always printable – even with those applications which are far too optimistic about the limits set by your printer (i.e. you can use a command like the above for those cases where the application's printer output in /etc/in.ps is too large for the printable area).

As another example, the commands

```
newbie@earth:~ > pstops '1:0@0.8(2cm,3cm)' /tmp/in.ps
    /tmp/out1.ps
newbie@earth:~ > psnup -2 /tmp/out1.ps /tmp/out.ps
```

place two heavily scaled-down pages on one sheet, leaving quite a lot of space between them.

To improve this, we need to include instructions to position each of the pages individually:

```
newbie@earth:~ > pstops '2:0L@0.6(20cm,2cm)+1L@0.6(20cm,15cm)' \
    /tmp/in.ps /tmp/out.ps
```

The above command needs to be entered as a single line, without the '\'.

The following is a step-by-step explanation of the page specifications as expressed by pstops '2:0L@0.6(20cm,2cm)+1L@0.6(20cm,15cm)':

2:0 ... +1 Two pages are merged into one, and pages are counted modulo 2, which means that each page gets the logical number 0 or 1, respectively.

0L@0.6(20cm,2cm) Pages with the logical number 0 are turned to the left by 90 degrees, and scaled down by a factor of 0.6. They are then shifted to the right by 20 cm and to the top by 2 cm.

1L@0.6(20cm,15cm) To match the above reformatting, pages with the logical number 1 are turned to the left by 90 degrees, and scaled down by a factor of 0.6. They are then shifted to the right by 20 cm and to the top by 15 cm.

Visualization of the pstops Example

In the case of PostScript files, the origin of coordinates is located in the bottom left corner of a page in normal position, as indicated by the '+'.

This is a page with the logical number 0 which has three lines of text:

After turning it to the left by 90 degrees, it looks like this:

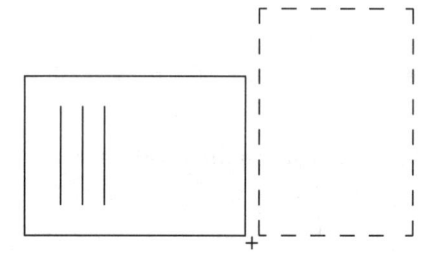

Now we scale it by a factor of 0.6:

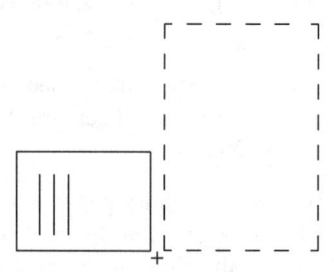

Finally, it gets moved to the right by 20 cm and up by 2 cm:

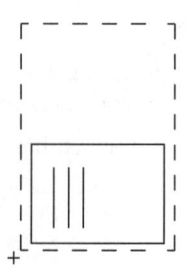

This is merged with the page that has the logical number 1, with two lines of text on it:

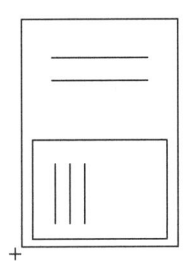

Now page 1 gets turned by 90 degrees to the left:

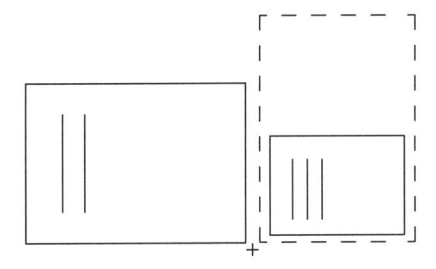

After scaling by factor 0.6, it looks like this:

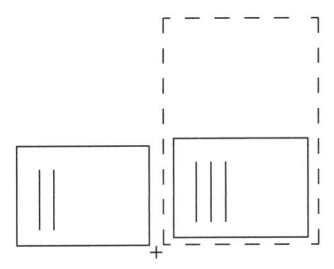

To finish up, page 1 is moved 20 cm to the right and 15 cm to the top:

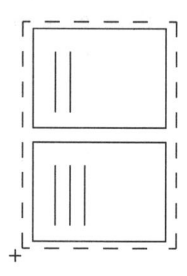

psselect

The `psselect` program allows you to select individual pages from a document.

With the command

newbie@earth:~ > **psselect -p2,3,4,5 /tmp/in.ps /tmp/out.ps**

or even

newbie@earth:~ > **psselect -p2-5 /tmp/in.ps /tmp/out.ps**

you can select pages 2, 3, 4, and 5 from the document in /tmp/in.ps, and write the selection into /tmp/out.ps.

While the commands

newbie@earth:~ > **psselect -p1,2,3,4 /tmp/in.ps /tmp/out.ps**

and

newbie@earth:~ > **psselect -p-4 /tmp/in.ps /tmp/out.ps**

select pages 1, 2, 3, and 4, with the command

newbie@earth:~ > **psselect -p2,2,2,5,5 /tmp/in.ps /tmp/out.ps**

page 2 gets selected three times and page 5 twice. The command

newbie@earth:~ > **psselect -p3- /tmp/in.ps /tmp/out.ps**

selects everything from page 3 up to the end, and

newbie@earth:~ > **psselect -p_1 /tmp/in.ps /tmp/out.ps**

only selects the last page. With

```
newbie@earth:~ >  psselect -p_4-_2 /tmp/in.ps /tmp/out.ps
```

you can select everything from the last but four to the last but two pages.
The command

```
newbie@earth:~ >  psselect -r -p3-5 /tmp/in.ps /tmp/out.ps
```

selects pages 3, 4, and 5 from `/tmp/in.ps` and writes them into `/tmp/out.ps` in the opposite order. Finally, the command

```
newbie@earth:~ >  psselect -r -p- /tmp/in.ps /tmp/out.ps
```

takes all pages and writes them to the output file in the opposite order.

Using Ghostscript to View the Output

On a graphical display, the PostScript file `/tmp/out.ps` can be viewed with `gs -r60 /tmp/out.ps`. You can scroll through the pages by pressing ⏎ in the terminal window from which you have started Gnostscript, and terminate with Ctrl + c.

As a graphical front-end for Ghostscript, you can use `gv`. To view the above-mentioned output file, for instance, enter `gv /tmp/out.ps`. The program is especially useful whenever there is a need to zoom in or out a document, or to view it in landscape orientation (though this has no effect on the file contents). It can also be used to select individual pages, which then can be printed directly from within `gv`.

ASCII Text Encoding

In plain text files, each character is represented as a certain numeric code. Characters and their matching codes are defined in code tables. Depending on the code table(s) used by an application and by the print filter, the same code may be represented as one character on the screen and as another one when printed.

Standard character sets only comprise the range from code 0 to code 255.

Of these, codes 0 through 127 represent the so-called pure ASCII set which is identical for every encoding (it comprises all "normal" letters as well as digits and some special characters, but none of the country-specific special characters).

Codes 128 through 255 of the ASCII set are reserved for country-specific special characters (e. g. umlauts).

However, the number of special characters in different languages is much bigger than 128. Therefore, codes 128 to 255 are not the same for each country. Rather, the same code may represent different country-specific characters, depending on the language being used.

The codes for Western European languages are defined by ISO-8859-1 (also called Latin 1), while the ISO-8859-2 encoding (alias Latin 2) defines the character sets for Central and Eastern European languages. Code 241 (octal), for instance, is defined as the (Spanish) inverted exclamation mark in ISO-8859-1, but the same code 241 is defined as an uppercase A with an ogonek in ISO-8859-2. The ISO-8859-15 encoding is basically the same as ISO-8859-1, but among other things it includes the Euro currency sign, defined as code 244 (octal). As an aside, German umlauts are defined the same way in ISO-8859-1 and ISO-8859-2. So if you happen to write in German, it would not matter which of these encodings are used, as long as you do not need the Euro sign.

A Sample Text

The commands below must be entered as a single line, and without any of the backslashes (`\`) if (and *only if*) they are at the end of line.

Create a sample text file with:

```
newbie@earth:~ >   echo -en "\rCode 241(octal):   \
    \241\r\nCode 244(octal):    \244\r\f" >example
```

Visualizing the Sample with Different Encodings

Under X, enter these commands to open three terminals:

```
newbie@earth:~ >   xterm -fn -*-*-*-*-*-*-14-*-*-*-*-*-iso8859-1 \
    -title iso8859-1 &
newbie@earth:~ >   xterm -fn -*-*-*-*-*-*-14-*-*-*-*-*-iso8859-15 \
    -title iso8859-15 &
newbie@earth:~ >   xterm -fn -*-*-*-*-*-*-14-*-*-*-*-*-iso8859-2 \
    -title iso8859-2 &
```

Now you can use the terminals to display the sample file in each of them, with:

```
newbie@earth:~ >   cat example
```

The "iso8859-1" terminal should display code 241 as the inverted (Spanish) exclamation mark, and code 244 as the general currency symbol.

The "iso8859-15" terminal should display code 241 as the inverted (Spanish) exclamation mark, and code 244 as the Euro symbol.

The "iso8859-2" terminal should display code 241 as an uppercase A with an ogonek, and code 244 as the general currency symbol.

Due to the fact that character encodings are defined as fixed sets, it is not possible to combine all the different country-specific characters with each other in an arbitrary way. For instance, the A with an ogonek cannot be used together with the Euro symbol in one and the same text file.

To obtain more information (including a correct representation of each character), consult the corresponding man page in each terminal, i.e. the the man page for `iso_8859-1` (`man iso_8859-1`) in the "iso8859-1" terminal, the the man page for `iso_8859-15` (`man iso_8859-15`) in the "iso8859-15" terminal, and the the man page for `iso_8859-2` (`man iso_8859-2`) in the "iso8859-2" terminal.

Printing the Sample with Different Encodings

When printed, ASCII text files such as the `example` file are treated in a similar way, i.e. according to the encoding which has been set for the print queue being used. However, word processor documents should not be affected by this, because their print output is in PostScript format (and not ASCII).

Consequently, when printing the above `example` file, characters will be represented in line with the encoding which has been set for ASCII files in your printing system.

But you can also convert the `example` file into PostScript beforehand, in order to change the character encoding as needed. The following `a2ps` commands achieve this:

```
newbie@earth:~ >   a2ps -1 -X ISO-8859-1 -o example-ISO-8859-1.ps
    example
newbie@earth:~ >   a2ps -1 -X ISO-8859-15 -o example-ISO-8859-
    15.ps example
newbie@earth:~ >   a2ps -1 -X ISO-8859-2 -o example-ISO-8859-2.ps
    example
```

You may then print the files `example-ISO-8859-1.ps`, `example-ISO-8859-15.ps`, and `example-ISO-8859-2.ps`, to get printouts with different encodings, as produced by `a2ps` before.

Printing in a TCP/IP Network

You can find extensive documentation about the LPRng printing system in the *LPRng-Howto*, under
`file:/usr/share/doc/packages/lprng/LPRng-HOWTO.html`,
and on the CUPS printing system in the *CUPS Software Administrators Manual*, under
`file:/usr/share/doc/packages/cups/sam.html`.

Terminology

Print server
> By "print server", we refer to a complete, dedicated printing host with the required CPU power, memory, and hard disk space.

Print server box, network printer

- By "print server box", we refer to a computer with relatively limited resources, which is equipped with both a TCP/IP network link and a local printer port. This includes "router boxes" which have a built-in printer port, and are treated just like print server boxes.

- By "network printer", we refer to a printer device which has its own TCP/IP port – basically a printer with an integrated print server box. Thus, network printers and print server boxes need to be handled in essentially the same way.

> There is an important distinction to be made between a network printer or a print server box on the one hand, and a true print server on the other. – As a somewhat special case, there are large printer devices which have a complete print server included with them to make them network-capable. But these are treated like print servers nevertheless, because clients will talk to the printer only through the server (and not directly).

TCP/IP Printing Protocols

Below we list the different methods which can be used to implement printing on a TCP/IP network. The decision which one to use will not so much depend on the hardware, but more on the possibilities offered by each protocol. Accordingly, the YaST2 printer configuration asks you to select a protocol and not a hardware device when setting up network printing.

Printing over the LPD protocol
Print jobs are forwarded to a remote queue over the LPD protocol. To allow this, the protocol must be supported both on the client and the server side.

Client side

LPRng

The `lpd` of LPRng supports the LPD protocol. For remote printing, a local queue must be set up through which the local `lpd` can forward the print job to a remote queue, using the LPD protocol.

LPRng also allows network printing without a local `lpd` running. With this method, the `lpr` included in package `lprng` uses the protocol to directly forward a print job to the remote queue.

CUPS

CUPS has support for the LPD protocol, but only through the CUPS daemon `cupsd`. To enable this, a local queue must be set up through which the print job can be relayed by the local `cupsd` to the remote queue, using the LPD protocol.

Server side

Print server

The printer must be connected locally to the print server, and the print server itself must support the LPD protocol.

Network printer or print server box

The print server box or network printer must support the LPD protocol (which should normally be the case).

Printing over the IPP protocol
Print jobs are forwarded to a remote queue over the IPP protocol. To allow this, the protocol must be supported both on the client and the server side.

Client side

LPRng

LPRng does not yet support the IPP protocol.

CUPS

CUPS supports the IPP protocol through `cupsd`. For this method, a local queue must be set up which can be used by `cupsd` to forward print jobs to a remote queue, using the IPP protocol.

CUPS also allows network printing without a local `cupsd` running. With this method, the program `lp` included in package `cups-client`, or the programs `xpp` or `kprinter` (a KDE program) can use the IPP protocol to directly forward a print job to a remote queue.

Server side

  Print server
  The printer must be connected locally to the print server, and the print server itself must support the IPP protocol.

  Network printer or print server box
  The print server box or network printer must support the IPP protocol, which is only the case with some devices shipped in more recent times.

Direct remote printing through TCP sockets

With this method, there is no print job that gets relayed to a remote queue – since no protocol capable of handling print jobs and queues is involved in the process (neither LPD nor IPP). Rather, printer-specific data are transferred to a remote TCP port via TCP sockets, which must be supported both on the client and on the server side.

Client side

  LPRng/lpdfilter
  The `lpd` of the LPRng printing system supports streaming data directly via TCP sockets. To enable this, there must be a local queue which can be used by the local `lpd` to convert the data of each print job into the printer-specific format (with the help of lpdfilter), and to transfer them to the remote TCP port via TCP sockets after conversion.
  With LPRng, it is also possible to implement this method without a local `lpd`. This requires that the `lpr` (included in package `lprng`) is called with the `-Y` option, to transfer data directly to the remote TCP port via TCP sockets. For details on this, see the the man page for `lpr` (`man lpr`). – Note however that in this case there is no print filter involved at all, which means that print data must be in the printer-specific format right from the beginning.

  CUPS
  CUPS supports the direct transfer of print data via TCP sockets, but only if `cupsd` is running. To enable this method, there must be a local queue which can be used by the local

`cupsd` to convert the data of each print job into the printer-specific format, and to stream data to the remote TCP port via TCP sockets after conversion.

Server side

Network printer or print server box

Print server boxes and network printers normally keep a TCP port open to transfer a data stream in the printer-specific format directly to the printer.

HP network printers, and in particular HP JetDirect print server boxes, use port 9100 as the default for this kind of data stream, and JetDirect print server boxes with two or three local printer ports listen on TCP ports 9100, 9101, and 9102. The same ports are used by many other print server boxes. If you are not sure about this, you might ask the manufacturer or consult the printer manual to find out which port is used by your device for raw socket printing. Additional information about this can be found in the *LPRng-Howto*, under
`file:/usr/share/doc/packages/lprng/LPRng-HOWTO.html`,
in particular the following sections:
`file:/usr/share/doc/packages/lprng/LPRng-HOWTO.html#SECNETWORK`
`file:/usr/share/doc/packages/lprng/LPRng-HOWTO.html#SOCKETAPI`
`file:/usr/share/doc/packages/lprng/LPRng-HOWTO.html#AEN4858`

Printing over the SMB protocol

With this method, print jobs are converted into the printer-specific format first, and then transferred via the SMB protocol to a remote share which represents a remote printer. Both the client and the server side must support the SMB protocol. Although neither LPRng/lpdfilter nor CUPS have direct support for the SMB protocol, they can support it indirectly with the help of `smbclient` and `smbspool`, respectively. (Both programs are included in package `samba-client`.)

Client side

LPRng/lpdfilter

LPRng needs lpdfilter to support the SMB protocol. There must be a local queue through which the local `lpd` can convert the print job into the printer-specific format with the help of lpdfilter. The latter then forwards the data with the help of `smbclient` to the remote share, using the SMB protocol.

CUPS
There must be a local queue which can be used by the local `cupsd` to convert data into the printer-specific format. After that, data are transferred to the remote share by `smbspool`, using the SMB protocol.

Server side

SMB print server
The printer must be connected to an SMB print server. The latter will usually be a DOS/Windows machine, though it could also be a Samba server powered by Linux.
The SMB print server must support the SMB protocol, and access to the printer (i.e. to the corresponding share) must have been enabled on the server side.

Filtering for Network Printers

This section describes the possible ways to implement filtering for network printers. Independently from the filtering method used, there should be exactly one point in the entire process chain where the input file is converted into the final format, i.e. the one which your printer requires to put the data on paper (PostScript, PCL, ESC/P).

Given that the conversion must be accomplished somehow somewhere by a printer filter, the latter should run on a machine which has sufficient CPU power and disk space to handle the task. This is especially true when using Ghostscript to convert data for high-res color and photo printouts on non-PostScript devices.

Network printers and print server boxes usually do not have any built-in filtering capabilities, so they will mostly require a print server.

If your printer is a PostScript model, you may be able to do without a print server. Also, PostScript printers are often able to autodetect whether their input is in ASCII or PostScript format, and switch accordingly. But if you expect to print ASCII texts with country-specific characters in them, it may be necessary to set the printer to a certain character encoding, and to use `a2ps` to convert the ASCII input into a PostScript file with that encoding. However, as long as the printing volume is not too high, a PostScript printer will usually not require that you have a dedicated print server for it, given that most applications are able to produce ASCII and/or PostScript output.

Network printers and print server boxes, on the other hand, often do not have the resources to handle higher printing volumes on their own. You will then need a dedicated print server which has sufficient disk space to temporarily store all the print jobs queued.

Prerequisites

The printer model must be supported by SuSE Linux, because print data must be converted into the printer-specific language by a filter, just in the same way as described for local printers (see *Manual Configuration of Local Printer Ports* on page 173 and the subsequent sections).

Terminology

- By "client", we refer to the host on which the print job is issued.

- With the term "print server box", we also refer to network printers (and not only print server boxes in the narrower sense), because both are treated the same way.

- By "print server", we refer to a central, dedicated host which handles all print jobs from all the network's clients. A print server can either send data to a locally connected printer, or transfer them to print server boxes through a TCP/IP network.

- By "forwarding (queue)", we refer to queue which forwards or relays print jobs to remote queues, but does not do any filtering.

- By "filter (queue)", we refer to a queue which filters (converts) print jobs.

- By "prefilter (queue)", we refer to a queue which filters print jobs and then transfers the resulting data to a forwarding queue on the same host.

- By "forwarding filter (queue)", we refer to a queue which filters print jobs and forwards the resulting data to a remote queue.

- By "streaming filter (queue)", we refer to a queue which filters print jobs and then streams the resulting data to a remote TCP port.

- The above terms may be combined with "LPD(-based)", "IPP(-based)", or "SMB(-based)", to indicate the protocol used in conjunction with the method.

Possible Filtering Methods for Network Printing

Print server box with filtering by client
> The filtering is performed on the client side, therefore a complete printing system must run on the client, either the LPRng/lpdfilter system or the complete CUPS printing system.
>
> **Client using the LPD protocol (LPRng or CUPS)**
>> **Prefilter followed by forwarding (LPRng only)**
>>> This is the classic remote-printing solution involving two queues on the client side, one for (pre)filtering and one for forwarding.
>>> 1. Client: The prefilter queue converts the print job into the printer format, and then transfers the data to the forwarding queue as a new print job.
>>> 2. Client: The forwarding queue relays the print data to the print server box (LPD-based forwarding).
>>> 3. LPD print server box: The print data are transferred to the printer.
>>
>> **Forwarding filter (LPRng or CUPS)** With this method, filtering and forwarding is performed by one and the same queue. If used with the LPRng printing system, the method is also called "lpr bounce" or "lpd bounce".
>>> 1. Client: The print job is converted into the printer format and forwarded to the print server box (LPD-based forwarding filter).
>>> 2. LPD print server box: The print data are transferred to the printer.
>
> **Client using the IPP protocol (CUPS only)**
>> **Forwarding filter (CUPS only)**
>>> 1. Client: The print job is converted into the printer format and forwarded to the print server box (IPP-based forwarding filter).
>>> 2. IPP print server box: The print data are transferred to the printer.
>
> **Client using TCP socket (LPRng or CUPS)**
>> **Streaming filter (LPRng or CUPS)**
>>> 1. Client: The print job is converted into the printer format and streamed to the print server box (streaming filter).

2. Print server box: The print data are transferred to the printer.

Print server box with filtering by print server

Given that the filtering is performed on the print server, the latter must run a complete printing system (including the corresponding daemon), either the LPRng/lpdfilter or the CUPS printing system.

On the other hand, running a complete printing system on the client side is not strictly required (again because the server does all the filtering), provided that the client issues print jobs with the `lpr` command (in the case of LPRng), or with `lp`, `xpp` or `kprinter` (in the case of CUPS), and provided that jobs are directly sent to the print server. In either case, the print server must support the protocol used by the client (either LPD or IPP).

When the print server receives a print job, it processes it in the same way as described above for a client, under the item *Print server box with filtering by client*.

The client may use one protocol to send print jobs to the print server, and the latter another protocol to send data to the print server box.

Client using the LPD protocol (LPRng only)

Direct print command (LPRng only)

1. Client: Sends the print job directly to the print server with the `lpr` command.
2. LPD print server: Converts the print job into the printer format, and sends the data to the print server box.

Forwarding (LPRng only)

1. Client: Forwards the print job to the print server (LPD-based forwarding).
2. LPD print server: Converts the print job into the printer format, and sends the data to the print server box.

Client using the IPP protocol (CUPS only)

Direct print command (CUPS only)

1. Client: Sends the print job directly to the print server, using the `lp` command, or the programs `xpp` or `kprinter`.
2. IPP print server: Converts the print job into the printer format, and sends the data to the print server box.

Printer connected to a print server, with filtering by print server
If the print server has a local printer connected to it, the procedure is the same as described under the item *Print server box with filtering by print server*, with the difference that the phrase "sends the data to the print server box" needs to be replaced with "sends the data to the printer".

Printer connected to a print server, with filtering by the client
This is probably not such a good idea, no matter whether you have an LPD or an IPP print server. To implement this, you would need to install and configure a complete printing system on each client host. As a better solution, consider the above method *Printer connected to a print server, with filtering by print server*.

SMB print server with filtering by client
Filtering cannot be easily implemented on an SMB print server. In that sense, an SMB print server is treated in the same way as a print server box.

Client using the SMB protocol (LPRng or CUPS)

SMB-based forwarding filter (LPRng or CUPS)

1. Client: Converts the print job into the printer format, and forwards the data to the SMB print server (SMB-based forwarding filter).
2. SMB-Print-Server: Sends the data to the printer.

Remote Printer Troubleshooting

Checking the TCP/IP network
First make sure that everything is in order with the TCP/IP network in general, including name resolution (see Chapter *Linux in the Network* on page 335).

Checking the filter configuration
Connect the printer to the first parallel port of your computer. To test the connection, initially set it up as a local printer, in order to exclude any network-related problems. Then find the correct Ghostscript driver and the other configuration options until the printer works without problem.

Testing a remote lpd
The command

```
earth:~ #  netcat -z host 515 && echo ok || echo failed
```

lets you test whether `lpd` can be reached via TCP on port 515 of `host`. If `lpd` cannot be reached in this way, it is either not running at all, or there is some basic network problem.

If you are logged in as `root`, you can enter the command

```
earth:~ #  echo -e "\004queue" | netcat -w 2 -p 722 host 515
```

to get a (possibly very long) status report about the `queue` on the (remote) `host`, provided that `lpd` is running, and provided that the host is reachable. If the daemon does not respond, it is either not running at all, or there is a basic network problem. If `lpd` does respond, though, the output should give you an idea why printing through the `queue` on `host` does not work. – These are some examples:

```
lpd: your host does not have line printer access
lpd: queue does not exist
printer: spooling disabled
printer: printing disabled
```

Output 6: lpd Status Messages

If you get messages like the ones above, the problem lies with the remote `lpd`.

Testing a remote cupsd

The command

```
earth:~ #  netcat -z host 631 && echo ok || echo failed
```

lets you test whether `cupsd` can be reached via TCP on port 631 of `host`. If `cupsd` cannot be reached in this way, it is either not running at all, or there is some basic network problem.

With the command

```
earth:~ #  lpstat -h host -l -t
```

you can get a (possibly very long) status report about all queues on `host`, provided that `cupsd` is running and that the host is reachable.

With the command

8 Printer Operation

SuSE Linux – Administration Guide   233

```
earth:~ #  echo -en "\r" | lp -d queue -h host
```

you can send a print job consisting of a single carriage return character, by which you can test whether the `queue` on `host` is accepting any jobs. This test command should not print out anything, or only cause the printer to eject an empty page.

Testing a remote SMB server

As a basic test of an SMB server, you can enter:

```
earth:~ #  echo -en "\r" | smbclient '//HOST/SHARE'
   'PASSWORD' \
   -c 'print -' -N -U 'USER' && echo ok || echo failed
```

This command must be entered as a single line, without the backslash ('\'). For HOST, enter the host name of the Samba server; for SHARE, the name of the remote queue ; for PASSWORD, the password string; for USER, the user name. This test command should not print out anything, or only cause the printer to eject an empty page.

The command

```
earth:~ #  smbclient -N -L host
```

will display any shares on the `host` which are currently available. Details on this can be obtained with the the man page for `smbclient` (`man smbclient`).

Troubleshooting an unreliable network printer or print server box

Spoolers on print server boxes often become unreliable when having to deal with relatively high printing volumes. As the cause of this lies with the server side spooler, there is mostly no way to fix this.

As a workaround, however, you can circumvent the spooler on the print server box, by using TCP sockets to directly stream data to the printer connected to the host.

This turns the print server box into a mere data converter between the two different data streams (TCP/IP network and local printer line), which effectively makes the printer behave very much like a local printer (even though it is connected to the print server box). Without the spooler acting as an intermediary, this method also gives you a much more direct control over the printer device in general.

To use this method, you need to know the corresponding TCP port on the print server box.

Provided that the printer is switched on and properly connected, you should be able to determine the TCP port a minute or so after booting the print server box, by using the program `nmap`.

Running `nmap` on the print server box may return an output similar to this:

```
Port        State       Service
23/tcp      open        telnet
80/tcp      open        http
515/tcp     open        printer
631/tcp     open        cups
9100/tcp    open        jetdirect
```

- You can log in on the above print server box with `telnet`, in order to look for important information, or to change basic configuration options.
- The above print server runs an HTTP daemon, which can provide detailed server information, or even allow you to set specific printing options.
- The print spooler running on the print server box can be reached over the LPD protocol on port 515.
- The print spooler running on the print server box can also be reached over the IPP protocol on port 631.
- The printer connected to the print server box can be accessed directly via TCP sockets on port 9100.

Print Servers Supporting Both LPD and IPP

Supporting Both Protocols through CUPS

By default, the CUPS daemon only supports the IPP protocol. However, the program `/usr/lib/cups/daemon/cups-lpd` from the package `cups` makes it possible for a CUPS daemon to accept print jobs arriving via the LPD protocol on port 515. This requires that the corresponding service is enabled for `inetd` – either with YaST2, or by enabling the corresponding line in `/etc/inetd.conf` manually.

Supporting Both Protocols by Using LPRng/lpdfilter together with CUPS

There may be situations where you want to run both LPRng/lpdfilter and CUPS on one and the same system, maybe because you want to enhance the functionality of LPD with some CUPS features, or because you need the LPRng/lpdfilter system as an add-on for certain special cases.

Running the two systems together on the same system will lead to a number of problems, however. Below we list the most important of these, and briefly explain the limitations resulting from them – though the topic is too complex to describe them in any greater detail here.

That said, there are several ways to solve these issues, depending on the individual case.

- You should not rely on YaST2 for configuration if you install both printing systems; the printer configuration module of YaST2 has not been written with this case in mind.

- There is a conflict between package `lprng` and package `cups-client`, because they contain a number of files with identical names, such as `/usr/bin/lpr` and `/usr/bin/lp`. You should therefore not install package `cups-client`. This however means that no CUPS-based command-line tools are available, but only those included with LPRng. You are still able to print through CUPS print queues from the X Window System with `xpp` or `kprinter`, though, as well as from all application programs which have built-in support for CUPS.

- By default, `cupsd` will create the `/etc/printcap` file when started, and write the names of CUPS queues to it. This is done to maintain compatibility with applications which expect queue names to be present in `/etc/printcap`, to offer them in their respective print dialogs. With both printing systems installed, you need to disable this `cupsd` feature, to reserve `/etc/printcap` for the exclusive use by the LPRng/lpdfilter printing system. As a result, applications which get queue names only from `/etc/printcap` can use only these local queues, but not the remote queues made available by CUPS through the network.

Hotplugging Services

Hardware components that can be connected and disconnected from the system while it is running are growing more common. As well as USB, the most prominent example for this kind of component, there are PCI, PCMCIA, Firewire, SCSI, and other interfaces.

Hotplug systems are responsible for recognizing newly-connected or installed hardware and automatically making it available for use. Components that will be removed again need, furthermore, to be prepared for this event. If removed without prior warning, resources must be freed again.

Hotplugging in Linux 238
Hotplugging and Coldplugging 238
USB 239
PCI and PCMCIA 240
Network 241
Firewire (IEEE1394) 242
Other Devices and Further Development 242

Hotplugging in Linux

Little programs called daemons watch parts of a system for external events. The inetd daemon, for example, watches incoming network requests. The daemon for hotplugging is the kernel itself. The driver for an interface must be able to recognize new devices and report them to the system in a standardized way. USB, PCMCIA, Firewire, the network subsystem, and, to some extent, PCI are able to do this in the 2.4 kernel. This part of hotplugging is firmly built into the corresponding modules and cannot be influenced without changing the kernel.

> **Note**
>
> PCMCIA devices are only being handled by the hotplugging service if they are CardBus cards and the PCMCIA system kernel was selected. They then appear as PCI devices. More detailed information about this can be found in the section on PCMCIA.
>
> **Note**

The second part of the hotplugging service initiates the necessary steps for the respective registration and release of devices and is a collection of scripts in the directory /etc/hotplug with the main script /sbin/hotplug. This script is the interface between the kernel and the collection of hotplugging scripts. These scripts are referred to as the "hotplug system" for the course of this chapter.

When a hot-pluggable device is connected or removed, the kernel calls the /sbin/hotplug/ script and passes additional information to the corresponding hardware component. This script directs the tasks — depending on the type of hardware — to additional scripts. These insert or remove the modules respectively and call other programs for the configuration of the components. These programs are located in /etc/hotplug and always end with .agent.

Hotplugging and Coldplugging

Although the kernel always passes hotplug events to /sbin/hotplug, the hotplug system needs to be started initially with the command rchotplug start. All hotplug events are discarded if hotplug has not been started.

Aside from this, there are components recognized by the kernel even before the file system can be accessed. These events are simply lost. This is why the scripts /etc/hotplug/*.rc attempt to create these events artificially for already existing hardware. The term "coldplugging" is used in this respect. If the USB base modules have not been loaded until then, they are loaded and the USB device file system usbdefs is mounted.

After hotplug has been stopped by calling rchotplug stop, no more events can be evaluated. Hot-plugging can be completely deactivated if the hardware configuration is never changed during operation. This, however, requires other methods of installing USB or PCMCIA devices.

The path /etc/sysconfig/hotplug contains a few variables that control the behavior of hotplug. For instance, the variable ⟨HOTPLUG_DEBUG⟩ influences the verbosity of hotplug. The variables ⟨HOTPLUG_START_USB⟩, ⟨HOTPLUG_START_PCI⟩, and ⟨HOTPLUG_START_NET⟩ determine that only events of a certain type are evaluated. All the other variables are explained in detail in the corresponding subsections. All the hotplug messages are logged in the file /var/log/messages — the system log.

USB

When a new USB device is connected, the script /etc/hotplug/usb.agent determines an appropriate driver and ensures that it is loaded. This driver is not necessarily a kernel module. Many USB cameras, for instance, are directly accessed by applications.

The assignment of drivers to hardware is multistaged: First, the file /etc/hotplug/usb.usermap is checked for an entry that specifies whether this hardware should be handled by an application or by a dedicated initialization script. If neither is the case, an individual assignment to a kernel module is searched for in /etc/hotplug/usb.handmap. If nothing is found there (which is most often the case), the assignment table of the kernel, /lib/modules/⟨*kernelversion*⟩/modules.usbmap, is queried. An additional USB hardware scan is run at this point, which triggers further actions if KDE is used. An appropriate YaST configuration module is presented, for instance, for devices connected for the first time or applications are run for using the new device. This mechanism runs in parallel to the other actions triggered by /etc/hotplug/usb.agent.

USB devices are differently by the usb.agent, according to type:

storage devices hard disks, for example, are handled by the script /usr/sbin/checkhotmounts as soon as the required drivers are loaded.

network devices create their own hotplug event in the kernel as soon as these are registered. The usb.agent merely records hardware information which is later used by the network event. This is only a transient solution for the 2.4 kernel and fails whenever more than one USB network devices are employed. This however happens only very rarely.

cameras are accessed by way of the hardware-scanning KDE mechanism. The access permissions of the device file are additionally set by /etc/hotplug/usb/usbcam to those of the logged-in user so he can access the device when using KDE.

mice only require a loaded module that, in this case, is loaded for immediate use.

keyboards needed during booting so are not handled by hotplug.

ISDN modem not installed automatically yet.

There are some USB-specific variables in /etc/sysconfig/hotplug. ⟨HOTPLUG_USB_HOSTCONTROLLER_LIST⟩ contains the driver for the USB controller in the order in which loading is attempted. When a driver is loaded successfully, those modules that need to be unloaded on removal of the component are listed in ⟨HOTPLUG_USB_MODULES_TO_UNLOAD⟩. All remaining USB modules are not unloaded, because it cannot be determined with certainty whether they are still required by a device. The variable ⟨HOTPLUG_USB_NET_MODULES⟩ contains the names of those modules that provide a network interface. A hardware descriptor for later reference on network events is stored when one of these modules is loaded. This process is logged in the system log.

PCI and PCMCIA

PCMCIA cards require a careful scrutiny because hotplug only handles Card-Bus cards. This handling is furthermore only done if the PCMCIA system of the kernel is activated. This condition is explained in more detail in the software section of the PCMCIA chapter.

CardBus cards are, technically-speaking, almost PCI devices. This is why both are handled by the same hotplug script — /etc/hotplug/pci.agent. It essentially determines a driver for the card and loads it. In addition to this, a record of where the new card has been connected (PCI bus or PCMCIA slots and the slot designator) is stored, so a later hotplug network event can read this information and select the correct configuration.

The determination of the drive is two-staged in this case: the file /etc/hotplug/pci.handmap is searched for individual settings and, if nothing was found, the PCI driver table of the kernel /lib/modules⟨*kernelversion*⟩/modules.pcimap is subsequently searched. To change the driver assignment, the file /etc/hotplug/pci.handmap should be altered, as the other list is overwritten on a kernel update.

Unlike with USB, no special actions are executed depending on the type of PCI or CardBus card. The kernel creates a hotplug network event for network cards, which induces the installation of the interface. Further action must ensue manually for all other cards. The hotplug system is, however, still being expanded in this respect.

As soon as the card is removed, the employed modules are unloaded again. Should this lead to problems with certain modules, this can be prevented by writing the names of those modules into ⟨*HOTPLUG_PCI_MODULES_NOT_TO_UNLOAD*⟩.

Network

When a new network interface is registered or unregistered in the kernel, the kernel creates a hotplug network event. This is evaluated by /etc/hotplug/net.agent. Only ethernet, token ring, and wireless LAN interfaces are currently taken into account. Other mechanisms exist for all other kinds of networks, like modems or ISDN. Network interfaces which are provided by PCMCIA cards and are handled by cardmanager instead of hotplug are likewise not handled here. A message then appears in the system log.

First, which hardware provides the interface is determined. Because the 2.4 kernel cannot provide such information, a record created following the USB or PCI event is used. Although this works well in most cases, it is regarded as a temporary quick fix only. For this reason, two network cards cannot be connected simultaneously. To use multiple hotplug-enabled network cards, connect them subsequently with the computer. A latency of a few seconds between connections is sufficient. This transmission of information is logged in /var/log/messages.

Insert additional individual actions to execute following the installation of a new network device in /sbin/ifup. Details about this can be found in the man page for ifup (man ifup). It is also possible to apply different default routing depending on the connected hardware. Refer to the man page for route (man route) for details.

If the probing of the hardware behind the interface fails and only one hotplug network device is used, the description of the network hardware in /etc/sysconfig/hotplug can be written to the variable ⟨HOTPLUG_NET_DEFAULT_HARDWARE⟩. This string must correspond to what should be used by /sbin/ifup for the allocation of the correct configuration. The variable ⟨HOTPLUG_NET_TIMEOUT⟩ determines for how long net.agent waits for a dynamically-created hardware desciption.

Firewire (IEEE1394)

Only the driver modules are currently loaded for firewire devices. SuSE is attempting to determine how widespread firewire hardware is with our customers. To assist with this, please contact us through our web feedback frontend at http://www.suse.de/feedback.

Other Devices and Further Development

All the kinds of hotplugging-enabled devices not described above are currently not handled. Hotplugging, however, is undergoing massive development that depends heavily on the abilities of the kernel. It is expected that better possibilities will be offered with the kernel 2.6.

10

Configuring and Using Laptop Computers

Laptop computers have unique needs. These include Power Management (APM and ACPI), infrared interfaces (IrDA), and PC cards (PCMCIA). Occasionally, such components can also be found in desktop computers. These are essentially no different than those used in laptops. For this reason, their use and configuration is summarized in this chapter.

> PCMCIA 244
> IrDA — Infrared Data Association 254

PCMCIA

PCMCIA stands for "Personal Computer Memory Card International Association." It is used as a general term for all hardware and software involved.

The Hardware

The essential component is the PCMCIA card. There are two distinct types:

PC cards These are currently the most used cards. They use a 16-bit bus for data transmission, are usually relatively cheap, are generally stable, and are fully supported.

CardBus Cards This is a more recent standard. It uses a 32-bit bus, which makes them faster, but also more expensive. Because the data transfer rate is frequently restricted at another point, it is often not worth the extra cost. There are now many drivers for these cards, although some are still unstable. This also depends on the available PCMCIA controller.

If the PCMCIA service is active, determine the type of the inserted card with the command `cardctl ident`. A list of supported cards can be found in SUPPORTED_CARDS in `/usr/share/doc/packages/pcmcia`. The current version of the PCMCIA-HOWTO is also located there.

The second necessary component is the PCMCIA controller or the PC card or CardBus bridge. This establishes the connection between the card and the PCI bus and, in older devices, the connection to the ISA bus as well. These controllers are almost always compatible with the Intel chip i82365. All common models are supported. The type of controller is shown with the command `probe`. If this is a PCI device, the command `lspci -vt` also shows some interesting information.

The Software

Differences Between PCMCIA Systems

There are currently two PCMCIA systems — external PCMCIA and kernel PCMCIA. The external PCMCIA system by David Hinds is the older system, which makes it better tested. It is still being developed. The sources of the modules used are not integrated in the kernel sources, which is why it is called an "external" system. From kernel 2.4, there are alternative modules in the kernel sources. These form the kernel PCMCIA system. The basic modules were written by Linus Torvalds. They support the more recent CardBus bridges better.

Unfortunately, these two systems are not compatible. There are various sets of card drivers in both systems. For this reason, only one system can be used, depending on the hardware involved. The default in SuSE Linux is the more recent kernel PCMCIA. It is possible to change the system, however. To do this, the variable ⟨*PCMCIA_SYSTEM*⟩ in the file /etc/sysconfig/pcmcia must be given either the value external or kernel. Then PCMCIA must be restarted with rcpcmcia restart. For temporary changes, use the commands rcpcmcia restart external or rcpcmcia restart kernel. If pcmcia is not running, use the option start instead of restart. Detailed information about this can be found in /usr/share/doc/packages/pcmcia/README.SuSE

The Base Module

The kernel modules for both systems are located in the kernel packages. In addition, the packages pcmcia and hotplug are required.

When PCMCIA is started, the modules pcmcia_core, i82365 (external PCMCIA) or yenta_socket (kernel PCMCIA), and ds are loaded. In some very rare cases, the module tcic is required instead of i82365 or yenta_socket. They initialize the existing PCMCIA controller and provide basic functionality.

The Card Manager

Because PCMCIA cards can be changed while the system is running, a daemon to monitor the activity in the slots is required. Depending on the PCMCIA system chosen and the hardware used, this task is performed by the card manager or the hotplug system of the kernel. With external PCMCIA, only the card manager is used. For kernel PCMCIA, the card manager only handles PC Card cards. CardBus cards are handled by hotplug. The card manager is started by the PCMCIA start script after the base modules have been loaded. Because hotplug manages other subsystems apart from PCMCIA, it has its own start script. (See also *Hotplugging Services* on page 237).

If a card is inserted, card manager or hotplug determines the type and function of the card then loads the corresponding modules. If this is successful, card manager or hotplug starts certain initialization scripts, depending on the function of the card, which in turn establish a network connection, mount partitions from external SCSI hard drives, or carry out other hardware-specific actions. The scripts for the card manager are located in /etc/pcmcia. The scripts for hotplug can be found in /etc/hotplug. If the card is removed, card manager or hotplug terminates the various card activities using the same scripts. Finally, those modules that are no longer required are unloaded.

Both the start process of PCMCIA and card events are recorded in the system log (/var/log/messages). Here, it is specified which PCMCIA system is currently being used and which daemons have been used by which scripts to set up things. In theory, a PCMCIA card can simply be removed. This works very well for network, modem, or ISDN cards as long as there are no open network connections. It does not work in connection with partitions mounted to an external hard drive or with NFS directories. Here, ensure that these units are synchronized and cleanly unmounted. This is no longer possible, of course, if the card has already been removed. In case of doubt, the command cardctl eject may be of help. This command deactivates all cards still in the laptop. To deactivate one card, also specify the slot number, for example, cardctl eject 0.

Configuration

Whether PCMCIA or hotplug is started when booting can be specified with the YaST2 runlevel editor or on the command line using chkconfig. In /etc/sysconfig/pcmcia, there are four variables:

⟨*PCMCIA_SYSTEM*⟩ Specifies which PCMCIA system to use.

⟨*PCMCIA_PCIC*⟩ Contains the name of the module that addresses the PCMCIA controller. Normally, the start script detects this name on its own. The module is only entered here if this goes wrong. Otherwise, this variable should be left empty.

⟨*PCMCIA_CORE_OPTS*⟩ Intended for parameters for the module pcmcia_core. They are only rarely required, however. These options are described in the man page for pcmcia_core (man pcmcia_core).

⟨*PCMCIA_PCIC_OPTS*⟩ Parameters for the module i82365. Refer to the man page for i82365 (man i82365). If yenta_socket is used, these options are ignored, because yenta_socket has no options.

The allocation of drivers to PCMCIA cards for the card manager can be found in the files /etc/pcmcia/config and /etc/pcmcia/*.conf. First, config is read then the *.conf in alphabetical order. The last entry to be found for a card is decisive. Details on the syntax of these files can be found in the man page for `pcmcia` (`man pcmcia`). The allocation of drivers to PCMCIA cards for hotplug is described in *Hotplugging Services* on page 237).

Network Cards (Ethernet, Wireless LAN, and Token Ring)

These can be set up with YaST2 like normal network cards. Select 'PCMCIA' as the card type. All other details about setting up the network can be found in the network chapter. Make sure you read the notes there about hotpluggable cards.

ISDN

Even for ISDN PC cards, configuration is done to a large extent using YaST2, as with other ISDN cards. It is not important which PCMCIA card offered there is chosen, but only that it is a PCMCIA card. When setting up hardware and provider, make sure the operating mode is set to `hotplug` and not to `onboot`.

ISDN modems also exist for PCMCIA cards. These are modem cards or multifunction cards with an additional ISDN connection kit. They are treated like an ordinary modem.

Modem

For modem PC cards there are normally no PCMCIA-specific settings. As soon as a modem is inserted, it is available under `/dev/modem`.

There are also "soft modems" for PCMCIA cards. As a rule, these are not supported. If there are some drivers, they must be integrated individually into the system.

SCSI and IDE

The corresponding driver module is loaded by the card manager or hotplug. When a SCSI or IDE card is inserted, the devices connected to it are available. The device names are detected dynamically. Information about existing SCSI or IDE devices can be found in `/proc/scsi` or `/proc/ide`.

External hard drives, CD-ROM drives, and similar devices must be switched on before the PCMCIA card is inserted into the slot. SCSI devices must be actively terminated.

> **Note**
>
> Before a SCSI or IDE card is removed, all partitions on the devices connected must be unmounted. If you have forgotten to do this, you can only access these devices again after rebooting the system, even if the rest of the system continues to run in a stable manner.
>
> **Note**

You can also install Linux entirely on these external hard drives. However, the boot process is then somewhat more complicated. A boot disk is required in all cases — containing the kernel and an initial ramdisk (initrd). More information about this can be found in *Booting with the Initial Ramdisk* on page 276. The initrd contains a virtual file system that includes all required PCMCIA modules and programs. The boot disk and boot disk images are constructed in the same way. With these, you could always boot your external installation. It is, however, tiresome to load the PCMCIA support every time by hand. More advanced users might create their own boot floppy disk, customized to their own particular system. Hints for doing this can be found in the English PCMCIA-HOWTO in the section *Booting from a PCMCIA Device*.

Switching Configurations — SCPM

Often with mobile computers, various configuration profiles are required. With PCMCIA devices, this was never a problem, thanks to the PCMCIA schemes. Because the users of the built-in network cards or USB and firewire devices would also like to use different profiles for system configuration, there is, from SuSE Linux 8.0, the package SCPM (System Configuration Profile Management). For this reason, SuSE no longer supports the PCMCIA schemes. To continue to use these, the configuration must be modified by hand under /etc/pcmcia. We recommend using SCPM instead, because any part of the system configuration can be administrated here — not just the PCMCIA parts.

Troubleshooting

Occasionally, there are problems with certain laptops and certain cards when using PCMCIA. Most difficulties can be solved with little trouble, if you approach the problem systematically.

> **Caution**
>
> Because both external PCMCIA and kernel PCMCIA are available in parallel in SuSE Linux, you must bear in mind one special feature when loading modules manually. The two PCMCIA systems use modules of the same name and are located in different subdirectories under /lib/modules/⟨*kernelversion*⟩. The subdirectories are named pcmcia for kernel PCMCIA and pcmcia-external for external PCMCIA. For this reason, the subdirectory must be specified when loading modules manually, either with insmod /lib/modules/⟨*kernel version*⟩/⟨*subdirectory*⟩/⟨*file name of module*⟩ or with modprobe -t ⟨*subdirectory*⟩ ⟨*module name*⟩.
>
> **Caution**

First, find out if the problem is with the card or with the PCMCIA-based system. For this reason, always start the computer first without the card inserted. Only insert the card when the base system appears to function correctly. All meaningful messages are recorded in /var/log/messages. The file should therefore be viewed, with tail -f /var/log/messages while the necessary tests are made. In this way, the error can be narrowed down to one of the two following cases.

Nonfunctional PCMCIA Base System

If the system hangs when booting, with the message PCMCIA: "Starting services", or other strange things happen, starting PCMCIA the next time the system is booted can be prevented by entering NOPCMCIA=yes at the boot prompt. To further isolate the error, the base modules of the PCMCIA system used are manually loaded.

These commands are used to do this:

earth:~ # **modprobe -t ⟨*dir*⟩ pcmcia_core**
earth:~ # **modprobe -t pcmcia-external i82365** (for external PCMCIA) or
earth:~ # **modprobe -t pcmcia yenta_socket** (for kernel PCMCIA)

or, in very rare cases,

earth:~ # **modprobe -t ⟨*dir*⟩ tcic**

and

earth:~ # **modprobe -t ⟨*dir*⟩ ds**

The critical modules are the first two.

If the error occurs when pcmcia_core is loaded, the manual pages for pcmcia_core can help. The options described there can first be tested using modprobe. As an example, switch off the APM support for the PCMCIA module. In a few cases, there could be problems with this. There is the option do_apm for this. With do_apm=0, power management is deactivated:

```
modprobe -t ⟨dir⟩ pcmciacore do_apm=0
```

If the chosen option is successful, it can be written to the variable ⟨PCMCIA_CORE_OPTS⟩ in the file /etc/sysconfig/pcmcia:

```
PCMCIA_CORE_OPTS="do_apm=0"
```

Checking free IO areas can lead to problems in isolated cases if other hardware components are disturbed by this. Get around this with probe_io=0. If several options should be used, they must be separated by spaces:

```
PCMCIA_CORE_OPTS="do_apm=0 probe_io=0"
```

If errors occur when loading the module i82365, refer to the man page for i82365 (man i82365).

A problem in this context is a resource conflict — if an interrupt, IO port or memory area is occupied twice. Although the module i82365 checks these resources before they are made available to a card, sometimes just this check will lead to problems. Thus, checking the interrupt 12 (PS/2 devices) on some computers leads to the mouse or keyboard hanging. In this case, the parameter irq_list=⟨List of IRQs⟩ can help. The list should contain all IRQs to use. For example, enter the command

```
modprobe i82365 irq_list=5,7,9,10
```

or permanently add the list of IRQs in /etc/sysconfig/pcmcia:

```
PCMCIA_PCIC_OPTS="irq_list=5,7,9,10"
```

In addition, there are /etc/pcmcia/config and /etc/pcmcia/config.opts. These files are evaluated by card manager. The settings made in them are only relevant when loading the driver modules for the PCMCIA cards. In /etc/pcmcia/config.opts, IRQs, IO ports, and memory areas can be included or excluded. The difference from the option irqlist is that the resources excluded in config.opts are not used for a PCMCIA card, but are still checked by the base module i82365.

Improperly Functioning or Nonfunctional PCMCIA Card

Here, there are basically three variations: the card is not detected, the driver cannot be loaded, or the interface made available by the driver is set up incorrectly.

Determine whether the card is managed by the card manager or hotplug. For external PCMCIA, card manager always takes control, for kernel PCMCIA, card manager manages PC card cards and hotplug manages CardBUS cards. Here, only card manager is discussed. Hotplug problems are discussed in *Hotplugging Services* on page 237.

- **Unrecognized Card**
  If the card is not recognized, the message "Unsupported Card in Slot x" appears in `/var/log/messages`. This message means only that the card manager cannot assign a driver to the card. To do this, `/etc/pcmcia/config` or `/etc/pcmcia/*.conf` are required. These files function as the driver database. This driver database can be easily extended if you take existing entries as a template. Find out, with the command `cardctl ident`, how the card identifies itself. More information about this can be found in the PCMCIA-HOWTO, Section 6 and in the man page for `pcmcia` (`man pcmcia`). After modifying `/etc/pcmcia/config` or `/etc/pcmcia/*.conf`, the driver allocation must be reloaded with the command `rcpcmcia reload`.

- **Driver Not Loaded**
  One reason for this occurring is that a wrong allocation has been made in the driver database. This can happen, for example, if a vendor uses a different chip in an apparently unchanged card model. Sometimes there are also alternative drivers that work better for certain models than the default driver. In these cases, precise information about the card is required. It can also be useful here to ask a mailing list or the Advanced Support Service.

  Another cause is a resource conflict. For most PCMCIA cards, it is irrelevant with which IRQ, IO port, or memory area they are operated, but there are exceptions. First test only one card and, if necessary, switch off other system components, such as the sound card, IrDA, modem, or printer. The allocation of system resources can be viewed with the command `lsdev` (it is quite normal that several PCI devices share the same IRQ).

  One possible solution would be to use a suitable option for the module `i82365` (see PCMCIA_PCIC_OPTS). Many card driver modules also have options. Find these using the command `modinfo`

/lib/modules/⟨*the correct pcmcia directory*⟩/⟨*driver*⟩.o (the complete path is needed to locate the correct driver). There is also a manual page for most modules. `rpm -ql pcmcia | grep man` lists all manual pages contained in pcmcia. To test the options, the card drivers can also be unloaded by hand. Again ensure that the module is using the correct PCMCIA system.

When a solution has been found, the use of a specific resource can, in general, be allowed or forbidden in the file `/etc/pcmcia/config.opts`. There is even room here for options for card drivers. If the module `pcnet_cs` should be operated exclusively with IRQ 5, for example, the following entry is required:

```
module pcnet_cs opts irq_list=5
```

One problem that sometimes occurs with 10/100-Mbit network cards is incorrect automatic identification of the transmission method. Use the command `ifport` or `mii_tool` to view and modify the transmission method. To have these commands run automatically, the script `/etc/pcmcia/network` must be individually adjusted.

- **Incorrectly Configured Interface**
  In this case, it is recommended to check the configuration of the interface to eliminate rare configuration errors. For network cards, the dialog rate of the network scripts can be increased by assigning the value `DEBUG=yes` to the variable in `/etc/sysconfig/network/config`. For other cards or if this is of no help, there is still the possibility to insert the line `set -x` into the script run by card manager (see `/var/log/messages`). With this, each individual command of the script is recorded in the system log. If you have found the critical part in a script, the corresponding commands can be entered in a terminal and tested.

Installation via PCMCIA

PCMCIA is already required for installation if you want to install via network or if the CD-ROM is operated via PCMCIA. To do this, start with a boot floppy disk. In addition, one of the module floppy disks is required.

After booting from floppy disk (or after selecting 'Manual Installation' booting from CD), the program `linuxrc` is started. Select 'Kernel Modules (Hardware Drivers)' → 'Load PCMCIA Module'. Two entry fields appear in which to enter options for the modules `pcmcia_core` and `i82365`. Normally, these fields can be left blank. The manual pages for `pcmcia_core` and `i82365` are available as text files on the first CD in the directory `docu`. Installation in SuSE Linux 8.1 is done with the external PCMCIA system.

During installation, system messages are sent to various virtual consoles. Switch to them using (Alt) + (function key).

During the installation, there are terminals on which commands can be run. As long as linuxrc is running, use console 9 (a very spartan shell). After YaST2 starts, there is a bash shell and many standard system tools on console 2.

If the wrong driver module for a PCMCIA card is loaded during installation, the boot floppy disk must be modified manually. This requires a detailed knowledge of Linux, however. When the first part of the installation is finished, the system is partially or completely rebooted. In rare cases, it is possible that the system will hang when the PCMCIA is started. At this point the installation is already at an advanced stage, so Linux can be started without PCMCIA using the boot option `NOPCMCIA=yes`, at least in text mode. See also *Troubleshooting* on page 248. It is possible that you can change some settings for the system on console 2 before the first part of the installation is completed, so the reboot will run successfully.

Other Utilities

cardctl is an essential tool for obtaining information from PCMCIA and carrying out certain actions. In cardctl, find many details. Enter just `cardctl` to obtain a list of the valid commands.

There is also a graphical front-end for this program — cardinfo, shown in Figure 10.1) — with which the most important things can be controlled. For this to work, the package `pcmcia-cardinfo` must be installed.

Figure 10.1: The cardinfo Program

Additional helpful programs from the `pcmcia` package are `ifport`, `ifuser`, `probe`, and `rcpcmcia`. These are not always required. To find out about everything contained in the package `pcmicia`, use the command `rpm -ql pcmcia`.

Updating the Kernel or PCMCIA Package

If you want to update the kernel, you should use the kernel packages provided by SuSE. If it is necessary to compile your own kernel, the PCMCIA modules must also be recompiled. It is important that the new kernel is already running when these modules are recompiled, because various information is extracted from it. The `pcmcia` package should already be installed, but not started. In case of doubt, run the command `rcpcmcia stop`. Install the PCMCIA source package and enter

`rpm -ba /usr/src/packages/SPECS/pcmcia.spec`

The new packages will be stored in `/usr/src/packages/RPMS`. The package `pcmcia-modules` contains the PCMCIA modules for external PCMCIA. This package must be installed with the command `rpm --force`, because the module files belong officially to the kernel package.

For More Information

For more information about specific laptops, visit the Linux Laptop home page at `http://linux-laptop.net`. Another good source of information is the Moblix home page at `http://mobilix.org/` (MobiliX — Mobile Computers and Unix). Apart from a lot of interesting information, also find a Laptop-Howto and an IrDA-Howto. In addition, there is also the article Laptops and Notebooks (PCMCIA) in the SuSE Support Database at `http://sdb.suse.de/en/sdb/html/laptop.html` (or locally at `file:/usr/share/doc/sdb/en/html/laptop.html`).

IrDA — Infrared Data Association

IrDA ("Infrared Data Association") is an industry standard for wireless communication with infrared light. Many laptops sold nowadays are equipped with an IrDA compatible transceiver that enables communication with other devices, such as printers, modems, LAN or other laptops. The transfer speed ranges from 2400 bps up to 4 Mbps.

There are two IrDA operation modes. The standard mode SIR accesses the infrared port through a serial interface. This mode works on almost all systems and is sufficient for most requirements. The faster mode FIR requires a special driver for the IrDA chip. There are however not such drivers for all chips. The desired mode furthermore needs to be set in the BIOS setup of the computer. This is also where it can be determined which serial interface is used for the SIR mode.

Information on IrDA can be found in the IrDA how-to by Werner Heuser at http://mobilix.org/Infrared-HOWTO/Infrared-HOWTO.html and on the web site of the Linux IrDA Project http://irda.sourceforge.net/.

Software

The necessary kernel modules are included in the kernel package. The package `irda` provides the necessary helper applications for supporting the infrared interface. The documentation can be found at `/usr/share/doc/packages/irda/README` after the installation of the package.

Configuration

The IrDA system service is not started automatically by the booting process. Use the YaST2 runlevel module for changing the settings of the system services. The application `chkconfig` can be used alternatively. Also refer to *Runlevel Editor* on page 79. IrDA unfortunately consumes noticeably more battery power since a "discovery packet" is sent every few seconds to automatically detect other peripheral devices. This is why IrDA should only be started when needed. The interface can always be activated manually with the command `rcirda start` or deactivated with the `stop` parameter. All necessary kernel modules are automatically loaded when the interface is activated.

The file `/etc/sysconfig/irda` contains only the one variable ⟨*IRDA_PORT*⟩. This is where the interface used in SIR mode is set. The script `/etc/irda/drivers` of the infrared support package sets this variable.

Usage

Data can be sent to the device file `/dev/irlpt0` for printing. The device file `/dev/irlpt0` acts just like the normal `/dev/lp0` cabled interface with the only difference that the printing data is sent wireless with infrared light.

Printers which are used with the infrared interface are installed just like printers connected to the parallel or serial ports. Make sure the printer is in visible range of the infrared interface and the infrared support is started.

Communication with other hosts and with mobile phones or other similar devices is conducted through the device file /dev/ircomm0. The Siemens S25 and Nokia 6210 mobile phones, for instance, can dial and connect to the Internet with the wvdial application using the infrared interface. A data synchronization with a Palm Pilot is equally possible in this way when the device setting of the corresponding application has been set to /dev/ircomm0.

Please note as well, that only those devices can be accessed without any other adjustments which support the printer or IrCOMM protocols. Devices that support the IROBEX protocol, such as the 3Com Palm Pilot, can be accessed with special applications like irobexpalm and irobexreceive. Refer to the IR-HOWTO on this subject. The protocols supported by the device are stated in brackets behind the name of the device in the output of irdadump. IrLAN protocol support is still a "work in progress" — it is unfortunately not stable yet but will surely be also available for Linux in the near future.

Troubleshooting

The superuser root can check with the command irdadump whether the other device has been recognized by the system in case that devices should not work at the infrared interface.

Something similar to Output 7 appears regularly when a Canon BJC-80 printer is in visible range of the computer:

```
21:41:38.435239 xid:cmd 5b62bed5 > ffffffff S=6 s=0 (14)
21:41:38.525167 xid:cmd 5b62bed5 > ffffffff S=6 s=1 (14)
21:41:38.615159 xid:cmd 5b62bed5 > ffffffff S=6 s=2 (14)
21:41:38.705178 xid:cmd 5b62bed5 > ffffffff S=6 s=3 (14)
21:41:38.795198 xid:cmd 5b62bed5 > ffffffff S=6 s=4 (14)
21:41:38.885163 xid:cmd 5b62bed5 > ffffffff S=6 s=5 (14)
21:41:38.965133 xid:rsp 5b62bed5 < 6cac38dc S=6 s=5 BJC-80
                        hint=8804 [ Printer IrCOMM ] (23)
21:41:38.975176 xid:cmd 5b62bed5 > ffffffff S=6 s=* erde
                        hint=0500 [ PnP Computer ] (21)
```

Output 7: IrDA: irdadump

Check the configuration of the interface in case of no output or the other device does not reply. Are you using the correct interface at all? The infrared interface is sometimes located at /dev/ttyS2 or at /dev/ttyS3 and another interrupt than IRQ 3 is used sometimes. These settings can be checked and modified in the BIOS setup menu of almost every laptop.

A simple CCD video camera can also help in determining whether the infrared LED lights up at all. Most video cameras can see infrared light whereas the human eye cannot.

Part III

System

The Linux Kernel

The kernel is the heart of a Linux system. Although the following sections will not teach you how to be a kernel "hacker", they will tell you how to install a SuSE update kernel and introduce the basics of compiling a customized kernel. If you proceed as outlined in this chapter, you can keep your current functional kernel. Later, if your new kernel works as desired, change it to the default.

Kernel Update 262
Kernel Sources 262
Kernel Configuration 263
Kernel Modules 264
Settings in the Kernel Configuration 266
Compiling the Kernel 267
Installing the Kernel 267
Cleaning Your Hard Disk After Compilation 268

The standard SuSE kernel, located in the directory /boot, is configured to support as wide a range of hardware as possible. There is no need to compile your own kernel, unless you want to test experimental features and drivers. Several Makefiles are provided with the kernel to automate the process. All you need to do is select the hardware settings and other kernel features. As you need to know your computer system pretty well to make the right selections, we recommend modifying an existing and working configuration file for your first attempt.

Kernel Update

To install an official SuSE update kernel, download the update rpm from the SuSE FTP server or a mirror like ftp://ftp.gwdg.de/pub/linux/suse/. In the subdirectory ⟨version⟩_update/kernel, there are kernel rpm packages. "k_deflt-⟨version⟩.i586.rpm" is the typical name for the standard kernel. Before installing this package, it is recommended to save the current kernel and initrd under a different name. As root, enter the following two commands:

cp /boot/vmlinuz /boot/vmlinuz.old
cp /boot/initrd /boot/initrd.old

Now install the new kernel with the command

rpm -Uvh k_deflt-2.4.⟨version⟩.rpm.

Replace ⟨version⟩ with the number of the package to install. Since SuSE Linux 7.3, reiserfs is the standard file system. It requires the use of an "initial ramdisk". Therefore, use the command mk_initrd to write the new initial ramdisk.

To be able to boot the old kernel, configure the bootloader accordingly (for more information refer to *Booting and Boot Managers* on page 81). Finally, reboot to load the new Kernel.

To reinstall the original kernel from the SuSE Linux CDs the procedure is almost the same, except you copy the kernel rpm from the directory boot on CD 1 or the DVD. Now install as described above. If you receive an error message saying that a newer kernel rpm is already installed, add the option --force to the above rpm command.

Kernel Sources

To build a kernel, the package kernel-source must be installed. Additional packages, like the C compiler (package gcc), the GNU binutils (package `binutils`), and the include files for the C compiler (package `glibc-devel`), are selected for installation automatically by YaST2.

After installation, the kernel sources are located in `/usr/src/linux-`⟨*kernel-version*⟩`.SuSE`. If you plan to experiment with different kernels, unpack them in different subdirectories and create a symbolic link to the current kernel source. As there are software packages that rely on the sources being in `/usr/src/linux`, maintain this directory as a symbolic link to your current kernel source. YaST2 does this automatically.

Kernel Configuration

The most recently compiled configuration is stored in the file `/usr/src/linux/.config`. To edit the configuration of the currently-used kernel, go to the directory `/usr/src/linux` as user `root` and enter `cp /boot/vmlinuz.config .config`.

The kernel can be configured at the command line, in a menu in text-mode, or in a menu in the X Window System. The following is a short overview of these three methods.

> **Tip**
>
> To use an already existing `.config` without making changes, just type `make oldconfig` then proceed as described in Section *Compiling the Kernel* on page 267.
>
> **Tip**

Configuration on the Command Line

To configure the kernel, make sure your working directory is `/usr/src/linux` and enter `make config`. Choose the options you want supported by the kernel. There are two or three possibilities: (Y), (N), or (M). 'm' means that this device is not compiled directly into the kernel, but loaded as a module instead. Any driver needed to boot the system should be integrated into the kernel, not loaded as a module. With (↵), confirm the default settings read from the file `.config`. Pressing any other key accesses a short help text about the current option.

Configuration in Text Mode

A much more convenient way of configuring the kernel can be achieved using `make menuconfig`. With `menuconfig`, you do not have to go through all the questions. Instead, select the areas of interest from the menu. The default settings are read from the file `.config`. To load another configuration, select 'Load an Alternate Configuration File' and enter the file name.

Configuration in the X Window System

If you have installed and configured the X Window System (package `xf86`) and Tcl/Tk (package `tcl` and package `tk`), you can use `make xconfig`. It uses a GUI (Graphical User Interface) that makes kernel configuration very user-friendly. If you have not logged in to the X Window System as `root`, enter the command `xhost +localhost` (replacing `localhost` with the name of the local host) to allow `root` to take over the display.

The default settings are taken from the file `/usr/src/linux/.config`. After a SuSE standard installation, this file contains the settings for the SuSE kernel, but it will be overwritten with your own settings. If you do not want to compile a completely new kernel, click 'Load Configuration from File' in the main menu and enter the file name. The settings for the currently-installed kernel are in `/boot/vmlinuz.config`. For safety, copy this file to `/usr/src/linux/.config`. This reduces the risk of wrong settings.

Kernel Modules

There is a wide variety of PC hardware components. To use this hardware properly, you need a "driver" with which the operating system (in Linux, the "kernel"), can access this hardware. There are basically two ways of integrating drivers into your system:

- The drivers can be compiled directly into the kernel. Such a kernel ("in one piece") is referred to as a *monolithic* kernel. Some drivers are only available in this form.

- Drivers can be loaded into the kernel on demand. In this case, the kernel is referred to as a *modularized* kernel. This has the advantage that only those drivers that are really needed are loaded and the kernel thus contains nothing unnecessary.

Which drivers to compile into the kernel and which to load as run-time modules is defined in the kernel configuration. Basically, components not required for booting the system should be built as modules. This makes sure the kernel does not get too big to be loaded by the BIOS or a boot loader. Drivers for `ext2`, the SCSI drivers on a SCSI-based system, and similar drivers should be compiled into the kernel. In contrast, items such as `isofs`, `msdos`, or `sound`, which are not needed for starting your computer system, should definitely be built as modules. Kernel modules are located at `/lib/modules/⟨Version⟩`, where ⟨Version⟩ is the current kernel version.

Handling Modules

The following commands are available:

- `insmod`
  insmod loads the requested module after searching for it in a subdirectory of `/lib/modules/⟨Version⟩`. It is better, however, to use `modprobe` (see below) rather than `insmod`.

- `rmmod`
  Unloads the requested module. This is only possible if this module is no longer needed. For example, the isofs module cannot be unloaded while a CD is still mounted.

- `depmod`
  Creates the file `modules.dep` in `/lib/modules/⟨Version⟩` that defines the dependencies of all the modules. This is necessary to ensure that all dependent modules are loaded with the selected ones. If `START_KERNELD` is set in `/etc/rc.config`, this file will be rebuilt each time the system is started.

- `modprobe`
  Loads or unloads a given module while taking into account dependencies of this module. This command is extremely powerful and can be used for a lot of things (e.g., probing all modules of a given type until one is successfully loaded). In contrast to insmod, modprobe checks `/etc/modules.conf` and therefore is the preferred method of loading modules. For detailed information on this topic, refer to the corresponding man page.

- `lsmod`
  Shows which modules are currently loaded as well as how many other modules are using them. Modules started by the kernel daemon are

tagged with `autoclean`. This label denotes that these modules will automatically be removed once they reach their idle time limit.

- `modinfo`
  Shows module information.

/etc/modules.conf

`/etc/modules.conf` affects how modules are loaded. Refer to the man page for depmod (`man depmod`).

Enter the parameters for modules that access hardware directly in this file. Such modules may need system-specific options (e. g., CD-ROM driver or network driver). The parameters entered here are, for the most part, identical to those given to the boot prompt of the kernel, for example, for LILO . However, in many cases the names used at the boot prompt are different . If a module failed to load, try specifying the hardware in this file and use modprobe instead of insmod to load the module.

Kmod — the Kernel Module Loader

The kernel module loader is the most elegant way to use modules. Kmod performs background monitoring and makes sure the required modules are loaded by modprobe as soon as the respective functionality is needed in the kernel.

To use Kmod, set the corresponding variable in the kernel configuration 'Kernel module loader' (`CONFIG_KMOD`). Kmod is not designed to automatically unload modules. The potential saving in memory is only marginal for the RAM capacity of computers today. See also `/usr/src/linux/Documentation/kmod.txt`. For reasons of performance, it is better for server machines, which have special tasks to perform and need only a few drivers, to have a "monolithic" kernel.

Settings in the Kernel Configuration

All the kernel's configuration options cannot be covered here in detail. Make use of the numerous help texts available on kernel configuration. The latest kernel documentation is always in `/usr/src/linux/Documentation`.

Compiling the Kernel

We recommend compiling a "bzImage". As a rule, this avoids the problem of the kernel getting too large, as can easily happen if you select too many features and create a "zImage". You will then get error messages like "kernel too big" or "System is too big".

After customizing the kernel configuration, start compilation by entering:

```
earth:/usr/src/linux # make dep
earth:/usr/src/linux # make clean
earth:/usr/src/linux # make bzImage
```

These three commands can be entered on one line as well:

```
earth:/usr/src/linux # make dep clean bzImage
```

After a successful compilation, you will find the compressed kernel in `/usr/src/linux/arch/\suselxarch{}/boot`. The kernel image — the file that contains the kernel — is called `bzImage`. If you cannot find this file, an error probably occurred during the kernel compilation. In the bash shell, enter the following command to launch the kernel compilation again and write the output to a file `kernel.out`:

```
earth:/usr/src/linux # make bzImage 2>&1 | tee kernel.out
```

If you have configured parts of your kernel to load as modules, launch the module compilation. Do this with `make modules`.

Installing the Kernel

After the kernel is compiled, it must be installed so it can be booted. If you use LILO, LILO must be updated as well. To prevent unpleasant surprises, it is recommended that you keep the old kernel (e.g., as `/boot/vmlinuz.old`), so that you can still boot it if the new kernel does not function as expected:

```
earth:/usr/src/linux # cp /boot/vmlinuz /boot/vmlinuz.old
earth:/usr/src/linux # cp arch/i386/boot/bzImage /boot/vmlinuz
earth:/usr/src/linux # lilo
```

The Makefile target `make bzlilo` performs these three steps in one go. Now the compiled modules need to be installed. By entering:

```
earth:/usr/src/linux # make modules_install
```
copy these to the correct directories in /lib/modules/⟨Version⟩. This overwrites the old modules with the same kernel version. However, the original modules can be reinstalled together with the kernel from the CDs.

> **Tip**
>
> You should make sure that modules whose functionality may now have been directly compiled into the kernel are removed from /lib/modules/⟨Version⟩. Otherwise, unexpected effects could occur. This is one reason why the inexperienced user is *strongly* advised against compiling the kernel.
>
> **Tip**

To enable LILO to boot the old kernel (now /boot/vmlinuz.old), add an image entry with label Linux.old in your /etc/lilo.conf. This procedure is described in detail in Section *Booting and Boot Managers* on page 81. When you have adapted /etc/lilo.conf to your needs, enter lilo.

If you boot Linux from DOS via linux.bat (loadlin), you must copy the kernel to /dosc/loadlin/bzimage (or to the directory where you have installed loadlin) for it to be available for the next boot.

If you start Linux via the Windows NT boot manager, copy the LILO boot sector to the Windows NT start partition again (see Section *Windows NT or Windows 2000 and Linux* on page 98 for details).

The file /System.map contains kernel symbols required by the modules to ensure successful launching of kernel functions. This file depends on the current kernel. Therefore, once you have compiled and installed the kernel, copy /usr/src/linux/System.map to the directory (/boot). This file is regenerated each time the kernel is recompiled. If you create your kernel using make bzlilo or make zlilo, this is done for you automatically. If you get an error message like "System.map does not match current kernel", System.map probably has not been copied.

Cleaning Your Hard Disk After Compilation

If you are low on hard disk space, delete the object files generated during kernel compilation using make clean in the /usr/src/linux directory. If you have plenty of disk space and plan to reconfigure the kernel on a regular basis, you might want to skip this. Recompiling the kernel is considerably faster then, since only the parts affected by changes will actually be recompiled.

Special Features of SuSE Linux

This chapter provides information on the *Filesystem Hierarchy Standard* (FHS) and *Linux Standard Base* (LSB), various software packages, and special features such as booting with "initrd", linuxrc, and the "rescue system".

Linux Standards	270
Example Environments for FTP and HTTP	270
Hints on Special Software Packages	271
Booting with the Initial Ramdisk	276
linuxrc	280
The SuSE Rescue System	285
Virtual Consoles	291
Keyboard Mapping	291
Local Adjustments — I18N/L10N	292

Linux Standards

File System Hierarchy Standard (FHS)

SuSE Linux strives, as far as possible, to conform to the *File system Hierarchy Standard* (FHS, package `fhs`). See also `http://www.pathname.com/fhs/`. For this reason, it is sometimes necessary to move files or directories to their "correct" places in the file system.

Linux Standard Base (LSB)

SuSE supports the *Linux Standard Base* project. Current information on this can be found at `http://www.linuxbase.org`.

The LSB specification version for 8.1 is 1.2. From now on, the Filesystem Hierarchy Standard (FHS) is included in the specification and defines settings, such as the package format and the initialization of the system. See Chapter *The SuSE Linux Boot Concept* on page 295.

teTeX — TeX in SuSE Linux

TeX is a complete typesetting system which runs on various platforms. It is expandable with macro packages like LaTeX. It consists of very many single files that have to be assembled according to the *TeX Directory Structure* (TDS) (ref. `ftp://ftp.dante.de/tex-archive/tds/` teTeX is a compilation of current TeXapplications.

teTeX is employed in SuSE Linux with a configuration that complies with the requirements of both the TDS and the FHS.

Example Environments for FTP and HTTP

About FTP

To make it easier to set up an FTP server, the package `ftpdir` includes an example environment. This is installed in `/srv/ftp`.

About HTTP

Apache is the standard web server in SuSE Linux. Together with the installation of Apache, some example documents are made available in `/srv/httpd`. To set up your own web server, include your own DocumentRoot in `/etc/httpd/httpd.conf` and store your files (documents, picture files) accordingly.

Hints on Special Software Packages

Package bash and /etc/profile

1. `/etc/profile`
2. `~/.profile`
3. `/etc/bash.bashrc`
4. `~/.bashrc`

Users can make personal entries in `~/.profile` or in `~/.bashrc` respectively. To ensure the correct processing of these files, it is necessary to copy the basic settings from `/etc/skel/.profile` or `/etc/skel/.bashrc` respectively into the home directory of the user. It is recommended to copy the settings from `/etc/skel` following an update. Execute the following shell commands to prevent the loss of personal adjustments:

```
mv ~/.bashrc ~/.bashrc.old
cp /etc/skel/.bashrc ~/.bashrc
mv ~/.profile ~/.profile.old
cp /etc/skel/.profile ~/.profile
```

The personal adjustments then need to be copied back from the files `*.old`.

cron Package

The cron tables are now located in `/var/cron/tabs`. `/etc/crontab` serves as a system-wide cron table. Enter the name of the user who should run the command directly after the time table (see File 40, here `root` is entered). Package-specific tables, located in `/etc/cron.d`, have the same format. See the man page for `cron` (`man 8 cron`).

```
1-59/5 * * * * root test -x /usr/sbin/atrun && /usr/sbin/atrun
```

File 40: Example of an Entry in /etc/crontab

/etc/crontab cannot be processed with crontab -e. It must be loaded directly into an editor, modified, then saved.

A number of packages install shell scripts to the directories /etc/cron.hourly, /etc/cron.daily, /etc/cron.weekly, and /etc/cron.monthly, whose instructions are controlled by /usr/lib/cron/run-crons. /usr/lib/cron/run-crons is run every fifteen minutes from the main table (/etc/crontab). This guarantees that processes that may have been neglected can be run at the proper time. Do not be surprised if, shortly after booting, the user nobody turns up in the process tables and is highly active. This probably means that nobody is just updating the locate (see Section *Settings for the Files in /etc/sysconfig* on page 317).

The daily system maintenance jobs have been distributed to various scripts for reasons of clarity (package aaa_base). Apart from aaa_base, /etc/cron.daily thus contains for instance the components backup-rpmdb, clean-tmp or clean-vi.

Log Files — the Package logrotate

There are a number of system services ("daemons"), which, along with the kernel itself, regularly record the system status and specific events to log files. This way, the administrator can regularly check the status of the system at a certain point in time, recognize errors or faulty functions, and troubleshoot them with pinpoint precision. These log files are normally stored in /var/log as specified by FHS and grow on a daily basis. The package logrotate package helps control the growth of these files.

Changing to logrotate

The old settings listed below will be adopted when updating from a version older than SuSE Linux 8.0:

- Entries from /etc/logfile not associated with a particular package are moved to /etc/logrotate.d/aaa_base.

- The variable MAX_DAYS_FOR_LOG_FILES from the former rc.config file is mapped as dateext and maxage in the configuration file. Refer to the man page for logrotate (man 8 logrotate).

Configuration

Configure logrotate with the file `/etc/logrotate.conf`. In particular, the include specification primarily configures the additional files to read. SuSE Linux ensures that individual packages install files in `/etc/logrotate.d` (e.g., `syslog` or `yast`).

```
# see "man logrotate" for details
# rotate log files weekly
weekly

# keep 4 weeks worth of backlogs
rotate 4

# create new (empty) log files after rotating old ones
create

# uncomment this if you want your log files compressed
#compress

# RPM packages drop log rotation information into this directory
include /etc/logrotate.d

# no packages own lastlog or wtmp - we'll rotate them here
#/var/log/wtmp {
#    monthly
#    create 0664 root utmp
#    rotate 1
#}

# system-specific logs may be also be configured here.
```

File 41: Example for /etc/logrotate.conf

logrotate is controlled through cron and it is called daily by `/etc/cron.daily/logrotate`.

> **Note**
>
> The create option reads all settings made by the administrator in `/etc/permissions*`. Ensure that no conflicts arise from any personal modifications.

Man Pages

For some GNU applications (e. g., tar) the man pages are no longer maintained. They have been replaced by info files. info is GNU's hypertext system. Typing `info info` gives a starting help for using `info`. `info` can be launched via `emacs -f info` or on its own with `info`. The programs `tkinfo` and `xinfo` are easy to use or you can access the SuSE help system.

The Command ulimit

With the `ulimit` (*user limits*) command, it is possible to set limits for the use of system resources and to have these displayed. `ulimit` is especially useful for limiting the memory available for applications. With this, an application can be prevented from using too much memory on its own, which could bring the system to a standstill.

`ulimit` can be used with various options. To limit memory usage, use the options listed in Table 12.1.

-m	maximum size of physical memory
-v	maximum size of virtual memory (swap)
-s	maximum size of the stack
-c	maximum size of the core files
-a	display of limits set

Table 12.1: `ulimit`*: Setting Resources for the User*

System-wide settings can be made in `/etc/profile`. There, creating core files must be enabled, needed by programmers for "debugging". A normal user cannot increase the values specified in `/etc/profile` by the system administrator, but he can make special entries in his own `~/.bashrc`.

```
# Limits of physical memory:
ulimit -m 98304

# Limits of virtual memory:
ulimit -v 98304
```

File 42: ulimit: Settings in ~/.bashrc

Details of memory must be specified in KB. For more detailed information, see the man page for bash (`man bash`).

> **Note**
>
> Not all shells support `ulimit` directives. PAM (for instance, `pam_limits`) offers comprehensive adjustment possibilities should you depend on encompassing settings for these restrictions.
>
> **Note**

The free Command

The `free` command is somewhat misleading if your goal is to find out how much RAM is currently being used. The relevant information can be found in `/proc/meminfo`. These days, users, who have access to a modern operating system such as Linux, should not really have to worry much about memory. The concept of "available RAM" dates back to before the days of unified memory management. The slogan *free memory is bad memory* applies well to Linux. As a result, Linux has always made the effort to balance out caches without actually allowing free or unused memory.

Basically, the kernel does not have direct knowledge of any applications or user data. Instead, it manages applications and user data in a "page cache". If memory runs short, parts of it will be either written to the swap partition or to files, from which they can initially be read with the help of the `mmap` command (see the man page for `mmap` (`man 2 mmap`)).

Furthermore, the kernel also contains other caches, such as the "slab cache" where the caches used for network access are stored. This may explain differences between the counters in `/proc/meminfo`. Most, but not all of them, can be accessed via `/proc/slabinfo`.

The File /etc/resolv.conf

Domain name resolution is handled through the file `/etc/resolv.conf`. Refer to *DNS — Domain Name Service* on page 361 on this.

This file is updated by the script `/sbin/modify_resolvconf` exclusively, with no other program having permission to modify `/etc/resolv.conf` directly. Enforcing this rule is the only way to guarantee that the system's network configuration and the relevant files are kept in a consistent state.

Booting with the Initial Ramdisk

As soon as the Linux kernel has been booted and the root file system (/) mounted, programs can be run and further kernel modules can be integrated to provide additional functions.

To mount the root file system, certain conditions must be met. The kernel needs the corresponding drivers to access the device on which the root file system is located (especially SCSI drivers). The kernel must also contain the code needed to read the file system (`ext2`, `reiserfs`, `romfs`, etc.). It is also conceivable that the root file system is already encrypted. In this case, a password is needed to mount the file system.

If you just take a look at the problem of SCSI drivers, a number of different solutions are possible: the kernel could contain all imaginable drivers. This might be a problem because different drivers could conflict with each other. Also, the kernel will become very large because of this. Another possibility is to provide different kernels, each one containing just one or a few SCSI drivers. This method also has the problem that a large number of different kernels are required, a problem then increased by the differently optimized kernels (Pentium optimization, SMP).

The idea of loading the SCSI driver as a module leads to the general question answered by the concept of an *initial ramdisk*: creating a way of being able to run user space programs even before the root file system is mounted.

Concept of the Initial Ramdisk

The *initial ramdisk* (also called "initdisk" or "initrd") solves precisely the problems described above. The Linux kernel provides an option of having a small file system loaded to a RAM disk and running programs there before the actual root file system is mounted. The loading of `initrd` is taken over by the boot loader (LILO, loadlin, etc.). Boot loaders only need BIOS routines to load data from the boot medium. If the boot loader is able to load the kernel, it can also load the initial ramdisk. Special drivers are not required.

The Order of the Booting Process with initrd

The boot loader loads the kernel and the `initrd` to memory and starts the kernel. The boot loader informs the kernel that an `initrd` exists and where it is located in memory.

If the `initrd` was compressed (which is typically the case), the kernel decompresses the `initrd` and mounts it as a temporary root file system. A program called linuxrc is started on this in the `initrd`. This program can now do all the things necessary to mount the proper root file system. As soon as linuxrc finishes, the temporary `initrd` is unmounted and the boot process continues as normal with the mounting of the proper root file system. Mounting the `initrd` and running linuxrc can be seen as a short interlude during a normal boot process.

The kernel tries to remount `initrd` to the `/initrd` directly after the actual root partition is booted. If this fails because the mount point `/initrd` does not exist, for example, the kernel will attempt to unmount `initrd`. If this does not work, the system is fully functional, but the memory taken up by `initrd` can no longer be unlocked and thus will no longer be available.

linuxrc

These are the only requirements for the program linuxrc in the `initrd`. It must have the special name `linuxrc` and it must be located in the root directory of the `initrd`. Apart from this, it only needs to be executable by the kernel. This means that linuxrc may be dynamically linked. In this case, the "shared libraries" in `/lib` must be completely available in `initrd`. linuxrc can also be a shell script. For this to work, a shell must exist in `/bin`. In short, `initrd` must contain a minimal Linux system that allows the program linuxrc to be run. When SuSE Linux is installed, a statically linked linuxrc is used to keep `initrd` as small as possible (space on boot disks is very limited). linuxrc is run with `root` permissions.

The Real Root File System

As soon as linuxrc terminates, `initrd` is unmounted and discarded, the boot process carries on as normal, and the kernel mounts the real file system. What is mounted as the root file system can be influenced by linuxrc. It just needs to mount the `/proc` file system and write the value of the real root file system in numerical form to `/proc/sys/kernel/real-root-dev`.

Boot Loaders

Most boot loaders (above all, LILO, loadlin, and syslinux) can handle `initrd`. Individual boot loaders are given instructions on how to use `initrd` as follows:

1. LILO

Entering the following line in `/etc/lilo.conf`:

```
initrd=/boot/initrd
```

The file /boot/initrd is the *initial ramdisk*. It can be, but does not have to be, compressed.

2. **loadlin.exe**
   run with:

   ```
   C:> loadlin ⟨kernelimage⟩ initrd=C:\loadlin\initrd ⟨parameter⟩
   ```

3. **syslinux**
   Entering the following line in syslinux.cfg:

   ```
   append initrd=initrd ⟨further parameters⟩
   ```

Using initrd in SuSE

Installing the System

The initrd has already been used for some time for the installation: here the user can load modules and make the entries necessary for an installation (above all, for the source medium). linuxrc then starts YaST, which carries out the installation. When YaST has finished, it tells linuxrc where the root file system of the freshly installed system is located. linuxrc writes this value to /proc, terminates, and informs the kernel to continue booting into the newly installed system.

For an installation of SuSE Linux, you are, from the very beginning, booting the system being installed. A real reboot after installation only takes place if the kernel does not match the modules installed in the system. Since SuSE Linux uses a kernel for uniprocessor systems during installation, a reboot is only necessary if if an SMP kernel was installed in the system with the corresponding modules.

Booting the Installed System

In the past, YaST has provided more than forty kernels for installing in the system, with the only basic difference a specific SCSI driver. This was necessary to be able to mount the root file system after booting. Further drivers could then be loaded afterwards as modules. Because optimized kernels are now available, this concept is no longer feasible — by now, over one hundred kernel images would be needed.

This is why an `initrd` is used now, even to start the system normally. The way it is used is similar to that for an installation. The linuxrc used here, however, is simply a shell script with the task of loading a given module. Typically, this is just one single module — the very SCSI driver which is needed to access the root file system.

Creating an initrd

An `initrd` is created by means of the script `mkinitrd` (previously `mk_initrd`). In SuSE Linux, the modules to load are specified by the variable INITRD_MODULES in `/etc/sysconfig/kernel`. After installation, this variable is automatically occupied by the correct values (the installation linuxrc knows which modules were loaded). Here it should be mentioned that the modules were loaded in exactly the order in which they appear in INITRD_MODULES. This is especially important if a number of SCSI drivers are used, since otherwise the names of the hard disks would change. Strictly speaking, it would be sufficient just to load those drivers needed to access the root file system, because the automatic loading of additional SCSI drivers may cause problems (how should it be "triggered" if hard disks hang on the second SCSI adapter), we load all SCSI drivers needed at the installation by means of `initrd`.

The current `mkinitrd` checks if a SCSI driver is needed for the root file system. If you run `mkinitrd` on a system where / is found on EIDE hard disks, an `initrd` is not needed as the kernel used for SuSE Linux already contains the EIDE driver. As there are more and more special EIDE controllers coming onto the market, in the future it will probably be necessary, in such cases, to use an `initrd` to boot the installed system.

> **Note**
>
> Because the loading of the `initrd` with the boot loader runs in the same way as loading the kernel itself (LILO notices in its map file the location of the files), LILO must be reinstalled after every change in `initrd`. After every `mkinitrd`, a `lilo` is also necessary.

Possible Difficulties — Self-Compiled Kernels

A self-compiled kernel can often lead to the following problem: out of habit, the SCSI driver is hard-linked to the kernel, but the existing `initrd` remains unchanged. When you boot, the following occurs. The kernel already contains the SCSI driver, so the hardware is detected. `initrd`, however, now tries to load the driver again as a module. With some SCSI drivers, especially with `aic7xxx`, this leads to the system blocking. Strictly speaking, this is a kernel error. An already existing driver should not be allowed to be loaded again as a module. The problem is already known from another context, however (serial drivers).

There are several solutions to the problem: either configure the driver as a module (then it will be correctly loaded in the `initrd`) or remove the entry for `initrd` from the file `/etc/lilo.conf`. An equivalent to the latter solution is to remove the variable INITRD_MODULES then run `mkinitrd`, which then realizes that no `initrd` is needed.

Prospects

It is quite possible in the future that an `initrd` will be used for many more and much more sophisticated things than loading modules needed to access `/`.

- High-end EIDE drivers
- Root file system on RAID software (linuxrc sets up the `md` devices)
- Root file system on the LVM
- Root file system is encrypted (linuxrc asks for the password)
- Root file system on a SCSI hard disk on a PCMCIA adapter.

For More Information

`/usr/src/linux/Documentation/ramdisk.txt`
`/usr/src/linux/Documentation/initrd.txt`
the man page for `initrd` (man 4 initrd)

linuxrc

linuxrc is started during the boot of the kernel, usually as a prelude to a Linux system installation, before the "actual" booting commences (the kernel must first be properly configured, of course). This allows you to boot a small, modularized kernel and to load the few drivers needed as modules from a floppy disk.

If needed, linuxrc assists in loading the related drivers.

You can also use linuxrc as a boot tool for an already installed system. You can even start a totally independent RAM disk–based rescue system, for example, if something serious should happen to your hard disk or you have simply forgotten your `root` password. More about this below, in Section *The SuSE Rescue System* on page 285.

Main Menu

After you have selected the language and keyboard, find yourself in linuxrc's main menu (see Figure 1.2 on page 10). Normally, linuxrc is used to start Linux. Go to the start menu to start an installation ('Start installation / system').

Settings / Preferences

Specify your settings in respect to 'Language', 'Screen' (Color/monochrome), 'Keyboard Layout', and 'Debug (Experts)'.

System Information

In 'System Information' (Figure 12.1 on the next page), check a number of other things, besides kernel messages, such as the I/O addresses of PCI cards or the size of the main memory recognized by Linux.

You can check some system information in 'System information'. Here, check the used interrupts, I/O ports used, main memory, and recognized PCI devices as detected by Linux.

The next lines show how a hard disk and a CD-ROM connected to an (E)IDE controller announce their start. In this case, you do not need to load additional modules:

```
hda: ST32140A, 2015MB w/128kB Cache, LBA, CHS=1023/64/63
hdb: CD-ROM CDR-S1G, ATAPI CD-ROM drive
Partition check:
 hda: hda1 hda2 hda3 < hda5 >
```

If you booted a kernel that already had a SCSI driver compiled, you do not need this SCSI driver as a module as well. Quite typical announcements when loading SCSI adapters and connected devices might look like this:

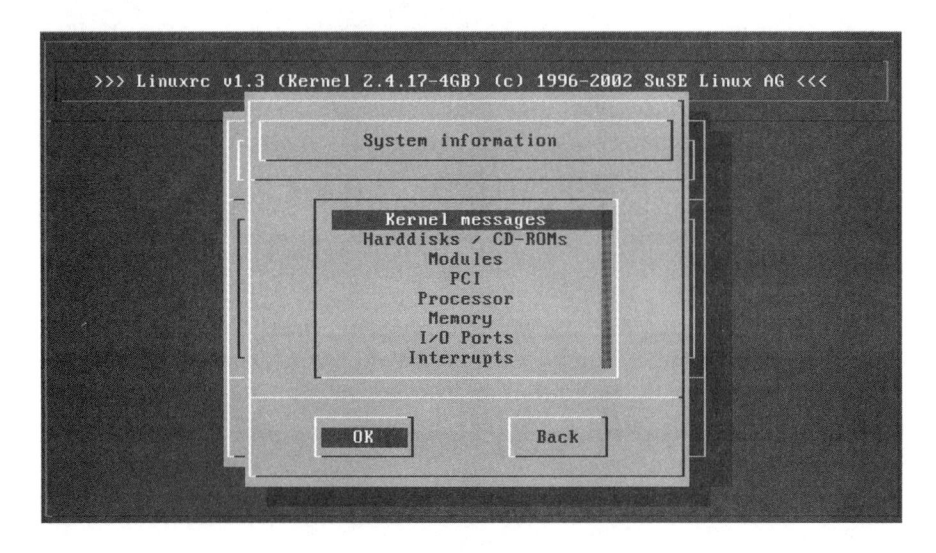

Figure 12.1: System Information

```
scsi : 1 host.
Started kswapd v 1.4.2.2
scsi0 : target 0 accepting period 100ns offset 8 10.00MHz FAST SCSI-II
scsi0 : setting target 0 to period 100ns offset 8 10.00MHz FAST SCSI-II
  Vendor: QUANTUM    Model: VP32210           Rev: 81H8
  Type:   Direct-Access                       ANSI SCSI revision: 02
Detected scsi disk sda at scsi0, channel 0, id 0, lun 0
scsi0 : target 2 accepting period 236ns offset 8 4.23MHz synchronous SCSI
scsi0 : setting target 2 to period 248ns offset 8 4.03MHz synchronous SCSI
  Vendor: TOSHIBA    Model: CD-ROM XM-3401TA Rev: 0283
  Type:   CD-ROM                              ANSI SCSI revision: 02
scsi : detected 1 SCSI disk total.
SCSI device sda: hdwr sector= 512 bytes. Sectors= 4308352 [2103 MB] [2.1 GB]
Partition check:
 sda: sda1 sda2 sda3 sda4 < sda5 sda6 sda7 sda8 >
```

Loading Modules

Select which kinds of modules you need. If you booted via disk, the corresponding data must be read by linuxrc and displayed in a list.

If you have booted from CD or from DOS (via loadlin), these modules are already set in linuxrc. This saves tedious loading, but requires additional memory.

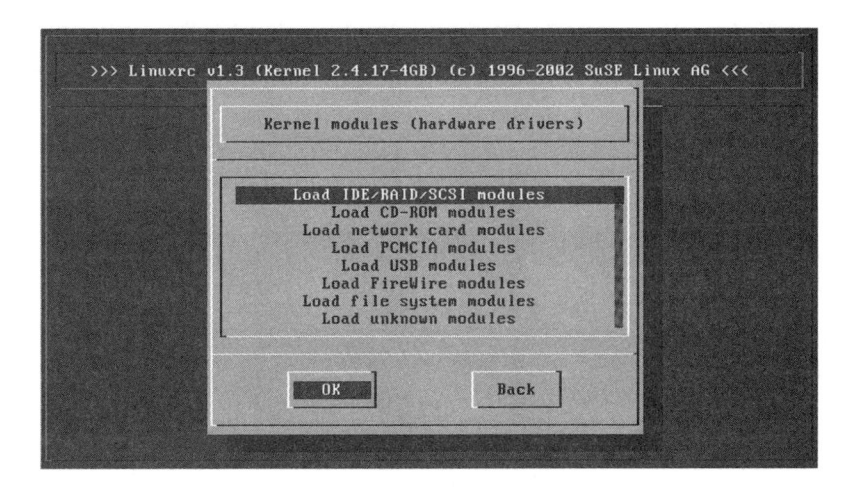

Figure 12.2: Load Modules

linuxrc offers a list of available drivers. On the left is the name of the module and, on the right, a short description of its usage. For some components, there are a variety of drivers from which to choose (even newer alpha drivers).

Passing Parameters

When you have found a suitable driver, move to it with the cursor and press ⏎. This opens a dialog box in which to add additional parameters for this module.

Beware that — in contrast to entering the parameters at the kernel prompt (as in MILO, LILO, or SYSLINUX) — multiple parameters for the same module must be separated here by a blank space.

In most cases, it is not necessary to specify the hardware in detail. Most drivers find their components automatically. Specifying parameters is only necessary if you have a network card or an older CD-ROM drive with a proprietary controller card. If in doubt, just try pressing ⏎.

Recognizing and initializing certain hardware can take some time. Switching to virtual console 4 (Alt + F4) lets you watch the kernel messages while loading. SCSI drivers need a while, as they have to wait for each device to load.

The messages are displayed by linuxrc so you can verify that everything ran smoothly. If it fails, the messages might give a hint as to why.

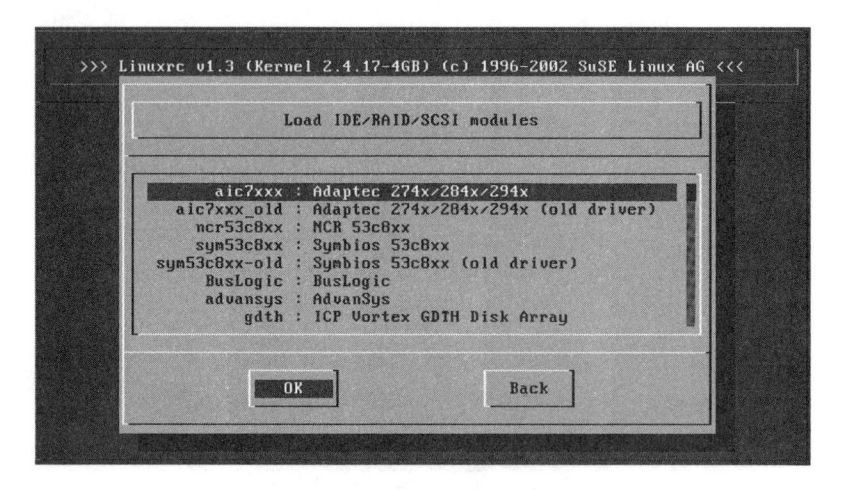

Figure 12.3: Selection of SCSI Drivers

Start Installation / System

Once you have set up hardware support via modules, proceed to the 'Start installation / system' menu.

From here, a number of procedures can be started: 'Start installation' (an update is also started from this item), 'Boot installed system' (the root partition must be known), 'Start rescue system' (refer to Section *The SuSE Rescue System* on the facing page), and 'Eject CD'.

'Start Live-CD' is only available if you booted a "LiveEval CD". Download ISO images from the FTP server (live-eval-\variable{VERSION}):

```
ftp://ftp.suse.com/pub/suse/i386/
```

--- Tip ---

The item 'Start Live-CD' can be of great use if, for example, you want to test, without actually installing, if the computer in question or the laptop you might want to buy is at all compatible with SuSE Linux — such a test ought to be possible in every modern PC shop, without any trouble.

--- Tip ---

For the installation (Figure 12.5 on page 286), choose various sources for the installation and similarly for the rescue system (see Figure 12.5 on page 286).

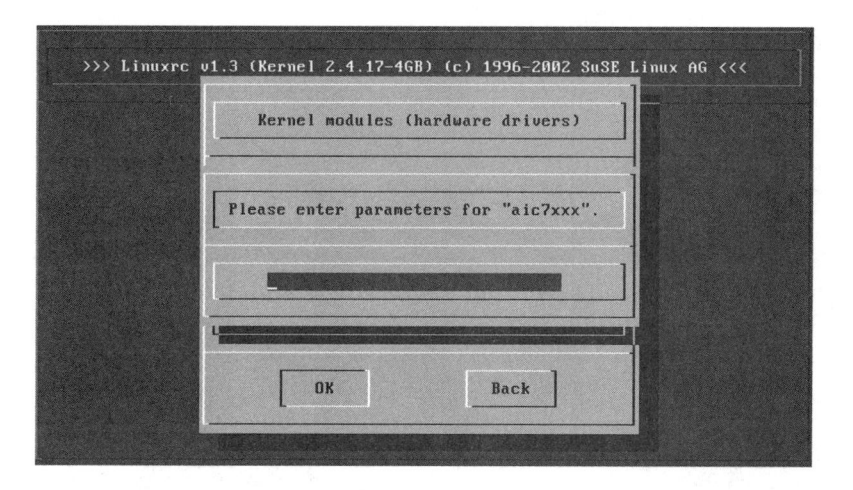

Figure 12.4: Entering Parameters for a Module to Load

The SuSE Rescue System

SuSE Linux contains several Linux rescue systems so that, in emergencies, your Linux partitions on the hard disks are reachable "from the outside": via a boot disk or the "Rescue" System, loaded from disk, CD, the network, or the SuSE FTP server. There is also a bootable SuSE Linux CD (the *"LiveEval CD"*) that can be used as a rescue system. The rescue system includes several help programs with which you can remedy large problems with inaccessible hard disks, misconfigured configuration files, or other similar problems.

Another aspect of the rescue system is Parted, which is used for modifying the partition size. This program can be launched from inside the rescue system itself, if you do not want to take advantage of the resizer integrated in YaST2. Information on Parted can be found at:

```
http://www.gnu.org/software/parted/
```

─ Tip ─────────────────────────────────────

Always have a boot and rescue disk at hand, because the slight effort for creating and maintaining the disk is negligible in comparison to the time wasted and work involved when, in the case of emergency, you cannot access your system or your CD-ROM drive.

─────────────────────────────────────── Tip ─

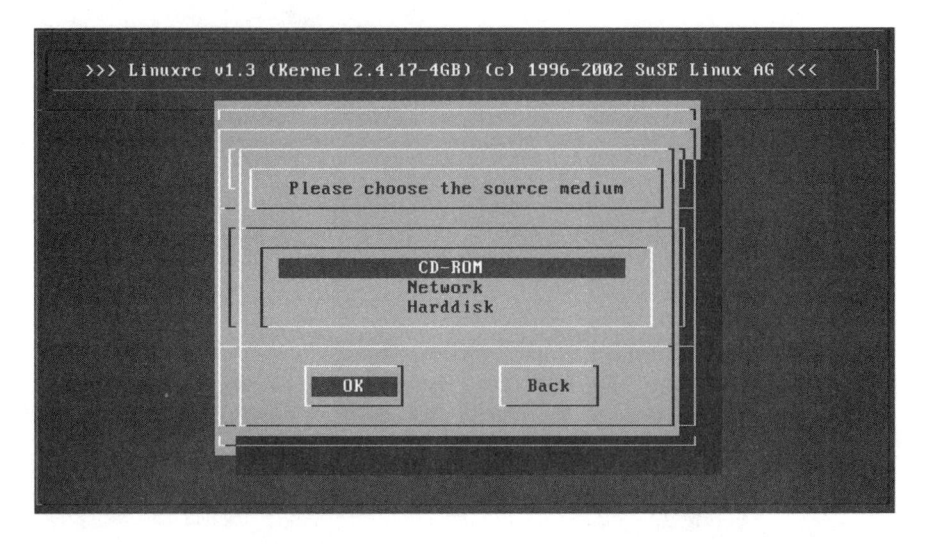

Figure 12.5: Selection of Source Media in linuxrc

Preparations

For setting up your rescue system, you need two disks free of errors: one as a future boot disk and the other for the compressed image of a small root file system. The image file `bootdisk` for booting the system and the file `rescue` for the root file system can be found on the first CD in the `boot` directory.

There are three ways to set up the root file system on the disk:

- with YaST

- in a console using the Linux commands

    earth:~ # **/sbin/badblocks -v /dev/fd0 1440**
    earth:~ # **dd if=/media/cdrom/boot/rescue of=/dev/fd0 bs=18k**

- at the DOS prompt (where the CD-ROM drive is Q:)

    Q:\> **cd \dosutils\rawrite** Q:\dosutils\rawrite> **rawrite.exe**

As of Version 8.0, the rescue disk is currently based on libc5 (SuSE Linux 5.3), since it is possible in this to save some programs, such as an editor, fdisk, or e2fsck to a disk.

> **Note**
>
> The rescue disk cannot be mounted, because it is not a file system. It only contains the compressed images of one. Directions for reading the file system are in the following paragraph.
>
> **Note**

To read the image, you will need to decompress the image file then mount the decompressed image as user `root`. If your Linux kernel support the *loop device*, the procedure is as follows:

```
earth:~ # cp /media/cdrom/boot/rescue /root/rescue.gz
earth:~ # gunzip /root/rescue.gz
earth:~ # mount -t ext2 -o loop /root/rescue /mnt
```

Starting the Rescue System

The rescue system is launched by the SuSE boot disk you created or by your bootable CD or DVD. It is required that the disk and CD-ROM or DVD drives are bootable. If necessary, change the boot series in the CMOS setup. Following are the steps for starting the rescue system:

1. Start your system with the SuSE boot disk created yourself or with the first SuSE Linux CD or DVD inserted into the corresponding drive.

2. Launch the entire system or choose 'Manual Installation' so that 'boot options' can be entered and kernel modules to load can be defined.

3. Make the respective settings for language and keyboard.

4. Select the item 'Installation/Start system' in the main menu.

5. If you started with the boot disk, now insert the installation CD or the `rescue` disk with the compressed image of the rescue system.

6. In the menu 'Start installation/system' select the item 'Start rescue system' (see Figure 1.3 on page 12) then specify the desired source medium (Figure 12.6 on the following page).

   Subsequently, we will introduce a few tips on selection options:

   'CD-ROM': When loading the rescue system, the path `/cdrom` is exported. This makes the installation from *this* CD possible.

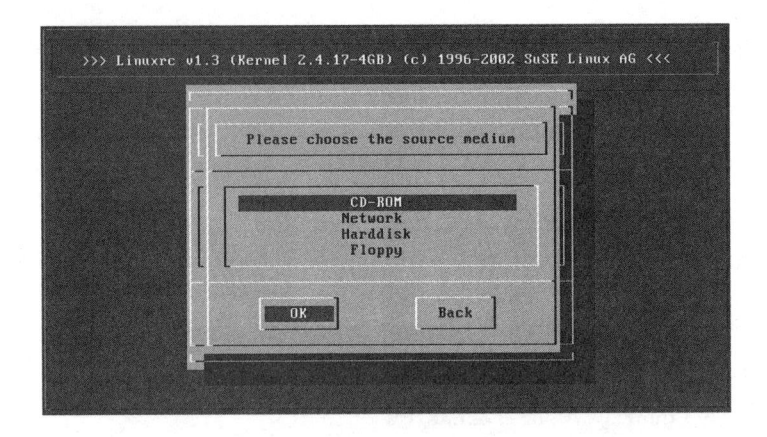

Figure 12.6: Source Medium for the Rescue System

- **'Network'**: For starting the `rescue` system over a network connection, the network card's driver must be loaded first. See the general information on this in Section *Installation from a Network Source* on page 16. Several protocols exist for this purpose (see Figure 12.7 on the facing page), such as NFS, FTP, or SMB.
- **'Hard disk'**: Load the `rescue` system from the hard disk.
- **'Floppy Disk'**: The `rescue` system can also be started from the floppy disk, especially if the computer only has a small amount of working memory.

Regardless of the medium chosen, the rescue system will be decompressed, loaded onto a RAM floppy disk as a new root file system, mounted, and started. Now it is ready for use.

Working with the Rescue System

The rescue system provides three virtual consoles on keys (Alt) + (F1) to (Alt) + (F3). Here, `root` may log in without a password. (Alt) + (F4) accesses the system console, where you can view the kernel and syslog messages.

A shell and lots of other useful utilities (net tools), such as the mount program, can be found in the /bin directory. In sbin, find important file and network utilities for reviewing and repairing the file system (e.g., e2fsck).

Furthermore, this directory contains the most important binaries for system maintenance, such as fdisk, mkfs, mkswap, mount, mount, init, and

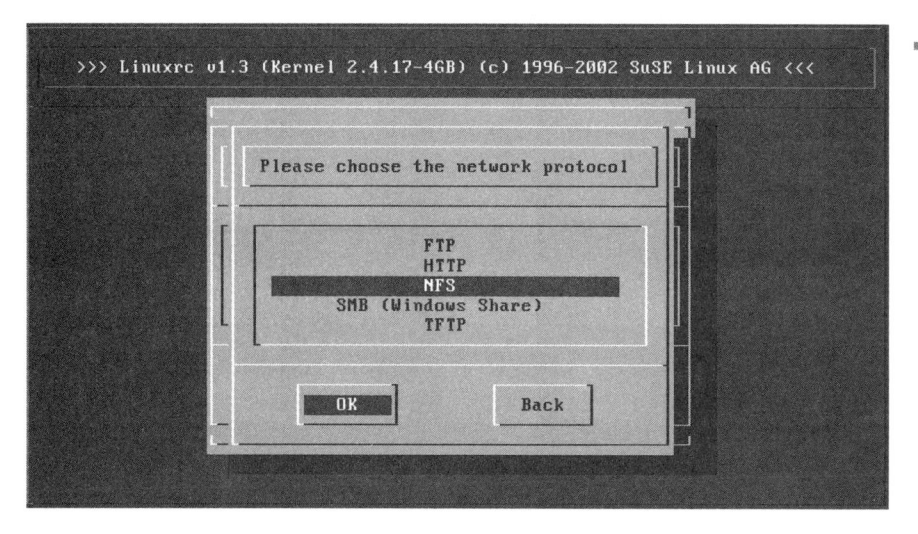

Figure 12.7: Network Protocols

shutdown, as well as ifconfig, route, and netstat for maintaining the network.

An editor, vi, is located in `/usr/bin`. Also, tools like grep, find, and less, along with telnet are available.

Accessing Your Normal System

To mount your SuSE Linux system using the rescue system, use the mount point `/mnt`. You can also use or create another directory.

As an example, assume your normal system is put together according to the `/etc/fstab` shown in the example File 43.

```
/dev/sdb5      swap      swap      defaults   0   0
/dev/sdb3      /         ext2      defaults   1   1
/dev/sdb6      /usr      ext2      defaults   1   2
```

File 43: Sample /etc/fstab

> **Caution**
>
> Pay attention to the order of steps outlined in the following section for mounting the various devices.

To access your entire system, mount it step-by-step in the /mnt directory using the following commands:

```
earth:/ #   mount /dev/sdb3 /mnt
earth:/ #   mount /dev/sdb6 /mnt/usr
```

Now, you can access your entire system and, for example, correct mistakes in configuration files such as /etc/fstab, /etc/passwd, and /etc/inittab. The configuration files are now located in the /mnt/etc directory instead of in /etc.

To recover even completely lost partitions with the fdisk program by simply setting it up again, determine where on the hard disk the partitions were previously located and make a printout of the /etc/fstab directory as well as the output of the command

```
earth:~ #   fdisk -l /dev/⟨disk⟩
```

Instead of the ⟨*disk*⟩ variable, insert, in order, the device names of your hard disks, such as hda.

Repairing File Systems Damaged file systems are tricky problems for the rescue system. This could happen after an unscheduled shutdown caused by power failure or a system crash. Generally, file systems cannot be repaired on a running system. If you encounter really severe problems, you may not even be able to mount your root file system so the system boot ends in a "kernel panic". Here, the only chance is to repair the system from the "outside" using a rescue system.

The SuSE Linux rescue system contains the utilities e2fsck and dumpe2fs (for diagnosis). These should remedy most problems.

In an emergency, man pages often are not available. That is why we have included them in this manual in Appendix B on page 469.

Example: If mounting a file system fails due to an *invalid* superblock, the e2fsck program would probably fail, too. If this were the case, your superblock may be corrupted, too. There are copies of the superblock located every 8192 blocks (8193, 16385, etc.). If your superblock is corrupted, try one of the copies instead. This is accomplished by entering the command:

```
earth:~ #   e2fsck -f -b 8193 /dev/damaged_partition
```

The -f option forces the file system check and overrides e2fsck's error so that — since the superblock copy is intact — everything is fine.

Virtual Consoles

Linux is a multiuser and multitasking system. The advantages of these features can be appreciated, even on a stand-alone PC system.

In text mode, there are six virtual consoles available. Switch between them using (Alt) + (F1) to (Alt) + (F6). The seventh console is reserved for X11. More or fewer consoles can be assigned by modifying the file /etc/inittab.

To switch to a console from X11 without leaving X11, use (Ctrl) + (Alt) + (F1) to (Ctrl) + (Alt) + (F6). (Alt) + (F7) then returns to X11.

Keyboard Mapping

To standardize the keyboard mapping of programs, changes were made to the following files:

```
/etc/inputrc
/usr/X11R6/lib/X11/Xmodmap
/etc/skel/.Xmodmap
/etc/skel/.exrc
/etc/skel/.less
/etc/skel/.lesskey
/etc/csh.cshrc
/etc/termcap
/usr/lib/terminfo/x/xterm
/usr/X11R6/lib/X11/app-defaults/XTerm
/usr/share/emacs/⟨VERSION⟩/site-lisp/term/*.el
/usr/lib/joerc
```

These changes only affect applications that make use of terminfo entries or whose configuration files are changed directly (vi, less, etc.). Other non-SuSE applications should be adjusted to these defaults.

Under X, the compose key ("multikey") can be accessed using the key combination (Ctrl) + (⇧ Shift) (right). Also see the corresponding entry in /usr/X11R6/lib/X11/Xmodmap.

Local Adjustments — I18N/L10N

SuSE Linux is, to a very large extent, internationalized and can be modified for local needs in a flexible manner. In other words, internationalization ("I18N") allows specific localizations ("L10N"). The abbreviations I18N and L10N are derived from the first and last letters of the words and, in between, the number of letters omitted.

Settings are made via LC_* variables defined in the file `/etc/sysconfig/language`. This refers not only to "native language support", but also to the categories *Messages* (Language), *Character Set*, *Sort Order*, *Time and Date*, *Numbers*, and *Money*. Each of these categories can be defined directly via its own variable or indirectly via a variable in the file `language` (see the man page for `locale` (`man 5 locale`)).

1. RC_LC_MESSAGES, RC_LC_CTYPE, RC_LC_COLLATE, RC_LC_TIME, RC_LC_NUMERIC, RC_LC_MONETARY: These variables are passed to the shell without the RC_ prefix and determine the above categories. The files concerned are listed below.

   The current setting can be shown with the command `locale`.

2. RC_LC_ALL: This variable (if set) overwrites the values of the variables mentioned in item 1.

3. RC_LANG: If none of the above variables are set, this is the "fallback". By default, SuSE Linux only sets RC_LANG. This makes it easier for users to enter their own values.

4. ROOT_USES_LANG: A `yes` or `no` variable. If it is set to `no`, root always works in the POSIX environment.

The other variables can be set via the `sysconfig` editor.

The value of such a variable contains the language code, country code, encoding, and modifier. The individual components are connected by special characters:

`LANG=⟨language⟩[[_⟨COUNTRY⟩].Encoding[@Modifier]]`

Some Examples

You should always set the language and country codes together. Language settings follow the standard ISO 639 (http://www.evertype.com/standards/iso639/iso639-en.html and http://www.loc

gov/standards/iso639-2/). Country codes are listed in ISO 3166, see (http://www.din.de/gremien/nas/nabd/iso3166ma/codlstp1/en_listp1.html). It only makes sense to set values for which usable description files can be found in `/usr/lib/locale`. Additional description files can be created from the files in `/usr/share/i18n` using the command `localedef`. A description file for `en_US.UTF-8` (for English and United States) can be created with:

```
earth:~ # localedef -i en_US -f UTF-8 en_US.UTF-8
```

LANG=en_US.ISO-8859-1

This sets the variable to English language, country to United States, and the character set to `ISO-8859-1`. This character set does not support the Euro sign, but it will be useful sometimes for programs that have not been updated to support `ISO-8859-15`. The string defining the charset (`ISO-8859-1` in our case) will then be evaluated by programs like Emacs.

LANG=en_US.UTF-8

If you use a Unicode xterm, it is necessary to specify `UTF-8` as well. To achieve this, make a small shell script called `uxterm` to start `xterm` with UTF-8 loaded each time. See File 44.

```
%

#!/bin/bash
export LANG=en_US.UTF-8
xterm -fn \
'-Misc-Fixed-Medium-R-Normal--18-120-100-100-C-90-ISO10646-1' \
-T 'xterm UTF-8' $*
```

File 44: uxterm to Start a Unicode xterm

SuSEconfig reads the variables in `/etc/sysconfig/language` and writes the necessary changes to `/etc/SuSEconfig/profile` and `/etc/SuSEconfig/csh.cshrc`. `/etc/SuSEconfig/profile` is read or "sourced" by `/etc/profile`. `/etc/SuSEconfig/csh.cshrc` is sourced by `/etc/csh.cshrc`. This makes the settings available system-wide.

Settings for Language Support

Files in the category *Messages* are, as a rule, only stored in the language directory (e. g., en) to have a fallback. If you set LANG to en,_US and the "message" file in /usr/share/locale/en_US/LC_MESSAGES does not exist, it will fall back to /usr/share/locale/en/LC_MESSAGES.

A fallback chain can also be defined, for example, for Breton → French or for Galician → Spanish → Portuguese:

```
LANGUAGE="br_FR:fr_FR"
LANGUAGE="gl_ES:es_ES:pt_PT"
```

If desired, use the Norwegian variants "nynorsk" and "bokmål" instead (with additional fallback to no):

```
LANG="nn_NO"
LANGUAGE="nn_NO:nb_NO:no"
```

or

```
LANG="nb_NO"
LANGUAGE="nb_NO:nn_NO:no"
```

Note that in Norwegian, LC_TIME is also treated differently.

Possible Problems

- The thousand comma is not recognized. LANG is probably set to en, but the description the glibc uses is located in /usr/share/locale/en_US/LC_NUMERIC. LC_NUMERIC, for example, must be set to en_US.

For More Information

- *The GNU C Library Reference Manual*, Chap. "Locales and Internationalization"; included in package glibc-info.

- Markus Kuhn, *UTF-8 and Unicode FAQ for Unix/Linux*, currently at http://www.cl.cam.ac.uk/~mgk25/unicode.html.

- *Unicode-Howto*, by Bruno Haible file:/usr/share/doc/howto/en/html/Unicode-HOWTO.html.

The SuSE Linux Boot Concept

Booting and initializing a UNIX system can challenge even an experienced system administrator. This chapter gives a short overview of the SuSE Linux boot concept. The new implementation is compatible with the *System Initialization* section of the LSB specification (Version 1.2). Refer to Section *Linux Standard Base (LSB)* on page 270 for more information on LSB.

The init Program	296
Runlevels	296
Changing Runlevels	298
Init Scripts	298
The YaST2 Runlevel Editor	301
SuSEconfig, /etc/sysconfig, and /etc/rc.config	301
Using the YaST2 sysconfig Editor	303
System Configuration: Scripts and Variables	303

The simple words "Uncompressing Linux..." signal that the kernel is taking control of your hardware. It checks and sets your console — more precisely: the BIOS registers of graphics cards and output format — to read BIOS settings and to initialize basic hardware interfaces. Next, your drivers "probe" existing hardware and initialize it accordingly. After checking the partitions and mounting the root file system, the kernel starts init, which "boots" (Unix jargon) the main system with all its programs and configurations. The kernel controls the entire system, including hardware access and the CPU time programs use.

The init Program

The program init is responsible for correctly initializing all system processes. Thus, it is the father of all processes in the entire system.

init takes a special role. It is started directly by the kernel and resists *signal 9*, which normally enables you to kill processes. All other programs are either started directly by init or by one of its "child" processes.

init is centrally configured via the /etc/inittab file. Here, the "runlevels" are defined (see Section *Runlevels* on the current page). It also specifies which services and daemons are available in each of the levels.

Depending on the entries in /etc/inittab, several scripts are invoked by init. For reasons of clarity, these scripts all reside in the directory /etc/init.d.

The entire process of starting the system and shutting it down is maintained by init. From this point of view, the kernel can be considered a background process whose task it is to maintain all other processes and to adjust CPU time and hardware access according to requests from other programs.

Runlevels

In Linux, *runlevels* define how the system is started. After booting, the system starts as defined in /etc/inittab in the line initdefault. Usually this is 3 or 5 (see Table 13.1 on the facing page). An alternative to this is assigning a special runlevel at boot time (e.g., at the boot prompt). The kernel passes any parameters it does not need directly to init.

To change runlevels while the system is running, enter init with the appropriate number. Only the superuser is allowed to do this. init 1 brings you

Runlevel	Meaning
0	System halt
S	Single user mode; from boot prompt with US keyboard layout
1	Single user mode
2	Local multiuser without remote network (standard)
3	Full multiuser with network
4	Unused
5	Full multiuser mode with network and xdm
6	System reboot

Table 13.1: Valid Runlevels in Linux

to *single user mode*, which is used for the maintenance and administration of your system. After finishing work in *S* mode, the system administrator can change the runlevel to 3 again by typing `init 3`. Now all essential programs are started and users can log in and work with the system.

Table 13.1 below gives an overview of available runlevels. Runlevel 2 should not be used on a system with a `/usr` partition mounted via NFS. You can halt the system using `init 0` or reboot it with `init 6`.

If you have already installed and configured the X Window System properly (Section *The X Window System* on page 113) and want users to log in via a graphical user interface, change the runlevel to 5. Try it first by typing `init 5` to see whether the system works as expected. Afterwards, set the default runlevel to 5 in YaST2.

Caution

Modifying `/etc/inittab`

If `/etc/inittab` is damaged, the system might not boot properly. Therefore, be extremely careful while editing `/etc/inittab` and always keep a backup of an intact version. To repair damage, try entering `init=/bin/sh` after the kernel name at the LILO boot prompt to boot directly into a shell. After that, replace `/etc/inittab` with your backup version using the `cp` command.

Caution

Changing Runlevels

Generally, a couple things happen when you change runlevels. First, *stop scripts* of the current runlevel are launched, closing down some programs essential for the current runlevel. Then *start scripts* of the new runlevel are started. Here, in most cases, a number of programs will be started.

To illustrate this, we will show you a change from runlevel 3 to 5:

- The administrator (root) tells init to change runlevels:

  root@earth:/ > **init 5**

- init now consults its configuration file (/etc/inittab) and realizes it should start /etc/init.d/rc with the new runlevel as a parameter.

- Now rc calls all the stop scripts of the current runlevel, but only for those where there is no start script in the selected new runlevel. In our example, these are all the scripts that reside in /etc/init.d/rc3.d (old runlevel was 3) and start with a 'K'. The number following 'K' guarantees a certain order to start, as there are some dependencies to consider.

  > **Note**
  >
  > The names of the stop scripts always begin with 'K' for kill. Start scripts begin with 'S' for start.
  >
  > **Note**

- The last thing to start are the start scripts of the new runlevel. These are (in our example) in /etc/init.d/rc5.d and begin with an 'S'. The same procedure regarding the order in which they are started is applied here.

When changing into the same runlevel as the current runlevel, init only checks /etc/inittab for changes and starts the appropriate steps (e.g., for starting a getty on another interface).

Init Scripts

Scripts in /etc/init.d are divided into two sections:

Option	Meaning
`start`	Starts service.
`stop`	Stops service.
`restart`	Stops service and restarts if service is already running. If it is not running, it starts the service.
`reload`	Load configuration of service again without stopping and restarting it.
`force-reload`	Load configuration of the service again if the service supports this. If not, a `restart` is carried out.
`status`	Show current status.

Table 13.2: Summary of init Script Options

- scripts executed directly by init. This only applies while booting and shutting down the system immediately (power failure or a user pressing Ctrl + Alt + Del).
- scripts started indirectly by init. These are run when changing the runlevel and always call the master script /etc/init.d/rc, which guarantees the correct order of the relevant scripts.

All scripts are located in `/etc/init.d`. Scripts for changing the runlevel are also found there, but are called via symbolic links from one of the subdirectories (`/etc/init.d/rc0.d` to `/etc/init.d/rc6.d`). This is just for clarity reasons and avoids duplicate scripts (e.g., if they are used in several runlevels). Since every script can be executed as both a start and a stop script, these scripts have to understand the parameters "start" and "stop". The scripts understand, in addition, the "restart", "reload", "force-reload", and "status" options. These different options are explained in Table 13.2.

After leaving runlevel 3, `/etc/init.d/rc3.d/K40network` is run. `/etc/init.d/rc` runs the `/etc/init.d/network` script with the `stop` parameter. After entering runlevel 5, the same script is started. This time, however, with the `start` parameter.

Links in these runlevel-specific subdirectories simply serve to assign the scripts to a certain runlevel. Adding and removing the required links is done by the program insserv (or by the link `/usr/lib/lsb/install_initd`) when installing and uninstalling packages. Refer to the man page for insserv (`man 8 insserv`).

Below is a short introduction to the boot and stop scripts launched first (or last, respectively) as well as an explanation of the maintaining script.

boot Executed while starting the system directly using init. It is independent of the chosen runlevel and is only executed once. Here, file systems are checked, the kernel daemon is launched, some unnecessary files in `/var/lock` are deleted, and the network is configured for the loopback device (if it has been selected in `/etc/rc.config`).

If an error occurs while automatically checking and repairing the file system, the system administrator can intervene after first entering the root password.

Last to be executed is the script boot.local.

boot.local Here, enter additional commands to execute at boot before changing into a runlevel. It can be compared to `AUTOEXEC.BAT` on DOS systems.

boot.setup General settings to make while changing from *single user mode* to another runlevel. Here, keyboard maps are loaded and the kernel daemon is started, which loads modules automatically.

halt This script is only executed while changing into runlevel 0 or 6. Here, it is executed either as `halt` or as `reboot`. Whether the system shuts down or reboots depends on how halt is called.

rc This script calls the appropriate stop scripts of the current runlevel and the start scripts of the newly selected runlevel.

With this concept in mind, you can create your own scripts. A skeleton has been prepared in `/etc/init.d/skeleton`. The exact format is described in the LSB outline. This defines specifically the order of steps and in which levels the script should be processed.

Now, create the links in the corresponding `rc?.d` to your script to make sure it is launched when you change runlevels (see Section *Changing Runlevels* on page 298 for script names). Refer to the man page for `init.d` (`man 7 init.d`) and the man page for `insserv` (`man 8 insserv`) for the necessary technical background. Use the YaST2 Runlevel Editor to create these links with a graphical front-end. See *The YaST2 Runlevel Editor* on the next page.

⌐ **Caution** ─────────────────────────────

Creating your own init scripts

Faulty init scripts may hang up your machine. Handle them with utmost care and, if possible, subject them to heavy testing in the multiuser environment. Some useful information on init scripts can be found in Section *Runlevels* on page 296.

────────────────────────────── **Caution** ⌐

The YaST2 Runlevel Editor

After this expert module starts, it is initialized. The current default runlevel is shown in the next dialog. This "operation mode" starts after your system boots. In SuSE Linux, this is usually runlevel 5 (full multiuser operation with network and KDM, the graphical login). Runlevel 3 also works well (full multiuser operation with network). With the help of YaST2, a different default runlevel can be set. See Table 13.1 on page 297.

'Edit' continues to an overview of all the services and daemons, supplemented with information as to whether they have been activated on your system and for which runlevels. Highlight a line with the mouse and activate the check boxes for runlevels '0', '1', '2', '3', '5', '6', and 'S' and, with that, state which service or daemon should be activated for which runlevel. Runlevel 4 is undefined — this is always reserved for custom settings.

With 'Start' and 'Stop', decide whether a server should be implemented. The current status is checked via 'Update', if this has not already been done automatically. 'Reset to default value' allows you to restore the default settings to their initial state following installation. 'Activate service' only appears if the service is currently disabled. 'Reset all services to default value' restores all services to their original state following installation. 'Finish' saves the system configuration.

> **Caution**
>
> **Changing runlevel settings**
> Faulty runlevel settings may render a system unusable. Before applying your changes, make absolutely sure you know about their consequences.
>
> Caution

SuSEconfig, /etc/sysconfig, and /etc/rc.config

The main configuration of SuSE Linux can be done via the configuration files in `/etc/sysconfig`. `/etc/rc.config`, formerly the main configuration file of SuSE Linux, is maintained as an empty file to allow your self-made scripts to source your settings and to apply your own variables globally.

The configuration files in /etc/sysconfig are interpreted by single scripts. For example, the network configuration files are only read by the network scripts.

Moreover, a large number of configuration files are generated from the settings in /etc/sysconfig. This is the task of /sbin/SuSEconfig. If you change the network configuration, for example, the file /etc/host.conf is regenerated, as it depends on the configuration made.

If you change anything in those files manually, you need to run /sbin/SuSEconfig afterwards to make sure all changes to the appropriate configuration files are made at the correct places. If you change the configuration with YaST2, it automatically executes /sbin/SuSEconfig and updates your configuration files.

This concept enables you to make basic changes to your configuration without having to reboot the system. Since some changes are rather complex, some programs must be restarted for the changes to take effect. If the network configuration has changed, the network programs can be restarted using the commands:

```
earth:    #   rcnetwork stop
earth:    #   rcnetwork start
```

As you can see, you can easily start and stop init scripts by hand.

Generally, we recommend the following steps for configuring your system:

- Bring the system into *single user mode* (Runlevel 1) with init 1.
- Change the configuration files as needed. This can be done using an editor of your choice or using the *Sysconfig editor* of YaST2.
- Execute /sbin/SuSEconfig to make the changes take effect. If you have changed the configuration files with YaST2, this is done automatically.
- Bring your system back to the previous runlevel with something like init 3.

This procedure is mainly relevant if you have changed system-wide settings (such as network configuration). It is not necessary to go into *single user mode* for small changes, but it ensures all relevant programs are correctly restarted.

> **Tip**
>
> To disable the automatic configuration of SuSEconfig, set the variable ⟨*ENABLE_SUSECONFIG*⟩ in `/etc/sysconfig/suseconfig` to no. Do not disable SuSEconfig if you want to use the SuSE installation support. It is also possible to disable the autoconfiguration partially.
>
> **Tip**

Using the YaST2 sysconfig Editor

The files where the most important SuSE Linux settings are stored are located in the `/etc/sysconfig` directory. This data used to be stored in a central file, `/etc/rc.config`. The sysconfig editor presents the settings options in an easy-to-read manner. The values can be modified and subsequently added to the individual configuration files in this directory. In general, it is not necessary to manually edit them, however, because these files are automatically adjusted when installing a package or configuring a service.

> **Caution**
>
> **Modifications of `/etc/sysconfig/` files**
> Do not modify the `/etc/sysconfig` files if you lack previous experience and knowledge. It could do considerable damage your system.
>
> **Caution**

System Configuration: Scripts and Variables

This section describes a selection of system parameters, including their default settings. If you do not use YaST2 to change the configuration files in `/etc/sysconfig`, make sure you set empty parameters as two quotation marks (e. g., ⟨*KEYTABLE=""*⟩) and surround parameters that contain a blank with quotation marks. Parameters consisting of only one word do not need to be quoted.

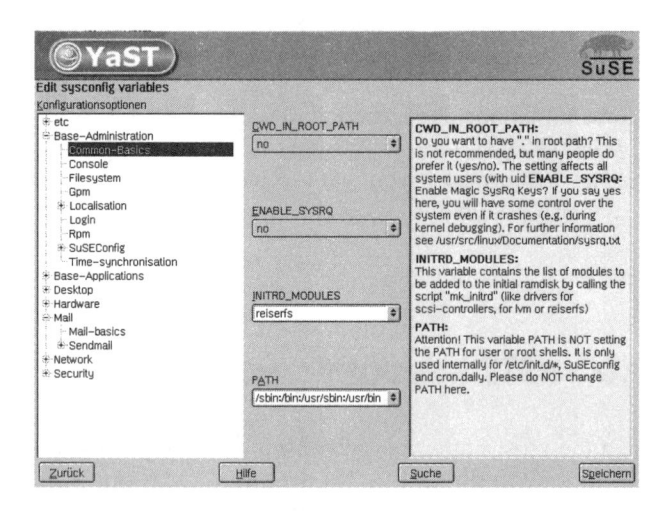

Figure 13.1: YaST2: Configuring with the sysconfig Editor

― **Note** ―――――――――――――――――――――――――――――――

Platform-specific variables in `/etc/sysconfig`

This is just an overview of variables and files in `/etc/sysconfig`. They are intended to represent those present on all supported platforms. Nevertheless, you might find some variables here that are not present on your specific hardware. Others, mostly highly specific ones, will probably not be mentioned here. Refer to the documentation in the appropriate `/etc/sysconfig` files.

――――――――――――――――――――――――――――――――― **Note** ―

Settings for the Files in /etc/sysconfig

3ddiag For 3Ddiag.

> **SCRIPT_3D="switch2mesasoft"**
> This variable specifies the script used to create the necessary symbolic links to the correct OpenGL libraries or extensions. These scripts are located in `/usr/X11R6/bin`. Possible values are:
>
> no execute no script
>
> switch2mesasoft emulation of Mesa Software (works with all graphics cards)

`switch2mesa3dfx` Mesa/Glide

`switch2nvidia_glx` XFree86 4.x/NVIDIA_GLX (NVIDIA_GLX/NVIDIA_kernel)

`switch2xf86_glx` XFree86 4.x/DRI

Use 3Ddiag to determine the correct settings.

`SuSEfirewall2` Activating firewall. See the readme file in package `SuSEfirewall2`.

`amavis` Activate the virus scanning facility AMaViS.

> **`USE_AMAVIS="yes"`**
> Set to `yes` if you want to use the e-mail virus scanning facility AMaViS within sendmail or postfix. If set to `yes`, SuSEconfig creates the correct sendmail or postfix configuration for using AMaViS. For details, see `README.SuSE` of the amavis package.

`apache` Configuration of the HTTP daemon Apache. This overview only covers the most important variables that need to be set by default or are vital for a basic understanding of Apache. Refer to the Apache documentation which you can install as package `apache-doc` for further information.

> **`HTTPD_PERFORMANCE="slim"`**
> Specify the performance class of your Apache. Choose from `slim`, `mid`, `thick`, and `enterprise` for the number of clients to server. SuSEconfig will set `MinSpareServers`, `MaxSpareServers`, `StartServers`, and `MaxClients` accordingly (see `/sbin/conf.d/SuSEconfig.apache`)

> **`HTTPD_START_TIMEOUT="2"`**
> Time-out during server start-up (in seconds). After this time, the stat script decides whether the httpd process has started without an error. You need to increase this value if you use `mod_ssl` and your certificate is passphrase protected.

> **`HTTPD_SEC_ACCESS_SERVERINFO="no"`**
> Enable or disable the status module to provide `server status` and `server info`.

> **`HTTPD_SEC_SAY_FULLNAME="no"`**
> Which information should be provided at the bottom of server-generated documents (e.g., error messages)? `yes` provides version number and server name. `email` adds a `mailto:` instruction to the version number and server name. This option correlates with the

`ServerSignature` directive of Apache. If no information should be revealed, set the parameter to `no`.

HTTPD_SEC_SERVERADMIN=""
Set the e-mail address of the server administrator (`ServerAdmin` directive) This address is added to the server's responses if ⟨*HTTPD_SEC_SAY_FULLNAME*⟩ is set to `email`. If empty, it defaults to `webmaster@$HOSTNAME`. `HOSTNAME` is set in `/etc/HOSTNAME`. Note that the `ServerAdmin` directives inside the `VirtualHost` statements are not changed, including the one for the SSL virtual host.

HTTPD_SEC_PUBLIC_HTML="yes"
Do you want to allow access to `UserDirs` (like `/home/*/public_html`)? If yes, this is defined in `/etc/httpd/suse_public_html.conf`.

HTTPD_CONF_INCLUDE_FILES=""
Here you can name files, separated by spaces, that should be included by `httpd.conf`. This allows you to add, for example, `VirtualHost` statements without touching `/etc/httpd/httpd.conf` itself, which means that SuSEconfig will continue doing its job (since it would not touch `httpd.conf` when it detects changes made by the admin via the md5sum mechanism).

HTTPD_AWSTATS_COMBINED_LOG="yes"
Should Apache write an extra combined log file? This is necessary for the awstats program (`yes` or `no`).

HTTPD_DDT="yes"
Should the DDT admin CGI be enabled? It is used to create and manage accounts on a local DDT (Dynamic DNS Tools) server.

MAILMAN_APACHE="yes"
Enable the web front-end for Mailman?

HTTPD_SEC_MOD_MIDGARD="yes"
Enable the `midgard` module. Midgard is an Open Source content management system.

HTTPD_SEC_MOD_PERL="yes"
Enable the Perl module.

HTTPD_SEC_MOD_PHP="yes"
Enable the PHP module.

HTTPD_SEC_MOD_PYTHON="yes"
Enable the Python module.

HTTPD_SEC_MOD_SSL="no"
Enable the SSL module. Before you can enable this module, you need a server certificate. A test certificate can be created by entering

```
cd /usr/share/doc/packages/mod_ssl
./certificate.sh
```

as `root`. Also, you need to set the ServerName inside the `<VirtualHost _default_:443>` block to the fully qualified domain name (see `$HOSTNAME` in `/etc/HOSTNAME`). If your server certificate is protected by a passphrase, increase the value of ⟨HTTPD_START_TIMEOUT⟩.

HTTPD_SEC_NAGIOS="yes"
Allow access to Nagios's web interface (configured in `/etc/httpd/nagios.conf`).

ZOPE_PCGI="no"
If unset, Zope runs as a stand-alone server. Remember Apache must be installed to use PCGI.

ZOPE_KEEP_HOMES="yes"
If Zope is handled by apache-pcgi and user home directories should be handled by Apache, set the variable to `yes`.

argoups This package allows you to control the actual condition of an ArgoUPS. If the power fails, the system performs a shutdown.

ARGO_TYPE="local"
Specify the connection type to the system to monitor. If the system should be monitored remotely (`net`), also specify the remote server at the ⟨ARGO_REMOTESERVER⟩ parameter.

ARGO_REMOTESERVER=""

ARGO_TTY="/dev/ttyS0"
Serial port to which ArgoUPS is attached.

ARGO_USERTIME="2"
Time to allow (in minutes) after a blackout until the script specified in ⟨ARGO_USERFILE⟩ is executed.

ARGO_USERFILE="/usr/sbin/argoblackout"

ARGO_SHUTDOWN="8"
Time after that when the shutdown should be started.

argus Server for Argus (a network monitor).

ARGUS_INTERFACE="eth0"
Interface to which argus should listen.

ARGUS_LOGFILE="/var/log/argus.log"
The Argus log file. It can get very large.

autofs With this daemon, it is possible to mount directories accessible via NFS or local directories (CD-ROM drives, disk drives, etc.) automatically. The package `autofs` must be installed and configured.

AUTOFS_OPTIONS=""
autofs daemon options, for example, `"--timeout 60"`. `--timeout` specifies the time (in seconds) after which directories should automatically be unmounted.

autoinstall AutoYast2 the autoinstaller of YaST2.

REPOSITORY="/var/lib/autoinstall/repository"
Repository with all profiles holding the configuration details of the hosts to install.

CLASS_DIR="/var/lib/autoinstall/classes"
Use classes to simplify the creation of profiles for complex installation scenarios. They will be stored in `/var/lib/autoinstall/classes`.

PACKAGE_REPOSITORY=""
Location in which to store the installation data and packages for SuSE Linux.

backup Backup of the RPM database

RPMDB_BACKUP_DIR="/var/adm/backup/rpmdb"
Where should cron.daily backups of the RPM database be stored? If you do not want backups, set the variable to `""`.

MAX_RPMDB_BACKUPS="5"
Number of backups of the RPM database.

RCCONFIG_BACKUP_DIR="/var/adm/backup/rpmdb"
If you want cron.daily to backup `/etc/rc.config` and the files in `/etc/sysconfig`, specify a directory where the backups will be stored. The backups will be made every time cron.daily is called and the the content of those files has changed. Setting the variable to `""` disables this feature.

MAX_RCCONFIG_BACKUPS="5"
Here, set the maximum number of backup files for the `/etc/rc.config` and `/etc/sysconfig` files.

`clock` time settings

`GMT=""`
If your hardware clock is set to GMT (*Greenwich Mean Time*), set this to `-u`. Otherwise, set it to `--localtime`. This setting is important for the automatic change from and to daylight savings time.

`TIMEZONE=""`
The time zone is also important for the change from and to daylight savings time. This sets `/usr/lib/zoneinfo/localtime`.

`console` Settings for the console.

`FB_MODULES=""`
You may want to load a framebuffer display driver into your kernel to change graphics modes and other things with fbset in console mode. Most people will not enter anything here, as it will not work with vesafb already active. It is advantageous to have framebuffer support compiled into your kernel. Some XFree86 drivers (especially in XFree86-4.x) do not work well if you enable framebuffer text mode.

`FBSET_PARAMS=""`
If your kernel has framebuffer support or loads it as a module, you might want to change the resolution or other parameters. These can be set with ⟨*FBSET_PARAMS*⟩. To get a list of possible parameters and their meanings, refer to the man page for `fbset` (`man fbset`) or enter `fbset -h` in the console.

> **Caution**
>
> **Setting framebuffer parameters**
> Framebuffer modes are extremely hardware dependent. A wrong decision here might damage your monitor. Consider the following things before setting framebuffer modes:
>
> vesafb does not (currently) support changing the display mode.
>
> Do not set modes your monitor cannot handle. Watch out for the maximum horizontal frequency. Old monitors might even be damaged if you exceed their capabilities.
>
> **Caution**

`CONSOLE_FONT=""`
Font for the console loaded at boot. Additional settings are: ⟨*CONSOLE_SCREENMAP*⟩, ⟨*CONSOLE_UNICODEMAP*⟩, and ⟨*CONSOLE_MAGIC*⟩.

CONSOLE_UNICODEMAP=""
Some fonts come without a unicode map. You can then specify the unicode mapping of your font explicitly. Find these maps under /usr/share/kbd/unimaps/. Normally, this variable is not needed.

CONSOLE_SCREENMAP=""
Does your console font need to be translated to unicode? Choose a screenmap from /usr/share/kbd/consoletrans/.

CONSOLE_MAGIC=""
For some fonts, the console has to be initialized with ⟨CONSOLE_MAGIC⟩. This option is normally not needed.

SVGATEXTMODE="80x25"
⟨SVGATEXTMODE⟩ comes from the package svgatext, which allows higher text resolutions (up to 160x60) on SVGA cards. The variable contains a valid mode from /etc/TextConfig. Configure this file to suit the needs of your graphics card. The procedure is explained in /usr/share/doc/packages/svgatext. The deefault is 80x25. SVGATextMode resolutions are used in runlevels 1, 2, 3, and 5.

cron Daily administration work on the system. The cron daemon automatically starts certain programs at specified times. It is recommended to activate it on computers that run all the time. An alternative or supplement is the AT daemon.

> **Note**
> A number of system settings require regular execution of certain programs. Therefore, the cron daemon should be active on every system.
> **Note**

MAX_DAYS_IN_TMP="0"
cron.daily can check for old files in tmp directories. It will delete all files not accessed for more than the days specified here. Leave it empty or set it to 0 to disable this feature.

TMP_DIRS_TO_CLEAR="/tmp /var/tmp"
Specify the directories from which old files should be deleted.

OWNER_TO_KEEP_IN_TMP="root"
Specify whose files should not be deleted, even after the time set.

CLEAR_TMP_DIRS_AT_BOOTUP="no"
Set this to yes to entirely remove (rm -rf) all files and subdirectories from the temporary directories defined in ⟨TMP_DIRS_TO_CLEAR⟩ on

boot. This feature ignores ⟨OWNER_TO_KEEP_IN_TMP⟩ — all files will be removed without exception.

DELETE_OLD_CORE="no"
Should old core files be deleted? If set to no, cron.daily will tell you if it finds old core files. This feature requires ⟨RUN_UPDATEDB⟩ be set to yes and package findutils-locate needs to be installed.

MAX_DAYS_FOR_CORE="7"
Maximum age of core files in days.

REINIT_MANDB="yes"
Should the manual page database (mandb and whatis) be recreated by cron.daily?

DELETE_OLD_CATMAN="yes"
Should old preformatted man pages (in /var/catman) be deleted?

CATMAN_ATIME="7"
How long (in days) should old preformatted man pages be kept before deleting them?

dhcpd Configure the DHCP server.

DHCPD_INTERFACE="eth0"
Enter a space-separated list of interfaces on which the DCHP server should be listening.

DHCPD_RUN_CHROOTED="yes"
Should dhcpd run in a "chroot jail"? Refer to dhcpd's README.SuSE (/usr/share/doc/packages/dhcp/README.SuSE) for further details.

DHCPD_CONF_INCLUDE_FILES=""
dhcpd.conf can contain include statements. If you enter the names of any include files here, *all* conf files will be copied to \$chroot/etc/ when dhcpd is started in the chroot jail. /etc/dhcpd.conf is always copied.

DHCPD_RUN_AS="nobody"
Leave empty or enter root to let dhcpd run as root. Enter nobody to run dhcpd as user nobody and group nogroup.

DHCPD_OTHER_ARGS=""
Other arguments with which dhcpd should be started. See man dhcpd for details.

dhcrelay DHCP Relay Agent. A DHCP relay agent allows you to relay DHCP (and Bootp) requests from one subnet without a DHCP server to one with a DHCP server.

DHCRELAY_INTERFACES=""
Interfaces on which the DHCP relay agent should listen (separarted by spaces).

DHCRELAY_SERVERS=""
Specify a space-separated list of DHCP servers to be used by the DHCP relay agent.

displaymanager Display manager configuration

DISPLAYMANAGER=""
Set the display manager for login. Possible values: console, xdm (traditional display manager of X Window System), kdm (display manager of KDE), gdm (display manager of GNOME), or wdm ("WINGs display manager").

DISPLAYMANAGER_REMOTE_ACCESS="no"
Allow remote access to your display manager. Default is no.

DISPLAYMANAGER_STARTS_XSERVER="yes"
Display manager starts a local X server. Set to no for remote access only.

KDM_SHUTDOWN="auto"
⟨KDM_SHUTDOWN⟩ determines who will be able to shutdown the system in kdm. Valid values are root, all, none, local, and auto.

KDM_USERS=""
Enter a space-separated list of users for whom icons should be displayed. If empty, the system defaults will be taken.

KDM_BACKGROUND=""
Specify a special background for KDM.

KDM_GREETSTRING=""
If you wish to be greeted by the system in a special way, enter the greeting words here.

dracd Settings for the dracd and mail relaying using "POP-before-SMTP."

DRACD_RELAYTIME="5"
Postfix, on a POP server, remembers the IP address of an authenticated host for a certain time (time to live) and allows this host to send e-mail. After the time has expired, a new authentication is necessary. This time to live is set in minutes.

DRACD_DRACDB="/etc/postfix/dracd.db"
This is where dracdb is stored.

dvb Settings for your DVB card.

DVB_SOUND_CHIP="ti"
Choose the sound chip on your DVB card — `ti` or `crystal`.

hardware Hardware settings

DEVICES_FORCE_IDE_DMA_ON=""
Switch on DMA for the listed IDE devices.

DEVICES_FORCE_IDE_DMA_OFF=""
Switch off DMA for the listed IDE devices.

hotplug Configuring the hotplug service.

HOTPLUG_DEBUG="default"
This variable controls the amount of output of the hotplug service. With `default`, `""`, or `no`, it prints only few messages and errors to `syslog`. Set it to `off` and it will be absolutely quiet. With `verbose` (or `yes`), it prints some extra debug output. With `max` it will pollute your `syslog` with every single detail.

HOTPLUG_START_USB="yes"
Enable or disable USB hotplug event handling.

> **Note**
>
> **Disabling USB hotplug**
> Disabling USB hotplug while having the USB input devices loaded as modules will render your keyboard unusable.
>
> **Note**

HOTPLUG_USB_HOSTCONTROLLER_LIST="usb-uhci uhci usb-ohci ehci-hcd"
The host controller drivers will be probed in this order.

HOTPLUG_USB_MODULES_TO_UNLOAD="scanner"
These modules should be unloaded on an USB "remove" event. For some devices, it is useful to reinitialize the hardware.

HOTPLUG_USB_NET_MODULES="pegasus usbnet catc kaweth CDCEther"
If one of these modules is loaded or unloaded, it is treated like a network device and the system creates a hardware description for the following "net event".

HOTPLUG_START_NET="yes"
Enable or disable NET hotplug event handling.

HOTPLUG_NET_DEFAULT_HARDWARE=""
One day in the future, there will be ways to obtain information on which type of hardware is behind a given network interface. Currently,

there is no easy way to get this information. At the moment, we use the following work-around: hardware descriptions are written at the USB or PCI hotplug events then read by the NET event. If you plug several devices at a time, this might cause race conditions. If the work-around fails, the string in ⟨HOTPLUG_NET_DEFAULT_HARDWARE⟩ is used when if{up,down} is called. Set it to what you use as hotplug NIC: `pcmcia`, `usb`, or `firewire`.

HOTPLUG_NET_TIMEOUT="8"
Specify how long to wait for a hardware description from a USB or PCI event (in seconds). If this value equals 0, the hotplug service will not wait for a hardware description and always use the value of ⟨HOTPLUG_NET_DEFAULT_HARDWARE⟩. The default value here is 8 since some PCMCIA NICs need a long time for some negotiation jobs.

HOTPLUG_START_PCI="yes"
Enable or disable PCI hotplug event handling.

HOTPLUG_PCI_MODULES_NOT_TO_UNLOAD=""
These modules should not be unloaded on a PCI "remove" event, because they cause too much trouble.

intermezzo Settings for the Intermezzo file system.

EXCLUDE_GID="63"
Specify the group to exclude from replication.

irda IrDA is the infrared interface used, for example, by notebooks. To activate it permanently, call `insserv /etc/init.d/irda`.

IRDA_PORT="/dev/ttyS1"
Currently, the UART (SIR) mode is supported in the normal configuration. The variable ⟨IRDA_PORT⟩ sets the used serial port. Check your BIOS setup to find out which is correct. If you have a supported FIR chipset, specify the name of the corresponding kernel module in ⟨IRDA_PORT⟩, for example, `IRDA_PORT="toshoboe"`. FIR must be enabled in the BIOS setup first. Sometimes, you additionally have to disable the serial port, which would be used in SIR mode via `setserial /dev/ttyS<x> uart none`

isdn/ Here you will find all the scripts needed for ISDN.

ispell Configuring the ispell spell checker.

ENGLISH_DICTIONARY="system american british"
SuSEconfig.ispell maintains a symbolic link from the `english` (default) dictionary to either `american` or `british`. If only one is in-

stalled, the link will point to this one. If both are installed, the space-separated value of ⟨ENGLISH_DICTIONARY⟩ takes effect. The magic word `system` expands to the system's default language (as defined in `/etc/sysconfig/language`'s ⟨RC_LANG⟩), if it is one of the English languages, and expands to the empty string otherwise. The symlink will point to the first installed dictionary in the list.

java Configuring Java.

CREATE_JAVALINK="yes"
SuSEconfig can automatically create the links `/usr/lib/java` and `/usr/lib/jre` that point to a suitable JDK or JRE respectively if you set ⟨CREATE_JAVALINK⟩ to `yes`. If you are not satisfied with the choice it makes, set ⟨CREATE_JAVALINK⟩ to `no` and set the link manually.

JAVA_JRE_THREADS_TYPE="green"
Configuration for the package `java-jre`. Set this to `native` if you want *real* multithreading, for example, in combination with SMP systems.

JAVA_THREADS_TYPE="green"
Configuration for the package `java`. Set this to `native` if you want *real* multithreading, for example, in combination with SMP systems.

joystick Joystick configuration

GAMEPORT_MODULE_0=""
Gameport module names, for example, `ns558` for legacy gameport support.

JOYSTICK_MODULE_0=""
Joystick module names, usually `analog`.

JOYSTICK_MODULE_OPTION_0=""
Joystick module options, such as `js=gameport` for analog.

JOYSTICK_CONTROL_0=""
Control name of sound driver to activate (via alsactl).

JOYSTICK_CONTROL_PORT_0=""
Port to use (via alsactl). Some sound cards, like ens1371, need the port address (typically 0x200).

kernel Kernel.

INITRD_MODULES=""
This variable contains the list of modules to add to the initial ramdisk with the script `mk_initrd` (like drivers for scsi controllers, lvm, or reiserfs).

SHMFS_SIZE=""
Size parameter for mounting the shmfs file system. The kernel defaults to half the available RAM size, but this might not be enough for some special setups.

keyboard Keyboard layout.

KEYTABLE="de-latin1-nodeadkeys"
Defines the key layout. If you use a US keyboard, this variable can remain empty.

KBD_RATE="24.0"
Rate of automatic keyboard repetition. Set this to a value between 2 and 30 times per second. The variable for the delay also needs to be set: ⟨KBD_DELAY⟩.

KBD_DELAY="500"
Set the delay after which the automatic key repetition starts. Possible values: 250, 500, 750, and 1000 in milliseconds. Also set the variable ⟨KBD_RATE⟩.

KBD_NUMLOCK="bios"
Set this to no and (NumLock) will not be enabled at boot. Other options are yes, "" , or bios for BIOS setting.

KBD_SCRLOCK="no"
Enable or disable (ScrollLock).

KBD_CAPSLOCK="no"
Do not enable (CapsLock) at boot time.

KBD_DISABLE_CAPS_LOCK="no"
Disable (CapsLock) and make it a normal Shift key?

KBD_TTY="tty1 tty2 tty3 tty4 tty5 tty6"
Limit (NumLock), (CapsLock), and (ScrollLock) to certain TTYs. "" means all.

COMPOSETABLE="clear winkeys shiftctrl latin1.add"
Compose tables to load. See /usr/share/doc/packages/kbd/README.SuSE for further details on key tables.

language Settings for language and locale.

RC_LANG="en_US"
Sets variable LANG for locale. This is the default for local users, as long as no ⟨RC_LC_*⟩ variables are used. The respective sysconfig variables are ⟨RC_LC_ALL⟩ (overwrites LC_* and LANG), ⟨RC_LC_MESSAGES⟩, ⟨RC_LC_CTYPE⟩, ⟨RC_LC_MONETARY⟩, ⟨RC_LC_NUMERIC⟩, ⟨RC_LC_TIME⟩, and ⟨RC_LC_COLLATE⟩. See Section *Local Adjustments — I18N/L10N* on page 292.

ROOT_USES_LANG="ctype"
Should locale settings be used for root? ctype means that root uses just ⟨LC_CTYPE⟩.

locate The locate database allows files on the system to be found quickly. It is usually updated shortly after booting the system.

RUN_UPDATEDB="no"
Should the database for locate (locate) get updated once a day? More detailed configuration of updatedb is possible with the following variables.

RUN_UPDATEDB_AS="nobody"
Specify the user executing updatedb. Default, for security reasons, is nobody.

UPDATEDB_NETPATHS=""
Normally, uptdatedb only scans local hard disks, but can include net paths in the database as well. If you specify directories here, they will be scanned.

UPDATEDB_PRUNEPATHS="/mnt /media/cdrom /tmp /usr/tmp /var/tmp /var/spool /proc /media"
Specify the directories to skip for the daily updatedb runs.

UPDATEDB_NETUSER=""
User, such as nobody, to search net paths.

UPDATEDB_PRUNEFS=""
Specify the type of file systems to exclude from the updatedb runs.

lvm The Logical Volume Manager.

mail Settings for e-mail.

FROM_HEADER=""
From: line defined for the whole system. If "", the FQDN is used. See Section *Domain Name System* on page 342.

MAIL_CREATE_CONFIG="yes"
Set this to no if SuSEconfig should not generate the configuration files (e.g., you want to generate /etc/sendmail.cf yourself). If you want to generate a sendmail configuration /etc/sendmail.cf from parameters given in /etc/sysconfig/sendmail, use yes.

NULLCLIENT=""
A null client is a machine that can only send mail. It receives no mail from the network and it does not deliver any mail locally. A null client typically uses POP or NFS for mailbox access.

SMTPD_LISTEN_REMOTE="no"
Set this to `yes` if external e-mails should be accepted. This is necessary for any mail server. If set to `no` or empty, only mails from the local host are accepted.

mouse Mouse settings

MOUSE=""
Specify the interface to which the mouse is connected (e.g., `/dev/ttyS0`). YaST2 or SuSEconfig sets a link `/dev/mouse` pointing to the device.

GPM_PROTOCOL=""
The gpm protocol for the mouse device from the variable MOUSE. The default value is defined by YaST2.

GPM_PARAM=" -t $GPM_PROTOCOL -m $MOUSE"
Default parameters for gpm.

network Directory for network configuration.

network/config Some general settings for network configuration.

DEFAULT_BROADCAST="+"
⟨DEFAULT_BROADCAST⟩ is read when a ⟨BROADCAST⟩ is not set elsewhere. Choose from the following values: `" "` for no broadcast address, `-` for ⟨IPADDR⟩ without host bits, or `+` for ⟨IPADDR⟩ with all host bits set.

CHECK_FOR_MASTER="yes"
To require an interface (master) to be up before an alias (labeled address) can be set up, set ⟨CHECK_FOR_MASTER⟩ to `yes`. Technically, this is not neccessary, because labeled and unlabeled adresses are equivalent. This setting serves just for the convenience of ifconfig users.

CHECK_DUPLICATE_IP="yes"
If ifup should check if an IP address is already in use, set this to `yes`. Make sure packet sockets (⟨CONFIG_PACKET⟩) are supported in the kernel, since this feature uses arping, which depends on that. Also be aware that this takes one second per interface. Consider that when setting up a lot of interfaces.

DEBUG="no"
Switch on and off debug messages for all network configuration scripts. If set to `no`, most scripts still can enable it locally with `-o debug`.

USE_SYSLOG="yes"
Should error messages from network configuration scripts go to `syslog`? If no, `stderr` is used.

MODIFY_RESOLV_CONF_DYNAMICALLY="yes"
There are some services (`ppp`, `ippp`, `dhcp-client`, `pcmcia`, and `hotplug`) that have to change `/etc/resolv.conf` dynamically at certain times. To prevent these services from changing `/etc/resolv.conf` at all, set this variable to `no`. If unsure, leave it at the default, which is `yes`.

MODIFY_NAMED_CONF_DYNAMICALLY="no"
Like ⟨MODIFY_RESOLV_CONF_DYNAMICALLY⟩, except it modifies `/etc/named.conf`. If unsure, leave it at the default, which is `no`.

network/dhcp Setting up DHCP (Dynamic Host Configuration Protocol).

> **Note**
>
> To configure one or more interfaces for DHCP configuration, you have to change the ⟨BOOTPROTO⟩ variable in `/etc/sysconfig/network/ifcfg-<interface>` to `dhcp` (and possibly set ⟨STARTMODE⟩ to `onboot`).
>
> **Note**

Most of these options are used only by `dhcpcd`, not by the ISC dhclient which uses a config file. Most of the options can be overridden by setting them in the `ifcfg-*` files, too.

DHCLIENT_BIN=""
Which DHCP client should be used? If empty, `dhcpcd` is tried, then `dhclient`. Other possible values are `dhcpcd` for the DHCP client daemon or `dhclient` for the ISC dhclient.

DHCLIENT_DEBUG="no"
Start in debug mode? Debug info will be logged to `/var/log/messages` for `dhcpcd` or to `/var/log/dhclient-script` for ISC dhclient.

DHCLIENT_SET_HOSTNAME="no"
Should the DHCP client set the host name? If `yes`, take care that the host name is not changed during a running X session or the ⟨DISPLAY⟩ variable cannot be read anymore. As a consequence, no new windows could be opened.

DHCLIENT_MODIFY_RESOLV_CONF="yes"
Should the DHCP client modify `/etc/resolv.conf` at all? If not, set this to `no`. The default is `yes`. `resolv.conf` will also stay untouched when ⟨MODIFY_RESOLV_CONF_DYNAMICALLY⟩ in `/etc/sysconfig/network/config` is set to `no`.

DHCLIENT_SET_DEFAULT_ROUTE="yes"
Should the DHCP client set a default route (default gateway)? When multiple copies of dhcpcd run, it would make sense that only one of them does it.

DHCLIENT_MODIFY_NTP_CONF="no"
Should the DHCP client modify the NTP configuration? If set to yes, /etc/ntp.conf is rewritten (and restored upon exit). If this is unwanted, set this variable to no. The default is no.

DHCLIENT_MODIFY_NIS_CONF="no"
Should the DHCP client modify the NIS configuration? If set to yes, /etc/yp.conf is rewritten (and restored upon exit). If this is unwanted, set this variable to no. The default is no.

DHCLIENT_SET_DOMAINNAME="yes"
Should the DHCP client set the NIS domain name? (Only valid if the server supplies the nis domain option).

DHCLIENT_KEEP_SEARCHLIST="no"
When writing a new /etc/resolv.conf, should the DHCP client take an existing search list and add it to the one derived from the DHCP server?

DHCLIENT_LEASE_TIME=""
Specifies (in seconds) the lease time suggested to the server. The default is infinite. For a mobile computer, you probably want to set this to a lower value.

DHCLIENT_TIMEOUT="999999"
This setting is only valid for dhcpcd. Specify a time-out in seconds after which dhcpcd terminates if it does not get a reply from the DHCP server.

DHCLIENT_REBOOT_TIMEOUT=""
This setting is only valid for dhcpcd. This time-out controls how long dhcpcd tries to reacquire a previous lease (init-reboot state), before it starts getting a new one.

DHCLIENT_HOSTNAME_OPTION="AUTO"
Specify a string used for the host name option field when dhcpcd sends DHCP messages. By default, the current host name is sent (AUTO), if one is defined in /etc/HOSTNAME. Use this variable to override this with another host name or leave empty not to send a host name.

DHCLIENT_CLIENT_ID=""
Specifies a client identifier string. By default, the hardware address of

the network interface is sent as client identifier string, if none is specified here.

DHCLIENT_VENDOR_CLASS_ID=""
Specifies the vendor class identifier string. `dhcpcd` uses the default vendor class identifier string (system name, system release, and machine type) if it is not specified.

DHCLIENT_RELEASE_BEFORE_QUIT="yes"
Send a ⟨DHCPRELEASE⟩ to the server (sign off the address)? This may lead to getting a different address and host name next time an address is requested. However, some servers require it.

DHCLIENT_SLEEP="0"
Some interfaces need time to initialize. Add the latency time in seconds so these can be handled properly. This setting should be made on a per interface basis, rather than here.

network/ifcfg-eth0 Configure the first network card. These settings can be done with YaST2.

STARTMODE=""
⟨STARTMODE⟩ tells ifup when a interface should be set up. Possible values are `onboot` for an automatic start at boot time, `manual` when ifup is called manually, and `hotplug` when ifup is called by `hotplug` or `pcmcia`.

BOOTPROTO=""
With ⟨BOOTPROTO⟩, choose between a `static` configuration with fixed IP addresses or dhcp.

IPADDR=""
Set the IP adress if static configuration is desired.

NETMASK=""
Specify the netmask of your net or subnet.

PREFIXLEN=""
Alternatively, specify the prefix length.

NETWORK=""
Specify the address of your network.

BROADCAST=""
Enter the broadcast address of your network.

network/ifcfg-lo The loopback device.

network/wireless Configuring wireless LANs. Use the YaST2 `network` modules.

news Settings for access to NNTP servers.

    ORGANIZATION=""
    The text entered here will appear in every news posting sent from this machine.

    NNTPSERVER="news"
    Address of the news server. If you receive news via UUCP and they are locally stored, set this variable to `localhost`.

nfs NFS server. The daemons rpc.nfsd and rpc.mountd are started simultaneously.

    REEXPORT_NFS="no"
    Set this variable to `yes` to reexport mounted NFS directories or NetWare volumes.

onlineupdate Settings for YaST2 Online Update.

    YAST2_LOADFTPSERVER="yes"
    When starting YOU (YaST2 Online Update), should the default FTP server list be updated via a call from `wget` to `www.suse.de`? This list is stored under `/etc/suseservers`. Set the variable to `no` if you do not want to reload the FTP server list.

    PROXY_USER=""
    Users of the proxy.

    PROXY_PASSWORD=""
    Password for the proxy.

pcmcia PCMCIA System and PC Cards.

    PCMCIA_SYSTEM="kernel"
    Set the variable to `external` or `kernel`. If only one of these systems is installed, this variable will be ignored.

    PCMCIA_PCIC=""
    Specify socket driver for the selected pcmcia system. Possible values are `i82365` or `tcic` for external pcmcia system or `yenta_socket`, `i82365`, or `tcic` for kernel pcmcia. If it is left empty, the start script will try to determine the correct driver or use a reasonable default.

    PCMCIA_PCIC_OPTS=""
    Socket driver timing parameters. These parameters are described in man page i82365 (or `man tcic`).

    PCMCIA_CORE_OPTS=""
    `pcmcia_core` options as described in `man pcmcia_core`. For more information, look for "CORE_OPTS" in the PCMCIA-HOWTO under `/usr/doc/packages/pcmcia`.

postfix Configuring postfix. Use the YaST2 `mail` module for this.

postgresql PostgreSQL.

POSTGRES_DATADIR="~postgres/data"
Specify the directory in which the PostgreSQL database is to reside.

POSTGRES_OPTIONS=""
Specify the options given to the PostgreSQL master daemon on start-up. See the manual pages for postmaster and postgres for valid options. Do not put `-D datadir` here since it is set by the start-up script based on the variable ⟨POSTGRES_DATADIR⟩ above.

powermanagement apmd.

APMD_WARN_LEVEL="10"
If you like to be warned when battery capacity goes below a certain level, you can set this level here in percent of maximum battery capacity. Set it to 0 to switch this and the following three options off. Default value is 10.

APMD_WARN_ALL="no"
For apmd warnings to be sent to all terminals, set this to yes. Otherwise the warnings will be logged in your syslog file. Default is no.

APMD_WARN_STEP="0"
This warning can be repeated every time the capacity has decreased by ⟨WARN_STEP⟩% of the maximum battery capacity. 0 means off. Default is 0.

APMD_CHECK_TIME="0"
By default apmd checks the battery status every time it receives an event from the BIOS. For it to be checked more often, set it to a value greater than 0 seconds. Note that this will wake up your disk at every check. Default value is 0.

APMD_DEBUG="no"
Make apmd and the apmd_proxy-script more verbose. Set this variable to yes to see when and how apmd_proxy is called. To see everything printed to stdout and stderr within apmd_proxy, set it to error. If you are interested in every single command within apmd_proxy, set it to all. Anything but no makes apmd itself verbose. Default value is no.

APMD_ADJUST_DISK_PERF="no"
For saving power, you should let your hard disk spin down after an idle time. That is not needed when on wall power. Set ⟨ADJUST_DISK_PERF⟩ to yes if apmd should check this. Note that

this does not help much if any process (like an text editor) writes frequently to your disk. Default value is no.

APMD_BATTERY_DISK_TIMEOUT="12"
Specify the time-out for your disk to be spun down when on battery. As this time-out is not just a matter of minutes or seconds, refer to the man page for hdparm (man hdparm). This option will only be valid if ⟨ADJUST_DISK_PERF⟩ has been set to yes. The default setting here is 12, which equals a time-out of one minute.

APMD_AC_DISK_TIMEOUT="0"
See ⟨BATTERY_DISK_TIMEOUT⟩, only that this setting concerns AC power. Default value is 0 for no spindown.

APMD_BATTERY_LOW_SHUTDOWN="0"
When the battery capacity becomes very low, some laptop BIOSes send a "battery low" message. You can then let your machine shut down a few minutes later. Set the number of minutes here. The minumum is 1 minute. A value of 0 switches off this behavior. The default value is 0.

APMD_SET_CLOCK_ON_RESUME="no"
If you have problems with wrong time settings after a standby or suspend, set ⟨SET_CLOCK_ON_RESUME⟩ to yes. The kernel time will be set according to the value stored in the GMT variable. Default is no.

APMD_SUSPEND_ON_AC="yes"
Set ⟨SUSPEND_ON_AC⟩ to no to avoid suspend and standby events when your machine is connected to AC power. By default, suspends can occur on either battery or AC power. A suspend requested by the user is executed anyway.

APMD_PCMCIA_SUSPEND_ON_SUSPEND="no"
If PCMCIA is compiled with APM support, cards are normally suspended before your system suspends. If you do not have APM support in PCMCIA, you can let apmd do this job. Default is no.

APMD_PCMCIA_EJECT_ON_SUSPEND="no"
PCMCIA cards can be more or less amenable to an APM suspend event. If you have a card that cannot be suspended properly (such as a SCSI card), it should be "ejected" before entering suspend mode. The cards are not physically ejected. Rather, the power to them is turned off via the cardctl eject command and is reactivated upon resume. Default value is no.

APMD_INTERFACES_TO_STOP=""
If you have a built-in NIC that does not survive a suspend and resume cycle properly, add the interface name to this variable. It will then be shut down before suspend and brought up after resume. Default is "".

`APMD_INTERFACES_TO_UNLOAD=""`
If it does not help to shut down the network interface via
⟨*APMD_INTERFACES_TO_STOP*⟩, unload the module driving your NIC
at suspend and restart the network at resume.

`APMD_LEAVE_X_BEFORE_SUSPEND="no"`
If your graphic device is not able to return properly from suspend,
switch to text console before suspend and return to your X console after resume. Default is `no`.

`APMD_LEAVE_X_BEFORE_STANDBY="no"`
Sometime, it is needed for standby. Default is `no`.

`APMD_LOCK_X_ON_SUSPEND="no"`
If you like apmd to lock your screen before suspend, set this variable
to `yes`. If only one X server is running and no one is logged in at any
virtual terminal, this can be considered a safe state. Together with an
encrypted partition for your data, no one can access your data when
your laptop is in this state. Default is `no`.

`APMD_STOP_SOUND_BEFORE_SUSPEND="no"`
Sometimes the sound modules do not survive a suspend and resume cycle. In this case, everything seems to be OK, but you
cannot hear anything. To avoid this, the sound modules can be
unloaded before suspend. A reload of these modules will only
be done if you use ALSA or OSS. If you use modules from the
kernel, they will be reloaded automatically. If you like that, set
⟨*APMD_STOP_SOUND_BEFORE_SUSPEND*⟩ to `alsa`, `oss` or `kernel`,
depending on what type of sound system you are using. To unload all
sound modules succesfully, all sound applications that are currently using some of them must be killed. Default value is `no`.

`APMD_KBD_RATE=""`
It might be neccessary to reset the key repetition rate and delay. You
can set the variables to any numeric value. The program kbdrate will
select the nearest possible values to these specified. To use the default
values, just leave the variable empty. Default for both is `""`.

`APMD_KBD_DELAY=""`

`APMD_TURN_OFF_IDEDMA_BEFORE_SUSPEND=""`
There are some notebooks that do not resume properly from suspend
when the hard disk was in DMA mode. Add every disk here that
needs DMA turned off. For `/dev/hda`, set it to `hda`. Several disks are
seperated by spaces. Default is `""`.

printer Printer

DEFAULT_PRINTER="lp"
Name of the printer queue used when `lpr` is invoked with no `-P`.

proxy Proxy settings

HTTP_PROXY=""
Some programs (e. g., lynx, arena, or wget) use a proxy server if this environment variable is set. SuSEconfig will set it in `/etc/SuSEconfig/*`. Example: `"http://proxy.provider.com:3128/"`.

FTP_PROXY=""
Proxy for FTP. Example: `"http://proxy.provider.com:3128/"`.

NO_PROXY="localhost"
Exclude domains or subdomains from proxy use. Example: `"www.me.de, do.main, localhost"`.

security Settings for system security

CHECK_PERMISSIONS="set"
Should SuSEconfig check file permissions using `/etc/permissions`? Value `set` will correct false settings. `warn` produces warnings. Disable this feature with `no`.

PERMISSION_SECURITY="easy local"
In `/etc/permissions.paranoid`, `/etc/permissions.secure`, and `/etc/permissions.easy`, three security levels are predefined. Enter `easy`, `secure`, or `paranoid`. If you select `paranoid`, some system sevices might not be available anymore. Explicitly enable them, if needed.

sendmail sendmail variables. Use the YaST2 `mail` module for configuration.

sound Sound configuration.

LOAD_SEQUENCER="yes"
Load ALSA sequencer modules at boot? Sequencer modules are necessary only for handling MIDI devices. If you do not need MIDI, disable this option. The modules can also be loaded automatically later if they are needed.

ssh Before starting the "Secure Shell Daemon", make sure a "host key" exists. Consult the documentation in `/usr/share/doc/packages/ssh` and the manual pages.

SSHD_OPTS=""
Options for sshd.

`suseconfig` Settings for SuSEconfig.

`ENABLE_SUSECONFIG="yes"`
Decide whether SuSEconfig should take care of updating the configuration. Do not disable SuSEconfig if you want to consult our Installation Support.

`MAIL_REPORTS_TO="root"`
Select the user to which SuSEconfig should send e-mail reports created during the automatic system administration.

`MAIL_LEVEL="warn"`
Set the variable to `warn` if only important messages should be sent. Set it to `all` if the log files should be mailed, too.

`CREATE_INFO_DIR="yes"`
Set the variable to `yes` if a perl script should be used to generate the file `/usr/share/info/dir` automatically. This file is the index for all info pages.

`CHECK_ETC_HOSTS="yes"`
Defines whether SuSEconfig should check and modify `/etc/hosts`.

`BEAUTIFY_ETC_HOSTS="no"`
Should `/etc/hosts` be sorted by SuSEconfig?

`SORT_PASSWD_BY_UID="no"`
If this variable is set to yes, SuSEconfig sorts your /etc/passwd and /etc/group by "uid" and "gid".

`CWD_IN_ROOT_PATH="no"`
Should the current working directory (".") be in the path of user `root`? For security reasons, this is not recommended. This setting is valid for all users with a "UID" below 100 (system users).

`CWD_IN_USER_PATH="yes"`
Should the current working directory (".") be in the path for normal users?

`CREATE_PERLLOCAL_POD="yes"`
May SuSEconfig modify your `perllocal.pod`?

`UPDATE_GROFF_CONF="yes"`
Update `DESC` to get page sizes correct?

`GROFF_PAGESIZE=""`
If the correct page size cannot be found in your `printcap`, this variable can be set to the following values: `letter`, `legal`, `a4`, or `b5`, supported by both groff and ghostscript

`sysctl` System control at the kernel level

IP_DYNIP="no"
Enable the "dynamic IP patch" at boot?

IP_TCP_SYNCOOKIES="yes"
Enable "syn flood protection"? See `/usr/src/linux/Documentation/Configure.help`.

IP_FORWARD="no"
If the host is supposed to forward to two network interfaces, set this variable to `yes`. This is usually applicable for routers or "masquerading". The script `/etc/init.d/boot.proc` enables IP forwarding with an entry in the `/proc` file system.

ENABLE_SYSRQ="no"
If you set this to `yes`, you will have some control over the system even if it crashes, for example, during kernel debugging. Consult `/usr/src/linux/Documentation/sysrq.txt` for further information.

DISABLE_ECN="yes"
If you have trouble connecting to some machines on the Internet with your 2.4 kernel but there are no problems with 2.2, this may be due to broken firewalls dropping network packets with the ECN (early congestion notification) flag set. Set this to `yes` to disable ECN at boot.

BOOT_SPLASH="yes"
Set to `no` to turn off the splash screen on console 1 at boot (after kernel load).

syslog Configuring the syslog daemon.

SYSLOGD_ADDITIONAL_SOCKET_DHCP="/var/lib/dhcp/dev/log"
The contents of this variable are added by the `dhcp-server` package. The file name mentioned here is added using `-a <filename>` as an additional socket via ⟨SYSLOGD_PARAMS⟩ when syslogd is started. This additional socket is needed in case syslogd is restarted. Otherwise, a chrooted dhcpd will not be able to continue logging.

KERNEL_LOGLEVEL="1"
Default log level for klogd.

SYSLOGD_PARAMS=""
Parameters for syslogd, for example, `-r -s my.domain.com`.

syslog-ng Configuring syslog-ng.

SYSLOG_NG_REPLACE="yes"
Replace the default syslog daemon? If set to `no`, syslog-ng will be started *in addition* to syslog.

SYSLOG_NG_PARAMS=""
Parameters for syslog-ng. Refer to `man 8 syslog-ng` for details.

tetex TEX/LATEX.

CLEAR_TEXMF_FONTS="no"
The automatic font generation of the TeX or LaTeX systems locate the bitmap font into the directory `/var/cache/fonts/`. If ⟨CLEAR_TEXMF_FONTS⟩ is set to `yes`, this directory will be cleared of fonts not used in the last twenty days.

windowmanager Window manager.

DEFAULT_WM="kde"
Here, set the default window manager, such as `kde`, `gnome`, or `fvwm`.

INSTALL_DESKTOP_EXTENSIONS="yes"
Install the SuSE extensions for new users (theme and additional functions).

KDM_SHUTDOWN="auto"
Specifies the users allowed to shut down or reboot the computer via kdm. Possible settings: `root`, `all`, `none`, `local`, and `auto`.

KDE_USE_FAM="no"
Should KDE use the fam daemon? It only makes sense on NFS mounted directories.

KDE_USE_FAST_MALLOC="no"
Use the improved malloc?

SUSEWM_UPDATE="yes"
Should SuSEconfig.wm create system-wide configuration files for the window managers?

SUSEWM_WM="all"
Space-separated list of window managers for which configuration files should be generated. Valid values are `fvwm`, `fvwm2`, `fvwm95`, `bowman`, `mwm`, `ctwm`, `kwm`, and `all`.

SUSEWM_XPM="yes"
Set ⟨SUSEWM_XPM⟩ to `yes` for pixmaps in menus. The package `3dpixms` must be installed.

xdmsc Using X terminals.

START_RX="no"
First, edit `/etc/inittab` to remove the comment from the line with `/sbin/init.d/rx`. Then ⟨RX_XDMCP⟩ and ⟨RX_RHOST⟩ must be set. Finally, set ⟨START_RX⟩ to `yes` to have an X terminal.

RX_XDMCP="broadcast"
xdm control protocol: `query`, `indirect`, or `broadcast`. For `query` or `indirect`, set ⟨*RX_RHOST*⟩.

RX_RHOST=""
xdm host, necessary if ⟨*RX_XDMCP*⟩ is set to `query` or `indirect`.

RX_DSP=""
Optional DISPLAY number, such as `:1` or `:2`. Default is DISPLAY `:0`.

RX_BPP=""
Optional color depth of the local X server.

RX_CLASS=""
This is an optional class name for naming a resource class in remote xdm configuration.

xntp   Starts the "Network Time Protocol (NTP) Daemon" of package `xntp`. Configuration is done in file `/etc/ntp.conf`.

XNTPD_INITIAL_NTPDATE="AUTO-2"
A space-separated list of NTP servers to query for current time and date before the local xntpd is started, for example, `"sun.cosmos.com"`. Set the value `AUTO` to query all servers and peers configured in `/etc/ntpd.conf`. The new default value is `AUTO-2`, which will query only the first two servers listed in `/etc/ntpd.conf`.
Radio and modem clocks have addresses in the form `127.127.T.U`, where T is the clock type and U is a unit number in the range 0–3. Most of these clocks require a serial port or special bus peripheral. The particular device is normally specified by adding a soft link from `/dev/device-U` to the particular hardware device involved, where U correspond to the unit number above. See `/usr/share/doc/packages/xntp/html/refclock.htm`.

ypbind   Configuration of an NIS client. Additional information: The domain name is set in `/etc/defaultdomain`. The server name will be entered in `/etc/yp.conf` directly during configuration with YaST2.

YPBIND_OPTIONS=""
Extra options for ypbind.

YPBIND_LOCAL_ONLY="no"
If this option is set, ypbind will only bind to the loopback interface and remote hosts cannot query it.

YPBIND_BROADCAST="no"
If this option is set to `yes`, ypbind will ignore `/etc/yp.conf` and use a broadcast call to find a NIS server in the local subnet. Avoid using this, as it is a big security risk.

YPBIND_BROKEN_SERVER="no"
Set this to yes if you have a NIS server in your network, which binds only to high ports over 1024. Since this is a security risk, you should consider replacing the NIS server with another implementation.

ypserv Configuration of an NIS server.

YPPWD_SRCDIR="/etc"
Specify the YP source directory where YP will search the source files for the passwd and group tables. Default is /etc

YPPWD_CHFN="no"
Should a user be allowed to change his GECOS field using ypchfn?

YPPWD_CHSH="no"
Should the user be allowed to change his default login shell using ypchsh?

zope Configuration of ZOPE systems.

ZOPE_FTP="yes"
Should Zope be accessible via FTP?

ZOPE_FTP_PORT="8021"
If so, on which port?

ZOPE_HTTP_PORT="8080"
If you run Zope as a stand-alone server, which port should it occupy?

Part IV

Network

14

Linux in the Network

Linux, really a child of the Internet, offers all the necessary networking tools and features for integration into all types of network structures. An introduction into the customary Linux protocol, TCP/IP, follows. The various services and special features of this protocol are discussed. Network access using a network card can be configured with YaST2. The central configuration files are discussed and some of the most essential tools described. Only the fundamental mechanisms and the relevant network configuration files are discussed in this chapter. The configuration of Internet access with PPP via modem, ISDN, or other connection can be completed with YaST2. It is described in the *Configuration Manual*.

TCP/IP — The Protocol Used by Linux	336
IPv6 — The Next Generation's Internet	344
Network Integration	349
Manual Network Configuration	352
Routing in SuSE Linux	359
DNS — Domain Name Service	361
NIS — Network Information Service	371
NFS — Shared File Systems	375
DHCP	379

TCP/IP — The Protocol Used by Linux

Linux and other Unix operating systems use the TCP/IP protocol. It not a single network protocol, but a family of network protocols that offer various services. TCP/IP was developed based on an application used for military purposes and was defined in its present form in an RFC in 1981. RFC stands for "Request for Comments". They are documents that describe various Internet protocols and implemenation procedures for the operating system and its applications. Since then, the TCP/IP protocol has been refined, but the basic protocol has remained virtually unchanged.

> **Tip**
>
> The RFC documents describe the setup of Internet protocols. To expand your knowledge about any of the protocols, the appropriate RFC document is the right place to start: `http://www.ietf.org/rfc.html`
>
> **Tip**

The services listed in Table 14.1 are provided for the purpose of exchanging data between two Linux machines via TCP/IP. Networks, combined by TCP/IP, comprising a world-wide network are also referred to, in their entirety, as "the Internet."

TCP	Transmission Control Protocol: A connection-oriented secure protocol. The data to transmit is first sent by the application as a stream of data then converted by the operating system to the appropriate format. The data arrives at the respective application on the destination host in the original data stream format in which it was initially sent. TCP determines whether any data has been lost during the transmission and that there is no mix-up. TCP is implemented wherever the data sequence matters.
UDP	User Datagram Protocol: A connectionless, insecure protocol. The data to transmit is sent in the form of packets already generated by the application. The order in which the data arrives at the recipient is not guaranteed and data loss is a possibility. UDP is suitable for record-oriented applications. It features a smaller latency period than TCP.

Table 14.1: continued overleaf...

ICMP	Internet Control Message Protocol: Essentially, this is not a user-friendly protocol, but a special control protocol that issues error reports and can control the behavior of machines participating in TCP/IP data transfer. In addition, a special echo mode is provided by ICMP that can be viewed using the program ping.
IGMP	Internet Group Management Protocol: This protocol controls the machine behavior when implementing IP multicast. The following sections do not contain more infomation regarding IP multicasting, because of space limitations.

Table 14.1: Several Protocols in the TCP/IP Protocol Family

Almost all hardware protocols work on a packet-oriented basis. The data to transmit is packaged in "bundles", as it cannot be sent all at once. This is why TCP/IP only works with small data packets. The maximum size of a TCP/IP packet is approximately sixty-four kilobytes. The packets are normally quite a bit smaller, as the network software can be a limiting factor. The maximum size of a data packet on an ethernet is about fifteen hundred bytes. The size of a TCP/IP packet is limited to this amount when the data is sent over an ethernet. If more data is transferred, more data packets need to be sent by the operating system.

Layer Model

IP (Internet Protocol) is where the insecure data transfer takes place. TCP (Transmission Control Protocol), to a certain extent, is simply the upper layer for the IP platform serving to guarantee secure data transfer. The IP layer itself is, in turn, supported by the bottom layer, the hardware-dependent protocol, such as ethernet. Professionals refer to this structure as the "layer model". See Figure 14.1 on the following page.

The diagram provides one or two examples for each layer. As you can see, the layers are ordered according to "degrees of abstraction". The bottommost layer is very close to the hardware. The uppermost layer, however, is almost a complete abstraction of the hardware. Every layer has its own special function, clarified in the following.

Host sun		Host earth
Application layer	Application	Application layer
Transport layer	TCP, UDP	Transport layer
Communication layer	IP	Communication layer
Security layer	Ethernet, FDDI, ISDN	Security layer
Bit transfer layer	Cable, Fiberglass	Bit transfer layer

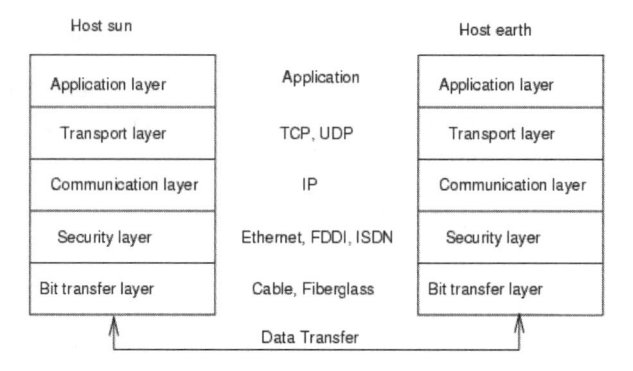

Figure 14.1: Simplified Layer Model for TCP/IP

The special functions of each layer are already implicit in their description. For example, the network used (e.g., ethernet) is depicted by the bit transfer and security layers.

- While layer 1 deals with cable types, signal forms, signal codes, and the like, layer 2 is responsible for accessing procedures (which host may send data?) and correcting errors. Layer 1 is called the bit transfer layer. Layer 2 is called security layer

- Layer 3 is the communication layer and is responsible for remote data transfer. The network layer ensures that the data arrives at the correct remote recipient and can be delivered.

- Layer 4, the transport layer, is responsible for application data. The transport layer ensures the data arrives in the correct order and none is lost. The security layer is only there to make sure that the data that has arrived is correct. The transport layer protects data from being lost.

- Finally, layer 5 is the layer where data is processed by the application itself.

For every layer to serve its designated function, additional information regarding each layer must be saved in the data packet. This takes place in the header of the packet. Every layer attaches a small block of data, called the protocol header, to the front of each emerging packet. A sample TCP/IP data packet travelling over an ethernet cable is illustrated in Figure 14.2 on the next page.

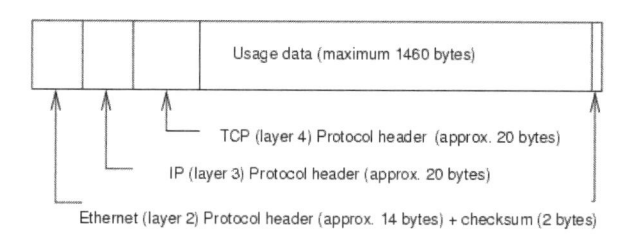

Figure 14.2: TCP/IP Ethernet Packet

The proof sum is located at the end of the packet, not at the beginning. This simplifies things for the network hardware. The largest amount of usage data possible in one packet is 1460 bytes in an ethernet network.

When an application sends data over the network, the data passes through each layer, all implemented in the Linux kernel except layer 1: network card. Each layer is responsible for preparing the data so it can be passed to the next layer below. The lowest layer is ultimately responsible for sending the data.

The entire procedure is reversed when data is received. Like the layers of an onion, in each layer the protocol headers are removed from the usage data. Finally, layer 4 is responsible for making the data available for use by the applications at the destination.

In this manner, one layer only commicates with the layer directly above or below it. For applications, it is irrelevant whether data is being transmitted via a 100 MBit/s FDDI network or via a 56-kbit/s modem line. Likewise, it is also irrelevant for the data transfer what data is being sent, as long as it has been properly compressed.

IP Addresses and Routing

IP Addresses

Every computer on the Internet has a unique 32-bit address. These 32 bits (or 4 bytes) are normally written as illustrated in the second row in Table 14.2 on the following page. In decimal form, the four bytes are written in the decimal number system, separated by periods. The IP address is assigned to a host or a network interface. It cannot be used anywhere else in the world. There are certainly exceptions to this rule, but these play a minimal role in the following passages.

IP Adress (binary):	11000000	10101000	00000000	00010100
IP Adress (decimal):	192.	168.	0.	20

Table 14.2: How an IP Address is Written

The ethernet card itself has its own unique address: the MAC (media access control) address. It is 48 bits long, internationally unique, and is programmed into the hardware by the network card vendor. There is, however, an unfortunate disadvantage of vendor-assigned addresses — the MAC addresses do not make up a hierarchical system, but are instead more or less randomly distributed. Therefore, they cannot be used for addressing remote machines. The MAC address plays an important role in communication between hosts in a local network and is the main component of the protocol header from layer 2.

The points in IP addresses indicate the hierarchical system. Until the 1990s, the IP addresses were strictly categorized in classes. However, this system has proven to be too inflexible and therefore was discontinued. Now, "classless routing" (or CIDR, Classless Inter Domain Routing) is used.

Netmasks and Routing

Netmasks were conceived for the purpose of informing the host with the IP address 192.168.0.20 of the location of the host with the IP address 192.168.0.1. To put it simply, the netmask on a host with an IP address defines what is "internal" and what is "external". Hosts located "internally" (professionals say, "in the same subnetwork") respond directly. Hosts located "externally" ("not in the same subnetwork") only respond via a gateway or router. Since every network interface can receive its own IP address, it can get quite complicated.

Before a network packet is sent, the following runs on the computer: the IP address is linked to the netmask via a logical AND, the address of the sending host is likewise connected to the netmask via the logical AND. If there are several network interfaces available, normally all possible sender addresses will be verified. The results of the AND links will be compared. If there are no discrepancies in this comparison, the destination, or receiving host, is located in the same subnetwork. Otherwise, it will have to be accessed via a gateway. That means that the more "1" bits are located in the netmask, the fewer hosts can be accessed directly and the more hosts can be reached via a gateway. Several examples are illustrated in Table 14.3 on the next page.

	binary representation
IP address:192.168.0.20	11000000 10101000 00000000 00010100
Netmask: 255.255.255.0	11111111 11111111 11111111 00000000
Result of the link	11000000 10101000 00000000 00000000
In the decimal system	192. 168. 0. 0
IP address: 213.95.15.200	11010101 10111111 00001111 11001000
Netmask: 255.255.255.0	11111111 11111111 11111111 00000000
Result of the link	11010101 10111111 00001111 00000000
In the decimal system	213. 95. 15. 0

Table 14.3: Linking IP Addresses to the Netmask

The netmasks appear, like IP addresses, in decimal form divided by periods. Since the netmask is also a 32-bit value, four number values are written next to each other. Which hosts are gateways or which address domains are accessible over which network interfaces must be entered in the user configurations.

To give another example: all machines connected with the same ethernet cable are usually located in the *same subnetwork* and are directly accessible. When the ethernet is divided by switches or bridges, these hosts can still be reached.

However, the economical ethernet is not suitable for covering larger distances. You will have to transfer the IP packets to another hardware (e.g., FDDI or ISDN). Devices for this transfer are called routers or gateways. A Linux machine can carry out this task. The respective option is referred to as ip_forwarding.

If a gateway has been configured, the IP packet will be sent to the appropriate gateway. This will then attempt to forward the packet in the same manner, from host to host, until it reaches the destination host or the packet's TTL (time to live) has expired.

The base network address	This is the netmask AND any address in the network, as shown in Table 14.3 under Result. This address cannot be assigned to any hosts.

Table 14.4: continued overleaf...

The broadcast address	Basically says, "Access all hosts in this sub-network". To generate this, the netmask is inverted in binary form and linked to the base network address with a logical OR. The above example therefore results in 192.168.0.255. This address cannot be assigned to any hosts.
The local host	The address `127.0.0.1` is strictly assigned to the "loopback device" on each host. A connection can be set up to your own machine with this address.

Table 14.4: Specific Addresses

Since IP addresses must be unique all over the world, you cannot just come up with your own random addresses. There are three address domains to use to set up a private IP-based network. With these, you cannot set up any connections to the rest of the Internet, unless you apply certain tricks, because these addresses cannot be transmitted over the Internet. These address domains are specified in RFC 1597 and listed in Table 14.5.

Network, Netmask	Domain
10.0.0.0, 255.0.0.0	10.x.x.x
172.16.0.0, 255.240.0.0	172.16.x.x - 172.31.x.x
192.168.0.0, 255.255.0.0	192.168.x.x

Table 14.5: Private IP Address Domains

Domain Name System

DNS

DNS serves to alleviate the burden of having to remember IP addresses: DNS assists in assigning an IP address to one or more names and, vice versa, assigning a name to an IP address. In Linux, this conversion is usually carried out by a special type of software known as bind. The machine that takes care of this conversion is called a name server.

The names make up a hierarchical system whereby each name component is divided by points. The name hierarchy is, however, independent of the IP address hierarchy described above.

Examine a complete name like `laurent.suse.de`. This is written in the format *host.domain*. A full name, referred to by experts as a "fully qualified domain name" or FQDN for short, consists of a host name and a domain name (*suse.de*), including the top level domain or TLD (*de*).

TLD assignment has become, for historical reasons, quite confusing. For instance, three-letter domain names are used in the USA. In the rest of the world, the two-letter ISO national codes are the standard.

In the early days of the Internet (before 1990), there was a file `/etc/hosts` for the purpose of storing the names of all the machines represented over the Internet. This quickly proved to be impractical in the face of the rapidly growing number of computers connected to the Internet. For this reason, a decentralized database was developed to store the host names in a widely distributed manner. This database, similar to the name server, does not have the data pertaining to all hosts in the Internet readily available, but can dispatch requests to other name servers.

The top of the hierarchy is occupied by "root name servers". These root name servers manage the top level domains. The root name servers are managed by the Network Information Center, or NIC for short. The root name server recognizes the name servers responsible for each top level domain. More information about top level domain NICs is available at `http://www.internic.net`.

For your machine to resolve an IP address, it has to recognize at least one name server with an IP address. Configure a name server with the help of YaST2. If you have a modem dial-up connection, you may not have to manually configure a name server at all. The dial-up protocol provides the name server address as the connection is being made.

DNS can do more than just resolve host names. The name server also "knows" which host is receiving e-mails for an entire domain, the mail exchanger (MX). The configuration of name server access with SuSE Linux is described in Section *DNS — Domain Name Service* on page 361.

whois

Closely related to DNS is the protocol whois. With this program, you can quickly find out who is responsible for any given domain.

IPv6 — The Next Generation's Internet

A New Internet Protocol

Due to the emergence of the WWW (World Wide Web), the Internet has experienced explosive growth with an increasing number of computers communicating via TCP/IP in the last ten years. Since Tim Berners-Lee at CERN (http://public.web.cern.ch/) invented the WWW in 1990, the number of Internet hosts has grown from a few thousand to about 100 million.

An IP address "only" consists of 32 bits. Since quite a few IP addresses cannot be used due to organizational circumstances, many IP addresses are lost. The Internet is divided into subnetworks. The number of addresses available in your subnet is the number of bits squared minus two. A subnetwork has, for example, two, six, or fourteen addresses available. To connect 128 hosts to the Internet, for instance, you will need a "Class C" subnetwork with 256 IP addresses, from which only 254 are usable. Two IP addresses are subtracted from the subnetwork — the broadcast address and the base network address.

Configuring a host in the TCP/IP network is relatively complicated. As you have already seen, you will have to configure the following items on your host: IP address, subnetmask, gateway address (if available), and a name server. You will already have to know this information or receive it from your provider.

Every IP packet contains a proof total that verifies each routing procedure and will have to be recalculated. This is why very fast routers require a lot of processor performance and are more expensive.

Some services have previously been implemented using broadcasts (for example, the Windows network protocol SMB). Hosts for which this service is irrelevant are, however, forced to process the packets and subsequently ignore them. This could lead to problems in high-speed networks.

The successor of the previous IP, IPv6, is a solution to all these problems. The main goal of its development was to expand significantly the rather limited address space, to simplify the configuration of workstations, and to automate them when possible. In this section, IPv4 or IP will be mentioned in reference to the Internet protocol currently used and IPv6 in reference to the new version 6.

IPv6 is defined in more detail in RFC 1752. IPv6 uses 128-bit addresses so features quadrillions of IP addresses, enough for even more general address distribution. This enormous amount of IPv6 addresses allows you to "enlarge" even the smallest subnetwork to 48 bits.

This enables you, then, to utilize the above mentioned MAC address as an address component. As this address is entirely unique and is strictly defined by the hardware vendor, this will make your host configuration a lot easier. In reality, an EUI-64 token will be consolidated down to the first 64 bits. In doing so, the last 48 bits of the MAC address will be removed and the remaining 24 bits will contain special information on the token type. This also enables the assignment of an EUI-64 token to devices without a MAC address (PPP and ISDN connections).

Furthermore, there has been a new development in IPv6: normally, several IP addresses are assigned to a network interface. This has the advantage that different networks can be made accessible. One of them can be turned into an automatically configured network. Specify the MAC address of the network card and a prefix and you will not have to configure anything else. All hosts in the local network will be accessible right after starting IPv6 ("link-local address").

Moreover, the remaining configuration tasks on a workstation can be carried out automatically to a greater extent. There is a special protocol for this purpose with which workstations can receive an IP address from a router.

All IPv6 supported hosts absolutely require "multicast" support. Multicast can aid several hosts in being accessible at the same time — they do not all have to be set to ("broadcast") or only one to ("unicast"), but, rather, a pair. Which of them that is depends on the application. However, a pair of well-defined multicast groups exists as well, for example, "all name servers multicast group" or "all routers multicast group."

As updating all hosts in the Internet from IPv4 to IPv6 is in no way feasible, there is a compatibility mode. This maps the previous addresses to IPv6 addresses. At the same time, there are mechanisms such as "tunneling" — here, IPv6 packets are sent in the form of IPv4 packets. Of course, it is also possible to convert IPv6 to IPv4. To reach an IPv6 host from a IPv4 host, the IPv6 host absolutely has to have a IPv4 compatibility address.

Structure of an IPv6 Address

An IPv6 address, conditional upon 128 bits, is significantly longer than an IPv4 address with its 32 bits. An IPv6 address is consequently 16 bytes long.

Due to the size factor, the new IPv6 addresses are written in a different format than the IPv4 addresses used previously. Look at the examples in Table 14.6 on the next page.

As you can see in the table, IPv6 addresses are represented by hexadecimal numbers. The hexadecimal numbers are represented in two-byte segments separated by a colon. Therefore, there can only be a maximum of eight

Local host	::1
IPv4-compatible IPv6 address	::10.10.11.102
	(IPv6 supported)
IPv4-mapped IPv6 address	::ffff:10.10.11.102
	(IPv6 is not supported)
random address	3ffe:400:10:100:200:c0ff:fed0:a4c3
Link-local address	fe80::10:1000:1a4
Site-local address	fec0:1:1:0:210:10ff:fe00:1a4
Multicast group "All link-local routers"	ff02:0:0:0:0:0:0:2

Table 14.6: Representation of Various IPv6 Addresses

groups and seven colons in one address. Zero-bytes in front of a group can be omitted, but not if these are in the middle or at the end of a group. More than four zero-bytes following one another can be skipped by the omission character ::. However, only one omission character is allowed in one address. This omission procedure is technically referred to as "collapsing". IPv4 compatibility addresses are a specific example of collapsing: here, the IPv4 address is simply attached to the predefined prefix for IPv4 compatibility addresses.

Every part of an IPv6 address has a set meaning. The first bytes comprise a prefix and specify the address type. The middle portion addresses a network or has no meaning. The last part of the address comprises the host segment. Table 14.7 on the facing page explains the meaning of some of the more common prefixes.

Prefix (hexadecimal)	Usage
00	IPv4 and IPv4 via IPv6 compatibility addresses. This is an IPv4-compatible address. The IPv6 packet will still need to be converted to an IPv4 packet via an appropriate router. Further special addresses (e.g., loopback devices) are likewise designated this prefix.
First digit 2 or 3	provider-based unicast addresses. As in the previous example, you can be designated a subnetwork in IPv6 from a provider.

Table 14.7: continued overleaf...

fe80 to febf	link-local addresses with this prefix cannot be routed and, therefore, cannot be accessed in the same subnetwork.
fec0 to feff	site-local. These addresses can be routed, but only internally within an organization. In this way, these addresses correspond to the previous "private" networks (for example, 10.x.x.x).
ff	multicast IPv6 addresses beginning with ff are multicast addresses.

Table 14.7: Various IPv6 Prefixes

As you can already see above, special unicast addresses can get quite long. These can no longer simply be memorized. A functional name server is therefore even more important for IPv6 than for IPv4. Name servers are so important that there is even an autoconfiguration protocol for them.

IPv6 Netmasks

Netmasks are represented by IPv6 in a slightly different way. The categorization of networks in classes is no longer practical, since classless routing is used from the beginning and the small subnetwork can already take up any number of hosts. Since netmasks would get quite long if written out in the previous manner, they will now be written in an entirely different format. The format

fec0:1:1:0:210:10ff:fe00:1a4/64

indicates that the last 64 bits make up the host segment and the first 64 bits are the network segment.

To be more precise, the 64 means that the netmask is filled up, as indicated at left, with 1 bits. Therefore, there are 64 one-bits in the netmask. As in IPv4, linking the netmask with the IP address with the logical AND defines whether a host is located in the same or in a different subnetwork.

For More Information About IPv6

Of course, the above overview cannot and is not intended to be a comprehensive introduction to the very extensive topic of IPv6. For a more in-depth introduction in IPv6, refer to http://www.ipv6.org/.

14

Network Integration

Currently TCP/IP is the standard network protocol. All modern operating systems can communicate via TCP/IP. Nevertheless, Linux also supports other network protocols, such as IPX (previously) implemented by Novell Netware or Appletalk used by Macintosh machines. Only the integration of a Linux machine into a TCP/IP network is discussed here. To integrate "exotic" arcnet, token rings, or FDDI network cards, refer to the kernel sources documentation at `/usr/src/linux/Documentation`. For information about network configuration changes made in SuSE Linux version 8.0, read the file `/usr/share/doc/packages/sysconfig/README`.

Preparing

The machine has to have a supported network card. Normally, the network card will already be recognized during installation and the appropriate driver loaded. See if your card has been integrated properly by entering the command `ifstatus eth0`. The output should show the status of the network device eth0.

If the kernel support for the network card is implemented as a module, as is usually the case with the SuSE kernel, the name of the module must be entered as an alias in `/etc/modules.conf`. For example, for the first ethernet card:

```
alias eth0 tulip
```

This will occur automatically if the driver support is started in the linuxrc during the first installation. Otherwise, start it via YaST2 at a later time.

If you are using a hotplug network card (e. g., PCMCIA or USB), the drivers are autodected when the card is plugged in. No configuration is necessary. Find more information in *Hotplugging Services* on page 237.

Configuration Assisted by YaST2

To configure the network card with YaST2, start the Control Center and select 'Network/Basic' → 'Network card configuration'. With 'Add', configure a new network card. With 'Delete', remove it from the configuration. With 'Edit', modify the network card configuration.

Activate the check box 'Hardware' to modify the hardware data for an already configured network card with 'Edit'. This opens the dialog for changing the settings of the network card, shown in Figure 14.3 on the following page.

SuSE Linux – Administration Guide   349

Normally, the correct driver for your network card is configured during installation and is activated. Therefore, manual hardware parameter settings are only needed if multiple network cards are used or if the network hardware is not automatically recognized. In this case, select 'Add' to specify a new driver module.

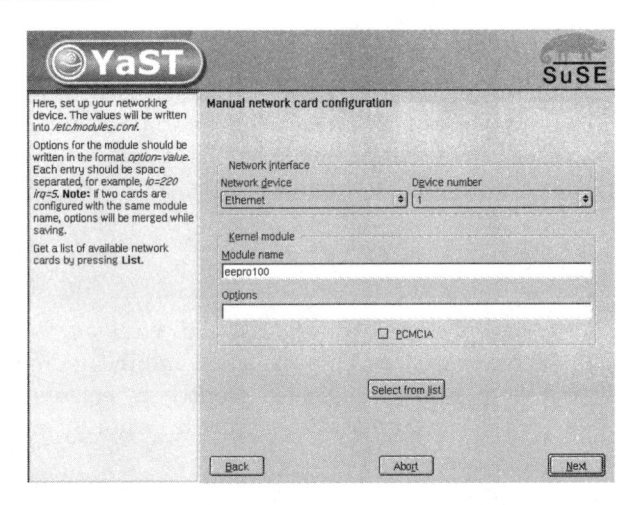

Figure 14.3: Configuring the Hardware Parameters

In this dialog, set the network card type and, for an ISA card, the interrupt to implement and the IO address. For some network drivers, also specify special parameters, such as the interface to use or whether it uses an RJ-45 or a BNC connection. For this, refer to the driver module documentation. To use PCMCIA or USB activate the respective check boxes.

After entering the hardware parameters, configure additional network interface data. Select 'Interface' in the dialog 'Network base configuration' to activate the network card and assign it an IP address. Select the card number then click 'Edit'. A new dialog will appear in which to specify the IP address and other IP network data. Find information about assigning addresses to your own network in Section *TCP/IP — The Protocol Used by Linux* on page 336 and Table 14.5 on page 342. Otherwise, enter the address assigned by your network administrator in the designated fields.

Configure a name server under 'Host Name and Name Server' so the name resolution functions as described in Section *DNS — Domain Name Service* on page 361. Via 'Routing', set up the routing. Select 'Configuration for Experts' to make advanced settings.

If you are using wireless lan network cards, activate the check box 'Wireless Device'. In the dialog window, set the most important options, like operation mode, network names, and the key for encrypted data transfer.

With that, the network configuration is complete. YaST2 starts SuSEconfig and transfers the settings to the corresponding files (see Section *Manual Network Configuration* on the following page). For the changes to take effect, the relevant programs must be reconfigured and the required daemons must be restarted. This is done by entering the command `rcnetwork restart`.

Hotplug and PCMCIA

Hotplug network cards, like PCMCIA or USB devices, are managed in a somewhat special way. Normal network cards are fixed components assigned a permanent device name, such as eth0. By contrast, PCMCIA cards are assigned a free device name dynamically on an as-needed basis. To avoid conflicts with fixed network cards, hotplug and PCMCIA services are loaded after the network has been started.

PCMCIA-related configuration and start scripts are located in the directory `/etc/sysconfig/pcmcia`. The scripts will be executed as soon as cardmgr, the PCMCIA Device Manager, detects a newly inserted PCMCIA card — which is why PCMCIA services do not need to be started before the network during boot.

Configuring IPv6

To configure IPv6, you will not normally need to make any changes on the individual workstations. However, the IPv6 support will have to be loaded. Do this most easily by entering the command `modprobe ipv6`.

Because of the autoconfiguration concept of IPv6, the network card is assigned an address in the "link-local" network. Normally, no routing table management takes place on a workstation. The network routers can be inquiried by the workstation, using the "router advertisement protocol", for what prefix and gateways should be implemented.

The radvd program out of package `radvd` can be used to set up an IPv6 router. This program informs the workstations which prefix to use for the IPv6 addresses and which routers.

To assign a workstation an IPv6 address easily, it is advisable to install and configure the router using the radvd program. The workstations will then automatically receive the IPv6 addresses assigned to them.

Manual Network Configuration

Manual configuration of the network software should always be the last alternative. We recommend using YaST2.

All network interfaces are set up with the script `/sbin/ifup`. To halt the interface, use `ifdown`. To check its status, use `ifstatus`.

If you only have normal, built-in network cards, configure the interfaces by name. With the commands `ifup eth0`, `ifstatus eth0`, and `ifdown eth0`, start, check, or stop the interface `eth0`. The respective configuration files are stored in `/etc/sysconfig/network/ifcfg-eth0`. `eth0` is the name of the interface and the name of the configuration.

The network can alternatively be configured in relation to the hardware address (MAC address) of a network card. In this case, a configuration file `ifcfg-<hardwareaddresswithoutcolon>` is used. Use lowercase characters in the hardware address, as displayed by the command `ip link` (`ifconfig` shows uppercase letters). If `ifup` finds a configuration file matching the hardware address, a possibly existing file `ifcfg-eth0` will be ignored.

Things are a little more complicated with hotplug network cards. If you do not use one of those cards, skip the following sections and continue reading *Configuration Files* on the next page.

Hotplug network cards are assigned the interface name arbitrarily, so the configuration for one of those cards cannot be stored under the name of the interface. Instead, a name is used that contains the kind of hardware and the connection point. In the following, this name is referred to as the hardware description. `ifup` has to be called with two arguments — the hardware description and the current interface name. `ifup` will then determine the configuration that best fits the hardware description.

For example, a laptop with two PCMCIA slots, a PCMCIA ethernet network card and a built-in network card configured as interface `eth0` is configured in the following way: The built-in network card is in slot 0 and its hardware description is `eth-pcmcia-0`. The program `cardmgr` or the hotplug network script runs the command `ifup eth-pcmcia-0 eth1` and `ifup` searches in `/etc/sysconfig/network/` for a file `ifcfg-eth-pcmcia-0`. If there is no such file, it looks for `ifcfg-eth-pcmcia`, `ifcfg-pcmcia-0`, `ifcfg-pcmcia`, `ifcfg-eth1` and `ifcfg-eth`. The first of these files found by `ifup` is used for the configuration. To generate a network configuration valid for all PCMCIA network cards in all slots, the configuration file must be named `ifcfg-pcmcia`. This file would then be used for the ethernet card in slot 0 (`eth-pcmcia-0`) as well as for a token ring card in slot

1 (`tr-pcmcia-1`). A configuration depending on the hardware address is treated with higher priority.

YaST2 lists the configurations for hotplug cards and accordingly writes the settings to `ifcfg-eth-pcmcia-<number>`. To use such a configuration file for all slots, a link `ifcfg-eth-pcmcia` points to this file. Keep this in mind if you sometimes configure the network with and sometimes without YaST2.

Configuration Files

This section provides an overview of the network configuration files and explains their purpose and the format used.

/etc/sysconfig/network/ifcfg-*

These files contain data specific to a network interface. They may be named after the network interface (`ifcfg-eth2`), the hardware address of a network card (`ifcfg-000086386be3`), or the hardware description (`ifcfg-usb`). If network aliases are used, the respective files are named `ifcfg-eth2:1` or `ifcfg-usb:1`. The script `ifup` gets the interface name and, if necessary, the hardware description as arguments then searches for the best matching configuration file.

The configuration files contain the IP address (BOOTPROTO="static", IPADDR="10.10.11.214") or the direction to use DHCP (BOOTPROTO="dhcp"). The IP address may also include the netmask (IPADDR="10.10.11.214/16") or the netmask can be specified separately (NETMASK="255.255.0.0"). Refer to the man page for `ifup` (`man ifup`) for the complete list of variables.

In addition, all the variables in the files `dhcp`, `wireless`, and `config` can be used in the `ifcfg-*` files, if a general setting is only to be used for one interface. By using the variables POST_UP_SCRIPT and PRE_DOWN_SCRIPT, individual scripts can be run after starting or before stopping the interface.

/etc/sysconfig/network/config, dhcp, wireless

The file `config` contains general settings for the behavior of `ifup`, `ifdown`, and `ifstatus`. `dhcp` contains settings for DHCP and `wireless` for wireless lan cards. The variables in all three configuration files are commented and can also be used in `ifcfg-*` files, where they are treated with higher priority.

/etc/hosts
In this file (see File 45), IP addresses are assigned to host names. If no name server is implemented, all hosts to which an IP connection will be set up must be listed here. For each host, a line consisting of the IP address, the fully qualified host name, and the host name (e. g., `earth`) is entered into the file. The IP address has to be at the beginning of the line, the entries divided by blanks and tabs. Comments are always preceeded by the '#' sign.

```
127.0.0.1 localhost
192.168.0.1 sun.cosmos.com sun
192.168.0.20 earth.cosmos.com earth
```

File 45: /etc/hosts

/etc/networks
Here, network names are converted to network addresses. The format is similar to that of the `hosts` file, except the network names preceed the addresses (see File 46).

```
loopback     127.0.0.0
localnet     192.168.0.0
```

File 46: /etc/networks

/etc/host.conf
Name resolution — the translation of host and network names via the *resolver* library — is controlled by this file. This file is only used for programs linked to the libc4 or the libc5. For current glibc programs, refer to the settings in /etc/nsswitch.conf. A parameter must always stand alone in its own line. Comments are preceeded by a '#' sign. Table 14.8 on the facing page shows the parameters available.

order *hosts, bind*	Specifies in which order the services are accessed for the name resolution. Available arguments are (separated by blank spaces or commas): *hosts*: Searches the /etc/hosts file *bind*: Accesses a name server

Table 14.8: continued overleaf...

	nis: Via NIS
multi *on/off*	Defines if a host entered in `/etc/hosts` can have multiple IP addresses.
nospoof *on*	These parameters influence the name server
alert *on/off*	*spoofing*, but, apart from that, do not exert any influence on the network configuration.
trim ⟨*domainname*⟩	The specified domain name is separated from the host name after host name resolution (as long as the host name includes the domain name). This option is useful if only names from the local domain are in the `/etc/hosts` file, but should still be recognized with the attached domain names.

Table 14.8: Parameters for /etc/host.conf

An example for `/etc/host.conf` is shown in File 47.

```
# We have named running
order hosts bind
# Allow multiple addrs
multi on
```

File 47: `/etc/host.conf`

/etc/nsswitch.conf

With the GNU C Library 2.0, the "Name Service Switch" (NSS) became more important. See the man page for `nsswitch.conf` or, for more details, *The GNU C Library Reference Manual*, Chap. "System Databases and Name Service Switch". Refer to package `libcinfo`.

In the `/etc/nsswitch.conf` file, the order of certain data is defined. An example of `nsswitch.conf` is shown in File 48. Comments are preceeded by '#' signs. Here, for instance, the entry under "database" `hosts` means that a request is sent to `/etc/hosts` (`files`) via DNS (see Section *DNS — Domain Name Service* on page 361).

```
passwd:      compat
group:       compat

hosts:       files dns
```

```
networks:     files dns

services:     db files
protocols:    db files

netgroup:     files
```

File 48: `/etc/nsswitch.conf`

The "databases" available over NSS are listed in Table 14.9. In addition, `automount`, `bootparams`, `netmasks`, and `publickey` are expected in the near future.

`aliases`	Mail aliases implemented by `sendmail`(8). See also the man page for `aliases`.
`ethers`	Ethernet addresses.
`group`	For user groups, used by `getgrent`(3). See also the man page for `group`.
`hosts`	For host names and IP addresses, used by `gethostbyname`(3) and similar functions.
`netgroup`	Valid host and user lists in the network for the purpose of controlling access permissions. See also the man page for `netgroup`.
`networks`	Network names and addresses, used by `getnetent`(3).
`passwd`	User passwords, used by `getpwent`(3). See also the man page for `passwd`.
`protocols`	Network protocols, used by `getprotoent`(3). See also the man page for `protocols`.
`rpc`	"Remote Procedure Call" names and addresses, used by `getrpcbyname`(3) and similar functions.
`services`	Network services, used by `getservent`(3).
`shadow`	"Shadow" user passwords, used by `getspnam`(3). See also the man page for `shadow`.

Table 14.9: Available Databases via /etc/nsswitch.conf

The configuration options for NSS databases are listed in Table 14.10 on the next page.

`files`	directly access files, for example, to `/etc/aliases`.
`db`	access via a database.
`nis`	NIS, see also Section *NIS — Network Information Service* on page 371.
`nisplus`	
`dns`	Only usable by `hosts` and `networks` as an extension.
`compat`	Only usable by `passwd`, `shadow`, and `group` as an extension.
`also`	It is possible to trigger various reactions with certain lookup results. Details can be found in the man page for `nsswitch.conf`.

Table 14.10: Configuration Options for NSS "Databases"

`/etc/nscd.conf`

The nscd (Name Service Cache Daemon) is configured in this file (see the man pages for `nscd` and `nscd.conf`). This effects the data resulting from `passwd`, `groups`, and `hosts`. The daemon must be restarted every time the name resolution (DNS) is changed by modifying the `/etc/resolv.conf` file. Use `rcnscd restart` to restart it.

> **Caution**
>
> If, for example, the caching for `passwd` is activated, it will usually take about fifteen seconds until a newly added user is recognized by the system. By resarting nscd, reduce this waiting period.
>
> **Caution**

`/etc/resolv.conf`

As is already the case with the `/etc/host.conf` file, this file, by way of the *resolver* library, likewise plays a role in host name resolution. The domain to which the host belongs is specified in this file (keyword search). Also listed is the status of the name server address (keyword name server) to access. Multiple domain names can be specified. When resolving a name that is not fully qualified, an attempt is made to generate one by attaching the individual search entries. Multiple name servers can be made known by entering several lines, each beginning with name server. Comments are preceeded by '#' signs.

An example of /etc/resolv.conf is shown in File 49.

```
# Our domain
search cosmos.com

name server 192.168.0.1
```

File 49: /etc/resolv.conf

Some services, like pppd (wvdial), ipppd (isdn), dhcp (dhcpcd and dhclient), pcmcia, and hotplug, modify the file /etc/resolv.conf. To do so, they rely on the script modify_resolvconf.

If the file /etc/resolv.conf has been temporarily modified by this script, it will contain a predefined comment giving information about the service by which it has been modified, about the location where the original file has been backed up, and hints on how to turn off the automatic modification mechanism.

If /etc/resolv.conf is modified several times, the file will include modifications in a nested form. These can be reverted in a clean way even if this reversal takes place in an order different from the order in which modifications where introduced. Services that may need this flexibility include isdn, pcmcia, and hotplug.

If it happens that a service was not terminated in a normal, clean way, modify_resolvconf can be used to restore the original file. Also, on system boot, a check will be performed to see whether there is an uncleaned, modified resolv.conf (e.g., after a system crash), in which case the original (unmodified) resolv.conf will be restored.

YaST2 uses the command modify_resolvconf check to find out whether resolv.conf has been modified and will subsequently warn the user that changes will be lost after restoring the file.

Apart from this, YaST2 will not rely on modify_resolvconf, which means that the impact of changing resolv.conf through YaST2 is the same as that of any manual change. In both cases, changes are made on purpose and with a permanent effect, while modifications requested by the above-mentioned services are only temporary.

/etc/HOSTNAME
Here is the host name without the domain name attached. This file is read by several scripts while the machine is booting. It may only contain one line where the host name is mentioned.

Start-Up Scripts

Apart from the configuration files described above, there are also various scripts that load the network programs while the machine is being booted. This will be started as soon as the system is switched to one of the *multiuser runlevels* (see also Table 14.11).

`/etc/init.d/network`	This script takes over the configuration for the network hardware and software during the system's start-up phase.
`/etc/init.d/inetd`	Starts inetd. This is only necessary if you want to log in to this machine over the network.
`/etc/init.d/portmap`	Starts the portmapper needed for the RPC server, such as an NFS server.
`/etc/init.d/nfsserver`	Starts the NFS server.
`/etc/init.d/sendmail`	Controls the sendmail process.
`/etc/init.d/ypserv`	Starts the NIS server.
`/etc/init.d/ypbind`	Starts the NIS client.

Table 14.11: Some Start-Up Scripts for Network Programs

Routing in SuSE Linux

The routing table is set up in SuSE Linux via the configuration files `/etc/sysconfig/network/routes` and `/etc/sysconfig/network/ifroute-*`.

All the static routes required by the various system tasks can be entered in the `/etc/sysconfig/network/routes` file: routes to a host, routes to a host via a gateway, and routes to a network. For each interface that need individual routing, define an additional configuration file: `/etc/sysconfig/network/ifroute-*`. Replace '*' with the name of the interface. The entries in the routing configuration files look like this:

```
DESTINATION           GATEWAY NETMASK   INTERFACE [ TYPE ] [ OPTIONS ]
DESTINATION           GATEWAY PREFIXLEN INTERFACE [ TYPE ] [ OPTIONS ]
DESTINATION/PREFIXLEN GATEWAY -         INTERFACE [ TYPE ] [ OPTIONS ]
```

To omit GATEWAY, NETMASK, PREFIXLEN, or INTERFACE, write '-' instead. The entries TYPE and OPTIONS may just be omitted.

- The route's destination is in the first column. This column may contain the IP address of a network or host or, in the case of *reachable* name servers, the fully qualified network or host name.

- The second column contains the default gateway or a gateway through which a host or a network can be accessed.

- The third column contains the netmask for networks or hosts behind a gateway. The mask is 255.255.255.255, for example, for a host behind a gateway.

- The last column is only relevant for networks connected to the local host such as loopback, ethernet, ISDN, PPP, and dummy device. The device name must be entered here.

The following scripts in the directory /etc/sysconfig/network/scripts/ assist with the handling of routes:

ifup-route for setting up a route

ifdown-route for disabling a route

ifstatus-route for checking the status of the routes

14

DNS — Domain Name Service

DNS (Domain Name Service) is needed to resolve the domain and host names into IP addresses. In this way, the IP address `192.168.0.20` is assigned to the host name `earth`, for example. Before setting up your own name server, read the general information on DNS in Section *Domain Name System* on page 342.

Starting the Name Server BIND

The name server BIND is already preconfigured in SuSE Linux, so you can easily start it right after installing the distribution.

If you already have a functioning Internet connection and have entered 127.0.0.1 as name server for the local host in `/etc/resolv.conf`, you should normally already have a working name resolution without having to know the DNS of the provider. BIND carries out the name resolution via the root name server, a notably slower process. Normally, the DNS of the provider should be entered with its IP address in the configuration file `/etc/named.conf` under forwarders to ensure effective and secure name resolution. If this works so far, the name server will run as a pure "caching-only" name server. Only when you configure its own zones will it become a proper DNS. A simple example of this can be found under `/usr/share/doc/packages/bind8/sample-config`. However, do not set up any official domains until assigned one by the responsible institution. Even if you have your own domain and it is managed by the provider, you are better off not to use it, as BIND would otherwise not forward any more requests for this domain. The provider's web server, for example, would not be accessible for this domain.

To start the name server, enter `rcnamed start` at the command line as root. If "done" appears to the right in green, `named`, as the name server process is called, has been started successfully. Immediately test the functionality of the name server on the local system with the `nslookup` program. The local host should appear as the default server with the address 127.0.0.1. If this is not the case, the wrong name server has probably been entered in `/etc/resolv.conf` or this file does not exist. For the first test, enter `nslookup` "localhost" or "127.0.0.1" at the prompt, which should always work. If you receive an error message instead, such as "No response from server", check to see if `named` is actually running using the command `rcnamed status`. If the name server is not starting or is exhibiting faulty behavior, find the possible causes of this logged in `/var/log/messages`.

SuSE Linux – Administration Guide   361

If you have a dial-up connection, be sure that BIND8, once it starts, will review the root name server. If it does not manage this because an Internet connection has not been made, this can cause the DNS requests not to be resolved other than for locally-defined zones. BIND9 behaves differently, but requires quite a bit more resources than BIND8.

To implement the name server of the provider or one already running on your network as "forwarder", enter one or more of these in the options section under forwarders. See File 50.

```
options {
        directory "/var/lib/named";
        forwarders { 10.11.12.13; 10.11.12.14; };
        listen-on { 127.0.0.1; 192.168.0.99; };
        allow-query { 127/8; 192.168.0/24; };
        notify no;
};
```

File 50: Forwarding Options in named.conf

Adjust the IP addresses to your personal environment.

After options follows the zone, "localhost", "0.0.127.in-addr.arpa", and "." entries. At least entries from "type hint" should exist. Their corresponding files never have to be modified, as they function in their present state. Also, be sure that a ";" follows each entry and that the curly braces are properly set.

If you have made changes to the configuration file /etc/named.conf or to the zone files, have BIND reread these files by entering `rcnamed reload`. Otherwise, completely restart the name server with `rcnamed restart`. To stop the name server, enter `rcnamed stop`.

The Configuration File /etc/named.conf

Make all the settings for the name server BIND8 and BIND9 in the /etc/named.conf file. The zone data, consisting of the host names, IP addresses, and similar, for the domains to administer are stored in separate files in the /var/lib/named directory.

The /etc/named.conf is roughly divided into two areas. One is the options section for general settings and the other consists of zone entries for the individual domains. Additional sections for logging and acl type entries can be added. Comment lines begin with a '#' sign or '//'. A minimalistic /etc/named.conf looks like File 51.

```
options {
        directory "/var/lib/named";
        forwarders 10.0.0.1; ;
        notify no;
};

zone "localhost" in {
        type master;
        file "localhost.zone";
};

zone "0.0.127.in-addr.arpa" in {
        type master;
        file "127.0.0.zone";
};

zone "." in {
        type hint;
        file "root.hint";
};
```

File 51: A Basic /etc/named.conf

This example works for both BIND8 and BIND9, because no special options are used that are only understood by one version or the other. BIND9 accepts all BIND8 configurations and makes note of options not implemented at start-up. Special BIND9 options are, however, not supported by BIND8.

Important Configuration Options

directory "/var/lib/named"; specifies the directory where BIND can find the files containing the zone data.

forwarders 10.0.0.1; ; is used to specify the name servers (mostly of the provider) to which DNS requests, which cannot be resolved directly, are forwarded.

forward first; causes DNS requests to be forwarded before an attempt is made to resolve them via the root name servers. Instead of forward first, forward only can be written to have all requests forwarded and none sent to the root name servers. This makes sense for firewall configurations.

listen-on port 53 127.0.0.1; 192.168.0.1; ; tells BIND to which network interface and port to listen. The port 53 specification can be left out, since

53 is the default port. If this entry is completely omitted, BIND accepts requests on all interfaces.

query-source address * port 53; This entry is necessary if a firewall is blocking external DNS requests. This tells BIND to post requests externally from port 53 and not from any of the ports greater than 1024.

allow-query 127.0.0.1; 192.168.1/24; ; defines the networks from which clients can post DNS requests. The /24 at the end is an abbreviated expression for the netmask, in this case 255.255.255.0.

allow-transfer ! *; ; controls which hosts can request zone transfers. This example cuts them off completely due to the ! *. Without this entry, zone transfers can be requested anywhere without restrictions.

statistics-interval 0; In the absence of this entry, BIND8 generates several lines of statistical information in /var/log/messages. Specifying 0 suppresses these completely. Otherwise the time in minutes can be given here.

cleaning-interval 720; This option defines at which time intervals BIND8 clears its cache. This triggers an entry in /var/log/messages each time it occurs. The time specification is in minutes. The default is 60 minutes.

interface-interval 0; BIND8 regularly searches the network interfaces for new or no longer existing interfaces. If this value is set to 0, this will not be carried out and BIND8 will only listen at the interfaces detected at start-up. Otherwise, the interval can be defined in minutes. The default is 60 minutes.

notify no; no prevents other name servers from being informed when changes are made to the zone data or when the name server is restarted.

The Configuration Section "Logging"

What, how, and where archiving takes place can be extensively configured in BIND8. Normally, the default settings should be sufficient. File 52 on the facing page represents the simplest form of such an entry and will completely suppress any logging:

```
logging {
        category default { null; };
};
```

File 52: Entry to Suppress Logging

Zone Entry Structure

```
zone "my-domain.de" in {
        type master;
        file "my-domain.zone";
        notify no;
};
```

File 53: Zone Entry for my-domain.de

After zone, the name of the domain to administer is specified, my-domain.de, followed by in and a block of relevant options enclosed in curly braces, as shown in File 53. To define a "slave zone", the type is simply switched to slave and a name server is specified that administers this zone as master (but can also be a "slave"), as shown in File 54.

```
zone "other-domain.de" in {
        type slave;
        file "slave/other-domain.zone";
        masters { 10.0.0.1; };
};
```

File 54: Zone Entry for other-domain.de

The options:

type master; master indicates that this zone is administered on this name server. This assumes that your zone file has been properly created.

type slave; This zone is transferred from another name server. Must be used together with masters.

type hint; The zone . of the type hint is used for specification of the root name servers. This zone definition can be left alone.

file "my-domain.zone" or file "slave/other-domain.zone"; This entry specifies the file where zone data for the domain is located. This file is not required by slaves, because its contents is read by another name server. To differentiate master and slave files, the directory `slave` is specified for the slave files.

masters { 10.0.0.1; }; This entry is only needed for slave zones. It specifies from which name server the zone file should be transferred.

allow-update { ! *; }; This options controls external write access, which would allow clients to make a DNS entry — something which is normally not desirable for security reasons. Without this entry, zone updates are not allowed at all. Note that with the above sample entry, the same would be achieved because ! * effectively bars any clients from such access.

Structure of Zone Files

Two types of zone files are needed: one serves to assign IP addresses to host names and the other does the reverse — supplies a host name for an IP address.

'.' has an important meaning in the zone files here. If host names are given without ending with a '.', the zone will be appended. Thus, complete host names specified with a complete domain must end with a '.' so the domain is not added to it again. A missing point or one in the wrong place is probably the most frequent cause of name server configuration errors.

The first case to consider is the zone file `world.zone`, responsible for the domain `world.cosmos`, as in File 55 on the next page.

```
1. $TTL 2D
2. world.cosmos.     IN SOA     gateway  root.world.cosmos. (
3.                   2001040901 ; serial
4.                   1D         ; refresh
5.                   2H         ; retry
6.                   1W         ; expiry
7.                   2D )       ; minimum
8.
9.                   IN NS      gateway
10.                  IN MX      10 sun
11.
12. gateway          IN A       192.168.0.1
13.                  IN A       192.168.1.1
14. sun              IN A       192.168.0.2
15. moon             IN A       192.168.0.3
16. earth            IN A       192.168.1.2
17. mars             IN A       192.168.1.3
```

File 55: The File /var/lib/named/world.zone

Line 1: $TTL defines the standard TTL that applies for all the entries in this file, here 2 days. TTL means "time to live".

Line 2: The SOA control record begins here:

- The name of the domain to administer is world.cosmos in the first position. This ends with a '.', because otherwise the zone would be appended a second time. Alternatively, a '@' can be entered here. Then, the zone would be extracted from the corresponding entry in /etc/named.conf.

- After IN SOA is the name of the name server in charge as master for this zone. The name is extended from gateway to gateway.world.cosmos, because it does not end with a '.'.

- Afterwards, an e-mail address of the person in charge of this name server will follow. Since the '@' sign already has a special significance, '.' is to be entered here instead, for root@world.cosmos, consequently root.world.cosmos..The '.' sign at the end cannot be neglected, otherwise, the zone will still be added here.

- A '(' follows at the end here, including the following lines up until ')' into the SOA record.

Line 3: The serial number is an arbitrary number that is increased each time this file is changed. It is needed to inform the secondary name servers (slave servers) of changes. For this, a ten-digit number of the date and run number, written as YYYYMMDDNN, has become the customary format.

Line 4: The refresh rate specifies the time interval at which the secondary name servers verify the zone serial number. In this case, 1 day.

Line 5: The retry rate specifies the time interval at which a secondary name server, in case of error, attempts to contact the primary server again. Here, 2 hours.

Line 6: The expiration time specifies the time frame after which a secondary name server discards the cached data if it has not regained contact to the primary server. Here, it is a week.

Line 7: The minimum time to live states how long the results of the DNS requests from other servers can be cached before they become invalid and have to be requested again.

Line 9: The IN NS specifies the name server responsible for this domain. The same is true here that gateway is extended to gateway.world.cosmos because it does not end with a '.'. There can be several lines like this, one for the primary and one for each secondary name server. If notify is not set to no in `/etc/named.conf`, all the name servers listed here will be informed of the changes made to the zone data.

Line 10: The MX record specifies the mail server that accepts, processes, and forwards e-mails for the domain world.cosmos. In this example, this is the host sun.world.cosmos. The number in front of the host name is the preference value. If there are multiple MX entries, the mail server with the smallest value is taken first and, if mail delivery to this server fails, an attempt will be made with the next higher value.

Line 12–17: These are now the actual address records where one or more IP addresses are assigned to the host names. The names are listed here without a '.', because they are entered without a domain added and can all be appended with world.cosmos. Two IP addresses are assigned to the host gateway, because it has two network cards.

The pseudodomain in-addr.arpa is used to assist the reverse lookup of IP addresses into host names. This will be appended, for this purpose, to the network components described here in reverse order. 192.168.1 is thus translated into 1.168.192.in-addr.arpa. See File 56.

```
1.  $TTL 2D
2.  1.168.192.in-addr.arpa. IN SOA  gateway.world.cosmos.
                                    root.world.cosmos. (
3.                          2001040901      ; serial
4.                          1D              ; refresh
5.                          2H              ; retry
6.                          1W              ; expiry
7.                          2D )            ; minimum
8.
9.                          IN NS           gateway.world.cosmos.
10.
11. 1                       IN PTR          gateway.world.cosmos.
12. 2                       IN PTR          earth.world.cosmos.
13. 3                       IN PTR          mars.world.cosmos.
```

File 56: Reverse Lookup

Line 1: $TTL defines the standard TTL that applies to all entries here.

Line 2: 'Reverse lookup' should be activated with this file for the network 192.168.1.0. Since the zone is called '1.168.192.in-addr.arpa' here, it is, of course, undesirable to add this to the host name. Therefore, these are all entered complete with domain and ending with '.'. The rest corresponds to the previous example described for world.cosmos.

Line 3–7: See the previous example for world.cosmos.

Line 9: This line also specifies the name server responsible for this zone. This time, however, the name is entered completely with domain and ending with '.'.

Line 11–13: These are the pointer records which are linked to an IP address at the respective host name. Only the last part of the IP address is entered at the beginning of the line missing the last '.'. Now, if the zone is appended to this and the .in-addr.arpa is neglected, the entire IP address will be backwards.

In this form, the zone files are usable both for BIND8 and BIND9. Zone transfers between different versions should not normally be an issue.

For More Information

- Documentation on package bind8: `file:/usr/share/doc/packages/bind8/html/index.html`.

- A sample configuration can be found at: `/usr/share/doc/packages/bind8/sample-config`

- the man page for `named` (`man 8 named`) in which the relevant RFCs are named and the the man page for `named.conf` (`man 5 named.conf`

14 NIS — Network Information Service

As soon as multiple UNIX systems in a network want to access common resources, you have to make sure, for example, that all user and group identities are the same for all machines in that network. The network should be transparent to the user: whatever machine a user uses, he will always find himself in exactly the same environment. This is made possible by means of NIS and NFS services. NFS distributes file systems over a network and is discussed in Section *NFS — Shared File Systems* on page 375.

NIS (Network Information Service) is a database service that enables access to /etc/passwd, /etc/shadow, and /etc/group across a network. NIS can be used for other, more specialized tasks (such as for /etc/hosts or /etc/services).

NIS Master and Slave Server

For installation, select 'Network/Advanced' in YaST2 then 'Configure NIS server'. If a NIS server does not exist on your network, first activate 'Create NIS Master Server' in the next screen. If you already have a NIS server (a "master"), add a NIS slave server if you are configuring a new subnetwork.

Enter the domain name at the top of the next configuration screen (Figure 14.4 on the following page). In the check box underneath, define whether the host should also be an NIS client.

Activate 'Active NIS Slave Server Exists' if your network has other NIS slave servers. Select 'Fast Map Distribution' to speed up the data transfer from the master to the slave server.

To allow users in your network to change their passwords on the NIS server with the command yppasswd, enable this option as well. "GECOS" means that the user can also change his name and address settings with the command ypchfn. "SHELL" allows a user to modify his default shell with the command ypchsh.

Under 'Other global settings...', a menu appears (Figure 14.5 on page 373) in which to change the default directory (/etc). In addition, passwords and groups can be consolidated here. The setting should be left at 'Yes' so the files (/etc/passwd and /etc/shadow as well as /etc/group and /etc/gshadow) can be synchronized. 'OK' returns to the previous screen. Click 'Next'.

If you previously enabled 'Active NIS Slave Server exists', give the host names to use as slaves. Specify the name and go to 'Next'. The menu that

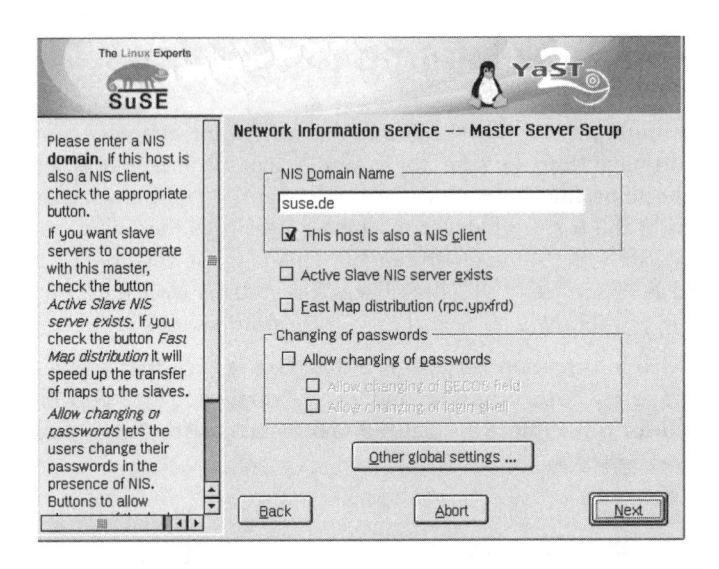

Figure 14.4: YaST2: NIS Server Configuration Tool

follows can be directly accessed, if you had not activated the slave server setting previously. Now the *maps*, the partial databases to transfer from the NIS server to the individual clients, can be configured. The default settings can be applied under most circumstances, so nothing usually needs to be changed here.

'Next' brings you to the last dialog, where you can define which networks are allowed to send requests to the NIS server (see Figure 14.6 on page 374). Normally, this is your internal network. If this is the case, there should be two entries:

```
255.0.0.0 127.0.0.0
0.0.0.0 0.0.0.0
```

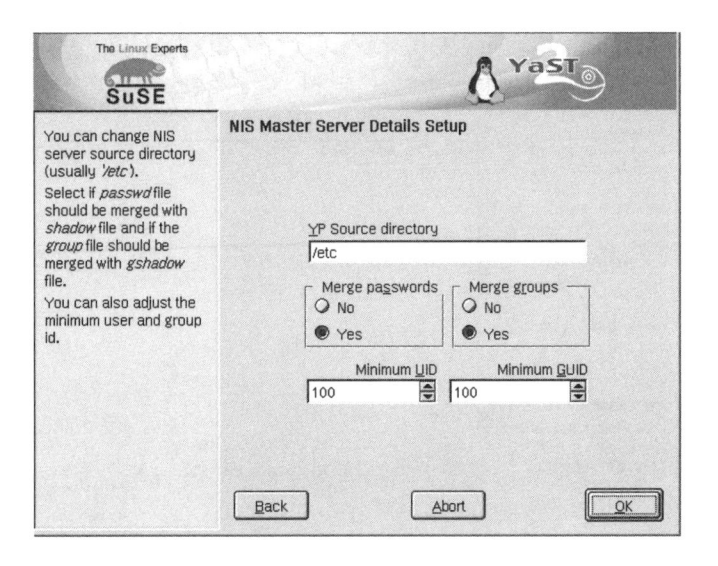

Figure 14.5: YaST2: NIS server: Changing the Directory and Synchronizing Files

The first one enables connections to your own host. The second one allows all hosts with access to your network to send requests to the server.

Manual Installation of an NIS Client

SuSE Linux contains all the packages needed to install a NIS client. Proceed as follows:

- Set the NIS domain in the file `/etc/defaultdomain`. The NIS domain name should not be confused with the DNS domain name. They have nothing to do with one another.

- The NIS server is set via `/etc/yp.conf`:

  `ypserver 192.168.0.1`

- NIS uses RPC (Remote Procedure Calls). Therefore, the RPC portmapper needs to be running. This server is started by `/etc/init.d/portmap`.

- Complete the entries in `/etc/passwd` and `/etc/group`. For a request to be sent to the NIS server, after the local files have been searched, a line beginning with a '+' has to be added to the relevant files.

SuSE Linux – Administration Guide   373

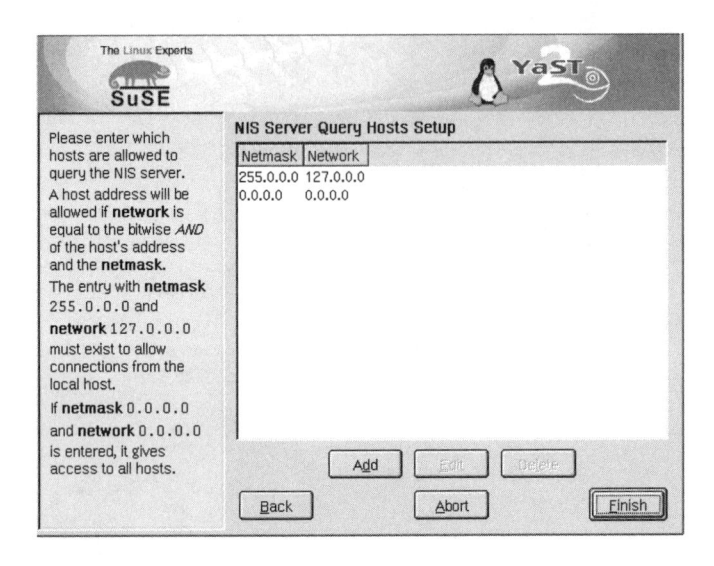

Figure 14.6: YaST2: NIS Server: Setting Request Permissions

- NIS allows you to set a multitude of other options in the file /etc/sysconfig/ypbind.

- The final step in activating the NIS server is to launch ypbind. This is what actually starts the NIS client.

- To activate your changes, either restart your system or enter:

    earth: # **rcnetwork restart**
    earth: # **rcypbind restart**

14

NFS — Shared File Systems

As mentioned in *NIS — Network Information Service* on page 371, NFS (together with NIS) makes a network transparent to the user. With NFS, it is possible to distribute file systems over the network. It does not matter at which terminal a user is logged in. He will always find himself in the same environment.

As with NIS, NFS is an asymmetric service. There are NFS servers and NFS clients. A machine can be both — it can supply file systems over the network (export) and mount file systems from other hosts (import). Generally, these are servers with a very large hard disk capacity, whose file systems are mounted by other clients.

Importing File Systems with YaST2

Any user who is authorized to do so can mount NFS directories from an NFS server into his own file tree. This can be achieved most easily using the YaST2 module 'NFS client'. Just enter the host name of the NFS server, the directory to import, and the mount point at which to mount this directory locally. All this is done after clicking 'Add' in the first dialog.

Importing File Systems Manually

To import file systems from an NFS server, the only requirement is that the RPC portmapper is already running. Starting this server has already been covered in connection with NIS (see *Manual Installation of an NIS Client* on page 373). If this is the case, other file systems can be mounted (as long as they are exported by the server) just as easily as local file systems using the program `mount` with the following syntax:

mount -t nfs ⟨host⟩:⟨remote path⟩ ⟨local path⟩

If user directories from the machine `sun`, for example, should be imported, the following command can be used:

earth:/ # **mount -t nfs sun:/home /home**

Exporting File Systems with YaST2

YaST2 enables you to quickly turn any host on your network into an NFS server. Select 'Network/Advanced' in YaST2 then 'NFS Server'.

Next, activate 'Start NFS Server' and click 'Next'. In the upper text field, enter the directories to export. Below, enter the hosts that should have access to them. This dialog is shown in Figure 14.7. There are four options that can be set for each host: ⟨single host⟩, ⟨netgroups⟩, ⟨wildcards⟩, and ⟨IP networks⟩. A more thorough explanation of these options is provided by the man page for `exports` (`man exports`).

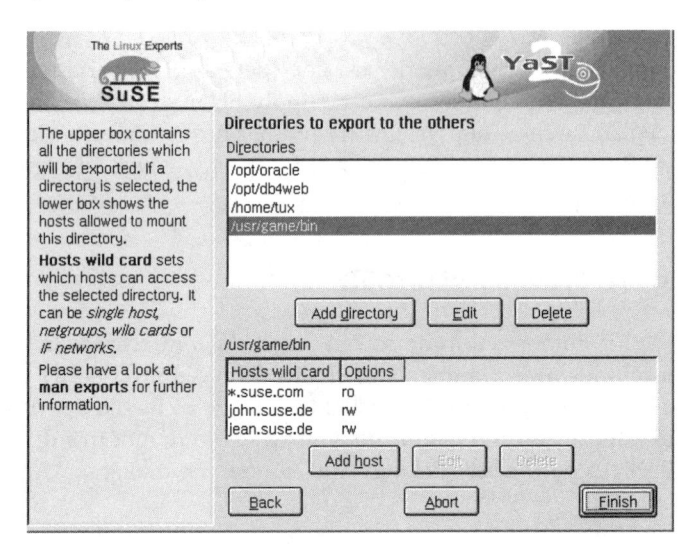

Figure 14.7: YaST2: NFS Server: Enter Export Directories and Hosts

'Exit' completes the configuration.

Exporting File Systems Manually

A machine that exports file systems is called an NFS server. On an NFS server, there are a few tools that need to be started:

- RPC portmapper (*rpc.portmap*)
- RPC mount daemon (*rpc.mountd*)
- RPC NFS daemon (*rpc.nfsd*)

These are started by the scripts /etc/init.d/portmap and /etc/init.d/nfsserver at boot. Starting the RPC portmapper was described in Section *Manual Installation of an NIS Client* on page 373. After these daemons have been started, the configuration file /etc/exports decides which directories should be exported to which machines.

For each directory to export, one line is needed to specify which machines may access that directory with what permissions. All subdirectories of this directory will automatically be exported as well. All authorized machines are usually denoted with their full names (including domain name), but it is possible to use wildcards like '*' or '?'. If no machine is specified here, any machine is allowed to import this file system with the given permissions.

Permissions of the file system to export are denoted in brackets after the machine name. The most important options are:

ro	file system is exported with read-only permission (default).
rw	file system is exported with read-write permission.
root_squash	This makes sure that the user root of the given machine does not have root specific permissions on this file system. This is achieved by assigning user ID 65534 to users with user ID 0 (root). This user ID should be set to nobody
no_root_squash	Does not assign user ID 0 to user ID 65534 (default).
link_relative	Converts absolute links (those beginning with '/') to a sequence of '../'. This is only useful if the whole file system of a machine is mounted (default).
link_absolute	Symbolic links remain untouched.
map_identity	User IDs are exactly the same on both client and server (default).
map-daemon	Client and server do not have matching user IDs. This tells nfsd to create a conversion table for user IDs. **ugidd** is required for this to work.

Table 14.12: Permissions for Exported File Systems

Your exports file might look like File 57.

```
#
# /etc/exports
#
/home              sun(rw)     venus(rw)
/usr/X11           sun(ro)     venus(ro)
/usr/lib/texmf     sun(ro)     venus(rw)
/                  earth(ro,root_squash)
/home/ftp          (ro)
# End of exports
```

File 57: `/etc/exports`

File /etc/exports is read by mountd. If you change anything in this file, restart mountd and nfsd for your changes to take effect. This can easily be done with rcnfsserver restart.

14

DHCP

The DHCP Protocol

The purpose of the "Dynamic Host Configuration Protocol" is to assign network settings centrally from a server rather than configuring them locally on each and every workstation. A client configured to use DHCP does not have control over its own static address. It is enabled to fully autoconfigure itself according to directions from the server.

One way to use DHCP is to identify each client using the hardware address of its network card (which is fixed in most cases) then supply that client with identical settings each time it connects to the server. DHCP can also be configured so the server assigns addresses to each "interested" host *dynamically* from an address pool set up for that purpose. In the latter case, the DHCP server will try to assign the same address to the client each time it receives a request from it (even over longer periods). This, of course, will not work if there are more client hosts in the network than network addresses available.

With these possibilities, DHCP can make life easier for system administrators in two ways. Any changes (even bigger ones) related to addresses and the network configuration in general can be implemented centrally by editing the server's configuration file. This is much more convenient than reconfiguring lots of client machines. Also it is much easier to integrate machines, particularly new machines, into the network, as they can be given an IP address from the pool. Retrieving the appropriate network settings from a DHCP server can be especially useful in the case of laptops regularly used in different networks.

A DHCP server not only supplies the IP address and the netmask, but also the host name, domain name, gateway, and name server addresses to be used by the client. In addition to that, DHCP allows for a number of other parameters to be configured in a centralized way, for example, a time server from which clients may poll the current time or even a print server.

The following section, gives an overview of DHCP without describing the service in every detail. In particular, we want to show how to use the DHCP server dhcpd in your own network to easily manage its entire setup from one central point.

DHCP Software Packages

SuSE Linux comes with three packages related to DHCP. The first of these is the DHCP server dhcpd distributed by the Internet Software Consortium, or

SuSE Linux – Administration Guide   379

ISC. This is the program that assigns and manages the corresponding information for the network. Normally with SuSE Linux, there is only this one program available as far as the server is concerned, but you can choose between two different DHCP client programs. SuSE Linux includes both the package `dhclient`, also from the ISC, and the "DHCP client daemon" provided by the package `dhcpcd`.

SuSE Linux installs `dhcpcd` by default. The program is very easy to handle and will be launched automatically on each system boot to watch for a DHCP server. It does not need a configuration file to do its job and should work out of the box in most standard setups.

If you administer a more complex network, you might need the ISC's dhclient, which can be controlled via the configuration file `/etc/dhclient.conf`. No matter whether you want to include an additional domain in the search list or even to emulate the behavior of a Microsoft DHCP client — if you are knowledgeable about networks, you will find that the dhclient gives all the possibilities to make it function according to your needs, down to the last detail.

The DHCP Server dhcpd

The core of any DHCP system is the *dynamic host configuration protocol daemon*. This server "leases" addresses and watches how they are used, according to the settings as defined in the configuration file `/etc/dhcpd.conf`. By changing the parameters and values in this file, a system administrator can influence the program's behavior in numerous ways.

Look at a basic sample `/etc/dhcpd.conf` file:

```
default-lease-time 600;         # 10 minutes
max-lease-time 7200;            # 2  hours

option domain-name "kosmos.all";
option domain-name-servers 192.168.1.1, 192.168.1.2;
option broadcast-address 192.168.1.255;
option routers 192.168.1.254;
option subnet-mask 255.255.255.0;

subnet 192.168.1.0 netmask 255.255.255.0
  {
    range 192.168.1.10 192.168.1.20;
    range 192.168.1.100 192.168.1.200;
  }
```

File 58: The Configuration File `/etc/dhcpd.conf`

This simple configuration file should be sufficient to get the DHCP server to assign IP addresses to the hosts of your network. One thing to remember, however, is to include a semicolon (;) at the end of each line. Without that character, dhcpd will not even start.

As you might have noticed, the above sample file can be subdivided into three different sections. The first one defines how many seconds an IP address is "leased" to a requesting host by default (`default-lease-time`) before it should apply for renewal. The section also includes a statement on the maximum period for which a machine may keep an IP address assigned by the DHCP server without applying for renewal (`max-lease-time`).

In the second part, some basic network parameters are defined on a global level:

- The line `option domain-name` defines the default domain of your network.

- With the entry `option domain-name-servers`, specify up to three values for the DNS servers used to resolve IP addresses into host names (and vice versa). Ideally, configure a name server on your machine or somewhere else in your network before setting up DHCP. That name server should also define a host name for each dynamic address and vice versa. To learn how to configure your own name server, read Section *DNS — Domain Name Service* on page 361.

- The line `option broadcast-address` defines the broadcast address to be used by the requesting host.

- With `option routers`, tell the server where to send data packets that cannot be delivered to a host on the local network (according to the source and target host address and the subnet mask provided). In most cases, especially in smaller networks, this router will be identical with the Internet gateway.

- With `option subnet-mask`, specify the netmask assigned to clients.

The last section of the file is there to define a network, including a subnet mask. To finish, specify the address range that the DHCP daemon should use to assign IP addresses to interested clients. In our example, clients may be given any address between `192.168.1.10` and `192.168.1.20`, as well as `192.168.1.100` and `192.168.1.200`.

After editing these few lines, you should be able to activate the DHCP daemon by issuing the command `rcdhcpd start`. The server is ready for use immediately after that. Do a basic check to see whether the configuration file is syntactically correct by entering the command rcdhcpd syntax-check. If you encounter any unexpected problems with your configuration — the server aborts with an error or does not return "done" on start — you should be able to find out what has gone wrong by looking for information either in the main system log /var/log/messages or on console 10 (Ctrl + Alt + F10).

Assigning Fixed IP Addresses to Hosts

Now that the server is set up to assign dynamic addresses, it is time to have a closer look at *static* addresses and the way to configure them. As mentioned above, with DHCP it is also possible to assign a predefined, fixed address to one host each time the latter sends a request to the server.

As might be expected, addresses assigned explicitly will always take priority over addresses from the pool of dynamic addresses. Furthermore, a static address will never expire in the way a dynamic address would, such as if there were not enough addresses available so the server needed to redistribute them among hosts.

To identify a host configured to get a *static* address, the DHCP daemon fetches the hardware address of that host. This is a numerical code consisting of six octet pairs, fixed in most cases, and unique to each network device sold in the world, e.g., 00:00:45:12:EE:F4.

If the appropriate lines, like the ones in 59, are added to the configuration file 58 on page 380, the DHCP daemon will assign the same set of data to the corresponding host under all circumstances.

```
host earth {
  hardware ethernet 00:00:45:12:EE:F4;
  fixed-address 192.168.1.21;
}
```

File 59: Entry Added to the Configuration File

The structure of this entry should be almost self-explanatory: The first line sets the DNS name of the newly defined host (host *host name*) and the second one its MAC address. On any network-enabled Linux host, this address can be determined very easily with the command ifstatus plus the network device, for example, eth0. If the network card is not enabled, use the command `ifup eth0` first. The output should contain something like *link/ether 00:00:45:12:EE:F4*.

In the above example, a host with a network card having the MAC address *00:00:45:12:EE:F4* is assigned the IP address `192.168.1.21` and the host name `earth` automatically.

The type of hardware to enter is `ethernet` in nearly all cases, though `token-ring`, which is often found on IBM systems, is also supported.

The Finer Points

As stated at the beginning of this chapter, these pages are only intended to provide a brief survey of what you can do with DHCP. For more information, the page of the *Internet Software Consortium* on the subject (`http://www.isc.org/products/DHCP/`) will prove a good source to read about the details of DHCP, including about version 3 of the protocol, currently in beta testing. Apart from that, you can always rely on the man pages for further help. Try `man dhcpd`, `man dhcpd.conf`, `man dhcpd.leases`, and `man dhcp-options`. Also, several books about *Dynamic Host Configuration Protocol* have been published over the years that take an in-depth look at the topic.

With `dhcpd`, it is even possible to offer a file to a requesting host, as defined with the parameter *filename*, and that this file may contain a bootable Linux kernel. This allows you to build client hosts which do not need a hard disk — they are enabled to load both their operating system and their network data over the network (*diskless clients*), which could be an interesting option for both cost and security reasons. Now add the package `alice` to all this and you can do some really amazing things.

Heterogenous Networks

In addition to connecting to other Linux systems, Linux is also able to connect to Windows and Macintosh computers and communicate over Novell networks. This chapter shows the requirements for and configuration of heterogenous networks.

Samba	386
Netatalk	394
Netware Emulation with MARSNWE	401

Samba

With the program package Samba, convert any UNIX machine into a powerful file and print server for DOS, Windows, and OS/2 machines. The *Samba Project* is run by the *Samba Team* and was originally developed by the Australian Andrew Tridgell.

Samba has now become a fully-fledged and rather complex product. This section presents an overview of its basic functionality. Samba offers plenty of online documentation. Enter `apropos samba` at the command line to display some manual pages or just browse the `/usr/share/doc/packages/samba` directory if Samba is installed. There, find some more online documentation and examples. A commented example configuration (`smb.conf.SuSE`) can be found in the `examples` subdirectory.

Samba uses the SMB protocol (Server Message Block) from the company Microsoft, based on the NetBIOS services. Due to pressure from IBM, Microsoft released the protocol so other software manufacturers could establish connections to a Microsoft domain network. Samba sets the SMB protocol on top of the TCP/IP protocol, so the TCP/IP protocol must also be installed on all clients.

NetBIOS

NetBIOS is a software interface (API) designed for communication between machines. Here, a name service is provided. It enables machines connected to the net to reserve names for themselves. After reservation, these machines can be addressed by name. There is no central process that checks names. Any machine on the network can reserve as many names as it wants, provided the name is not already in use. The NetBIOS interface can now be implemented for different network architectures. An implementation that works relatively closely with network hardware is called NetBEUI, but this is often referred to as NetBIOS. Network protocols implemented with NetBIOS are IPX from Novell (NetBIOS via TCP/IP) and TCP/IP.

The NetBIOS names sent via TCP/IP have nothing in common with the names used in `/etc/hosts` or those defined by DNS. NetBIOS uses its own, completely independent naming convention. However, it is recommended to use names that correspond to DNS host names to make administration easier. This is the default used by Samba.

Clients

All standard operating systems, such as DOS, Windows, and OS/2, support the SMB protocol. The TCP/IP protocol must be installed on all computers.

Samba can also be used with all the various UNIX "flavors".

SMB servers provide hardware space to their clients by means of shares. Here, a share includes a directory and its subdirectories. It is exported by means of a name and can be accessed by its name. The share name can be set to any name — it does not have to be the name of the export directory. A printer is also assigned a name. Clients can access the printer by its name.

Installing and Configuring the Server

First, install the package `samba`. The SMB services are started when the computer is booted. The services can be started manually with `rcsmb start`. With `rcsmb stop`, the services can be stopped.

The main configuration file of Samba is `/etc/samba/smb.conf`. Here, the entire service is configured. Basically, `smb.conf` is divided into two separate sections. In the `[global]` section, the central and general settings are made. The second section is the `[share]` section. Here, define the file and printer shares. If a specific value from the `[share]` section should be made valid for all shares, this can be taken over into the `[global]` section, making it valid for all shares system-wide and securing clarity of the configuration file. Since this central configuration file is accessed often, it is recommended to keep it as short and free of comments as possible. The shorter this file, the faster the server can respond.

The following sections provide an overview of some selected parameters.

The (global) Section

The following parameters of the `[global]` section need some adjustment to match the requirements of your network setup to let other machines access your Samba server via SMB in a Windows environment.

workgroup = TUX-NET This line assigns the Samba server to a work group. Replace `TUX-NET` with an appropriate work group of your networking environment. Your Samba server will appear under its DNS name unless this name has been assigned to any other machine in the net.

If the DNS name is not available, set the server name using `netbiosname=MYNAME`. See `man smb.conf` for more details about this parameter.

os level = 2 This parameter triggers whether your Samba server tries to become LMB "Local Master Browser" for its work group. Choose a very low value to spare the existing Windows net from any disturbances caused by a misconfigured Samba server. More information about this important topic can be found in the files BROWSING.txt and BROWSING-Config.txt under the textdocs subdirectory of the package documentation.

As long as there is no other SMB server present in your network, such as a Windows NT or 2000 server, and the Samba server should keep a list of all systems present in the local environment, set the os level to a higher value (for example, 65). Your Samba server will thus be chosen as LMB for your local network.

When changing this setting, consider carefully how this could affect an existing Windows network environment. A misconfigured Samba server can cause severe trouble when trying to become LMB for its work group. Contact your administrator and subject your configuration to some heavy testing either in an isolated network or at a noncritical time of day.

wins support and wins server If your Samba server should integrate into an existing Windows network with a running WINS server, remove the leading semicolon in front of the wins server parameter and adjust the IP address to the requirements of your network. If your Windows machines run in separate subnets, they should "see" each other, your Windows network does not have a WINS server running, and your Samba server should become the WINS server, uncomment the line holding the wins support = yes parameter. Make sure you activate this setting solely on a Samba server. Keep wins server inactive in this configuration.

Shares

The following examples illustrate how a CD-ROM drive and the user directories (home directories) are made available to the SMB clients.

CD-ROM

```
;[cdrom]
;          comment = Linux CD-ROM
;          path = /media/cdrom
;          locking = no
```

File 60: A CD-ROM Share

To avoid having the CD-ROM drive accidentally made available, these lines are commented by default.

- [cdrom] and comment [cdrom] is the name of the share that can be seen by all SMB clients on the net. An additional comment can be added to further describe the share.

- path=/media/cdrom exports the directory /media/cdrom.

By means of a very restrictive default configuration, this kind of share is only made available to the users present on this system. If this share should be made available to everybody, add a line guestok=yes to the configuration. This setting gives read permissions to anyone on the network. It is recommended to handle this parameter with great care. This applies even more to the use of this parameter in the [global] section.

[homes]

The [home] share is of special importance here. If the user has a valid account and password for the Linux file server and his own home directory, he can be connected to it.

```
[homes]
    comment = Home Directories
    valid users = %S
    browseable = no
    writeable = yes
    create mask = 0640
    directory mask = 0750
```

File 61: The [homes] *Share*

- [homes] As long as there is no other share using the share name of the user connecting to the SMB server, a share is dynamically generated using the [homes] share directives. The resulting name of the share is identical to the user name.

- valid users=%S %S is replaced by the concrete name of the share as soon as a connection has been successfully established. For a [homes] share, this is always identical to the user's name. As a consequence, access rights to a user's share are restricted exlusively to the user.

- browseable = no This setting enables the share to be invisible in the network environment.

- `writeable = yes` By default, Samba prohibits write access to any exported share by means of the `read only = yes` parameter. If a share should be made available as writeable, you must explicitly state this using the `writeable = yes` parameter. This is normally desired for user directories.

- `create mask = 0640` Windows machines do not understand the concept of UNIX permissions, so cannot assign permissions when creating a file. The parameter `create mask` assigns what permissions to use when a new file is created. This only applies to shares with write permissions. In detail, this setting means that the owner of this file holds both read and write permissions. The members of his group have read access to this file. `valid users = %S` prevents read access by the other members of the group.

Security Levels

The SMB protocol comes from the DOS and Windows world and directly takes into consideration the problem of security. Each share access can be protected with a password. SMB has three possible ways of achieving this:

- **Share Level Security:** A password is firmly allocated to a share. Everyone who knows this password has access to that share.

- **User Level Security:** This variation introduces the concept of the user in the SMB. Each user must register with the server with his own password. After registering, the server can grant access to individual exported shares independently of user names.

- **Server Level Security:** To its clients, Samba pretends to be working in User Level Mode. However, it passes on all password queries to another User Level Mode Server, which takes care of authentication. This setting expects an additional parameter (`password server =`).

The differentiation between share, user, and server level security must be made for the entire server. It is not possible to export some shares by Share Level Security and others by User Level Security. More information on this subject can be found in the file `/usr/share/doc/packages/samba/textdocs/security_level.txt`.

> **Tip**
>
> For simple administration tasks with the Samba server, there is also the program swat. It provides a simple web interface with which to conveniently configure the Samba server. In a web browser, open http://localhost:901 and log in as user root. swat is also activated in the files /etc/inetd.conf and /etc/services. More information about swat can be found in its man page.
>
> **Tip**

Samba as Login Server

In networks where predominantly Windows clients are found, it is often preferable that users may only register with a valid account and password. This can be brought about with the help of a Samba server. In a pure Windows network, a Windows NT server takes on this task. This is configured as a Primary Domain Controller (PDC). The following entries must be made in the [global] section of the smb.conf.

```
[global]
  workgroup = TUX-NET
  domain logons = yes
  domain master = yes
```

File 62: [Global] Section in smb.conf

If encrypted passwords are used for verification purposes, the Samba server must be able to handle these. The entry `encrypt passwords = yes` in the [global] section enable this functionality. In addition, it is necessary to prepare user accounts and passwords in an encryption format that conforms with Windows. This is done with the command `smbpasswd -a name`. Since, in accordance with the Windows NT domain concept, the computers themselves need a domain account, this is created with the following commands:

```
useradd -m machinename
smbpasswd -a -m machinename
```

File 63: Adding a Machine Account

With the `useradd` command, a dollar sign, masked by a backslash, is added. The command `smbpasswd` includes this automatically when the -m parameter is used. See the commented sample configuration for the settings needed to automate this task.

```
add user script = /usr/sbin/useradd -g machines \
                  -c "NT Machine Account" -d
/dev/null -s /bin/false %m$
```

File 64: Automated Adding of a Machine Account

Installing Clients

First, it should be mentioned that clients can only access the Samba server via TCP/IP. NetBEUI and NetBIOS via IPX are not available at the moment. Since TCP/IP is becoming more and more popular, even with Novell and Microsoft, it is not certain whether this is going to change in the near future.

Windows 9x/ME

Windows 9x/ME already has built-in support for TCP/IP. However, this is not installed as the default. To add TCP/IP, go to 'Control Panel' → 'System' and choose 'Add' → 'Protocols' → 'TCP/IP from Microsoft'. Be sure to enter your network address and network mask correctly. After rebooting your Windows machine, find the properly configured Samba server in networks (double-click the network icon on your desktop).

> **Tip**
>
> To use a printer on the Samba server, install the standard or Apple-PostScript printer driver from the corresponding Windows version. It is best to link this to the Linux printer queue, which includes an automatic apsfilter recognition.

Optimization

`socket options` is one possible optimization provided with the sample configuration that ships with your Samba version. Its default configuration refers to a local Ethernet network. To get further information about `socket options`, refer to the man page for `smb.conf` (`man smb.conf`), section "socket options" and to the man page for `socket` (`man 7 socket`). Additional optimization tips regarding speed can be found under `/usr/share/doc/packages/samba/textdocs/Speed.txt` and `/usr/share/doc/packages/samba/textdocs/Speed2.txt`.

The standard configuration under `/etc/samba/smb.conf` is designed to provide sensible settings for most purposes. The settings here differ from all default settings made by the Samba team. Providing reasonable settings is very difficult or rather impossible with regards to the network configuration or the name of the work group. Check the commented sample configuration under `examples/smb.conf.SuSE` for further directions about the adjustment of the configuration to local requirements.

> **Tip**
>
> The Samba team offers `textdocs/DIAGNOSIS.txt`, which is a step-by-step guide to check your configuration.
>
> **Tip**

Netatalk

With the package `netatalk`, obtain a high-performance file and print server for MacOS clients. With it, access data on a Linux machine from a Macintosh or print to a connected printer.

Netatalk is a suite of Unix programs that run on kernel-based DDP (Datagram Delivery Protocol) and implement the AppleTalk protocol family (ADSP, ATP, ASP, RTMP, NBP, ZIP, AEP, and PAP). AppleTalk is, in effect, an equivalent to the more familiar protocol known as TCP (Transmission Control Protocol). It has counterparts to many services available on TCP/IP, including services for resolving host names and time synchronization. For example, the command `nbplkup` (NBP, Name Binding Protocol) is used instead of `nslookup` (DNS, Domain Name Service) and `aecho` (AEP, AppleTalk Echo Protocol) instead of `ping` (ICMP ECHO_REQUEST, Internet Control Message Protocol).

The three daemons described below are normally started on the server:

- atalkd ("AppleTalk Network Manager") that somewhat correlates with the programs ifconfig and routed
- afpd (AppleTalk Filing Protocol daemon), which provides an interface for Macintosh clients to Unix file systems
- papd (Printer Access Protocol daemon), which makes printers available in the (AppleTalk) network.

Of course, you can export server directories not only via Netatalk, but also, at the same time, via Samba for Windows clients (see Section *Clients* on page 386) and via NFS (see *NFS — Shared File Systems* on page 375), which is very useful in heterogeneous network environments. This centralizes the management of data backup and user permissions on the Linux server.

Note:

- Due to Macintosh client restrictions, the user passwords on the server cannot be longer than eight characters.
- Macintosh clients cannot access Unix files with names longer than 31 characters.
- File names may not contain colons (':') because they serve as path name separators in MacOS.

The package `netatalk` has to be installed.

Configuring the File Server

In the default configuration, Netatalk is already fully functional as a file server for home directories of the Linux system. To use the extended features, define some settings in the configuration files. These are located in the `/etc/atalk` directory.

All configuration files are pure text files. Text that follows a hash mark '#' (comments) and empty lines can be disregarded.

Configuring the Network — `atalkd.conf`

Define, in `/etc/atalk/atalkd.conf`, over which interfaces services are provided. This is usually `eth0`, which means that it suffices if the only value entered here is `eth0`. In the example file that comes with Netatalk, this is the case. Enter additional interfaces to use several network cards at the same time. When the server is started, it will search the network for already existing zones and servers and modify the corresponding lines by entering the set AppleTalk network addresses. You will then find a line such as

```
eth0 -phase 2 -net 0-65534 -addr 65280.57
```

at the end of the file. To make more complex configurations, find examples for this in the configuration file. Find documentation on additional options in the manual page of afpd.

Defining File Servers — `afpd.conf`

The `afpd.conf` file contains definitions for how your file server appears on MacOS machines as an item under the 'Chooser' dialog. As is the case with the other configuration files, these also contain detailed comments explaining the wide variety of options.

If you do not change anything here, the default server will simply be started and displayed with the host name in the 'Chooser'. Therefore, you do not necessarily have to enter anything. However, you can give additional file servers a variety of names and options here. For instance, to provide a specific "guest server" where everybody can save files as "guest",

```
"Guest server" -uamlist uams_guest.so
```

Define a server that denies guests access, but which is only accessible for users who already exist in the Linux system with:

```
"Font server" -uamlist uams_clrtxt.so,uams_dhx.so
```

This behavior is controlled by the option `uamlist`, followed by a list of authentication modules to use, separated by commas. If you do not provide this option, all procedures are active by default.

An AppleShare server not only provides its services by default via AppleTalk, but also ("encapsulated") via TCP/IP. The default port is 548. Assign dedicated ports to additional AppleShare servers (on the same machine) if these are to likewise run via TCP. The availability of the service via TCP/IP enables access to the server even over non-AppleTalk networks, such as the Internet.

In this case, the syntax would read:

```
"Font server" -uamlist uams_clrtxt.so,uams_dhx.so -port 12000
```

The AppleShare server, set to the port 12000, then appears in the network with the name "Font server" and will not allow guest access. In this way, it is also accessible via TCP/IP routers.

The file `AppleVolumes.default` (described in detail below) defines which directories located on the server are made available by each AppleShare server as network "volumes". Define other files containing unique descriptions for each AppleShare server using the option `-defaultvol`, such as with (in one line):

```
"Guest server" -uamlist uams_guest.so -defaultvol
/etc/atalk/AppleVolumes.guest
```

Further options are explained in the `afpd.conf` file itself.

Directories and Access Permissions — `AppleVolumes.default`

Here, define directories to export. The access permissions are defined via the customary Unix user and group permissions. This is configured in the `AppleVolumes.default` file.

> **Note**
>
> Here, the syntax has partially changed. Take this into consideration if you are updating this version from a previous one. For example, it is now `allow:` instead of `access=` (a typical symptom would be if, instead of the drive descriptions, you were to see a display of the drive options on the Mac clients in the 'Chooser'.) Since the new files are created with the `.rpmnew` endings during an update, it is possible that your previous settings may no longer function as a result of the modified syntax. We recommend creating backups of your configuration files, copying your old configurations from them into your new files, then renaming these files to the proper names. This way, you will benefit from the current comments contained in the configuration files, which provide a detailed explanation of the diverse options.
>
> **Note**

Along with `AppleVolumes.default`, additional files can be created, such as `AppleVolumes.guest`, used by some servers (by giving the option `-defaultvol` in the `afpd.conf` file — see previous section).

The syntax

```
/usr/local/psfonts "PostScript Fonts"
```

indicates that the Linux directory `/usr/local/psfonts` located in the root directory is available as an AppleShare volume with the name "PostScript Fonts".

Options are separated by a space and attached to the end of a line. A very useful option is the access restriction:

```
/usr/local/psfonts "PostScript Fonts" allow:User1,@group0
```

which restricts access to the volume "PostScript Fonts" to the user "User1" and all members of the group "group0". The users and groups entered here have to be known, of course, to the Linux system. Likewise, explicitly deny users access with `deny:User2`.

These restrictions only apply to access via AppleTalk and not to the normal access rights users have if they can log in to the server itself.

Netatalk maps the customary Resource Fork of MacOS files to `.AppleDouble` directories in the Linux file system. Using the `noadouble` option, set these directories to be created only when they are actually needed. Syntax:

```
/usr/local/guests "Guests" options:noadouble
```

Additional options and features can be found in the explanations included in the file itself.

The tilde ('~') in this configuration file stands for the home directory for each and every user on the server. This way, every user can easily access his home directory without each one having to be explicitly defined here. The example file installed already includes a tilde, which is why Netatalk makes the home directory available by default as long as you do not modify anything in this file.

afpd also searches for a file Applevolumes or .Applevolumes in the home directory of a user logged on to the system. Entries in this file supplement the entries in the server files AppleVolumes.system and AppleVolumes.default to enable individual type and creator file specifications and to access specific directories. These entries are extensions and do not allow access for the user for whom access permission is denied from the server side.

The netatalk.pamd file is used, via PAM (pluggable authentication modules), for authentication purposes. Using PAM is, however, irrelevant in this context.

File Specifications — AppleVolumes.system

In the AppleVolumes.System file, define which customary MacOS type and creator specifications are assigned to certain file endings. An entire series of default values are already predefined. If a file is displayed by a generic white icon, there is not yet an entry for it in this file. If you encounter a problem with a text file belonging to another system, which cannot be opened properly in MacOS or vice versa, check the entries there.

Configuring the Print Server

A laserwriter service is made available by configuring the papd.conf file. The printer must be already functioning locally via lpd, so configure a printer as described in the Reference Manual. If you can print a text file locally using the command lpr file.txt, the first step has been successfully completed.

You do not necessarily need to enter anything in papd.conf if a local printer is configured in Linux, because print jobs can simply be forwarded to the print daemon lpd without additional specifications. The printer registers itself in the AppleTalk network as Laserwriter. You can, however, extend your printer entries by referring to File 65.

```
Printer_Reception:pr=lp:pd=/etc/atalk/kyocera.ppd
```

File 65: `papd.conf`

This causes the printer named Printer_Reception to appear as a 'Chooser' item. The corresponding printer description file is usually provided by the vendor. Otherwise, refer to the file `Laserwriter` located in the 'System Extensions' folder. However, using this file, often you cannot use all of the printer's features.

Starting the Server

The server can be started at system boot time via its "init script" or manually with `rcatalk start`. The init script is located at `/etc/init.d/atalk`.

The actual starting of the server takes place in the background. It takes about a minute until the AppleTalk interfaces are set up and responsive. Check for the status as shown in the following (all servers are running if OK is reported three times):

```
earth:~ # rcatalk status
Checking for service atalk:OKOKOK
```

Now it is time to go to a Mac running MacOS. Check for AppleTalk activation, choose 'Filesharing', double-click 'AppleShare'. The names of the servers should then appear in the window. Double-click a server and log in. Choose the volume and there is your shared net volume, accessible from within MacOS.

The procedure is a bit different for AppleShare servers configured to use TCP only (and no DDP). To connect, press the 'Server IP address' button and enter the respective IP address. If necessary, append the port number, separated by a colon (':').

Additional Information

To take full advantage of all the options netatalk offers, read the corresponding manual pages. Find them by entering the command

```
earth:~ # rpm -qd netatalk
```

The `/etc/atalk/netatalk.conf` file is not used in our netatalk version, so disregard it.

Helpful URLs:

- `http://netatalk.sourceforge.net/`
- `http://www.umich.edu/~rsug/netatalk/`
- `http://thehamptons.com/anders/netatalk/`
- `http://cgi.zettabyte.net/fom-serve/netatalk/cache/1.html`

We do not currently recommend trying to access an AppleShare file system hosted on a Macintosh from a Linux machine. Software is available, but it is in early development stages. For more information, refer to

- `http://www.panix.com/~dfoster/afpfs/`

Netware Emulation with MARSNWE

The Netware emulator MARSNWE can easily replace the file and print services of a Novell Netware 2.2 or 3.11 server. It can also be used in this manner as an IPX router. However, it does not offer the features of newer Netware versions, such as NDS (Netware Directory Services). Workstations running DOS or Windows already configured to access a Netware 2.2, 3.11, or 3.12 server can use the Linux server with the Netware emulator MARSNWE as a server without having to change the configuration much. Administration is best taken care of in Linux, because Novell system administration applications can only be utilized under certain conditions and have licensing issues as well.

Starting the Netware Emulator MARSNWE

MARSNWE in SuSE Linux can be started immediately after installation, because it is already preconfigured for initial testing. The required IPX support on the part of the kernel is available as a loadable kernel module and is automatically loaded by the start script. The IPX interface is automatically set up by MARSNWE. At this point, the network number and the protocol to use will both be read from the extensively commented configuration file /etc/nwserv.conf. MARSNWE is started via the command rcnwe start. The done message to the right of the screen in green indicates that MARSNWE has been successfully started. Use rcnwe status to check whether the Netware emulator is running. Halt it with rcnwe stop.

The Configuration File /etc/nwserv.conf

The configuration options are summarized in enumerated sections. Every configuration line starts with the number of the corresponding section. Only sections 1 to 22 are relevant here. Not all numbers are used, however. Most of the time, the following sections are enough for the configuration:

1 Netware Volumes

2 Server Name

4 IPX Network

13 User Names

21 Printers

After modifying the configuration, MARSNWE must be restarted with the command `rcnwe restart`.

The configuration options in detail:

Volumes (Section 1):

```
1    SYS    /usr/local/nwe/SYS/    kt    711 600
```

Here, the volumes to export are defined. Every line begins with the section number (here 1), followed by the volume name and the server directory path. In addition, various options can be specified represented by specific letters and a UMASK for the generation of both directories and files. If a UMASK is not specified, the default value from Section 9 is used. The volume for SYS is already entered. To avoid problems with uppercase and lowercase letters in the file names, it is recommended to use the k option, so all the file names will be converted to lowercase letters.

Server Name (Section 2):

```
2    MARS
```

This specification is optional. The host name will be used by default.

Internal Network Number (Section 3):

```
3    auto
```

The internal network number is generated from the network card's MAC address if auto is specified here. This setting is usually retained.

IPX Configuration (Section 4):

```
4    0x0     *       AUTO           1
4    0x22    eth0    ethernet_ii    1
```

Here, the Netware network number is specified as well as to which network interface using which protocol the bind should be made. The first example sets up everything automatically, while the second binds the network number 0x22 to the network card eth0 with the frame type Ethernet-II. If you have several network cards and enter all these with different network numbers, IPX will be routed between them.

Create Mode (Section 9):

    9   0751   0640

Enters the default permission with which directories and files are created.

GID and GID with minimal permissions (Section 10, 11):

    10   65534
    11   65534

Group ID and user ID for users not logged in. Here nogroup and nobody.

Supervisor Login (Section 12):

    12   SUPERVISOR   root

The supervisor is mapped to user `root`.

User Logins (Section 13):

    13   LINUX   linux

Netware users are assigned to Linux users. A static password can optionally be entered here.

Automatic User Mapping (Section 15):

    15   0   top-secret

If 1 is specified here instead of 0, Linux logins will automatically be made available as Netware logins. In this case, the password is "top-secret".

Printer Queues (Section 21):

    21   LP   -   lpr -

The first parameter LP is the name of the Netware printer. Second, the name of the spool directory can be given. The print command is listed last.

Print Server (Section 22):

```
22    PS_NWE    LP_PS    1
```

Printers can be defined here that are accessed over the pserver by the package `ncpfs`.

Access to Netware Servers and Their Administration

The package `ncpfs` is a collection of small programs that can be used to administer a Netware 2.2 or 3.11 server from Linux, mount Netware volumes, or manage printers. To access Netware servers newer than version 4, the bindery emulation and IPX must be enabled on them.

The following programs are available. Refer to the man pages for their functions:

nwmsg	ncopy	ncpmount	ncpumount
nprint	nsend	nwauth	nwbocreate
nwbols	nwboprops	nwborm	nwbpadd
nwbpcreate	nwbprm	nwbpset	nwbpvalues
nwdir	nwdpvalues	nwfsctrl	nwfsinfo
nwfstime	nwgrant	nwpasswd	nwpurge
nwrevoke	nwrights	nwsfind	nwtrustee
nwtrustee2	nwuserlist	nwvolinfo	pqlist
pqrm	pqstat	pserver	slist

`ncpmount`, for example, is an essential program used to mount volumes from a Netware server in Linux. In turn, `ncpumount` is used to unmount them. package `ncpfs` contains tools for configuring the IPX protocol and IPX routing:

```
ipx_cmd
ipx_configure
ipx_interface
ipx_internal_net
ipx_route
```

With `ipx_configure` and `ipx_interface`, configure the the network card's IPX. If you already have MARSNWE running, however, it will take care of this configuration automatically.

IPX Router with ipxrip

Another package for converting Linux into an IPX router is package `ipxrip`. Usually, it is not needed, because an IPX router can be configured with MARSNWE or the tools from package `ncpfs`.

Internet

A lot could be written about the Internet, but the scope of this book is confined to two aspects: the manual configuration of ADSL access, in case problems arise with the YaST2 configuration, and the configuration of the Squid proxy.

Configuring an ADSL or T-DSL Connection 408
Proxy Server: Squid 409

Configuring an ADSL or T-DSL Connection

Default Configuration

Currently, SuSE Linux supports DSL connections which work with the point-to-point over ethernet protocol (PPPoE) used by most major providers. If you are not sure what protocol is used for your DSL connections, ask your provider.

If you have a single-user workstation with a graphical interface, the DSL connection should be set up with the YaST2 modules ADSL/T-DSL .

1. The `ppp` and `smpppd` packages must be installed. It is best to use YaST2 for this purpose.

2. Configure your network card with YaST2. Do not activate dhcp, but set a fixed IP address instead, e.g. `192.168.2.22`.

3. The parameters set with YaST2 will be saved in the file `/etc/sysconfig/network/providers/dsl-provider0`. In addition, there are configuration files for the SuSE meta ppp daemon and its frontends kinternet and cinternet. Please consult the man page `man smpppd`.

4. Start the network with the command `rcnetwork start`.

5. With the commands `cinternet -start` and `cinternet -stop` the connection can be established or terminated on a non graphical system and On a graphical desktop use kinternet that is started automatically if you used YaST2 to set up DSL. Click on the gear icon in the control panel. Select 'Communication/Internet' → 'Internet Tools' → 'kinternet'. A plug icon will appear in the control panel. Start the connection by clicking on it once and, by clicking on it again, terminate the connection.

DSL Connection by Dial-on-Demand

Dial-on-demand means that the connection will automatically be set up when the user goes online, for example, when visiting a web site in a browser or when sending an e-mail. After a certain amount of idle time when no data is being sent or received, the connection will automatically be dropped. Since the dial-up connection via PPPoE, the protocol for ADSL, is quite fast, it is almost as if you had an ongoing Internet connection.

However, this really only makes sense if you have a flat-rate connection. If your Internet access is billed by the length of time online, make sure that there are not any interval processes, such as a cronjob, which may be periodically establishing a connection. This could get quite expensive.

Although a permanent online connection would also be possible using a DSL flat-rate connection, there are certain advantages to having a connection which only exists for a short amount of time when needed:

- Most providers drop the connection after a certain period of time.

- A permanent connection can be considered as a drain on resources (e. g. IP addresses).

- Being online permanently is a security risk, because hackers may be able to systematically comb the system for vulnerable areas. A system that is only accessible over the Internet when necessary and is always changing IP addresses is significantly more difficult to attack.

Dial-on-demand can be enabled using YaST2 (also refer to the *User Guide*) or set it up manually:

Set the parameter DEMAND="yes" in the `/etc/sysconfig/network/providers/dsl-provider0` file then define an idle time via the variable IDLETIME="60". This way, an unused connection will be dropped after 60 seconds.

Proxy Server: Squid

The following chapter describes how caching web sites assisted by a proxy server works and what the advantages of using proxy servers are. The most popular proxy cache for Linux and UNIX platforms is Squid. We will discuss its configuration, the specifications required to get it running, how to configure the system to do transparent proxying, how to gather statistics about the cache's use with the help of programs like Calamaris and cachemgr, and how to filter web contents with squidgrd.

About Proxy Caches

Squid acts as a proxy cache. It behaves like an agent that receives requests from clients, in this case web browsers, and passes them to the specified server provider. When the requested objects arrive at the agent, it stores a copy in a disk cache.

Benefits arise when different clients request the same objects: these will be served directly from the disk cache, much faster than obtaining them from the Internet and, at the same time, saving overall bandwidth for the system.

> **Tip**
>
> Squid covers a wide range of features, including intercommunicating hierarchies of proxy servers to divide the load, defining strict access control lists to all clients accessing the proxy, and, with the help of other applications, allowing or denying access to specific web pages. It also can obtain statistics about the most visited web sites, user usage of the Internet, and others.
>
> *Tip*

Squid is not a generic proxy. It proxies normally only between HTTP connections. It does also support the protocols FTP, Gopher, SSL, and WAIS, but it does not support other Internet protocols, such as Real Audio, news, or videoconferencing. Because Squid only supports the UDP protocol to provide communication between different caches, many other multimedia programs will not be supported.

Some Facts About Cache Proxying

Squid and Security

It is also possible to use Squid together with a firewall to secure internal networks from the outside using a proxy cache. The firewall denies all external services except for Squid, forcing all World Wide Web connections to be established by the proxy.

If it is a firewall configuration including a DMZ, set the proxy there. In this case, it is important that all computers in the DMZ send their log files to hosts inside the secured network.

One way to implement this feature is with the aid of a "transparent" proxy. It will be covered in Section *Transparent Proxy Configuration* on page 419.

Multiple Caches

"Multiple Caches" means configuring different caches so objects can be exchanged between them, reducing the total system load and increasing the chances of finding an object already in the local network. It enables the configuration of cache hierarchies so a cache is able to forward object requests to sibling caches or to a parent cache. It can get objects from another cache in the local network or directly from the source.

Choosing the appropriate topology for the cache hierarchy is very important, because we do not want to increase the overall traffic on the network. For example, in a very large network, it is possible to configure a proxy server for every subnetwork and connect it to a parent proxy, connected in its turn to the proxy cache from the ISP.

All this communication is handled by ICP (Internet Cache Protocol) running on top of the UDP protocol. Data transfers between caches are handled using HTTP (Hyper Text Transmission Protocol) based on TCP, but for these kinds of connections, it is preferable to use faster and simpler protocols capable of reacting to incoming requests within a maximum of one or two seconds.

To find the most appropriate server from which to get the objects, one cache sends an ICP request to all sibling proxies. These will answer the requests via ICP responses with a HIT code if the object was detected or a MISS if it was not. If multiple HIT responses were found, the proxy server will decide which server to download depending on factors such as which cache sent the fastest answer or which one is closer. If no satisfactory responses have been sent, the request will be sent to the parent cache.

Tip

To avoid duplication of objects in different caches in our network, other ICP protocols are used such as CARP (Cache Array Routing Protocol) or HTCP (HyperText Cache Protocol). The more objects maintained in the network, the greater the possibility of finding the one we want.

Tip

Caching Internet Objects

Not all objects available in our network are static. There are a lot of dynamically generated CGI pages, visitor counters, or encrypted SSL content documents. This is the reason objects like this are not cached: every time you access one, it will have changed.

The question remains as to how long all the other objects stored in the cache should stay there. To determine this, all objects in the cache are assigned one of three states.

Web and proxy servers find out the status of an object by adding headers to these objects such as "Last modified" or "Expires" and the corresponding date. Other headers specifying that objects must not be cached are used as well.

Objects in the cache are normally replaced, due to a lack of free hard disk space, using algorithms such as LRU (Last Recently Used). It consists of first replacing the less requested objects.

System Requirements

The most important thing is to determine the maximum load the system will have to bear. It is, therefore, important to pay more attention to the load picks, because these might be more than four times the day's average. When in doubt, it would be better to overestimate the system's requirements, because having Squid working close to the limit of its capabilities could lead to a severe loss in the quality of the service.

Speed: Choosing Fast Hard Disks

Speed plays an important role in the caching process, so should be of utmost concern. In hard disks, this parameter is described as "random seek time", measured in milliseconds. As a rule of thumb, the lower this value, the better.

Size of the Disk Cache

It depends on a few factors. In a small cache, the probability of a HIT (finding the requested object already located there) will be small, because the cache is easily filled so the less requested objects will be replaced by newer ones. On the other hand, if 1 GB is available for the cache and the users only surf 10 MB a day, it will take more than 100 days to fill the cache.

Probably the easiest way to determine the needed cache size is to consider the maximum transfer rate of our connection. With a 1 MB/s connection, the maximum transfer rate will be 125 KB/s. If all this traffic ends up in the cache, in one hour it will add up to 450 MB and, assuming that all this traffic is generated in only 8 working hours, it will reach 3.6 GB in one day. Because the connection was not used up to its maximum capacity, we could assume that the total amount of data going through the cache is about 2 GB. In the example, to keep all the browsed data of *one* day in the cache, we will require 2 GB of disk space for Squid. Summing up, Squid tends to read and write smaller blocks from or to the disk, making it more important how fast it detects these objects on the disk than having a fast disk.

RAM

The amount of memory required by Squid directly correlates to the amount of objects allocated in the cache. Squid also stores cache object references and frequently requested objects in memory to speed up the retrieving of this data. The memory is one million times faster than a hard disk. Compare the seek time of a hard disk, about 10 milliseconds, with the 10 nanoseconds access time of the newer RAM memories.

It is very important to have more than enough memory for the Squid process, because the system performance will be dramatically reduced if it has to be swapped to disk. To assist in cache memory management, use the tool cachemgr.cgi, as discussed in Section *cachemgr.cgi* on page 422.

CPU

Squid is not a program that requires intensive CPU usage. The load of the processor is only increased while the contents of the cache are being loaded or checked. Using a multiprocessor machine does not increase the performance of the system. To increase efficiency, it is better to buy faster disks or add more memory.

Some examples of configured systems running Squid are available at `http://wwwcache.ja.net/servers/squids.html`.

Starting Squid

Squid is already preconfigured in SuSE Linux, so you can start it easily right after installation. A prerequisite for a smooth start is an already configured network, at least one name server and, of course, Internet access. Problems can arise if a dial-up connection is used with dynamic DNS configuration. In cases such as this, at least the name server should be clearly entered, since Squid will not start if it does not detect a DNS in the `/etc/resolv.conf`.

To start Squid, enter `rcsquid start` at the command line as `root`. For the initial start-up, the directory structure must first be defined in `/var/squid/cache`. This is done by the start script `/etc/init.d/squid` automatically and can take a few seconds or even minutes. If `done` appears to the right in green, Squid has been successfully loaded. Test Squid's functionality on the local system by entering `localhost` and `Port 3128` as proxy in the browser. To allow all users to access Squid and thus the Internet, change the entry in the configuration file `/etc/squid.conf` from `http_access deny all` to `http_access allow all`. However, in doing so, consider that Squid is made completely accessible to anyone by this action. Therefore, define ACLs that control access to the proxy. More on this is available in Section *Options for Access Controls* on page 417.

If you have made changes in the configuration file `/etc/squid.conf`, instruct Squid to load the changed file. Do this by entering `rcsquid reload` or restart Squid with `rcsquid restart`. With `rcsquid status`, determine whether the proxy is running and with `rcsquid stop` halt Squid. The latter can take a while, since Squid waits up to half a minute (`shutdown_lifetime` option in `/etc/squid.conf`) before dropping the connections to the clients then will still have to write its data to the disk. If Squid is halted with `kill` or `killall`, this can lead to the destruction of the cache, which will then have to be fully removed to restart Squid.

If Squid dies after a short period of time, although it has seemingly been started successfully, it can be the result of a faulty name server entry or a missing `/etc/resolv.conf` file. The cause of the start failure would then be logged by Squid in the `/var/squid/logs/cache.log` file.

If Squid should be loaded automatically when the system boots, reset the entry `START_SQUID=no` to `START_SQUID=yes` in the `/etc/sysconfig/squid` file.

An uninstall of Squid will neither remove the cache or the log files. Manually delete the `/var/cache/squid` directory.

Local DNS Server

Setting up a local DNS server, such as BIND-8 or BIND-9, makes absolute sense even if the server does not manage its own domain. It will then simply act as a "caching-only DNS" and will also be able to resolve DNS requests via the root name server without requiring any special configuration. If you enter this in the `/etc/resolv.conf` with the IP address `127.0.0.1` for localhost, Squid will detect a valid name server when it starts up. Configuring a name server is discussed in Section *DNS — Domain Name Service* on page 361. It is sufficient, however, to install the package and to boot it. The name server of the provider should be entered in the configuration file `/etc/named.conf` under forwarders along with its IP address. If you have a firewall running, even if it is just personal-firewall, make sure the DNS requests will be sent.

The Configuration File /etc/squid.conf

All Squid proxy server settings are made in the `/etc/squid.conf` file. To start Squid for the first time, no changes will be necessary in this file, but

external clients will initially be denied access. The proxy needs to be made
available for the localhost, usually with 3128 as port. The options are extensive and therefore provided with ample documentation and examples in the
preinstalled /etc/squid.conf file. Nearly all entries begin with a # sign
(the lines are commented out) and the relevant specifications can be found at
the end of the line. The given values almost always correlate with the default
values, so removing the comment signs without changing any of the parameters actually has little effect in most cases. It is better to leave the sample as
it is and reinsert the options along with the modified parameters in the line
below. In this way, easily interpret the default values and the changes.

If you have updated an earlier Squid version, it is recommended to edit the
new /etc/squid.conf and only apply the changes made in the previous
file. If you try to implement the old squid.conf again, you are running a
risk that the configuration will no longer function, because options are sometimes modified and new changes added.

General Configuration Options

http_port 3128 This is the port where Squid listens for client requests. The
default port is 3128, but 8080 is also common. You have the option
here of specifying several port numbers separated by blank spaces.

cache_peer <hostname> <type> <proxy-port> <icp-port> Here, enter a parent proxy as "parent", for example, or use that of the provider. As
<hostname>, the name and IP address of the proxy to use are entered
and, as <type>, parent. For <proxy-port>, enter the port number that is also specified by the operator of the parent for use in the
browser, usually 8080. Set the <icp-port> to 7 or 0 if the ICP port
of the parent is not known and its use is irrelevant to the provider. In
addition, default and no-query should be specified after the port
numbers to strictly prohibit the use of the ICP protocol. Squid will then
behave like a normal browser as far as the provider's proxy is concerned.

cache_mem 8 MB This entry defines the amount of memory Squid can use
for the caches. The default is 8 MB.

cache_dir ufs /var/cache/squid/ 100 16 256 The entry cache_dir defines
the directory where all the objects are stored on disk. The numbers at
the end indicate the maximum disk space in MB to use and the number
of directories in the first and second level. The ufs parameter should
be left alone. The default is 100 MB occupied disk space in the /var/
cache/squid directory and creation of 16 subdirectories inside it, each

containing 256 more subdirectories. When specifying the disk space to use, leave sufficient reserve disk space. Values from a minimum of fifty to a maximum of eighty percent of the available disk space make the most sense here. The last two numbers for the directories should only be increased with caution, because too many directories can also lead to performance problems. If you have several disks that share the cache, enter several `cache_dir` lines.

cache_access_log /var/squid/logs/access.log   path for log messages

cache_log /var/squid/logs/cache.log   path for log messages

cache_store_log /var/squid/logs/store.log   path for log messages

> These three entries specify the path where Squid will log all its actions. Normally, nothing is changed here. If Squid is experiencing a heavy usage burden, it might make sense to distribute the cache and the log files over several disks.

emulate_httpd_log off   If the entry is set to `on`, obtain readable log files. Some evaluation programs cannot interpret this, however.

client_netmask 255.255.255.255   With this entry, mask the logged IP addresses in the log files to hide the clients' identity. The last digit of the IP address will be set to zero if you enter `255.255.255.0` here.

ftp_user Squid@   With this, set the password Squid should use for the anonymous FTP login. It can make sense, however, to specify a valid e-mail address here, because some FTP servers can check these for validity.

cache_mgr webmaster   An e-mail address to which Squid sends a message if it unexpectedly crashes. The default is `webmaster`.

logfile_rotate 0   If you run `squid -k rotate`, Squid can rotate secured log files. The files will be enumerated in this process and after reaching the specified value, the oldest file at that point will be overwritten. This value here normally stands for 0 because archiving and deleting log files in SuSE Linux is carried out by a cronjob found in the configuration file `/etc/logrotate.d/syslog`. The period of time after which the files are deleted is defined in the `/etc/sysconfig/aaa_base` file via the `MAX_DAYS_FOR_LOG_FILES` entry.

append_domain <domain>   With `append_domain`, specify which domain to append automatically when none is given. Usually, your own domain is entered here, so entering `www` in the browser accesses your own web server.

forwarded_for on If you set the entry to off, Squid will remove the IP address and the system name of the client from the HTTP requests.

negative_ttl 5 minutes; negative_dns_ttl 5 minutes Normally, you do not need to change these values. If you have a dial-up connection, however, the Internet may, at times, not be accessible. Squid will make a note of the failed requests then refuse to issue new ones, although the Internet connection has been reestablished. In a case such as this, change the minutes to seconds then, after clicking on Reload in the browser, the dial-up process should be reengaged after a few seconds.

never_direct allow <acl_name> To prevent Squid from taking requests directly from the Internet, use the above command to force connection to another proxy. You need to have previously entered this in cache_peer. If all is specified as the <acl_name>, force all requests to be forwarded directly to the parent. This might be necessary, for example, if you are using a provider that strictly stipulates the use of its proxies or denies its firewall direct Internet access.

Options for Access Controls

Squid provides an intelligent system that controls access to the proxy. By implementing ACLs, it can be configured easily and comprehensively. This involves lists with rules that are processed sequentially. ACLs must be defined before they can be used. Some default ACLs, such as all and localhost, already exist. After defining an ACL, implement it, for example, in conjunction with http_access.

acl <acl_name> <type> <data> An ACL requires at least three specifications to define it. The name <acl_name> can be chosen arbitrarily. For <type>, select from a variety of different options which can be found in the ACCESS CONTROLS section in the /etc/squid.conf file. The specification for <data> depends on the individual ACL type and can also be read from a file, for example, via host names, IP addresses, or URLs. The following are some simple examples:

```
acl mysurfers srcdomain .my-domain.com
acl teachers src 192.168.1.0/255.255.255.0
acl students src 192.168.7.0-192.168.9.0/255.255.255.0
acl lunch time MTWHF 12:00-15:00
```

http_access allow <acl_name> http_access defines who is allowed to use the proxy and who can access what on the Internet. For this, ACLs will have to be given. `localhost` and `all` have already been defined above, which can deny or allow access via `deny` or `allow`. A list containing any number of `http_access` entries can be created, processed from top to bottom, and, depending on which occurs first, access will be allowed or denied to the respective URL. The last entry should always be `http_access deny all`. In the following example, the `localhost` has free access to everything while all other hosts are denied access completely.

```
http_access allow localhost
http_access deny all
```

Another example, where the previously defined ACLs are used:
The group `teachers` always has access to the Internet. The group `students` only gets access Monday to Friday during lunch time.

```
http_access deny localhost
http_access allow teachers
http_access allow students lunch time
http_access deny all
```

The list with the `http_access` entries should only be entered, for the sake of readability, at the designated position in the `/etc/squid.conf` file. That is, between the text

```
# INSERT YOUR OWN RULE(S) HERE TO ALLOW ACCESS FROM YOUR CLIENTS
```

and the last

```
http_access deny all
```

redirect_program /usr/bin/squidGuard With this option, a redirector, such as SquidGuard, which is able to block unwanted URLs, can be specified. Internet access can be individually controlled for various user groups with the help of proxy authentication and the appropriate ACLs. SquidGuard is a package in and of itself that can be separately installed and configured.

authenticate_program /usr/sbin/pam_auth If users must be authenticated on the proxy, a corresponding program, such as pam_auth, can be specified here. When accessing pam_auth for the first time, the user will see a login window where the user name and password must be entered. In addition, an ACL is still required so only clients with a valid login can use the Internet:

```
acl password proxy_auth REQUIRED

http_access allow password
http_access deny all
```

The `REQUIRED` after `proxy_auth` can be replaced with a list of permitted user names or with the path to such a list.

ident_lookup_access allow <acl_name> With this, have an ident request run for all ACL-defined clients to find each user's identity. If you apply `all` to the `<acl_name>`, this will be valid for all clients. Also, an ident daemon must be running on all clients. For Linux, install the pidentd package for this purpose. For Windows, there is free software available to download from the Internet. To ensure that only clients with a successful ident lookup are permitted, a corresponding ACL will also have to be defined here:

```
acl identhosts ident REQUIRED

http_access allow identhosts
http_access deny all
```

Here, too, replace the `REQUIRED` with a list of permitted user names. Using `ident` can slow down the access time quite a bit, because ident lookups will be repeated for each request.

Transparent Proxy Configuration

The usual way of working with proxy servers is the following: the web browser sends requests to a certain port in the proxy server and the proxy provides these required objects, whether they are in its cache or not. When working in a real network, several situations may arise:

- For security reasons, it is recommended that all clients use a proxy to surf the Internet.
- All clients must use a proxy whether they are aware of it or not.
- In larger networks already using a proxy, it is possible to spare yourself the trouble of reconfiguring each machine whenever changes are made in the system.

In all these cases, a transparent proxy may be used. The principle is very easy: the proxy intercepts and answers the requests of the web browser, so that the web browser receives the requested pages without knowing from where they are coming. This entire process is done transparently, hence the name.

Kernel Configuration

First, make sure the proxy server's kernel has support for transparent proxying. Otherwise, add this option to the kernel and compile it again. More on this topic is available in *The Linux Kernel* on page 261.

Kernel modules change sometimes from version to version. Check the current state in the Transparent Proxy mini-howto installed in your SuSE Linux system at `/usr/share/doc/howto/en/html/mini/TransparentProxy-3.html` or online at the Linux Documentation Project web page (`http://www.tldp.org/HOWTO/mini/TransparentProxy-3.html`).

Now, save the new configuration, compile the new kernel, install it, and reconfigure GRUB or LILO, if necessary. Finally, restart the system.

Configuration Options in /etc/squid.conf

The options to activate in the `/etc/squid.conf` file to get the transparent proxy up and running are:

- httpd_accel_host virtual
- httpd_accel_port 80 # the port number where the actual HTTP server is located
- httpd_accel_with_proxy on
- httpd_accel_uses_host_header on

Firewall Configuration with SuSEfirewall2

Now redirect all incoming requests via the firewall with help of a port forwarding rule to the Squid port.

To do this, use the SuSE-provided tool SuSEfirewall2. Its configuration file can be found in `/etc/sysconfig/scripts/SuSEfirewall2-custom`. Again, the configuration file consists of well-documented entries. Even to set only a transparent proxy, you must configure a couple firewall options In our example:

- Device pointing to the Internet: FW_DEV_WORLD="eth1"
- Device pointing to the network: FW_DEV_INT="eth0"

Set ports and services (see /etc/exports) on the firewall being accessed from untrusted networks such as the Internet. In this example, only web services are offered to the outside:

FW_SERVICES_EXTERNAL_TCP="www"

Define ports or services (see /etc/exports) on the firewall to be accessed from the secure network, both TCP and UDP services:

FW_SERVICES_INTERNAL_TCP="domain www 3128"

FW_SERVICES_INTERNAL_UDP="domain"

We are accessing web services and Squid (whose default port is 3128).

The service "domain" specified before stands for DNS or Domain Name Server. It is most common to use this service, otherwise we simply take it out of the above entries and set the following option to no:

FW_SERVICE_DNS="yes"

The most important option is number 15:

```
#
# 15.)
# Which accesses to services should be redirected to a localport
# on the firewall machine?
#
# This can be used to force all internal users to surf via your
# squid proxy, or transparently redirect incoming webtraffic to
# a secure webserver.
#
# Choice: leave empty or use the following explained syntax of
# redirecting rules, separated by a space.
# A redirecting rule consists of 1) source IP/net,
# 2) destination IP/net, 3) original destination port and
# 4) local port to redirect the traffic to, separated by a colon,
# e.g. "10.0.0.0/8,0/0,80,3128 0/0,172.20.1.1,80,8080"
#
```

File 66: Option 15 der Firewallkonfiguration

The comments above show the syntax to follow. First, the IP address and the netmask of the "internal networks" accessing the proxy firewall. Second, the

IP address and the netmask to which these clients "send" their requests. In the case of web browsers, specify the networks 0/0, a wild card that means "to everywhere". After that, enter the "original" port to which these requests are sent and, finally, the port to which all these requests are "redirected". As Squid supports more protocols than HTTP, redirect requests from other ports to our proxy, such as FTP (port 21), HTTPS, or SSL (port 443). The example uses the default port 3128. If there are more networks or services to add, they only need to be separated by a single blank character in the corresponding entry.

FW_REDIRECT_TCP="192.168.0.0/16,0/0,80,3128 192.168.0.0/16,0/0,21,3128"

FW_REDIRECT_UDP="192.168.0.0/16,0/0,80,3128 192.168.0.0/16,0/0,21,3128"

To start the firewall and the new configuration with it, change an entry in the `/etc/sysconfig/SuSEfirewall2` file. The entry START_FW must be set to "yes".

Start Squid as shown in Section *Starting Squid* on page 413. To check if everything is working properly, take a look at the Squid logs in `/var/log/squid/access.log`.

To verify that all ports are correctly configured, perform a port scan on the machine from any computer outside your network. Only the web services port (80) should be open. Do the port scan with `nmap`:

```
nmap -O IP_address
```

Squid and Other Programs

In the following section, see how other applications interact with Squid. `cachemgr.cgi` enables the system administrator to check the amount of memory needed for caching objects. squidgrd filters web pages. Calamaris is a report generator for Squid.

cachemgr.cgi

The cache manager (cachemgr.cgi) is a CGI utility for displaying statistics about the memory usage of a running Squid process. It is also a more convenient way to manage the cache and view statistics without logging the server.

Setup

First, a running web server on your system is required. To check if Apache is already running, type, as `root`, `rcapache status`.

If a message like this appears:

```
Checking for service httpd: OK
Server uptime: 1 day 18 hours 29 minutes 39 seconds
```

Apache is running on your machine. Otherwise, type `rcapache start` to start Apache with the SuSE Linux default settings.

The last step to set it up is to copy the file `cachemgr.cgi` to the Apache directory `cgi-bin`:

```
cp /usr/share/doc/packages/squid/scripts/cachemgr.cgi
/usr/local/httpd/cgi-bin
```

Cache Manager ACLs in /etc/squid.conf

There are some default settings in the original file required for the cache manager:

```
acl manager proto cache_object
acl localhost src 127.0.0.1/255.255.255.255
```

With the following rules:

```
http_access allow manager localhost
http_access deny manager
```

the first ACL is the most important, as the cache manager tries to communicate with Squid over the cache_object protocol.

The following rules assume that the web server and Squid are running on the same machine. If the communication between the cache manager and Squid originates at the web server on another computer, include an extra ACL as in Figure 67.

```
acl manager proto cache_object
acl localhost src 127.0.0.1/255.255.255.255
acl webserver src 192.168.1.7/255.255.255.255 # IP of webserver
```

File 67: Access Rules

Then add the rules as in Figure 68.

```
http_access allow manager localhost
http_access allow manager webserver
http_access deny manager
```

File 68: Access Rules

Configure a password for the manager for access to more options like closing the cache remotely or viewing more information about the cache. For this, configure the entry cachemgr_passwd with a password for the manager and the list of options to view. This list appears as a part of the entry comments in `/etc/squid.conf`.

Restart Squid with the option `-k reconfigure` every time the configuration file is changed.

Viewing the Statistics

Go to the corresponding web site:
`http://webserver.example.org/cgi-bin/cachemgr.cgi`

Press 'continue' and browse through the different statistics. More details on each entry shown by the cache manager is in the Squid FAQ at `http://www.squid-cache.org/Doc/FAQ/FAQ-9.html`

SquidGuard

This section is not intended to go through an extensive configuration of SquidGuard, only to introduce it and give some advice on using it. For more in-depth configuration issues, refer to the SquidGuard web site at `http://www.squidguard.org`

SquidGuard is a free (GPL), flexible, and fast filter, redirector, and access controller plug-in for Squid. It lets you define multiple access rules with different restrictions for different user groups on a Squid cache. SquidGuard uses Squid's standard redirector interface.

SquidGuard can be used for the following:

- limit the web access for some users to a list of accepted or well-known web servers or URLs

- block access to some listed or blacklisted web servers or URLs for some users

- block access to URLs matching a list of regular expressions or words for some users

- redirect blocked URLs to an "intelligent" CGI-based info page

- redirect unregistered users to a registration form

- redirect banners to an empty GIF
- have different access rules based on time of day, day of the week, date, etc.
- have different rules for different user groups
- and much more

Neither SquidGuard or Squid can be used to:

- Edit, filter, or censor text inside documents
- Edit, filter, or censor HTML-embedded script languages such as JavaScript or VBscript

Using SquidGuard

Install the package `squidgrd`. Edit a minimal configuration file `/etc/squidguard.conf`. There are plenty of configuration examples in `http://www.squidguard.org/config/`. Experiment later with more complicated configuration settings.

The following step is to create a dummy "access denied" page or a more or less intelligent CGI page to redirect Squid if the client requests a blacklisted web site. Using Apache is strongly recommended.

Now, tell Squid to use SquidGuard. Use the following entry in the `/etc/squid.conf` file:

redirect_program /usr/bin/squidGuard

There is another option called redirect_children configuring how many different "redirect" (in this case SquidGuard) processes are running on the machine. SquidGuard is fast enough to cope with lots of requests (SquidGuard is quite fast: 100,000 requests within 10 seconds on a 500MHz Pentium with 5900 domains, 7880 URLs, 13780 in sum). Therefore, it is not recommended to set more than 4 processes, because this may lead to an unnecessary increase of memory for the allocation of these processes.

redirect_children 4

Last of all, send a HUP signal to Squid to have it read the new configuration:

squid -k reconfigure

Test your settings with a browser.

Cache Report Generation with Calamaris

Calamaris is a Perl script used to generate reports of cache activity in ASCII or HTML format. It works with native Squid access log files. The Calamaris Home Page is located at `http://Calamaris.Cord.de/`

The use of the program is quite easy. Log in as `root`, then:

`cat access.log.files | calamaris [options] > reportfile`

It is important when piping more than one log file that the log files are chronologically ordered, with older files first.

The various options:

-a normally used for the output of available reports

-w an HTML report

-l a message or logo in the header of the report

More information on the various options can be found in the manual page `man calamaris`.

A typical example is:

```
cat access.log.2 access.log.1 access.log | calamaris -a -w \
 >/usr/local/httpd/htdocs/Squid/squidreport.html
```

This puts the report in the directory of the web server. Apache is required to view the reports.

Another powerful cache report generator tool is SARG (Squid Analysis Report Generator). More information on this can be found in the relevant Internet pages at `http://web.onda.com.br/orso/`

More Information on Squid

Visit the home page of Squid at `http://www.squid-cache.org/`. Here, find the Squid User Guide and a very extensive collection of FAQs on Squid.

There is a Mini-Howto regarding transparent proxies in the package `howtoen`, under `/usr/share/doc/howto/en/mini/TransparentProxy.gz`

In addition, mailing lists are available for Squid at: `squid-users@squid-cache.org`.

The archive for this is located at: `http://www.squid-cache.org/mail-archive/squid-users/`

17

Network Security

Masquerading, firewall, and Kerberos provide the foundation for a secure network and ensure a controlled flow of data. The secure shell (SSH) offers the user the possibility to log in to a remote host over an encrypted connection. The following sections describe how these vast possibilities can be used.

Masquerading and Firewalls 428
SSH — Secure Shell, the Safe Alternative 433
Network Authentication — Kerberos 438
Security and Confidentiality 445

Masquerading and Firewalls

Because of its outstanding network capabilities, Linux is frequently used as a router operating system for dial-up or dedicated lines. "Router," in this case, refers to a host with multiple network interfaces that transmits any packets not destined for one of its own network interfaces to another host communicating with it. This router is often called a gateway. The packet filtering mechanism provided by the Linux kernel allows precise control over which packets of the overall traffic are transferred.

In general, defining the exact rules for a packet filter requires at least some experience on the part of the administrator. For the less experienced user, SuSE Linux includes a separate package package `SuSEfirewall2` intended to make it easier to set up these rules.

SuSEfirewall2 is highly configurable, making it a good choice for a more complex packet filtering setup.

With this packet filter solution, a Linux machine can be used as a router with masquerading to link a local network through a dial-up or dedicated connection where only one IP address is visible to the outside world. Masquerading is accomplished by implementing rules for packet filtering.

> **Caution**
>
> This chapter only describes standard procedures that should work well in most situations. Although every effort has been made to provide accurate and complete information, no guarantee is included. SuSE cannot be responsible for the success or failure of your security measures. We do appreciate your criticism and comments. Although you might not receive a direct answer from us, rest assured that suggestions for improvement will be taken seriously.
>
> **Caution**

Masquerading Basics

Masquerading is the Linux-specific form of NAT (Network Address Translation). The basic principle is not very complicated: Your router has more than one network interface, typically a network card and a separate interface to the Internet (e.g an ISDN interface). While this interfaces links with the outside world, the remaining ones are used to connect this router with the other hosts in your network. For example, the dial-up is conducted via ISDN and the network interface is `ippp0`. Several hosts in your local network are connected to the network card of your Linux router, in this example, `eth0`. Hosts in the network should be configured to send packets destined outside the local network to this gateway.

> **Note**
>
> Make sure that both the broadcast addresses and the network masks are the same for all the hosts when configuring your network.
>
> **Note**

When one of the hosts sends a packet destined for an Internet address, this packet is sent to the network's default router. The router needs to be configured to actually forward such packets. SuSE Linux does not enable this with a default installation for security reasons. Set the variable IP_FORWARD, defined in the file `/etc/sysconfig/network/options`, to IP_FORWARD=yes. The forwarding mechanism is enabled after rebooting or issuing the command `echo 1 > /proc/sys/net/ipv4/ip_forward`.

The router has only one IP address visible from the outside, such as the IP address of the connected ISDN interface. The source address of transmitted packets must be replaced with the router's address to enable reply. The target host only knows your router, not hosts in your internal network. Your internal host disguises itself behind the router, which is why the technique is called "masquerading".

The router, as the destination of any reply packets, has to identify the incoming packets, change the target address to the intended recipient, and forward it to that host in the local network. The identification of packets belonging to a connection handled by a masquerading router is done with the help of a table kept in the kernel of your router while connected. By using the `ipchains` and the `iptables` commands, the superuser (`root`) can view these tables. Read the man pages for these commands for detailed instructions. For the identification of single masqueraded connections, the source and target addresses, the port numbers, and the protocols involved are relevant. A router is capable of hiding many thousand connections per internal host simultaneously.

With the routing of inbound traffic depending on the masquerading table, there is no way to open a connection to an internal host from the outside. For such a connection, there would be no entry in the table because it is only created if an internal host opens a connection with the outside. In addition, any established connection is assigned a status entry in the table and this entry cannot be used by another connection. A second connection would require another status record. As a consequence of all this, you might experience some problems with a number of applications, such as ICQ, cucme,

IRC (DCC, CTCP), Quake, and FTP (in PORT mode). Netscape, as well as the standard ftp program and many others, uses the PASV mode. This passive mode is much less problematic as far as packet filtering and masquerading is concerned.

Firewalling Basics

"Firewall" is probably the most widely used term to describe a mechanism to control the data traffic between two networks and to provide and manage the link between networks. There are various types of firewalls, which mostly differ in regard to the abstract level on which traffic is analyzed and controlled. Strictly speaking, the mechanism described in this section is called a "packet filter." Like any other type of firewall, a packet filter alone does not guarantee full protection from all security risks. A packet filter implements a set of rules related to protocols, ports, and IP addresses to decide whether data may pass through. This blocks any packets that, according to the address or destination, are not supposed to reach your network. Packets sent to the telnet service of your hosts on port 23, for example, should be blocked, while you might want people to have access to your web server and therefore enable the corresponding port. A packet filter will not scan the contents of any packets as long as they have legitimate addresses (e. g., directed to your web server). Thus, packets could attack your CGI server, but the packet filter would let them through.

A more effective, more complex mechanism is the combination of several types of systems, such as a packet filter interacting with an application gateway or proxy. In this case, the packet filter rejects any packets destined to disabled ports. Only packets directed to the application gateway are allowed through. This gateway or proxy pretends to be the actual client of the server. In a sense, such a proxy could be considered a masquerading host on the protocol level used by the application. One example for such a proxy is Squid, an HTTP proxy server. To use Squid, the browser needs to be configured to communicate via the proxy, so that any HTTP pages requested would be served from the proxy cache rather than directly from the Internet. As another example, the SuSE proxy suite (the package proxy-suite in series sec) includes a proxy for the FTP protocol.

The following section focuses on the packet filter that come with SuSE Linux. For more information and links, read the Firewall HOWTO included in package `howtoen`. If this package is installed, read the HOWTO with `less /usr/share/doc/howto/en/Firewall-HOWTO.gz`.

17

SuSEfirewall2

The configuration of SuSEfirewall2 requires a certain degree of experience and understanding. Find documentation about SuSEfirewall2 in `/usr/share/doc/packages/SuSEfirewall2`.

The configuration of SuSEfirewall2 is stored in the file `/etc/sysconfig/SuSEfirewall2`. This firewall can also be configured with YaST2 ('Security' → 'Firewall'). In the following we demonstrate a successful configuration step-by-step. For each configuration item, find a note as to whether it is relevant for firewalling or masquerading. Aspects related to the DMZ (or "demilitarised zone") are not covered here.

If your requirements are strictly limited to masquerading, only fill out items marked *masquerading*.

- First, use the YaST2 runlevel editor to enable SuSEfirewall2 in your runlevel (3 or 5 most likely). It sets the symlinks for the SuSEfirewall2_* scripts in the `/etc/init.d/rc?.d/` directories.

- FW_DEV_WORLD (firewall, masquerading): The device linked to the Internet, such as `eth0` or `ippp0`.

- FW_DEV_INT (firewall, masquerading): The device linked to the internal, "private" network. Leave this blank if there is no internal network and the firewall is supposed to protect only the one host.

- FW_ROUTE (firewall, masquerading): If you need the masquerading function, enter `yes` here. Your internal hosts will not be visible to the outside, because their private network addresses (e.g., 192.168.x.x) are ignored by Internet routers.

  For a firewall without masquerading, only set this to `yes` to allow access to the internal network. Your internal hosts need to use officially registered IPs in this case. Normally, however, you should *not* allow access to your internal network from the outside.

- FW_MASQUERADE (masquerading): Set this to `yes` if you need the masquerading function. It is more secure to have a proxy server between the hosts of the internal network and the Internet.

- FW_MASQ_NETS (masquerading): Specify the hosts or networks to masquerade, leaving a space between the individual entries. For example, FW_MASQ_NETS="192.168.0.0/24 192.168.10.1".

SuSE Linux – Administration Guide   431

- **FW_PROTECT_FROM_INTERNAL** (firewall): Set this to `yes` to protect your firewall host from attacks originating in your internal network. Services will only be available to the internal network if explicitly enabled. See also FW_SERVICES_INTERNAL_TCP and FW_SERVICES_INTERNAL_UDP.

- **FW_AUTOPROTECT_GLOBAL_SERVICES** (firewall): This should normally be `yes`.

- **FW_SERVICES_EXTERNAL_TCP** (firewall): Enter the services that should be available, for example, `"www smtp ftp domain 443"`. Leave this blank for a workstation at home that is not intended to offer any services.

- **FW_SERVICES_EXTERNAL_UDP** (firewall): Leave this blank if you do not run a name service that you want to make available to the outside. Otherwise, enter the ports to use.

- **FW_SERVICES_INTERNAL_TCP** (firewall): This defines the services available to the internal network. The notation is the same as for external TCP services, but, in this case, refers to the *internal* network.

- **FW_SERVICES_INTERNAL_UDP** (firewall): See above.

- **FW_TRUSTED_NETS** (firewall): Specify the hosts you *really* trust ("trusted hosts"). Note, however, that these need to be protected from attacks, too.

    `"172.20.0.0/16 172.30.4.2"` means that all hosts which have an IP address beginning with `172.20.x.x` and the host with the IP address `172.30.4.2` are allowed to pass information through the firewall.

- **FW_SERVICES_TRUSTED_TCP** (firewall): Here, specify the port addresses that may be used by the "trusted hosts". For example, to grant them access to all services, enter `1:65535`. Usually, it is sufficient to enter `ssh` as the only service.

- **FW_SERVICES_TRUSTED_UDP** (firewall): Just like above, but for UDP ports.

- **FW_ALLOW_INCOMING_HIGHPORTS_TCP** (firewall): Set this to `ftp-data` if you intend to use normal (active) FTP services.

- **FW_ALLOW_INCOMING_HIGHPORTS_UDP** (firewall): Set this to `dns` to use the name servers registered in `/etc/resolv.conf`. If you enter `yes` here, all high ports will be enabled.

- **FW_SERVICE_DNS** (firewall): Enter `yes` if you run a name server that should be available to external hosts. At the same time, enable port 53 under FW_TCP_SERVICES_*.

- **FW_SERVICE_DHCLIENT** (firewall): Enter `yes` here if you use dhclient to assign your IP address.

- **FW_LOG_*** (firewall): Specify the firewall's logging activity. For normal operation, it is sufficient to set FW_LOG_DENY_CRIT to `yes`.

- **FW_STOP_KEEP_ROUTING_STATE** (firewall): Insert `yes` if you have configured your dial-up procedure to work automatically via diald or ISDN (dial-on-demand).

Now that you have configured SuSEfirewall2, do not forget to test your setup (for example, with `telnet` from an external host). Have a look at `/var/log/messages`, where you should see something like:

```
Feb  7 01:54:14 www kernel: Packet log: input DENY eth0
PROTO=6 129.27.43.9:1427 195.58.178.210:23 L=60 S=0x00
I=36981 F=0x4000 T=59 SYN (#119)
```

SSH — Secure Shell, the Safe Alternative

In these times of increasing networks, accessing a remote system also becomes more common. Regardless of the activity, the person accessing the system must be authenticated.

Most users should know by now that the user name and password are only intended for individual use. Strict confidence pertaining to personal data is usually guaranteed between the employer, computer center, or service provider. However, the ongoing practice of authenticating and transferring data in clear text form is a frightening phenomenon. Most directly affected are the commonly used services Post Office Protocol (POP) for retrieving mail and telnet for logging in on remote systems. Using these methods, user information and data considered sensitive, such as the contents of a letter or a chat via the talk command, travel openly and unsecured over the network. This encroaches on the user's privacy and leaves such access methods open to misuse. Usually, this misuse occurs by accessing one system to attack another or to obtain administrator or root permissions.

Any device involved in data transfer or operating on the local network, such as firewall, router, switch, mail servers, or workstations, can also access the data. There are laws prohibiting such behavior, but it is difficult to detect.

The SSH software provides the necessary protection. Complete authentication, usually user name and password, as well as the communication is encrypted. Even here, snatching the transferred data is possible, but the contents cannot be deciphered by intruders without the key. This enables secure communication via unsafe networks, such as the Internet. SuSE Linux provides the package OpenSSH.

The OpenSSH Package

SuSE Linux installs the package OpenSSH by default. The programs ssh, scp, and sftp are then available as alternatives to telnet, rlogin, rsh, rcp, and ftp.

The ssh Program

Using the ssh program, it is possible to log in to remote systems and work interactively. It replaces both telnet and rlogin. The symbolic name slogin points to ssh. For example, it is possible to log in to the host sun with the command `ssh sun`. The host then prompts for the password on sun.

Following successful authentication, work from the command line there or use interactive applications. If the local user name is different from the remote user name, log in using a different login name with `ssh -l augustine sun` or `ssh augustine@sun`.

Furthermore, ssh offers the option of running commands on another system, as does rsh. In the following example, we will run the command uptime on the host sun and create a directory with the name tmp. The program output will be displayed on the local terminal of the host earth.

```
newbie@earth:~ >  ssh sun"uptime; mkdir tmp"
newbie@sun's password:
1:21pm up 2:17, 9 users, load average:   0.15, 0.04, 0.02
```

Quotation marks are necessary here to send both instructions with one command. It is only by doing this that the second command is likewise executed on sun.

scp — Secure Copy

scp copies files to a remote machine. It is the secure and encoded substitute for rcp. For example, `scp MyLetter.tex sun:` copies the file `MyLetter.tex` from the machine `earth` to the machine `sun`. To give a different user name, use the `username@machine` format.

After the correct password is entered, scp starts the data transfer and shows a series of stars, gradually marking the progress from left to right. In addition, the estimated time of arrival will be shown in the right margin. All output can be suppressed by giving the option `-q`.

scp also provides a recursive copying feature for entire directories. `scp -r src/ sun:backup/` copies the entire contents of the directory `src/` including all subdirectories to the machine `sun` in the subdirectory `backup/`. If this subdirectory does not exist yet, it will be created automatically.

Via the option `-p`, scp leaves the time stamp of the files unchanged. `-C` compresses the data transfer. This minimizes the data volume to be transferred, but creates heavier burden on the processor.

sftp — Secure File Transfer

Instead of scp, sftp can be used for secure file transfer. During the session, sftp provides many of the commands used by ftp. This may be an advantage over scp, especially when transferring data for which the file names are unknown.

The SSH Daemon (sshd) — Server-Side

To work with the SSH client programs ssh and scp, a server, the SSH daemon, has to be running in the background. This waits for its connections on TCP/IP port 22.

The daemon generates three key pairs when starting for the first time. The key pairs consist of a private and a public key. Therefore, this procedure is referred to as public key–based. To guarantee the security of the communication via SSH, only the system administrator can see the private key files. The file permissions are restrictively defined by the default setting. The private keys are only required locally by the SSH daemon and must not be given to anyone else. The public key components (recognizable by the name extension .pub) are sent to the communication partner and are readable for all users.

SuSE Linux – Administration Guide

A connection is initiated by the SSH client. The waiting SSH daemon and the requesting SSH client exchange identification data comparing the protocol and software versions and preventing connection to the wrong port. Since a child process of the original SSH daemon replies to the request, several SSH connections can be made simultaneously.

The SSH protocol is available in two versions, 1 and 2, for the communication between SSH server and SSH client. When using SSH with version 1, the server sends its public host key and a server key, regenerated by the SSH daemon every hour. Both allow the SSH client to encrypt a freely chosen session key then send it to the SSH server. The SSH client also tells the server which encryption method (cipher) to use.

SSH in version 2 does not require a server key. A Diffie-Helman algorithm is employed instead for exchanging the keys.

The private host and server keys absolutely necessary for decoding the session key cannot be derived from the public parts. Only the SSH daemon contacted can decipher the session key using its propietary keys (see also /usr/share/doc/packages/openssh/RFC.nroff). This initial connection phase can be watched closely using the SSH client program's error search option -v. Version 2 of the SSH protocol is used by default, which however can be overridden to use version 1 of the protocol with the -1 switch. By storing all public host keys after initial contact in ~/.ssh/known_hosts on the client side, so-called "man-in-the-middle" access attempts can be prevented. SSH servers that try to fraudulently use names and IP addresses of others will be exposed by a clear indicator. They will either be noticed due to a wrong host key which differs from ~/.ssh/known_hosts or they cannot decipher the session key in the absence of an appropriate private counterpart.

It is recommended to securely archive the private and public keys stored in /etc/ssh/ externally. In this way, key modifications can be detected and the old ones can be used again after a new installation. This spares users the unsettling warning. If it is verified that, despite the warning, it is indeed the correct SSH server, the existing entry regarding this system will have to be removed from ~/.ssh/known_hosts.

SSH Authentication Mechanisms

Now the actual authentication will take place, which, in its simplest form, consists of entering a password as mentioned above. The goal of SSH was to introduce a secure software that is also easy to use. As it is meant to replace rsh and rlogin programs, SSH must also be able to provide an authentication method good for daily use. SSH accomplishes this by way of another key pair generated by the user. The SSH package also provides a help program, ssh-keygen, for this. After entering `ssh-keygen -t rsa` or `ssh-keygen -t dsa`, the key pair will be generated and you will be prompted for the base file name in which to store the keys:

```
Enter file in which to save the key (/home/newbie/.ssh/id_rsa):
```

Confirm the default setting and answer the request for a passphrase. Even if the software suggests an empty passphrase, a text from ten to thirty characters is recommended for the procedure described here. Do not use short and simple words or phrases. Confirm by repeating the passphrase. Subsequently, you will see where the private and public keys are stored, in our example, the files `id_rsa` and `id_rsa.pub`.

```
Enter same passphrase again:  Your identification has been
saved in /home/newbie/.ssh/id_rsa Your public key has been
saved in /home/newbie/.ssh/id_rsa.pub.  The key fingerprint is:
79:c1:79:b2:e1:c8:20:c1:89:0f:99:94:a8:4e:da:e8 newbie@sun
```

Use `ssh-keygen -p -t rsa` or `ssh-keygen -p -t dsa` to change your old passphrase.

Copy the public key component (`id_rsa.pub` in our example) to the remote machine and save it there at the location `~/.ssh/authorized_keys2`. You will be asked to authenticate yourself with your passphrase the next time you establish a connection. If this does not occur, verify the location and contents of these files.

In the long run, this procedure is more troublesome than giving your password each time. Therefore, the SSH package provides another tool, the ssh-agent, which retains the private keys for the duration of an X session. The entire X session will be started as a child process of ssh-agents. The easiest way to do this is to set the variable `usessh` at the beginning of the `.xsession` file to `yes` and log in via a display manager such as KDM or XDM. Alternatively, enter ssh-agent startx.

Now you can use `ssh` or `scp` as usual. If you have distributed your private key as described above, you are no longer prompted for your password. Take care of terminating your X session or locking it with a password-protection, for instance xlock.

All the relevant changes which resulted from the introduction of version 2 of the SSH protocol have also been documented in the file `/usr/share/doc/packages/openssh/README.SuSE`.

X, Authentication, and Other Forwarding Mechanisms

Beyond the previously described security-related improvements, ssh also simplifies the use of remote X applications. If you run `ssh` with the option `-X`, the DISPLAY variable will automatically be set on the remote machine and all X output will be exported to the remote machine over the existing ssh connection. At the same time, X applications started remotely and locally viewed with this method cannot be intercepted by unauthorized persons.

By adding the option `-A`, the ssh-agent authentication mechanism will be carried over to the next machine. This way, you can work from different machines without having to enter a password, but only if you have distributed your public key to the destination hosts and properly saved it there.

Both mechanisms are deactivated in the default settings, but can be permanently activated at any time in the system-wide configuration file `/etc/ssh/sshd_config` or the user's `~/.ssh/config`.

ssh can also be used to redirect TCP/IP connections. In the following example, the SMTP and POP3 port is redirected through ssh: `ssh -L 25:sun:25 sun`. Here, each connection directed to "`earth` port 25", SMTP is redirected to the SMTP port on `sun` via an encrypted channel. This is especially useful for those using SMTP servers without SMTP-AUTH or POP-before-SMTP features. From any arbitrary location connected to a network, e-mail can be transferred to the "home" mail server for delivery. In a similar manner, the following command forwards all port 110 and POP3 requests on `earth` to the POP3 port of `sun`: `ssh -L 110:sun:110 sun`.

Both examples must be carried out by user `root`, because the connection is made to privileged local ports. E-mail is sent and retrieved by normal users in an existing SSH connection. The SMTP and POP3 host must be set to `localhost` for this.

Additional information can be found in the manual pages for each of the programs described above and also in the files under `/usr/share/doc/packages/openssh`.

Network Authentication — Kerberos

An open network provides no means to ensure that a workstation can identify its users properly except for the usual password mechanisms, which are inherently insecure. This means anyone could start any service pretending to be someone else and fetch his mail or browse his private data. As a consequence, your networking environment must meet the following requirements to be secure:

- Let all users prove their identity for each desired service and make sure no one can take the identity of someone else.

- Make sure each network server also proves its identity. If you do not, an attacker might be able to impersonate the server and obtain sensitive information transmitted to the server. This concept is called "mutual authentication", because the client authenticates to the server and vice versa.

Kerberos helps you meet the above requirements by providing strongly encrypted authentication. The following sections show how this is achieved. Only the basic principles of Kerberos are discussed here. For detailed technical instruction, refer to the documentation provided with your implementation of Kerberos.

Note

The original Kerberos was designed at the MIT. Besides the MIT Kerberos, there exist several other implementations of Kerberos. SuSE Linux ships with a free implementation of Kerberos 5, the so-called Heimdal Kerberos 5 from KTH. Since the following text covers features common to all versions, we will refer to the program itself as Kerberos as long as no Heimdal-specific information is presented.

Note

Kerberos Terminology

The following glossary will help you cope with Kerberos terminology.

credential Users or clients need to present some kind of credentials that authorize them to request services. Kerberos knows two kinds of credentials — tickets and authenticators.

ticket A ticket is a per server credential used by a client to authenticate at a server from which it is requesting a service. It contains the name of the server, the client's name, the client's Internet address, a timestamp, a lifetime, and a random session key. All this data is encrypted using the server's key.

authenticator Combined with the ticket, an authenticator is used to prove that the client presenting a ticket is really the one it claims to be. An authenticator is built of the client's name, the workstation's IP address, and the current workstation's time all encrypted with the session key which is only known to the client and the server from which it is requesting a service. An authenticator can only be used once, unlike a ticket. A client can build an authenticator itself.

principal A Kerberos principal is unique entity (a user or service) to which it can assign a ticket. A principal consists of the following components:

- **primary** — the first part of a the principal, which can be the same as your user name in the case of a user
- **instance** — some optional information characterizing the primary. This string is separated from the primary by a '/'.
- **realm** — this specifies your Kerberos realm. Normally, your realm is your domain name in upper-case letters.

mutual authentication Kerberos ensures that both client and server can be sure of each others identity. They will share a (session) key, which they can use to comminicate securely.

session key Session keys are temporary private keys generated by Kerberos. They are known to the client and used to encrypt the communication between the client and the server for which it requested and received a ticket.

replay Almost all messages passed on in a network can get eavesdropped, stolen, and resent. In Kerberos context, this would be most dangerous if an attacker manages to obtain your request for a service containing your ticket and authenticator. He could then try to resend it ("replay") and to impersonate you. However, Kerberos implements several mechanisms to deal with that problem.

server or service "Service" is used when we talk of a specific action to perform. The process behind this action is referred to as a "server".

How Kerberos Works

Kerberos is often called a third party trusted authentication service, which means all its clients trust Kerberos judgement of another client's identity. Kerberos keeps a database of all its users and their private keys.

To ensure Kerberos is worth all the trust put in it, run both the authentication and ticket-granting server must be run on a dedicated machine. Make sure only the administrator can access this machine both physically and over the network. Reduce the (networking) services run on it to the absolute minimum — do not even run sshd.

First contact Your first contact with Kerberos is quite similar to any login procedure at a normal networking system. Enter your user name. This piece of information and the name of the ticket-granting service are sent to the authentication server (Kerberos). If the authentication server knows about your existence, it will generate a (random) session key for further use between your client and the ticket-granting server. Now the authentication server will prepare a ticket for the ticket-granting server. The ticket contains the following information — all encrypted with a session key only the authentication server and the ticket-granting server know:

- the names both of the client and the ticket-granting server
- the current time
- a lifetime assigned to this ticket
- the client's IP address
- the newly-generated session key

This ticket is then sent back to the client together with the session key, again in encrypted form, but this time the private key of the client is used. This private key is only known to Kerberos and the client, because it is derived from your user password. Now that the client has received this response, you are prompted for your password. This password is converted into the key that can decrypt the package sent by the authentication server. The package is "unwrapped" and password and key are erased from the workstation's memory. As long as the lifetime given to the ticket used to obtain other tickets does not expire, your workstation can prove your identity.

Requesting a service To request a service from any server in the network, the client application needs to prove its identity to the server. Therefore, the application generates an authenticator. An authenticator consists of the following components:

- the client's principal
- the client's IP address
- the current time
- a checksum (chosen by the client)

All this information is encrypted using the session key that the client has already received for this special server. The authenticator and the ticket for the server are sent to the server. The server uses its copy of the session key to decrypt the authenticator, which gives him all information needed about the client requesting its service to compare it to that contained in the ticket. The server verifies that the same client has sent both.

Without any security measures implemented on the server side, this stage of the process would be an ideal target for replay attacks. Someone could try to resend a request stolen off the net some time before. To prevent this, the server will not accept any request with a timestamp and ticket received previously. In addition to that, a request with a timestamp differing too much from the time the request is received can be ignored.

Mutual authentication Kerberos authentication can be used in both directions. It is not only a question of the client being the one it claims to be, the server should also be able to authenticate itself to the client requesting its service. Therefore, it sends some kind of authenticator itself. It adds one to the checksum it received in the client's authenticator and encrypts it with the session key, which is shared between it and the client. The client takes this response as a proof of the server's authenticity and they both start cooperating.

Ticket-granting — getting into contact with all servers Tickets are designed to be used for one server at a time. This implies that you have to get a new ticket each time you request another service. Kerberos implements a mechanism to obtain tickets for individual servers. This service is called the "ticket-granting service". The ticket-granting service is a service just like any other service mentioned before, so uses the same access protocols that have already been outlined. Any time an application needs a ticket that has not already been requested, it contacts the ticket-granting server. This request consists of the following components:

- the requested principal
- the ticket-granting ticket
- an authenticator

Like any other server, the ticket-granting server now checks the ticket-granting ticket and the authenticator. If they are considered valid, the ticket-granting server builds a new session key to be used between the original client and the new server. Then the ticket for the new server is built, containing the following information:

- the client's principal
- the server's principal
- the current time
- the client's IP address
- the newly-generated session key

The new ticket is assigned a lifetime, which is the lesser of the remaining lifetime of the ticket-granting ticket and the default for the service. The client receives this ticket and the session key, which are sent by the ticket-granting service, but this time the answer is encrypted with the session key that came with the original ticket-granting ticket. The client can decrypt the response without requiring the user's password when a new service is contacted. Kerberos can thus acquire ticket after ticket for the client without bothering the user more than once at login time.

Compatibility to Windows 2000 Windows 2000 contains a Microsoft implementation of Kerberos 5. As SuSE Linux makes use of the Heimdal implementation of Kerberos 5, you will find useful information and guidance in the Heimdal documentation. See *For More Information* on the following page.

Users' View of Kerberos

Ideally, a user's one and only contact with Kerberos happens during login at his workstation. The login process includes obtaining a ticket-granting ticket. At logout, a user's Kerberos tickets are automatically destroyed, which hinders anyone else from impersonating this user when not logged in. The automatic destruction of tickets can lead to a somewhat awkward situation when a user's login session lasts longer than the maximum lifespan given to the ticket-granting ticket (a reasonable setting is 10 hours). However, the user can get a new ticket-granting ticket by running kinit. He simply needs to type in his password again and Kerberos will make sure he gets access to any service he wants without being further troubled by authentication. Those interested in a list of all the tickets silently acquired for them by Kerberos should run klist.

Here is a short list of some applications that use Kerberos authentication. These applications can be found under `/usr/lib/heimdal/bin`. They all have the full functionality of their common UNIX and Linux brothers plus the additional bonus of transparent authentication managed by Kerberos:

- telnet, telnetd
- rlogin
- rsh, rcp, rshd
- popper, push
- ftp, ftpd
- su
- imapd
- pine

You will notice that you no longer have to type your password for using these applications because Kerberos has already proven your identity. ssh — if compiled with Kerberos support — can even forward all the tickets acquired for one workstation to another one. If you use ssh to log in to another workstation, ssh makes sure the encrypted contents of the tickets are adjusted to the new situation. Simply copying tickets between workstations is not sufficient as the ticket contains workstation specific information (the IP address). XDM and KDM offer Kerberos support, too. Read more about the Kerberos network applications in the *Kerberos V5 UNIX User's Guide* at http://web.mit.edu/kerberos/www/krb5-1.2/krb5-1.2.5/doc/user-guide_toc.html

For More Information

SuSE Linux contains a free implementation of Kerberos called Heimdal. Its documentation is installed along with the package `heimdal` under `/usr/share/doc/packages/heimdal/doc/heimdal.info`. It is also available at the project's home page at http://www.pdc.kth.se/heimdal/

This is the official site of the MIT Kerberos is http://web.mit.edu/kerberos/www/. There you will find links to any other relevant resource concerning Kerberos.

A "classical" dialogue pointing out the principles of Kerberos is available at http://web.mit.edu/kerberos/www/dialogue.html. It is a less technical but still comprehensive read.

The paper at `ftp://athena-dist.mit.edu/kerberos/doc/usenix.PS` gives quite an extensive insight to the basic principles of Kerberos without being too much of a hard read. It also provides a lot of opportunities for further investigation and reading on Kerberos.

These links provide a short introduction to Kerberos and answer many questions regarding Kerberos installation, configuration, and administration:
`http://web.mit.edu/kerberos/www/krb5-1.2/krb5-1.2.5/doc/user-guide_toc.html`
`http://www.lns.cornell.edu/public/COMP/krb5/install/install_toc.html`
`http://web.mit.edu/kerberos/www/krb5-1.2/krb5-1.2.5/doc/admin_toc.html`
The official Kerberos FAQ is available at `http://www.nrl.navy.mil/CCS/people/kenh/kerberos-faq.html`.

The book *Kerberos — A Network Authentication System* by Brian Tung (ISBN 0-201-37924-4) offers extensive information.

Security and Confidentiality

Basic Considerations

One of the main characteristics of a Linux or UNIX system is its ability to handle several users at the same time (multiuser) and to allow these users to perform several tasks (multitasking) on the same computer simultaneously. Moreover, the operating system is network transparent. The users often do not know whether the data and applications they are using are provided locally from their machine or made available over the network.

With the multiuser capability the respective data of different users must be stored separately. Security and privacy need to be guaranteed. "Data security" was already an important issue, even before computers could be linked through networks. Just like today, the most important concern was the ability to keep data available in spite of a lost or otherwise damaged data medium, a hard disk in most cases.

This chapter is primarily focused on confidentiality issues and on ways to protect the privacy of users, but it cannot be stressed enough that a comprehensive security concept should always include procedures to have a regularly updated, workable, and tested backup in place. Without this, you could have a very hard time getting your data back — not only in the case of some hardware defect, but also if the suspicion arises that someone has gained unauthorized access and tampered with files.

Local Security and Network Security

There are several ways of accessing data:

- Personal communication with people who have the desired information or access to the data on a computer
- directly from the console of a computer (physical access)
- over a serial line
- using a network link

In all these cases, a user should be authenticated before accessing the resources or data in question. A web server might be less restrictive in this respect, but you still would not want it to disclose all your personal data to any surfer out there.

In the list above, the first case is the one where the highest amount of human interaction is involved, such as when you are contacting a bank employee and are required to prove that you are the person owning that bank account. Then you will be asked to provide a signature, a PIN, or a password to prove that you are the person you claim to be. In some cases, it might be possible to elicit some intelligence from an informed person just by mentioning known bits and pieces here and there to win the confidence of that person by using clever rhethoric. The victim could be led to gradually reveal more information, maybe without even becoming aware of it. Among hackers, this is called "social engineering". You can only guard against this by educating people and by dealing with language and information in a conscious way. Before breaking into computer systems, attackers often try to target receptionists, service people working with the company, or even family members. In many cases, such an attack based on social engineering will only be discovered at a much later time.

A person wanting to obtain unauthorized access to your data could also use the traditional way and try to get at your hardware directly. Therefore, the machine should be protected against any tampering so that no one can remove, replace, or cripple its components. This also applies to backups and even any network cable or the power cord. Likewise, secure the boot procedure, as there are some well-known key combinations which invoke special reactions during booting. Protect yourself against this by setting passwords for the BIOS and the bootloader.

Serial terminals connected to serial ports are still used in many places. Unlike network interfaces, they do not rely on a network protocol to communicate with the host. A simple cable or an infrared port is used to send plain characters back and forth between the devices. The cable itself is the weakest point of such a system: with an older printer connected to it, it is easy to record anything that runs over the wires. What can be achieved with a printer can also be accomplished in other ways, depending on the effort that goes into the attack.

Reading a file locally on a host requires other access rules than opening a network connection with a server on a different host. There is a distinction between local security and network security. The line is drawn where data has to be put into packets to be sent somewhere else.

Local Security

Local security starts with the physical environment in the location where the computer is running. Set up your machine in a place where security is in line with your expectations and needs.

The main goal of "local security" is to keep users separate from each other, so that no user can assume the permissions or the identity of another. This is a general rule to be observed, but it is especially true for the user `root` who holds the supreme power on the system. User `root` can take on the identity of any other local user without being prompted for the password and read any locally stored file.

Passwords

On a Linux system, passwords are, of course, *not* stored as plain text and the text string entered is not simply matched with the saved pattern. If this were the case, all accounts on your system would be compromised as soon as someone got access to the corresponding file. Instead, the stored password is encrypted and, each time it is entered, is encrypted again and the two encrypted strings are compared. Naturally, this will only work if the encrypted password cannot be reverse-computed into the original text string. This is actually achieved by a special kind of algorithm, also called "trapdoor algorithm," because it only works in one direction. An attacker who has obtained the encrypted string will not be able to get your password by simply applying the same algorithm again. Instead, it would be necessary to test all the possible character combinations until a combination is found which looks like your password when encrypted. As you can imagine, with passwords eight characters long, there are quite a number of possible combinations to calculate.

In the seventies, it was argued that this method would be more secure than others due to the relative slowness of the algorithm used, which took a few seconds to encrypt just one password. In the meantime, however, PCs have become powerful enough to do several hundred thousand or even millions of encryptions per second. Because of this, encrypted passwords should not be visible to regular users (`/etc/shadow` cannot be read by normal users). It is even more important that passwords are not easy to guess, in case the password file becomes visible due to some error. Consequently, it is not really useful to "translate" a password like "tantalise" into "t@nt@1ls3".

Replacing some letters of a word with similar looking numbers is not safe enough. Password cracking programs which use dictionaries to guess words also play with substitutions like that. A better way is to make up a word with no common meaning, something which only makes sense to you personally, like the first letters of the words of a sentence or the title of a book, such as "The Name of the Rose" by Umberto Eco. This would give the following safe password: "TNotRbUE9". By contrast, passwords like "beerbuddy" or "jasmine76" are easily guessed even by someone who has only some casual knowledge about you.

The Boot Procedure

Configure your system so it cannot be booted from a floppy or from CD, either by removing the drives entirely or by setting a BIOS password and configuring the BIOS to allow booting from a hard disk only. Normally, a Linux system will be started by a boot loader, allowing you to pass additional options to the booted kernel. This is crucial to your system's security. Not only does the kernel itself run with root permissions, but it is also the first authority to grant root permissions at system start-up. Prevent others from using such parameters during boot by setting an additional password in `/etc/lilo.conf` (see *Booting and Boot Managers* on page 81).

File Permissions

As a general rule, always work with the most restrictive privileges possible for a given task. For example, it is definitely not necessary to be `root` to read or write e-mail. If the mail program has a bug, this bug could be exploited for an attack which will act with exactly the permissions of the program when it was started. By following the above rule, minimize the possible damage.

The permissions of the more than 200,000 files included in a SuSE distribution are carefully chosen. A system administrator who installs additional software or other files should take great care when doing so, especially when setting the permission bits. Experienced and security-conscious system administrators always use the `-l` option with the command `ls` to get an extensive file list, which allows them to detect any wrong file permissions immediately. An incorrect file attribute does not only mean that files could be changed or deleted. These modified files could be executed by `root` or, in the case of configuration files, that programs could use such files with the permissions of `root`. This significantly increases the possibilities of an attacker. Attacks like this are called cuckoo eggs, because the program (the egg) is executed (hatched) by a different user (bird), just like a cuckoo tricks other birds into hatching its eggs.

A SuSE Linux system includes the files `permissions`, `permissions.easy`, `permissions.secure`, and `permissions.paranoid`, all in the directory `/etc`. The purpose of these files is to define special permissions, such as world-writable directories or, for files, the setuser ID bits, which means the corresponding program will not run with the permissions of the user that has launched it, but with the permissions of the file owner, `root` in most cases. An administrator may use the file `/etc/permissions.local` to add his own settings. To define which of the above files is used by SuSE's configuration programs to set permissions accordingly use the submenu 'Security' in YaST2. To learn more about the topic, read the comments in `/etc/permissions` or consult the manual page of `chmod` (`man chmod`).

Buffer Overflows and Format String Bugs

Special care must be taken whenever a program is supposed to process data that can or could be changed by a user, but this is more of an issue for the programmer of an application than for regular users. The programmer has to make sure that his application will interpret data in the correct way, without writing them into memory areas that are too small to hold them. Also, the program should hand over data in a consistent manner, using the interfaces defined for that purpose.

A "buffer overflow" can happen if the actual size of a memory buffer is not taken into account when writing to that buffer. There are cases where this data (as generated by the user) uses up some more space than what is available in the buffer. As a result, data is written beyond the end of that buffer area, which, under certain circumstances, makes it possible that a program will execute program sequences influenced by the user (and not by the programmer), rather than just processing user data. A bug of this kind may have serious consequences, in particular if the program is being executed with special privileges (see Section *File Permissions* on the facing page).

"Format string bugs" work in a slightly different way, but again it is the user input which could lead the program astray. In most cases, these programming errors are exploited with programs executed with special permissions

— setuid and setgid programs — which also means that you can protect your data and your system from such bugs by removing the corresponding execution privileges from programs. Again, the best way is to apply a policy of using the lowest possible privileges (see Section *File Permissions* on page 448).

Given that buffer overflows and format string bugs are bugs related to the handling of user data, they are not only exploitable if access has been given to a local account. Many of the bugs that have been reported can also be exploited over a network link. Accordingly, buffer overflows and format string bugs should be classified as being relevant for both local and network security.

Viruses

Contrary to what some people will tell you, there *are* viruses that run on Linux. However, the viruses that are known were released by their authors as "proof of concept" to prove that the technique works as intended. None of these viruses have been spotted "in the wild" so far.

Viruses would not be able to survive and spread without a host on which they could live. In our case, the host would be a program or an important storage area of the system, such as the master boot record, which needs to be writable for the program code of the virus. Owing to its multiuser capability, Linux can restrict write access to certain files, especially important with system files. Therefore, if you did your normal work with `root` permissions, you would increase the chance of the system being infected by a virus. By contrast, if you follow the principle of using the lowest possible privileges as mentioned above, chances of getting a virus are slim.

Apart from that, you should never rush into executing a program from some Internet site that you do not really know. SuSE's RPM packages carry a cryptographic signature as a digital label that the necessary care was taken to build them. Viruses are a typical sign that the administrator or the user lacks the required security awareness, putting at risk even a system that should be highly secure by its very design.

Viruses should not be confused with worms which belong to the world of networks entirely. Worms do not need a host to spread.

Network Security

Network security is important for protecting from an attack originating in the network. The typical login procedure requiring a user name and a password for user authentication is a local security issue. However, in the particular case of logging in over a network, we need to differentiate between both security aspects. What happens until the actual authentication is network security and anything that happens afterwards is local security.

X Window System and X11 Authentication

As mentioned at the beginning, network transparency is one of the central characteristics of a UNIX system. X11, the windowing system of UNIX operating systems, can make use of this feature in an impressive way. With X11, it is basically no problem to log in at a remote host and start a graphical program that will then be sent over the network to be displayed on your computer.

For an X client to be displayed remotely using our X server, the latter is supposed to protect the resource managed by it (i.e. the display) from unauthorized access. In more concrete terms, certain permissions must be given to the client program. With the X Window System, there are two ways to do this, called host-based access control and cookie-based access control. The former relies on the IP address of the host where the client is supposed to run. The program to control this is `xhost`. `xhost` enters the IP address of a legitimate client into a tiny database belonging to the X server. However, relying on IP addresses for authentication is not very secure. For example, if there were a second user working on the host sending the client program, that user would have access to the X server as well — just like someone stealing the IP address. Because of these shortcomings, we will not describe this authentication method in more detail here, but you can learn about it from `man xhost`.

In the case of cookie-based access control, a character string is generated which is only known to the X server and to the legitimate user, just like an ID card of some kind. This cookie (the word goes back not to ordinary cookies, but to Chinese fortune cookies which contain an epigram) is stored on login in the file `.Xauthority` in the user's home directory and is available to any X Window client wanting to use the X server to display a window. The file `.Xauthority` can be examined by the user with the tool `xauth`. If you were to rename `.Xauthority` or if you deleted the file from your home directory by accident, you would not be able to open any new windows or X clients. Read more about X Window security mechanisms in the man page of `Xsecurity` (`man Xsecurity`).

`ssh` (secure shell) can be used to completely encrypt a network connection and forward it to an X server transparently without the encryption mechanism being perceived by the user. This is also called X forwarding. X forwarding is achieved by simulating an X server on the server side and setting a DISPLAY variable for the shell on the remote host. Further details

SuSE Linux – Administration Guide   451

about `ssh` can be found in Section *SSH — Secure Shell, the Safe Alternative* on page 433.

⌈─ **Caution** ──

If you do not consider the host where you log in to be a secure host, do not use X forwarding. With X forwarding enabled, an attacker could authenticate via your ssh connection to intrude on your X server and sniff your keyboard input, for instance.

── **Caution** ─⌋

Buffer Overflows and Format String Bugs

As discussed on on page 449, buffer overflows and format string bugs should be classified as issues concerning both local and network security. As with the local variants of such bugs, buffer overflows in network programs, when successfully exploited, are mostly used to obtain `root` permissions. Even if that is not the case, an attacker could use the bug to gain access to an unprivileged local account to exploit any other vulnerabilities which might exist on the system.

Buffer overflows and format string bugs exploitable over a network link are certainly the most frequent form of remote attacks in general. Exploits for these — programs to exploit these newly-found security holes — are often posted on the security mailing lists. They can be used to target the vulnerability without knowing the details of the code. Over the years, experience has shown that the availability of exploit codes has contributed to more secure operating systems, obviously due to the fact that operating system makers were forced to fix the problems in their software. With free software, anyone has access to the source code (SuSE Linux comes with all available source codes) and anyone who finds a vulnerability and its exploit code can submit a patch to fix the corresponding bug.

DoS — Denial of Service

The purpose of this kind of attack is to force down a server program or even an entire system, something which could be achieved by various means: overloading the server, keeping it busy with garbage packets, or exploiting a remote buffer overflow.

Often a DoS attack is done with the sole purpose of making the service disappear. However, once a given service has become unavailable, communications could become vulnerable to so-called "man-in-the-middle attacks" (sniffing, TCP connection hijacking, spoofing) and DNS poisoning.

Man in the Middle: Sniffing, Hijacking, Spoofing

In general, any remote attack performed by an attacker who puts himself between the communicating hosts is called a "man-in-the-middle attack". What almost all types of man-in-the-middle attacks have in common is that the victim is usually not aware that there is something happening. There are many possible variants, for example, the attacker could pick up a connection request and forward that to the target machine himself. Now the victim has unwittingly established a connection with the wrong host, because the other end is posing as the legitimate destination machine.

The simplest form of a man-in-the-middle attack is called "sniffer" — the attacker is "just" listening to the network traffic passing by. As a more complex attack, the "man in the middle" could try to take over an already established connection (hijacking). To do so, the attacker would have to analyze the packets for some time to be able to predict the TCP sequence numbers belonging to the connection. When the attacker finally seizes the role of the target host, the victims will notice this, because they get an error message saying the connection was terminated due to a failure. The fact that there are protocols not secured against hijacking through encryption, which only perform a simple authentication procedure upon establishing the connection, makes it easier for attackers.

"Spoofing" is an attack where packets are modified to contain counterfeit source data, mostly the IP address. Most active forms of attack rely on sending out such fake packets — something that, on a Linux machine, can only be done by the superuser (`root`).

Many of the attacks mentioned are carried out in combination with a DoS. If an attacker sees an opportunity to abruptly bring down a certain host, even if only for a short time, it will make it easier for him to push the active attack, because the host will not be able to interfere with the attack for some time.

DNS poisoning

DNS poisoning means that the attacker corrupts the cache of a DNS server by replying to it with spoofed DNS reply packets, trying to get the server to send certain data to a victim who is requesting information from that server. Many servers maintain a trust relationship with other hosts, based on IP addresses or host names. The attacker will need a good understanding of the actual structure of the trust relationships between hosts to dusguise itself as one of the trusted hosts. Usually, the attacker analyzes some packets received from the server to get the necessary information. The attacker often needs to target a well-timed DoS attack at the name server as well. Protect yourself by using encrypted connections that are able to verify the identity of the hosts to which to connect.

Worms

Worms are often confused with viruses, but there is a clear difference between the two. Unlike viruses, worms do not need to infect a host program to live. Rather, they are specialized to spread as quickly as possible on network structures. The worms that appeared in the past, such as Ramen, Lion, or Adore, make use of well-known security holes in server programs like `bind8` or `lprNG`. Protection against worms is relatively easy. Given that some time will elapse between the discovery of a security hole and the moment the worm hits your server, there is a good chance that an updated version of the affected program will be available on time. Of course, that is only useful if the administrator actually installs the security updates on the systems in question.

Some General Security Tips and Tricks

Information: To handle security competently, it is important to keep up with new developments and to stay informed about the latest security issues. One very good way to protect your systems against problems of all kinds is to get and install the updated packages recommended by security announcements as quickly as possible. SuSE security announcements are published on a mailing list to which you can subscribe by following the link `http://www.suse.de/security`. The list `suse-security-announce@suse.de` is a first-hand source of information regarding updated packages and includes members of SuSE's security team among its active contributors.

The mailing list `suse-security@suse.de` is a good place to discuss any security issues of interest. Subscribe to it under the URL as given above for `suse-security-announce@suse.de`.

`bugtraq@securityfocus.com` is one of the best-known security mailing lists worldwide. We recommend reading this list, which receives between 15 and 20 postings per day. More information can be found at `http://www.securityfocus.com`.

The following is a list of rules which you may find useful in dealing with basic security concerns:

- According to the rule of using the most restricive set of permissions possible for every job, avoid doing your regular jobs as `root`. This reduces the risk of getting a cuckoo egg or a virus and protects you from your own mistakes.

- If possible, always try to use encrypted connections to work on a remote machine. Use ssh (secure shell) to replace `telnet`, `ftp`, `rsh`, and `rlogin`.

- Avoid using authentication methods based on IP addresses alone.

- Try to keep the most important network-related packages up-to-date and subscribe to the corresponding mailing lists to receive announcements on new versions of such programs (`bind`, `sendmail`, `ssh`, etc.). The same should apply to software relevant to local security.

- Change the `/etc/permissions` file to optimize the permissions of files crucial to your system's security. If you remove the setuid bit from a program, it might well be that it cannot do its job anymore in the way it is supposed to. On the other hand, consider that, in most cases, the program will also have ceased to be a potential security risk. You might take a similar approach with world-writable directories and files.

- Disable any network services you do not absolutely require for your server to work properly. This will make your system safer. Open ports, with the socket state LISTEN, can be found with the program `netstat`. As for the options, we suggest that you use `netstat -ap` or `netstat -anp`. The `-p` option allows you to see which process is occupying a port under which name.

  Compare the `netstat` results with those of a thorough port scan done from outside your host. An excellent program for this job is `nmap`, which not only checks out the ports of your machine, but also draws some conclusions as to which services are waiting behind them. However, port scanning may be interpreted as an aggressive act, so do not do this on a host without the explicit approval of the administrator. Finally, remember that it is important not only to scan TCP ports, but also UDP ports (options `-sS` and `-sU`).

- To monitor the integrity of the files of your system in a reliable way, use the program `tripwire`, available on the SuSE Linux distribution. Encrypt the database created by `tripwire` to prevent someone from tampering with it. Furthermore, keep a backup of this database available outside your machine, stored on an external data medium not connected to it by a network link.

- Take proper care when installing any third-party software. There have been cases where a hacker had built a trojan horse into the tar archive of a security software package, which was fortunately discovered very quickly. If you install a binary package, have no doubts about the site from which you downloaded it.

  Note that SuSE's RPM packages are gpg-signed. The key used by SuSE for signing reads as follows:

ID:9C800ACA 2000-10-19 SuSE Package Signing Key <build@suse.de>

Key fingerprint = 79C1 79B2 E1C8 20C1 890F 9994 A84E DAE8 9C80 0ACA

The command `rpm --checksig package.rpm` shows whether the checksum and the signature of an uninstalled package are correct. Find the key on the first CD of the distribution and on most key servers worldwide.

- Check your backups of user and system files regularly. Consider that if you do not test whether the backup will work, it might actually be worthless.

- Check your log files. Whenever possible, write a small script to search for suspicious entries. Admittedly, this is not exactly a trivial task. In the end, only you can know which entries are unusual and which are not.

- Use `tcp_wrapper` to restrict access to the individual services running on your machine, so you have explicit control over which IP addresses can connect to a service. For further information regarding `tcp\_wrappers`, consult the manual page of `tcpd` and `hosts\_access` (man 8 tcpd, man hosts_access).

- Use SuSEfirewall to enhance the security provided by `tcpd` (tcp_wrapper).

- Design your security measures to be redundant: a message seen twice is much better than no message at all.

Using the Central Security Reporting Address

If you discover a security-related problem (please check the available update packages first), write an e-mail to `security@suse.de`. Please include a detailed description of the problem and the version number of the package concerned. SuSE will try to send a reply as soon as possible. You are encouraged to pgp encrypt your e-mail messages. SuSE's pgp key is as follows:

ID:3D25D3D9 1999-03-06 SuSE Security Team <security@suse.de>

Key fingerprint = 73 5F 2E 99 DF DB 94 C4 8F 5A A3 AE AF 22 F2 D5

This key is also available for download from: `http://www.suse.de/security`

Part V

Appendixes

File Systems in Linux

There are a number of file systems supported by Linux. This chapter presents a brief overview of the most popular Linux file systems, elaborating on their design concept, advantages, and fields of application. Some additional information on LFS "Large File Support" in Linux is also provided.

Glossary 460
Major File Systems in Linux 460
Some Other Supported File Systems 465
Large File Support in Linux 466
For More Information 467

Glossary

metadata A file system internal data structure that assures all the data on disk is properly organized and accessible. Essentially, it is "data about the data." Almost every file system has its own structure of metadata, which is partly why the file systems show different performance characteristics. It is of major importance to maintain metadata intact, because otherwise the whole file system could be corrupted.

inode Inodes contain all sorts of information about a file, including name, size, number of links, date, and time of creation, modification, and access, as well as pointers to the disk blocks where the file is actually stored.

journal In the context of a file system, a journal means an on-disk structure containing a kind of log where the file system driver enters what it is about to change in the file system's metadata. "Journaling" greatly reduces the recovery time of a Linux system as the file system driver does not need to initiate an exhaustive search for corrupt metadata all over the disk. Instead, the journal entries are replayed.

Major File Systems in Linux

Unlike two or three years ago, choosing a file system for your Linux system is no longer a matter of a few seconds ("Ext2 or ReiserFS?"). Kernels starting from 2.4 offer a variety of file systems from which to choose. The following is an overview of how those file systems basically work and which advantages they offer.

It is very important to bear in mind that there may be no file system that best suits all kinds of applications. Each file system has its particular strengths and weaknesses, which have to be taken into account. Even the most sophisticated file system in the world will never substitute for a reasonable backup strategy.

The terms "data integrity" or "data consistency", when used in this chapter, do not refer to the consistency of the user space data (the data your application writes to its files). Whether this data is consistent or not must be controlled by the application itself.

Ext2

The origins of Ext2 go back to the early days of Linux history. Its predecessor, the Extended File System, was implemented in April 1992 and integrated in Linux 0.96c. Extended File System underwent a number of modifications and, as Ext2, became the most popular Linux file system for years. With the creation of journaling file systems and their astonishingly short recovery times, Ext2 became less important.

A brief summary of Ext2's strenghts might help you to understand why it was — and in some areas still is — the favorite Linux file system of many a Linux user.

Solidity Being quite an "old–timer", Ext2 underwent many improvements and was heavily tested. This may be the reason why people often refer to it as "rock–solid". After a system outage when the file system could not be cleanly unmounted, e2fsck starts to analyze the file system data. Metadata is brought into a consistent state and pending files or data blocks are written to a designated directory (called `lost+found`). In contrast to (most of) the journaling file systems, e2fsck analyzes the whole file system and not just the recently modified bits of metadata. This takes significantly longer than the checking of the log data of a journaling file system. Depending on file system size, this procedure can take half an hour or more. Therefore, you would not choose Ext2 for any server that needs to be highly available. Yet, as Ext2 does not maintain a journal and uses significantly less memory, it is sometimes faster than other file systems.

Easy upgradability The code Ext2 is the strong foundation on which Ext3 could become a highly-acclaimed next-generation file system. Its reliability and solidity were elegantly combined with the advantages of a journaling file system.

Ext3

Ext3 was designed by Stephen Tweedie. In contrast to all other "next-generation" file systems, Ext3 does not follow a completely new design principle. It is based on Ext2. These two file systems are very closely related to each other. An Ext3 file system can be easily built on top of an Ext2 file system. The most important difference between Ext2 and Ext3 is that Ext3 supports journaling.

Summed up, Ext3 has three major advantages to offer:

Easy and highly reliable file system upgrades from Ext2 As Ext3 is based on the Ext2 code and shares its on-disk format as well as its metadata format, upgrades from Ext2 to Ext3 are incredibly easy. They can even be transformed while your Ext2 file systems are mounted. Unlike transitions to other journaling file systems, such as ReiserFS, JFS, or XFS, which can be quite tedious (making backups of the whole file system and recreating it from scratch), a transition to Ext3 is a matter of minutes. It is also very safe, as the recreation of a whole file system from scratch might not work flawlessly. Considering the number of existing Ext2 systems that await an upgrade to a journaling file system, you can easily figure out why Ext3 might be of some importance to many system administrators. Downgrading from Ext3 to Ext2 is as easy as the upgrade. Just perform a clean unmount of the Ext3 file system and remount it as an Ext2 file system.

Reliability and performance Other journaling file systems follow the "metadata-only" journaling approach. This means your metadata will always be kept in a consistent state but the same cannot be automatically guaranteed for the file system data itself. Ext3 is designed to take care of both metadata and data. The degree of "care" can be customized. Enabling Ext3 in the data=journal mode offers maximum security (i.e., data integrity), but can slow down the system as both metadata and data are journaled. A relatively new approach is to use the data=ordered mode, which ensures both data and metadata integrity, but uses journaling only for metadata. The file system driver collects all data blocks that correspond to one metadata update. These blocks are grouped as a "transaction" and will be written to disk before the metadata is updated. As a result, consistency is achieved for metadata and data without sacrificing performance. A third option to use is data=writeback which allows data to be written into the main file system after its metadata has been committed to the journal. This option is often considered the best in performance. It can, however, allow old data to reappear in files after crash and recovery while internal file system integrity is maintained. Unless you specify something else, Ext3 is run with the data=ordered default.

ReiserFS

Officially one of the key features of the 2.4 kernel release, ReiserFS has been available as a kernel patch for 2.2.x SuSE kernels since SuSE Linux version 6.4. ReiserFS was designed by Hans Reiser and the Namesys development team. ReiserFS has proven to be a powerful alternative to the old Ext2. Its key assets are better disk space utilization, better disk access performance, and faster crash recovery. However, there is a minor drawback: ReiserFS pays great care to metadata but not to the data itself. Future generations of ReiserFS will include data journaling (both metadata and actual data are written to the journal) as well as ordered writes.

ReiserFS's strengths, in more detail, are:

Better disk space utilization In ReiserFS, all data is organized in a structure called B*-balanced tree. The tree structure contributes in better disk space utilization as small files can be stored directly in the B*tree leaf nodes instead of being stored elsewhere and just maintaining a pointer to the actual disk location. In addition to that, storage is not allocated in chunks of 1 or 4 kB, but in portions of the exact size that is needed. Another benefit lies in the dynamic allocation of inodes. This keeps the file system more flexible in contrast to traditional file systems, like Ext2, where the inode density has to be specified at file system creation time.

Better disk access performance For small files, you will often find that both file data and "stat_data" (inode) information are stored next to each other. They can be read with a single disk IO operation, meaning that only one access to disk is required to retrieve all the information needed.

Fast crash recovery Using a journal to keep track of recent metadata changes makes a file system check a matter of seconds, even for huge file systems.

JFS

JFS, the "Journaling File System" was developed by IBM. The first beta version of the JFS Linux port reached the Linux community in the summer of 2000. Version 1.0.0 was released in 2001. JFS is tailored to suit the needs of high throughput server environments where performance is the ultimate goal. Being a full 64-bit file system, JFS supports both large files and partitions which is another pro for its use in server environments.

A closer look at JFS shows why this file system might prove a good choice for your Linux server:

Efficient journaling JFS follows a "metadata only" approach like ReiserFS. Instead of an extensive check, only metadata changes generated by recent file system activity get checked, which saves a great amount of time in recovery. Concurrent operations requiring multiple concurrent log entries can be combined into one group commit, greatly reducing performance loss of the file system through multiple write operations.

Efficient directory organization JFS holds to different directory organizations. For small directories, it allows the directory's content to be stored directly into its inode. For larger directories, it uses B$^+$trees, which greatly facilitate directory management.

Better space usage through dynamic inode allocation For Ext2, you have to define the inode density in advance (the space occupied by management information), which restricted the maximum number of files or directories of your file system. JFS spares you these considerations — it dynamically allocates inode space and frees it when it is no longer needed.

XFS

Originally intended as file system for their IRIX OS, SGI started XFS development back in the early 1990s. The idea behind XFS was to create a high-performance 64-bit journaling file system to meet the extreme computing challenges of today. XFS is very good at manipulating large files and performs well on high-end hardware. However, you will find a drawback even in XFS. Like ReiserFS, XFS takes a great deal of care of metadata integrity, but less of data integrity.

A quick review XFS's key features explains why it may prove a strong competitor for other journaling file systems in high-end computing.

High scalability through the use of allocation groups At creation time of an XFS file system, the block device underlying the file system is divided into eight or more linear regions of equal size. Those are referred to as "allocation groups". Each allocation group manages its own inodes and free disk space. Practically, allocation groups can be seen as "file systems in a file system." As allocation groups are rather independent of each other, more than one of them can be addressed by the kernel simultaneously. This feature is the key to XFS's great scalability. Naturally, the concept of independent allocation groups suits the needs of multiprocessor systems.

High performance through efficient management of disk space Free space and inodes are handled by B$^+$ trees inside the allocation groups. The use of B^+ trees greatly contributes to XFS's performance and scalability. A feature truly unique to XFS is "delayed allocation". XFS handles allocation by breaking the process into two pieces. A pending transaction is stored in RAM and the appropriate amount of space is reserved. XFS still does not decide where exactly (speaking of file system blocks) the data should be stored. This decision is delayed until the last possible moment. Some short-lived temporary data may never make its way to disk since they may be obsolete at the time XFS decides where to actually save them. Thus XFS increases write performance and reduces file system fragmentation. Since delayed allocation results in less frequent write events than in other file systems, it is likely that data loss after a crash during a write is more severe.

Preallocation to avoid file system fragmentation Before writing the data to the file system, XFS "reserves" (preallocates) the free space needed for a file. Thus, file system fragmentation is greatly reduced. Performance is increased as the contents of a file will not be distributed all over the file system.

User defined metadata — Extended attributes XFS offers a neat feature called "extended attributes", which will remind those familiar with MacOS of the "resource forks" on their systems. In XFS with extended attributes enabled, it is possible to associate any type of user-defined data (up to 64 kB) with a file system object. Those attributes will not be seen by any standard file operations, but with special function calls used by certain applications. Extended attributes help to distinguish between the file data and the metadata contained, such as comments.

Some Other Supported File Systems

Table A.1 on the following page summarizes some other file systems supported by Linux. They are supported mainly to ensure compatibility and interchange of data with different kinds of media or foreign operating systems.

`cramfs`	*Compressed ROM file system*: A compressed read-only file system for ROMs.
`hpfs`	*High Performance File System*: the IBM OS/2 standard file system — only supported in read-only mode.

Table A.1: continued overleaf...

iso9660	Standard file system on CD-ROMs.
minix	This file system originates from academic projects on operating systems and was the first file system used for Linux. Nowadays, it is used as a file system for floppy disks.
msdos	*fat*, the file system originally used DOS, used today by various operating systems.
ncpfs	file system for mounting Novell volumes over networks.
nfs	*Network File System*: Here, data can be stored on any machine in a network and access may be granted via a network.
smbfs	*Server Message Block*: used by products, such as Windows, to enable files to be accessed over a network.
sysv	Used on SCO UNIX, Xenix, and Coherent (commercial UNIX systems for PCs).
ufs	Used by BSD, SunOS, and NeXTstep. Only supported in *read-only* mode.
umsdos	*UNIX on MSDOS*: applied on top of a normal fat file system. Achieves UNIX functionality (permissions, links, long file names) by creating special files.
vfat	*Virtual FAT*: extension of the fat file system (supports long file names).
ntfs	*Windows NT file system*, read-only.

Table A.1: File System Types in Linux

Large File Support in Linux

Originally, Linux supported a maximum file size of 2 GB. This was enough as long as no one tried to manipulate huge databases on Linux. Becoming more and more important for server computing, the kernel and C library were modified to support file sizes larger than 2 GB when using a new set of interfaces that applications must utilize. Nowadays, (almost) all major file systems offer LFS support allowing you to perform high-end computing.

Table A.2 on the next page offers an overview of the current limitations of Linux files and file systems for Kernel 2.4. Hopefully the figures below will become outdated, with future kernel releases offering support for even larger files and file systems.

File System	File Size Limit	File System Size Limit
Ext2 or Ext3 (1 kB block size)	16448 MB (~16 GB)	2048 GB (2 TB)
Ext2 or Ext3 (2 kB block size)	256 GB	8192 GB (8 TB)
Ext2 or Ext3 (4 kB block size)	2048 GB (2 TB)	16384 GB (16 TB)
Ext2 or Ext3 (8 kB block size) Systems with 8 kB pages only (like Alpha)	65568 GB (~64 TB)	32768 GB (32 TB)
ReiserFS 3.5	4 GB	16384 GB (16 TB)
ReiserFS 3.6 (as in Linux 2.4)	2^{60} Bytes (1 EB)	16384 GB (16 TB)
XFS	2^{63} Bytes (8 EB)	2048 GB (2 TB) (Linux kernel limitation)
JFS (512 Bytes block size)	4194304 GB (4 PB)	512 TB
JFS (4 kB block size)	33554432 GB (32 PB)	4 PB

Table A.2: Maximum Sizes of File Systems

For More Information

Each of the file system projects described above maintains its own home page where you can find mailing list information as well as further documentation and FAQs.

```
http://e2fsprogs.sourceforge.net/ext2.html
http://www.zipworld.com.au/~akpm/linux/ext3/
http://www.namesys.com/
http://oss.software.ibm.com/developerworks/opensource/jfs/
http://oss.sgi.com/projects/xfs/
```

A comprehensive multipart tutorial on Linux file systems can be found at *IBM developerWorks*:
http://www-106.ibm.com/developerworks/library/l-fs.html

For a comparison of the different journaling file systems in Linux, look at Juan I. Santos Florido's article at *Linuxgazette*: http://www.linuxgazette.com/issue55/florido.html.

Those interested in an in-depth analysis of LFS in Linux should try Andreas Jaeger's LFS site: http://www.suse.de/~aj/linux_lfs.html.

Manual Page of e2fsck

E2FSCK(8)   E2FSCK(8)

NAME
       e2fsck - check a Linux second extended file system

SYNOPSIS
       e2fsck [-pacnyrdfvstFSV] [-b superblock] [-B block-
       size] [-l|-L bad_blocks_file] [-C fd] [-j external-
       journal] [device

DESCRIPTION
       e2fsck is used to check a Linux second extended file sys-
       tem (e2fs). E2fsck also supports ext2 filesystems coun-
       taining a journal, which are also sometimes known as ext3
       filesystems.

       device is the special file corresponding to the device
              (e.g /dev/hdc1).

OPTIONS
       -a   This option does the same thing as the -p option.
              It is provided for backwards compatibility only; it
              is suggested that people use -p option whenever
              possible.

       -b superblock
              Instead of using the normal superblock, use an
              alternative superblock specified by superblock.
              This option is normally used when the primary
              superblock has been corrupted. The location of the
              backup superblock is dependent on the filesystem's
              blocksize. For filesystems with 1k blocksizes, a
              backup superblock can be found at block 8193; for
              filesystems with 2k blocksizes, at block 16384; and
              for 4k blocksizes, at block 32768.

Additional backup superblocks can be determined by using the mke2fs program using the -n option to print out where the superblocks were created. The -b option to mke2fs, which specifies blocksize of the filesystem must be specified in order for the superblock locations that are printed out to be accurate.

If an alternative superblock is specified and the filesystem is not opened read-only, e2fsck will make sure that the primary superblock is updated appropriately upon completion of the filesystem check.

-B blocksize
    Normally, e2fsck will search for the superblock at various different block sizes in an attempt to find the appropriate block size. This search can be fooled in some cases. This option forces e2fsck to only try locating the superblock at a particular blocksize. If the superblock is not found, e2fsck will terminate with a fatal error.

-c   This option causes e2fsck to run the badblocks(8) program to find any blocks which are bad on the filesystem, and then marks them as bad by adding them to the bad block inode.

-C   This option causes e2fsck to write completion information to the specified file descriptor so that the progress of the filesystem check can be monitored. This option is typically used by programs which are running e2fsck. If the file descriptor specified is 0, e2fsck will print a completion bar as it goes about its business. This requires that e2fsck is running on a video console or terminal.

-d   Print debugging output (useless unless you are debugging e2fsck).

-f   Force checking even if the file system seems clean.

-F   Flush the filesystem device's buffer caches before beginning. Only really useful for doing e2fsck time trials.

-j external-journal
    Set the pathname where the external-journal for this filesystem can be found.

-l filename

Add the blocks listed in the file specified by filename to the list of bad blocks. The format of this file is the same as the one generated by the badblocks(8) program.

-L filename
Set the bad blocks list to be the list of blocks specified by filename. (This option is the same as the -l option, except the bad blocks list is cleared before the blocks listed in the file are added to the bad blocks list.)

-n Open the filesystem read-only, and assume an answer of 'no' to all questions. Allows e2fsck to be used non-interactively. (Note: if the -c, -l, or -L options are specified in addition to the -n option, then the filesystem will be opened read-write, to permit the bad-blocks list to be updated. However, no other changes will be made to the filesystem.)

-p Automatically repair ("preen") the file system without any questions.

-r This option does nothing at all; it is provided only for backwards compatibility.

-s This option will byte-swap the filesystem so that it is using the normalized, standard byte-order (which is i386 or little endian). If the filesystem is already in the standard byte-order, e2fsck will take no action.

-S This option will byte-swap the filesystem, regardless of its current byte-order.

-t Print timing statistics for e2fsck. If this option is used twice, additional timing statistics are printed on a pass by pass basis.

-v Verbose mode.

-V Print version information and exit.

-y Assume an answer of 'yes' to all questions; allows e2fsck to be used non-interactively.

EXIT CODE
The exit code returned by e2fsck is the sum of the following conditions:
    0 - No errors
    1 - File system errors corrected
    2 - File system errors corrected, system should be rebooted if file system was mounted
    4 - File system errors left uncorrected

```
       8    - Operational error
      16    - Usage or syntax error
     128    - Shared library error
```

SIGNALS
       The following signals have the following effect when sent
       to e2fsck.

       SIGUSR1
              This signal causes e2fsck to start displaying a
              completion bar. (See discussion of the -C option.)

       SIGUSR2
              This signal causes e2fsck to stop displaying a com-
              pletion bar.

REPORTING BUGS
       Almost any piece of software will have bugs. If you man-
       age to find a filesystem which causes e2fsck to crash, or
       which e2fsck is unable to repair, please report it to the
       author.

       Please include as much information as possible in your bug
       report. Ideally, include a complete transcript of the
       e2fsck run, so I can see exactly what error messages are
       displayed. If you have a writeable filesystem where the
       transcript can be stored, the script(1) program is a handy
       way to save the output of e2fsck to a file.

       It is also useful to send the output of dumpe2fs(8). If a
       specific inode or inodes seems to be giving e2fsck trou-
       ble, try running the debugfs(8) command and send the out-
       put of the stat(1u) command run on the relevant inode(s).
       If the inode is a directory, the debugfs dump command will
       allow you to extract the contents of the directory inode,
       which can sent to me after being first run through uuen
       code(1).

       Always include the full version string which e2fsck dis-
       plays when it is run, so I know which version you are run-
       ning.

AUTHOR
       This version of e2fsck was written by Theodore Ts'o
       <tytso@mit.edu>.

SEE ALSO
       mke2fs(8), tune2fs(8), dumpe2fs(8), debugfs(8)

E2fsprogs version 1.25   September 2001   E2FSCK(8)

The GNU General Public License

GNU General Public License

Copyright (C) 1989, 1991 Free Software Foundation, Inc.

59 Temple Place, Suite 330, Boston, MA 02111-1307, USA

Copyright (C) 1989, 1991 Free Software Foundation, Inc. 675 Mass Ave, Cambridge, MA 02139, USA Everyone is permitted to copy and distribute verbatim copies of this license document, but changing it is not allowed.

Foreword

The licenses for most software are designed to take away your freedom to share and change it. By contrast, the *GNU General Public License* is intended to guarantee your freedom to share and change free software — to make sure the software is free for all its users. This *General Public License* applies to most of the *Free Software Foundation's* software and to any other program whose authors commit to using it. (Some other *Free Software Foundation* software is covered by the *GNU Library General Public License* instead.) You can apply it to your programs, too.

When we speak of *"free" software*, we are referring to freedom, not price. Our General Public Licenses are designed to make sure that you have the freedom to distribute copies of free software (and charge for this service if you wish), that you receive source code or can get it if you want it, that you can change the software or use pieces of it in new free programs; and that you know you can do these things.

To protect your rights, we need to make restrictions that forbid anyone to deny you these rights or to ask you to surrender the rights. These restrictions translate to certain responsibilities for you if you distribute copies of the software, or if you modify it.

For example, if you distribute copies of such a program, whether gratis or for a fee, you must give the recipients all the rights that you have. You must make sure that they, too, receive or can get the source code. And you must show them these terms so they know their rights.

We protect your rights with two steps: (1) copyright the software, and (2) offer you this license which gives you legal permission to copy, distribute and/or modify the software.

Also, for each author's protection and ours, we want to make certain that everyone understands that there is no warranty for this free software. If the software is modified by someone else and passed on, we want its recipients to know that what they have is not the original, so that any problems introduced by others will not reflect on the original authors' reputations.

Finally, any free program is threatened constantly by software patents. We wish to avoid the danger that redistributors of a free program will individually obtain patent licenses, in effect making the program proprietary. To prevent this, we have made it clear that any patent must be licensed for everyone's free use or not licensed at all.

The precise terms and conditions for copying, distribution and modification follow.

GNU General, Public License

Terms and Conditions for Copying, Distribution and Modification

0. This License applies to any program or other work which contains a notice placed by the copyright holder saying it may be distributed under the terms of this *General Public License*. The "Program", below, refers to any such program or work, and a *work based on the Program* means either the Program or any derivative work under copyright law: that is to say, a work containing the Program or a portion of it, either verbatim or with modifications and/or translated into another language. (Hereinafter, translation is included without limitation in the term "modification".) Each licensee is addressed as "you".

Activities other than copying, distribution and modification are not covered by this License; they are outside its scope. The act of running the Program is not restricted, and the output from the Program is covered only if its contents constitute a work based on the Program (independent of having been made by running the Program). Whether that is true depends on what the Program does.

1. You may copy and distribute verbatim copies of the Program's source code as you receive it, in any medium, provided that you conspicuously and appropriately publish on each copy an appropriate copyright notice and disclaimer of warranty; keep intact all the notices that refer to this License and to the absence of any warranty; and give any other recipients of the Program a copy of this License along with the Program.

You may charge a fee for the physical act of transferring a copy, and you may at your option offer warranty protection in exchange for a fee.

2. You may modify your copy or copies of the Program or any portion of it, thus forming a work based on the Program, and copy and distribute such modifications or work under the terms of Section 1 above, provided that you also meet all of these conditions:

   a) You must cause the modified files to carry prominent notices stating that you changed the files and the date of any change.

   b) You must cause any work that you distribute or publish, that in whole or in part contains or is derived from the Program or any part thereof, to be licensed as a whole at no charge to all third parties under the terms of this License.

   c) If the modified program normally reads commands interactively when run, you must cause it, when started running for such interactive use in the most ordinary way, to print or display an announcement including an appropriate copyright notice and a notice that there is no warranty (or else, saying that you provide a warranty) and that users may redistribute the program under these conditions, and telling the user how to view a copy of this License. (Exception: if the Program itself is interactive but does not normally print such an announcement, your work based on the Program is not required to print an announcement.)

These requirements apply to the modified work as a whole. If identifiable sections of that work are not derived from the Program, and can be reasonably considered independent and separate works in themselves, then this License, and its terms, do not apply to those sections when you distribute them as separate works. But when you distribute the same sections as part of a whole which is a work based on the Program, the distribution of the whole must be on the terms of this License, whose permissions for other licensees extend to the entire whole, and thus to each and every part regardless of who wrote it.

Thus, it is not the intent of this section to claim rights or contest your rights to work written entirely by you; rather, the intent is to exercise the right to control the distribution of derivative or collective works based on the Program.

In addition, mere aggregation of another work not based on the Program with the Program (or with a work based on the Program) on a volume of a storage or distribution medium does not bring the other work under the scope of this License.

3. You may copy and distribute the Program (or a work based on it, under Section 2) in object code or executable form under the terms of Sections 1 and 2 above provided that you also do one of the following:

- a) Accompany it with the complete corresponding machine–readable source code, which must be distributed under the terms of Sections 1 and 2 above on a medium customarily used for software interchange; or,

- b) Accompany it with a written offer, valid for at least three years, to give any third party, for a charge no more than your cost of physically performing source distribution, a complete machine–readable copy of the corresponding source code, to be distributed under the terms of Sections 1 and 2 above on a medium customarily used for software interchange; or,

- c) Accompany it with the information you received as to the offer to distribute corresponding source code. (This alternative is allowed only for noncommercial distribution and only if you received the program in object code or executable form with such an offer, in accord with Subsection b above.)

The source code for a work means the preferred form of the work for making modifications to it. For an executable work, "complete source code" means all the source code for all modules it contains, plus any associated interface definition files, plus the scripts used to control compilation and installation of the executable. However, as a special exception, the source code distributed need not include anything that is normally distributed (in either source or binary form) with the major components (compiler, kernel, and so on) of the operating system on which the executable runs, unless that component itself accompanies the executable.

If distribution of executable or object code is made by offering access to copy from a designated place, then offering equivalent access to copy the source code from the same place counts as distribution of the source code, even though third parties are not compelled to copy the source along with the object code.

4. You may not copy, modify, sublicense, or distribute the Program except as expressly provided under this License. Any attempt otherwise to copy, modify, sublicense or distribute the Program is void, and will automatically terminate your rights under this License. However, parties who have received copies, or rights, from you under this License will not have their licenses terminated so long as such parties remain in full compliance.

5. You are not required to accept this License, since you have not signed it. However, nothing else grants you permission to modify or distribute the Program or its derivative works. These actions are prohibited by law if you do not accept this License. Therefore, by modifying or distributing the Program (or any work based on the Program), you indicate your acceptance of this License to do so, and all its terms and conditions for copying, distributing or modifying the Program or works based on it.

6. Each time you redistribute the Program (or any work based on the Program), the recipient automatically receives a license from the original licensor to copy, distribute or modify the Program subject to these terms and conditions. You may not impose any further restrictions on the recipients' exercise of the rights granted herein. You are not responsible for enforcing compliance by third parties to this License.

7. If, as a consequence of a court judgment or allegation of patent infringement or for any other reason (not limited to patent issues), conditions are imposed on you (whether by court order, agreement or otherwise) that contradict the conditions of this License, they do not excuse you from the conditions of this License. If you cannot distribute so as to satisfy simultaneously your obligations under this License and any other pertinent obligations, then as a consequence you may not distribute the Program at all. For example, if a patent license would not permit royalty-free redistribution of the Program by all those who receive copies directly or indirectly through you, then the only way you could satisfy both it and this License would be to refrain entirely from distribution of the Program.

If any portion of this section is held invalid or unenforceable under any particular circumstance, the balance of the section is intended to apply and the section as a whole is intended to apply in other circumstances.

It is not the purpose of this section to induce you to infringe any patents or other property right claims or to contest validity of any such claims; this section has the sole purpose of protecting the integrity of the free software distribution system, which is implemented by public license practices. Many people have made generous contributions to the wide range of software distributed through that system in reliance on consistent application of that system; it is up to the author/donor to decide if he or she is willing to distribute software through any other system and a licensee cannot impose that choice.

This section is intended to make thoroughly clear what is believed to be a consequence of the rest of this License.

8. If the distribution and/or use of the Program is restricted in certain countries either by patents or by copyrighted interfaces, the original copyright holder who places the Program under this License may add an explicit geographical distribution limitation excluding those countries, so that distribution is permitted only in or among countries not thus excluded. In such case, this License incorporates the limitation as if written in the body of this License.

9. The *Free Software Foundation* may publish revised and/or new versions of the *General Public License* from time to time. Such new versions will be similar in spirit to the present version, but may differ in detail to address new problems or concerns.

Each version is given a distinguishing version number. If the Program specifies a version number of this License which applies to it and "any later version", you have the option of following the terms and conditions either of that version or of any later version published by the *Free Software Foundation*. If the Program does not specify a version number of this License, you may choose any version ever published by the *Free Software Foundation*.

10. If you wish to incorporate parts of the Program into other free programs whose distribution conditions are different, write to the author to ask for permission. For software which is copyrighted by the *Free Software Foundation*, write to the *Free Software Foundation*; we sometimes make exceptions for this.

Our decision will be guided by the two goals of preserving the free status of all derivatives of our free software and of promoting the sharing and reuse of software generally.

No Warranty

11. Because the program is licensed free of charge, there is no warranty for the program, to the extent permitted by applicable law. Except when otherwise stated in writing the copyright holders and/or other parties provide the program "as is" without warranty of any kind, either expressed or implied, including, but not limited to, the implied warranties of merchantability and fitness for a particular purpose. The entire risk as to the quality and performance of the program is with you. Should the program prove defective, you assume the cost of all necessary servicing, repair or correction.

12. In no event unless required by applicable law or agreed to in writing will any copyright holder, or any other party who may modify and/or redistribute the program as permitted above, be liable to you for damages, including any general, special, incidental or consequential damages arising out of the use or inability to use the program (including but not limited to loss of data or data being rendered inaccurate or losses sustained by you or third parties or a failure of the program to operate with any other programs), even if such holder or other party has been advised of the possibility of such damages.

End of Terms and Conditions

How to Apply These Terms to Your New Programs

If you develop a new program, and you want it to be of the greatest possible use to the public, the best way to achieve this is to make it free software which everyone can redistribute and change under these terms.

To do so, attach the following notices to the program. It is safest to attach them to the start of each source file to most effectively convey the exclusion of warranty; and each file should have at least the "copyright" line and a pointer to where the full notice is found.

> *one line to give the program's name and a brief idea of what it does.*
> Copyright (C) 19*yy* *name of author*
>
> This program is free software; you can redistribute it and/or modify it under the terms of the GNU General Public License as

published by the Free Software Foundation; either version 2 of the License, or (at your option) any later version.

This program is distributed in the hope that it will be useful, but WITHOUT ANY WARRANTY; without even the implied warranty of MERCHANTABILITY or FITNESS FOR A PARTICULAR PURPOSE. See the GNU General Public License for more details.

You should have received a copy of the GNU General Public License along with this program; if not, write to the Free Software Foundation, Inc., 675 Mass Ave, Cambridge, MA 02139, USA.

Also add information on how to contact you by electronic and paper mail.

If the program is interactive, make it output a short notice like this when it starts in an interactive mode:

Gnomovision version 69, Copyright (C) 19*yy* *name of author*
Gnomovision comes with ABSOLUTELY NO WARRANTY; for details type 'show w'. This is free software, and you are welcome to redistribute it under certain conditions; type 'show c' for details.

The hypothetical commands `show w` and `show c` should show the appropriate parts of the General Public License. Of course, the commands you use may be called something other than `show w` and `show c`; they could even be mouse-clicks or menu items — whatever suits your program.

You should also get your employer (if you work as a programmer) or your school, if any, to sign a "copyright disclaimer" for the program, if necessary. Here is a sample; alter the names:

Yoyodyne, Inc., hereby disclaims all copyright interest in the program 'Gnomovision' (which makes passes at compilers) written by James Hacker.
Signed by Ty Coon, 1 April 1989
Ty Coon, President of Vice

This *General Public License* does not permit incorporating your program into proprietary programs. If your program is a subroutine library, you may consider it more useful to permit linking proprietary applications with the library. If this is what you want to do, use the *GNU Library General Public License* instead of this License.

Bibliography

[Alm94] ALMESBERGER, Werner: *LILO User's guide*, 1994. – (see file `/usr/doc/lilo/user.dvi`)

[Bai97] BAILEY, Edward C.: *Maximum RPM*. Red Hat, 1997. – (ISBN 1-888172-78-9)

[CAR93] COSTALES, Bryan; ALLMAN, Eric ; RICKERT, Neil: *sendmail*. O'Reilly & Associates, Inc., 1993. – (ISBN 1-56592-056-2)

[CB96] CHESWICK, William R.; BELLOVIN, Steven M.: *Firewalls und Sicherheit im Internet*. Addison Wesley GmbH, 1996. – (ISBN 3-89319-875-x)

[CR91] CAMERON, Debra; ROSENBLATT, Bill: *Learning GNU Emacs*. O'Reilly & Associates, Inc., 1991. – (ISBN 0 937175-84-6)

[CZ96] CHAPMAN; ZWICKY: *Einrichten von Internet Firewalls. Sicherheit im Internet gewährleisten.*. O'Reilly & Associates, Inc., 1996. – (ISBN 3-930673312)

[Daw95] DAWSON, Terry: *Linux NET-2/NET-3 HOWTO*, v2.8, 07 Jan 1995. – (see file `/usr/doc/howto/NET-2-HOWTO`)

[FCR93] FANG, Chin; CROSSON, Bob ; RAYMOND, Eric S.: *The Hitchhiker's Guide to X386/XFree86 Video Timing (or, Tweaking your Monitor for Fun and Profit)*, 1993. – (see file `/usr/X11/lib/X11/doc/VideoModes.doc`)

[Fri93] FRISCH, Æleen: *Essential System Administration*. O'Reilly & Associates, Inc., 1993. – (ISBN 0-937175-80-3)

[Gil92] GILLY, Daniel: *UNIX in a nutshell: System V Edition*. O'Reilly & Associates, Inc., 1992. – (ISBN 1-56592-001-5)

[GMS93] GOOSSENS, Michel; MITTELBACH, Frank ; SAMARIN, Alexander: *The LaTeX Companion*. Addison Wesley GmbH, 1993. – (ISBN 3-54199-8)

[Gri94] GRIEGER, W.: *Wer hat Angst vorm Emacs?*. Addison Wesley GmbH, 1994. – (ISBN 3-89319-620-X)

[GS93] GARFINKEL, Simson; SPAFFORD, Gene: *Practical UNIX Security*. O'Reilly & Associates, Inc., 1993. – (ISBN 0-937175-72-2)

[Her92] HEROLD, H.: *UNIX Grundlagen*. Addison Wesley GmbH, 1992. – (ISBN 3-89319-542-8)

[HHMK96] HETZE, Sebastian; HOHNDEL, Dirk; MÜLLER, Martin ; KIRCH, Olaf: *Linux Anwenderhandbuch*. 6. LunetIX Softfair, 1996. – (ISBN 3-929764-05-9)

[Hof97] HOFFMANN, Erwin: EMail-Gateway mit qmail. In: *iX* 12 (1997), S. 108ff

[Hun95] HUNT, Craig: *TCP/IP Netzwerk Administration*. O'Reilly & Associates, Inc., 1995. – (ISBN 3-930673-02-9)

[Kie95] KIENLE, Micheal: TIS: Toolkit für anwendungsorientierte Firewall-Systeme. In: *iX* 8 (1995), S. 140ff

[Kir95] KIRCH, Olaf: *LINUX Network Administrator's Guide*. O'Reilly & Associates, Inc., 1995. – (ISBN 1-56592-087-2)

[Kof95] KOFLER, M.: *Linux*. Addison Wesley GmbH, 1995. – (ISBN 3-89319-796-6)

[Kop94] KOPKA, Helmut: *LaTeX-Einführung*. Addison Wesley GmbH, 1994. – (ISBN 3-89319-664-1)

[Kun95] KUNITZ, Ulrich: Sicherheit fast kostenlos: Einrichtung eines kostenlosen Firewall-Systems. In: *iX* 9 (1995), S. 176ff

[Lam90] LAMB, Linda: *Learning the vi Editor*. O'Reilly & Associates, Inc., 1990. – (ISBN 0-937175-67-6)

[Lam94] LAMPORT, Leslie: *LaTeX User's Guide and Reference Manual*. Addison Wesley GmbH, 1994. – (ISBN 0-201-52983-1)

[Lef96a] LEFFLER, Sam: *HylaFAX Home Page*, 1996

[Lef96b] LEFFLER, Sam: *TIFF Software*, 1996

[OT92]   O'REILLY, Tim; TODINO, Grace: *Manging UUCP and Usenet*.
          O'Reilly & Associates, Inc., 1992. – (ISBN 0-937175-93-5)

[Per94]   PERLMAN, G.: *Unix For Software Developers*. Prentice-Hall, 1994. –
          (ISBN 13-932997-8)

[Pug94]   PUGH, K.: *UNIX For The MS-DOS User*. Prentice-Hall, 1994. –
          (ISBN 13-146077-3)

[SB92]   SCHOONOVER, M.; BOWIE, J.: *GNU Emacs*. Addison Wesley
          GmbH, 1992. – (ISBN 0-201-56345-2)

[Sch98]   SCHEIDERER, Jürgen: Sicherheit Kostenlos - Firewall mit Linux.
          In: *iX* 12 (1998)

[Sto98]   STOLL, Clifford: *Kuckucksei; Die Jagd auf die deutschen Hacker, die
          das Pentagon knackten*. Fischer-TB.-Vlg., 1998. – (ISBN 3596139848)

[SuS02a] *SuSE Linux. Basics*. 1. Nürnberg : SuSE Linux AG, 2002

[SuS02b] *SuSE Linux. User Guide*. 1. Nürnberg : SuSE Linux AG, 2002

[SuS02c] *SuSE Linux. Applications*. 1. Nürnberg : SuSE Linux AG, 2002

[The96]   THE XFREE86™-TEAM: *XF86Config(4/5) - Configuration File for
          Xfree86™*, 1996. – Manual-Page zu XFree86™

[TSP93]   TODINO, Grace; STRANG, John ; PEEK, Jerry: *Learning the UNIX
          operating system*. O'Reilly & Associates, Inc., 1993. – (ISBN 1-
          56592-060-0)

[Wel94]   WELSH, Matt: *Linux Installation and Getting Started*. 2. SuSE Linux
          AG, 1994. – (ISBN 3-930419-03-3)

[WK95]   WELSH, Matt; KAUFMAN, Lars: *Running Linux*. O'Reilly & Associates, Inc., 1995. – (ISBN 1-56592-100-3)

Index

symbols
3D 146–150
   - SaX2 and 117
   - testing 149
   - troubleshooting 149
3Ddiag 148, 149

A
addresses
   - IP 339
   - MAC 339
ADSL
   - configuring 408
   - dial-on-demand 408
   - starting 408
ALSA 151–156
   - MIDI 154
   - PCM types 152
Apache 271
   - Squid 422
APM 323
   - kernel parameters 41
AppleTalk .... see Netatalk
apsfilter
   - network printer 224

B
Bash
   - .bashrc 271
   - .profile 271
   - profile 271
BIND 361–369
   - BIND8 363
   - BIND9 363
BIOS 82
   - LILO and 86

   - virus protection 14
boot disks
   - creating in a Unix-related system 20
   - creating in DOS 19
   - creating with rawrite 19
   - installing with 9, 18
booting 81–111, 295–331
   - BIOS 82
   - boot disks 13
   - boot graphics 93
   - boot loaders 42, 277
   - boot managers 81–111
   - boot sectors 82–83
   - CD2 18
   - chaining 84
   - CMOS 82
   - concepts 83
   - DOS 83
   - floppy, from 83
   - graphic 15
     · disabling 15
   - GRUB 100–102
   - initial ramdisk 276
   - LILO 14, 85
   - loadlin 14, 104–111
   - logical partitions 87
   - message files 93
   - methods 13
   - sample configurations 97
   - securing 90, 94
   - system freezes ...... see BIOS, virus protection
   - viruses 86
   - Windows 83

C

cardctl 244
cardmgr 351
cards
 - network
  · hotplugging 241
  · testing 349
 - PCMCIA 244–254, 351
  · removing 246
 - wireless 351
CD-ROM
 - ATAPI 21
 - parallel port drives 23
 - supported drives 21
clients
 - diskless 383
CMOS 82
color depths
 - SaX2 and 122
commands
 - cardctl 253
 - free 275
 - ifport 252
 - lpr 172
 - mii_tool 252
compressing
 - audio data 152
configuration files 353
 - .Xmodmap 127
 - .bashrc 271, 274
 - .config 263
 - .profile 271
 - .xsession 437
 - afpd.conf 395
 - AppleVolumes.default 396
 - AppleVolumes.system 398
 - atalk 395
 - atalkd.conf 395
 - crontab 271
 - csh.cshrc 293
 - defaultdomain 373
 - dhcp 353
 - dhcpd.conf 380
 - exports 377, 378, 421
 - fstab 289
 - group 327
 - groups 373
 - host.conf 302, 354
  · alert 355
  · multi 355
  · nospoof 355
  · order 354
  · trim 355
 - HOSTNAME 358
 - hosts 327, 354
 - hotplug 240, 241
 - httpd.conf 271
 - ifcfg-* 353
 - inetd.conf 391
 - inittab 291, 296–298, 329
 - kernel 279
 - language 292, 293
 - lilo.conf 88–94, 133, 268
 - localtime 309
 - logrotate.conf 273
 - lpd.conf 180
 - lpd.perms 180
 - lpdfilter 185, 186
 - menu.lst 100
 - modules.conf 173–175, 265–266
 - named.conf 361–369, 414
 - netatalk.conf 400
 - network 353
 - networks 354
 - nscd.conf 357
 - nsswitch.conf 355
 - ntp.conf 330
 - nwserv.conf 401
 - options 429
 - papd.conf 398
 - passwd 327, 373
 - pcmcia 245, 246, 248, 250
 - permissions 455
 - printcap 179, 185, 327
 - profile 271, 274, 293
 - rc.config 265, see configuration files, sysconfig
  · START variables 41
 - resolv.conf 275, 357, 413
 - routes 359
 - sendmail.cf 317
 - services 391
 - smb.conf 386, 387
 - squid 414
 - squid.conf 413–420, 423, 425
 - squidguard.conf 425
 - sshd_config 438
 - suseconfig 303
 - SuSEfirewall2 431–433
 - suseservers 322
 - sysconfig 41, 301–304
 - syslinux.cfg 18
 - TextConfig 310
 - wireless 353
 - XF86Config 115, 120, 134, 138
  · device 141

```
             · monitor ....................... 142
             · screen ........................ 140
           - yp.conf ..................... 330, 373
           - ypbind .......................... 374
        configuring ............................ 301
           - DHCP ........................... 380
           - DNS ............................ 361
           - IPv6 ............................ 351
           - Netatalk ........................ 395
           - networks
             · manually ................. 352-360
           - printing ..................... 165-172
           - routing ........................ 359
           - Samba ..................... 387-392
           - Squid .......................... 414
           - system ......................... 303
           - YaST2 ........................... 61
        console background
           - graphical  see SuSE screen, deactivate
        consoles
           - assigning ....................... 291
           - fonts ........................... 309
           - framebuffer ..................... 309
           - switching ................. 116, 291
        core files ............................ 274
        cron ............................. 271, 310
           - removing core files ............. 311
           - removing temporary files ....... 310

        D
        daemons
           - autofs .......................... 308
           - lpd ............................. 179
           - ssh ............................. 326
        depmod ................................ 265
        DHCP ........................ 319, 379-383
           - configuring ................. 380-383
           - dhcpd ....................... 380-382
           - packages ....................... 379
           - server ...................... 380-382
           - starting ........................ 381
           - static .......................... 382
        digital cameras
           - hotplugging ..................... 240
        Direct3D .............................. 146
        disks
           - boot
             · creating ...................... 102
        DMA
           - disabling ....................... 313
           - enabling ........................ 313
        DNS .............................. 342-343
           - BIND ....................... 361-369

           - configuring ................. 361-370
           - forwarding ..................... 362
           - logging ......................... 364
           - mail exchanger .................. 343
           - NIC ............................. 343
           - options ......................... 363
           - reverse lookup .................. 368
           - security and .................... 453
           - server ........................... 77
           - Squid and ....................... 414
           - starting ........................ 361
           - top level domain ................ 343
           - troubleshooting ................. 361
           - zones ........................... 365
             · files .......................... 366
        DOS
           - sharing files ................... 386
        DVB cards ............................. 312
        Dynamic Host Configuration Protocol ... see
                           DHCP

        E
        e-mail
           - configuring with YaST2 .......... 76
        e2fsck
           - man page ....................... 469
        environment variables
           - CUPS_SERVER ................... 199
           - PRINTER ........................ 181

        F
        FHS ................... see file systems, FHS
        file systems ....................... 459-468
           - Ext2 ............................ 461
           - Ext3 ........................ 461-462
           - FHS ............................. 270
           - intermezzo ...................... 314
           - JFS ......................... 463-464
           - limitations ..................... 466
           - ReiserFS .................... 462-463
           - repairing ....................... 290
           - selecting ....................... 460
           - supported ................... 465-466
           - terms ........................... 460
           - TeX and ......................... 270
           - usbdefs ......................... 239
           - XFS ......................... 464-465
        files
           - large ....................... 466-467
           - ogg ............................. 153
           - printing .............. 181, 183, 205
        firewalls ....................... 428-430, 433
           - packet filters .............. 428, 430
```

SuSE Linux – Administration Guide   487

```
              - Squid and ......................  420
              - SuSEfirewall2 ..... 305, 428, 431–433
                · configuring ............. 431–433
firewire
              - hotplugging ..................... 242
fonts
              - Asian ........................... 143
              - encodings ....................... 144
              - LaTeX ........................... 329
              - TeX ............................. 329
              - Unicode ......................... 145
              - X ............................... 143
framebuffer ............................. 133
FTP
              - server
                · path ........................... 42
              - servers ......................... 270

G
GDM ..................................... 312
Ghostscript ............................. 210
              - drivers ......................... 161
GLIDE ............................. 146–150
GNU
              - GPL ......................... 473–480
graphical console background .... see SuSE
                    screen, deactivate
graphics
              - 3D
                · diagnosing .................... 149
                · testing ....................... 149
                · troubleshooting ............... 149
graphics cards
              - 3D ......................... 146–150
                · drivers ....................... 146
                · installation support for ...... 150
                · support for ................... 146
              - configuring with SaX2 .......... 122
              - FireFL ........................... 8
              - unsupported .................... 133
graphics tablets
              - configuring with SaX2 .......... 129
groups
              - changes in names ............... 42
gs .......................... see Ghostscript

H
hardware
              - CD-ROM drives .................. 21
              - DMA ............................ 313
              - hotplug ........................ 313
              - pcmcia ......................... 322
              - power management ............. 323
```

```
              - Promise Controller .............. 31
              - YaST2 and ....................... 65
help
              - info pages ...................... 274
              - man pages ...................... 274
              - X ............................... 142
hotplugging ....................... 237–242
              - cameras ........................ 240
              - coldplugging ................... 238
              - configuring .................... 239
              - firewire ....................... 242
              - keyboards ...................... 240
              - mice ........................... 240
              - network devices ................ 240
              - network interfaces ............. 241
              - PCI ............................ 240
              - PCMCIA ......................... 240
              - storage devices ................ 239
              - USB ............................ 239

I
I18N .................................... 292
id ...................................... 148
info pages .............................. 274
              - index .......................... 327
init .................................... 296
              - inittab ........................ 296
              - scripts .................... 298–300
initrd ............................ 276, 315
              - boot loaders and ............... 277
              - creating ....................... 279
              - linuxrc and .................... 277
insmod .................................. 265
installing
              - autoinstaller .................. 308
              - boot disk ....................... 18
              - boot methods .................... 13
              - CD2 ............................. 18
              - FTP ............................. 16
              - linuxrc .......................... 9
              - modules ......................... 11
              - net as source medium ........... 16
              - NFS ............................. 16
              - PCMCIA ......................... 252
              - special installations ........... 16
              - YaST2 ............................ 8
IP addresses ...................... 339–343
              - classes ........................ 340
              - dynamic ........................ 328
              - IPv6 ....................... 344–348
                · configuring ................... 351
                · netmasks ...................... 348
                · prefixes ...................... 346
```

· structure 345
- masquerading 428–430
- netmasks 340–342
- private 342
IPX .... see MARSNWE
IrDA 254, 314

J
Java 315
joysticks
 - configuring 315

K
KDM 312
 - shutting down 329
kernels 261–268
 - caches 275
 - compiling 261–268
 - configuring 263–266
 - errors messages 267
 - installing 267–268
 - Kmod 266
 - modules 264–267
  · loading 315
  · network card 349
  · parport 173
  · PCMCIA 244
 - modules.conf 266
 - problems 279
 - sources 262–263
 - System.map 268
 - transparent proxies and 420
keyboard
 - CapsLock 316
 - configuring with SaX2 121
 - delay 316
 - layout 291, 316
 - mapping 291
  · compose 291
  · multikey 291
 - NumLock 316
 - repetition rate 316
Kmod 266

L
L10N 292
Lame 152
LANs
 - configuring 349–360
 - wireless 351
laptops 243–254
 - IrDA 254
LILO 85–99

- BIOS and 86
- boot sector, in 87
- booting DOS 97
- booting Windows 95/98 97
- booting with another boot manager . 87
- components 85
- configuring 14, 87–94
- floppy, from 86
- installing 94–95
- lilo.conf 88–94
- locations for 86
- map files 86
- MBR 87
- memory test 91
- message files 86, 93
- other systems 91
- overview 85
- parameters 89
- passwords 94
- reinstalling 95–96
- sample configurations 97
- troubleshooting 99
- uninstalling 96–97
- Windows 2000 98
- Windows NT 98
- YaST2 88
Linux
 - networks and 335
 - sharing files with another OS .. 386, 394
Linux Standard Base 270
linuxrc 9
 - initrd and 277
loadlin 104–111
 - configuring 14
 - files 105
 - problems 23
Local Area Networks .... see LANs
locale 316
locate 41, 317
 - updatedb 317
log files 272
 - Argus 308
 - boot.msg 175
 - managing 41
 - messages 239, 241, 246, 361, 433
 - SaX.log 132
 - Squid 414, 416, 422
 - X 130
 - XFree86.0.log 115, 132
logging
 - logrotate 272

· configuring 273
Logical Volume Manager
  - YaST2 67
logrotate 272
lprsetup 179
LSB .... see Linux Standard Base
  - installing packages 43
lsmod 265

M

MacOS
  - sharing files 394
mail
  - mail relay 312
mailman 43
majordomo 43
man pages 274
  - database 311
MARSNWE 401–405
  - configuring 401–404
  - IPX 401, 404
  - permissions 403
  - printing 403
  - starting 401
masquerading 428–430
  - configuring with SuSEfirewall2 . 431
  - IP forwarding 328
  - ipchains 429
  - iptables 429
  - problems 429
Master Boot Record .... see MBR
MBR 82
  - LILO 87
memory
  - RAM 275
MIDI 154
modinfo 266
modprobe 265
modules
  - loading 282
  - parameters 283
monitors
  - configuring with SaX2 122
mountd 378
mouse
  - configuring with SaX2 ..... 120, 136
  - controlling with keyboard 118
  - interface 318
  - pine 42
MP3s
  - encoding 152
multihead
  - SaX2 and 128

N

name servers .... see DNS
Name Service Cache Daemon 357
NAT .... see masquerading
Netatalk 394–400
  - afpd 394
  - AppleDouble 397
  - atalkd 394
  - configuring 395–398
  - guest servers 395
  - papd 394
  - permissions 396
  - printing 398–399
  - restrictions 394
  - starting 399
  - TCP/IP and 396
Netware
  - administering from Linux 404
  - emulating 401–405
network
  - DHCP relay agent 311
  - DHCP server 311
  - YaST2 and 76
Network File System .... see NFS
Network Information Service .... see NIS
network monitors
  - Argus 307
networks 335
  - authentication
    · Kerberos 438–445
  - base network address 341
  - broadcast address 342
  - configuration files 353–358
  - configuring 318, 349, 352–360
    · IPv6 351
  - DNS 342–343
  - integrating 349–360
  - IP addresses 339–343
  - ISDN 314
  - local host 342
  - mail 317
  - monitors
    · ArgoUPS 307
  - netmasks 340
  - NFS 322
  - printing 201
  - routing 339–342
  - SSH 326
  - TCP/IP 336
  - testing cards 349
news
  - servers 322

NFS 375–378
    - clients 375
    - exporting 376
    - importing 375
    - mounting 375
    - permissions 377
    - RPC 373
    - server 322
    - servers 77, 375, 376
nfsd 378
NIS 371–374
    - autofs 41
    - client 330
    - configuring 77
    - installing 373
    - masters 371–373
    - server 373
    - Server 331
    - slaves 371–373
NNTP
    - servers 322
notebooks .... *see* laptops
NSS 355
    - databases 356
nVidia 146

O

Ogg Vorbis
    - encoding 153
    - playing 153
    - support 153
OpenGL 146–150
    - drivers 146
    - testing 149
OpenSSH .... *see* SSH
OS/2
    - sharing files 386

P

package
    - 3dpixms 329
    - a2ps 167
    - aaa_base 38, 272
    - alice 383
    - allman 40
    - alsa, pmidi, aseqview,
        vkeybd 154
    - alsa-devel 44
    - apache 37
    - awesfx 155
    - awesfx, snd_sf2, kalsatools .
        154
    - bind8 369

    - binutils 263
    - bzip 43
    - bzip2 43
    - cdparanoia 152
    - cron 37
    - cups 166, 200, 203, 205, 235
    - cups-client ... 166, 167, 172, 205,
        226, 236
    - cups-drivers 166, 171, 200
    - cups-drivers-stp . 166, 171, 200,
        203
    - cups-libs 166, 167
    - dhclient 380
    - dhcpcd 380
    - docbktls 40
    - docbook-dsssl-stylesheets . 39
    - docbook_3 39
    - docbook_4 39
    - dochost 38
    - emacs-auctex 39
    - emacs-el 39
    - emacs-info 39
    - emacs-nox 39
    - emacs-x11 39
    - fhs 270
    - file 167
    - findutils-locate 311
    - ftpdir 270
    - gcc 262
    - ghostscript-fonts-std 167
    - ghostscript-library 167
    - ghostscript-x11 167
    - gimp-devel 44
    - glibc-devel 263
    - glibc-info 294
    - glx 150
    - gnuserv 39
    - howtoen 426, 430
    - ipxrip 405
    - irda 255
    - isapnp 41, 175
    - jade_dsl 39
    - kbd 41
    - kdelibs-devel 44
    - kernel-source 35, 262
    - kernmod 35
    - kernmods 35
    - libc 49
    - libcinfo 355
    - libz 43
    - logrotate 272
    - lpdfilter 167
    - lprng 167, 179, 225, 226, 236

- lvm	41	- zlib-devel	43
- makewhat	36	packages	
- mesa	149, 150	- changes in 8.1	43
- mesa3dfx	150	- compiling	49
- mesasoft	148	- installing	44
- mod_php	39	- LSB	43
- mod_php4	39	- managing	43
- mutt	38	- RPMs	43–51
- mysql-Max	40	- uninstalling	44
- ncpfs	404, 405	- verifying	44
- netatalk	394	partitions	
- nkit	49	- expert partitioning	24
- nkitb	39	- partition table	82
- openldap	43	- swap	24
- openldap2	43	- YaST2 and	66
- openssh	37	PCI	
- pcmcia-cardinfo	253	- hotplugging	240
- pcmcia-modules	254	PCMCIA	244–254, 322
- pcmicia	254	- card manager	245
- pg_datab	37	- cardctl	253
- phpdoc	37	- configuring	246–248
- popt	43	- driver assignment	251
- popt-devel	43	- hotplugging	240
- postgres	31, 37	- IDE	247
- psgml	39	- installing with	252
- psutils	187, 216	- IrDA	254
- radvd	351	- ISDN	247
- rpm	43, 49	- modems	247
- rpm-devel	43	- modules	245
- rzsz	39	- network cards	247, 351
- samba-client	201, 203, 227	- problems	248
- sdb_en	34	- removing cards	246
- squidgrd	425	- restarting	245
- SuSEfirewall2	305, 428	- SCSI	247
- susehelp	38	- starting	
- syslinux	18, 103	· preventing	249
- tcl	264	- supported cards	244
- tk	264	- switching configurations	248
- ttmkfdir	145	- systems	244
- vorbis-tools	152	- troubleshooting	248
- wget	48	- utilities	253
- xf86	150, 264	permissions	326
- xfsetup	114	- file permissions	273
- xkeycaps	127	pine	42
- xntp	330	ports	
- yast2-trans-*	43	- IrDA	178
- yast2-trans-cs	43	- parallel	173–176
- yast2-trans-de	43	- scanning	422
- yast2-trans-es	43	- serial	179
- ypclient	39	- USB	176–178
- ypserv	37	postfix	43
- yudit	145	PostgreSQL	323
- zlib	43	- updating	31

492 _____ Index

power management
- apmd 323
printing 65–66, 157–236
- applications, from 172
- banners 171
- basics 158–160
- command line, from 172, 205
- configuring 165–172
  · CUPS 199–200
  · LPRng and lpdfilter 179
  · ports 173–179
  · YaST2 166–172
- CUPS 198–205
- default queue 326
- drivers 162–163
- files 181, 183, 205
- filters 158
  · configuring 186
  · custom 194–198
  · customizing 187
  · lpdfilter 184–194
  · troubleshooting 194
- GDI printers 163–165
  · configuring 192
  · supported 164
- Ghostscript
  · drivers 161–163
- IPP 198
- jobs 158–159
  · processing 202
  · removing 181, 183, 206
  · status 181, 183, 206
- languages 158
- lpc 182
- lpq 183
- lpr 181, 183
- lprsetup 179
- network printers 201, 224
  · prefiltering 224
  · print filters 224
- PPD 200
- print server 224
- print server box 224
- printer languages 158
  · ASCII 158
  · ESC 158
  · PCL 158
  · PostScript 158
- processing 158, 202
- protocols 224
- queues 158, 165
  · controlling 182
  · lp 165

· managing 181–184, 205
· names 169
· options 207
· raw 185
· remote 183–184
· removing jobs 181, 183
· selecting queues 172
· status 181, 183, 206
- requirements 161
- Samba 387
- spoolers 158
  · lpd 179–180
- supported printers 161
- systems 159
- troubleshooting 160, 184
protocols
- IPP 198
- SMB 386
proxies
- advantages 410
- caches 409
- FTP 326
- HTTP 326
- Squid 409–426
- transparent 419

R
RAID
- soft 72
rc.config .... see sysconfig
rescue system 285
- preparing 286
- starting 287
- using 288
resolutions
- configuring with SaX2 122
RFCs 336
rmmod 265
root
- locale 317
- remote login 41
- working directory 327
routing 339, 359–360
- IP forwarding 328
- masquerading 428–430
- netmasks 340–342
- routes 359
- static 359
RPM 43–51
- database 43, 308
  · rebuilding 46, 48
- dependencies 44
- installing 44

SuSE Linux – Administration Guide   493

- queries 46
- security 455
- SRPMS 49
- tools 50
- uninstalling 44, 45
- updating 44
- verify 48
- verifying 44
runlevels 296–298
- changing 298
- editing in YaST2 .... 78, 301

S

Samba 386–393
- clients 386–387, 392
- configuring 387–392
- help 393
- installing 387
- login 391
- names 386
- NetBIOS 386
- optimizing 393
- permissions 390
- printers 387
- printing 392
- security 390–391
- servers 387–392
- shares 387, 388
- SMB 386
- starting 387
- stopping 387
- swat 391
- TCP/IP and 386
SaX2 115–137
- 3D and 117
- 3D graphics 148
- color depth 122
- configuration 134
- configuring graphics cards 122
- display problems 135
- FAQ 133
- fastpaths 127
- graphics cards 133, 134
- graphics tablets 129
- hardware recognition 117
- image geometry 125
- keyboard configuration 121
- laptops and 127
- loading old configuration 120
- monitor configuration 122
- mouse configuration 120, 136
- multihead configuration 128
- notebooks and 127

- resolutions 122
- saving configuration 117
- starting 117, 133
- support 135
- testing configuration 124
- touch screens 130
- troubleshooting 133
SCPM 248
scripts
- checkhotmounts 239
- hotplug 238, 240, 246
- ifup 241
- init.d 296, 298–300, 359
  · atalk 399
  · boot 41, 300
  · boot.local 300
  · boot.proc 328
  · boot.setup 300
  · halt 300
  · inetd 359
  · lpd 179
  · network 359
  · nfsserver 359, 377
  · portmap 359, 373, 377
  · rc 298–300
  · sendmail 359
  · skeleton 300
  · squid 413
  · ypbind 359
  · ypserv 359
- lpdfilter 185
  · guess 185
  · if 185
- mkinitrd 279
- modify_resolvconf 275, 358
- pcmcia 246, 351
  · network 252
- rchotplug 239
- running from current directory . 327
- SuSEconfig 301–303
  · disabling 303, 327
- switch2mesasoft 304
- ypbind 374
security 428–433, 445, 456
- attacks 452–454
- booting 446, 448
- bugs and 449, 452
- DNS 453
- firewalls 78, 428–433
- local 447–450
- network 450–454
- passwords 447–448
- permissions 448–449

494 ———— Index

- reporting problems 456
- RPM signatures 455
- Samba 390
- serial terminals 446
- social engineering 446
- Squid 410
- SSH 433–438
- tcpd 456
- tips and tricks 454
- viruses 450
- worms 454
- X and 451
sendmail 43, 326
series
- d 35
- doc 34
shell
- problems after updating 33
SMB .... see Samba
Soft RAID .... see YaST2,Soft RAID
software
- compiling 49
- installing with YaST2 64
- removing with YaST2 64
sound
- ALSA 151–156
- buffering 153–154
- compressing audio data 152
- configuring 326
- latencies 153–154
- MIDI 154
- Ogg Vorbis 153
- sound fonts 155
source code
- compiling 49
spell checker 314
spm 49
Squid 409–426
- access controls 417, 423
- Apache 422
- cache size 412
- cachemgr.cgi 422–424
- caches 409, 410
- Calamaris 426
- configuring 414–419
- CPU and 413
- directories 413
- DNS 414
- features 410
- firewalls and 420
- log files 414, 416, 422
- object status 411
- permissions 413, 417

- protocols 410
- RAM and 413
- reports 426
- SARG 426
- security 410
- SquidGuard 424–425
- starting 413
- statistics 422–424
- stopping 414
- system requirements 412
- transparent proxies 419–422
- troubleshooting 414
- uninstalling 414
SSH 433–438
- authentication mechanisms 436
- daemon 435
- key pairs 435, 437
- scp 435
- sftp 435
- ssh 434
- ssh-agent 437, 438
- ssh-keygen 437
- sshd 326, 435
- X and 438
sudo 154
SuSEconfig 327
switch2mesasoft 148
switch2nv 148
sysconfig 79
SYSLINUX 18
syslog 328
syslog-ng 328
system
- configuring 303
- freezes ... see BIOS, virus protection
- information 281
- limiting resource use 274
- localizing 292
- rescuing 285
- time 309
- updating 29–51
- updating with YaST2 64

T
T-DSL .... see ADSL
TCP/IP 336–339
- ICMP 337
- IGMP 337
- layer model 337–339
- packets 337, 338
- services 336
- TCP 336
- UDP 336

time zones 309
touch screens
    - configuring with SaX2 130
Tridgell, Andrew 386

U

ulimit 274
    - options 274
updating 29–51
    - base system 32
    - from console 63
    - loadlin 33
    - patch CD 64
    - problems 31, 33
    - YaST2 64
USB
    - connecting devices 239
    - file system 239
users
    - changes in names 42
    - nobody 272
    - working directory 327

V

Variable
    - CUPS_SERVER 199
    - HOME 30
    - LANG 316
    - LC_* 316
    - MANPATH 36
    - PATH 3
    - PRINTER 181
    - run_ldconfig 37
variables
    - environment 292
viruses
    - AIRCOP 86

W

WDM 312
web servers
    - Apache 305
    - path 42
    - setting up 271
whois 343
window managers
    - X and 116
Windows
    - booting Linux from 104–111
    - sharing files 386

X

X 113

- blank screen on start 137
- color depth 330
- configuration 66
- configuring 137
- configuring with SaX2 115–137
- control protocols 330
- default window manager 329
- display managers 312
- display numbers 330
- drivers 142
- fonts 143
- GDM 312
- history 113
- KDM 312
- log file 130
- optimizing 138
- security 451
- shutdown 329
- SSH and 438
- starting 126, 132
- troubleshooting 133
- virtual screen 141
- WDM 312
- window managers and 116
- XFree86 113
X Window System .... see X
XFine2 125

Y

YaST .... see YaST2
YaST Online Update .... see YOU
YaST2 41
    - 3D 146
    - configuring system 61
    - DNS server 77
    - firewall 78
    - graphics card 66
    - hardware 65
    - Logical Volume Manager 67
    - LVM 67
    - network 76
    - network configuration 349–351
    - NFS server 77
    - NIS server 77
    - partitioning 66
    - patch CD update 64
    - postfix 76
    - printers 65–66
    - printing 166–172
        · suppressing autodetection 166
    - rc.config 79
    - routing 77
    - runlevel editor 78, 301

- sendmail 76
- Soft RAID 72
- software installation 64
- software removal 64
- sysconfig editor 79, 303
- text mode 55–60
  · modules 59
  · starting 56
- text-based 8
- update 64
- updating 32
- X configuration 66

- YaST Online Update 63
- Yellow Pages . *see* YaST2, NIS server
- YOU 63
  · cron 59–60
YOU .... *see* YaST2,YOU, 146
- from console 63
- server list 322
YP .... *see* NIS

Z
Zope
  - configuring 331

Notice

Notice

Notice

Notice

Notice

Notice

Notice

Notice

Notice

Notice

Notice

Notice

Notice

Notice

Notice

Notice

Notice

Made in Germany

SuSE

SuSE Inc. · USA
318 Harrison Street, Suite 301
Oakland, CA 94607

Phone: (888) 875-4689
       (510) 628-3380
Fax: (510) 628-3381
WWW: http://www.suse.com
E-Mail: info@suse.com

**Installation support
(support key needed):**
E-Mail: support@suse.com

SuSE Linux Ltd. · UK
The Kinetic Centre · Theobald Street
Borehamwood, Herts. WD6 4PJ

Phone: +44 208 387 4088
Fax: +44 208 387 4010
WWW: http://www.suse.co.uk/
E-Mail: info@suse.co.uk

**Installation support
(support key needed):**
E-Mail: support@suse.co.uk

SuSE Linux AG · Germany
Deutschherrnstr. 15-19
90429 Nuernberg

Phone: +49 911 74 05 33 9
WWW: http://www.suse.de/en
E-Mail: info@suse.de

**Installation support
(support key needed):**
E-Mail: support@suse.de

ISBN 3-935922-79-5